# CARRYING
# THE WORD

# MESOAMERICAN WORLDS: FROM THE OLMECS TO THE DANZANTES

*After Monte Albán*, JEFFREY P. BLOMSTER, EDITOR

*The Apotheosis of Janaab' Pakal*, GERARDO ALDANA

*Carrying the Word: The Concheros Dance in Mexico City*, SUSANNA ROSTAS

*Commoner Ritual and Ideology in Ancient Mesoamerica*, NANCY GONLIN AND JON C. LOHSE, EDITORS

*Conquered Conquistadors*, FLORINE ASSELBERGS

*Empires of Time*, ANTHONY AVENI

*Encounter with the Plumed Serpent*, MAARTEN JANSEN AND GABINA AURORA PÉREZ JIMÉNEZ

*In the Realm of Nachan Kan*, MARILYN A. MASSON

*Invasion and Transformation*, REBECCA P. BRIENEN AND MARGARET A. JACKSON, EDITORS

*The Kowoj*, PRUDENCE M. RICE AND DON S. RICE, EDITORS

*Life and Death in the Templo Mayor*, EDUARDO MATOS MOCTEZUMA

*Maya Daykeeping*, JOHN M. WEEKS, FRAUKE SACHSE, AND CHRISTIAN M. PRAGER

*The Madrid Codex*, GABRIELLE VAIL AND ANTHONY AVENI, EDITORS

*Maya Worldviews at Conquest*, LESLIE G. CECIL AND TIMOTHY W. PUGH, EDITORS

*Mesoamerican Ritual Economy*, E. CHRISTIAN WELLS AND KARLA L. DAVIS-SALAZAR, EDITORS

*Mesoamerica's Classic Heritage*, DAVÍD CARRASCO, LINDSAY JONES, AND SCOTT SESSIONS, EDITORS

*Mockeries and Metamorphoses of an Aztec God*, GUILHEM OLIVIER, TRANSLATED BY MICHEL BESSON

*Rabinal Achi*, ALAIN BRETON, EDITOR; TRANSLATED BY TERESA LAVENDER FAGAN AND ROBERT SCHNEIDER

*Representing Aztec Ritual*, ELOISE QUIÑONES KEBER, EDITOR

*Ruins of the Past*, TRAVIS W. STANTON AND ALINE MAGNONI, EDITORS

*Skywatching in the Ancient World*, CLIVE RUGGLES AND GARY URTON, EDITORS

*Social Change and the Evolution of Ceramic Production and Distribution in a Maya Community*, DEAN E. ARNOLD

*The Social Experience of Childhood in Mesoamerica*, TRACI ARDREN AND SCOTT R. HUTSON, EDITORS

*Stone Houses and Earth Lords*, KEITH M. PRUFER AND JAMES E. BRADY, EDITORS

*The Sun God and the Savior*, GUY STRESSER-PÉAN

*Sweeping the Way*, CATHERINE R. DiCESARE

*Tamoanchan, Tlalocan: Places of Mist*, ALFREDO LÓPEZ AUSTIN

*Thunder Doesn't Live Here Anymore*, ANATH ARIEL DE VIDAS; TRANSLATED BY TERESA LAVENDER FAGAN

*Topiltzin Quetzalcoatl*, H. B. NICHOLSON

*The World Below*, JACQUES GALINIER

# CARRYING
### THE CONCHEROS DANCE IN MEXICO CITY
# THE WORD

S U S A N N A    R O S T A S

UNIVERSITY PRESS OF COLORADO

Published by the University Press of Colorado
5589 Arapahoe Avenue, Suite 206C
Boulder, Colorado 80303

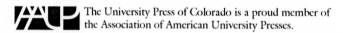 The University Press of Colorado is a proud member of
the Association of American University Presses.

The University Press of Colorado is a cooperative publishing enterprise supported, in part,
by Adams State College, Colorado State University, Fort Lewis College, Mesa State College,
Metropolitan State College of Denver, University of Colorado, University of Northern
Colorado, and Western State College of Colorado.

∞ The paper used in this publication meets the minimum requirements of the American
National Standard for Information Sciences—Permanence of Paper for Printed Library
Materials. ANSI Z39.48-1992

Library of Congress Cataloging-in-Publication Data

Rostas, Susanna.
  Carrying the word : the Concheros dance in Mexico City / Susanna Rostas.
    p. cm.
  Includes bibliographical references and index.
  ISBN 978-0-87081-960-5 (hardcover : alk. paper) — ISBN 978-1-60732-138-5 (pbk. :
alk. paper)
    1. Folk dancing—Mexico—Mexico City. 2. Religious dance—Mexico—Mexico City. I.
Title.
  GV1628.M49R67 2009
  793.3'10972—dc22

                                                                    2009023099

Design by Daniel Pratt

21   20   19   18   17   16   15   14   13   12          10   9   8   7   6   5   4   3   2   1

Cover: Dancer probably from a country group playing his *concha* at Tlatelolco.

# ILLUSTRATIONS

In December 1998, I was one of a reported 6 million pilgrims and other visitors who made their way to the Basilica of Guadalupe in the northern suburbs of Mexico City to celebrate the annual feast day of the Virgin of Guadalupe (December 12). Over a three-day period, the huge atrium in front of the basilica was packed with dance groups from all over central Mexico. As many as thirty groups performed at a time, often competing with one another for physical space and musical audibility. By far the most popular, in numbers of both participants and watching crowds, were the Mexica dances. Men (and, to a lesser extent, women), in costumes loosely based on pictures of Mexica warriors and dancers from the old codices, performed to the loud and insistent rhythm of *huehuetl* and *teponaztli* drums. Similar in underlying form, but clearly different in conception, were the *danzas de los concheros*, whose quieter music was played on *conchas*, stringed instruments made from armadillo shells or, in some cases, from gourds. The Concheros have been around much longer in central Mexico, but on that feast day outside the basilica they were fewer in number and tended to draw smaller crowds than the noisier and more flamboyant Mexica dancers. (There were, of course, many other *danzantes* besides.)

I knew about the Concheros, both from having seen them dance elsewhere and from reading (among other things) Martha Stone's classic *At the Sign of Midnight: The Concheros Dance Cult of Mexico* (1975). I had seen the Mexica dances, too—I first watched a small group dance, to prerecorded music, in

Chalma in January 1972—but I had never seen so many Mexica in one place before. Moreover, I had not yet read any coherent explanation of the Mexica dancers' intent or popularity. For understanding, I later turned to an article by Susanna Rostas, one of many published while she was working on *Carrying the Word: The Concheros in Mexico City*. Rostas's article confirmed my sense that the Mexica dances had developed from those of the Concheros, that they were performed for the most part by urban mestizos with a New Age sensibility, and that they embodied, as Rostas called it, a kind of "invented ethnicity."

I relied heavily on Rostas's article when I wrote about this aspect of the *Día de Guadalupe* festivities. It is therefore with considerable pleasure that I have responded to the unexpected request to write a foreword to her book.

*Carrying the Word* is an important and much-needed study of the Concheros and their relationship to the newer Mexica dancers who (unlike the Concheros) aggressively invoke an imagined and revindicated Aztec past. Rostas's book updates and, in many ways, moves far beyond Stone's *At the Sign of Midnight*. Stone's work is dated, not because she was an amateur (but very observant) ethnographer, nor because her work is "anecdotal," as Rostas puts it, rather than rigorously scholarly, but because the *danza de los concheros* itself has changed so much since the twenty-five-year period (ca. 1945–1970) during which Stone studied and took part in the dance. One of the great virtues of Rostas's book is her close attention to the fluidity of the dance, to the changes in its social organization and modes of performance, to its part in shaping the nascent Mexica dance, and, in turn, to its own capacity to be influenced by the Mexica's dancing (while still largely dismissing them as inauthentic and ill-disciplined).

Rostas is an acute participant observer. She danced frequently with the Concheros group of Santo Niño de Atocha. She attended its vigils and other religious and social rituals. She sat through sometimes tense organizational meetings. She talked at length to members of the group and, rather than trying to homogenize their responses, has been careful to allow individual differences of interpretation to remain. To my mind, one of the more surprising developments that she uncovers is the apparently easy movement of some dancers between the Concheros dances, which are distinctly Mexican in character, and imported Sufi dance traditions. Both, according to the explanations offered by some of the more middle-class Concheros, emphasize the embodied transcendence reportedly possible for the initiate during the dance. This is language that I suspect was not much used by Stone's informants fifty years ago. Rostas explores such claims both as an observant scholar and as an active participant.

Rostas is well-versed in both ritual theory and performance theory and grounds her discussion firmly in current scholarship in these fields. Happily, however, she does not privilege the language of the academy over that of the dancers themselves, allowing the two different forms of discourse to stand alongside one another as equal partners in her effort to document and understand the present state of the dance of the Concheros in Mexico City. Her book will be of considerable value not only to those who are particularly interested in the rich and varied forms of traditional dance in central Mexico but also to those wanting more generally to understand the ways in which traditional dance can both resist and adapt to a cultural context that is always shifting.

MAX HARRIS
Madison, Wisconsin

# PREFACE & ACKNOWLEDGMENTS

Most in Mexico City know something about the Concheros, who are to be seen performing their dances—circular in form—in a variety of public places throughout the year. The Concheros contribute dramatically to the vibrant cultural life of the city and forge a direct link between rural religious practices and urban postmodern innovation. Few, however, know much about who the dancers are, what their dancing signifies, and the other activities in which they are involved (such as their all-night vigils). Despite the Concheros' distinct religio-social identity, it is often assumed that the dancers are part of the Catholic Church. However, although their practices are indeed synergistic (and many dancers are at least outwardly Catholics), the dance as a tradition has retained its autonomy, thereby preserving many elements of a rural religiosity that goes back at the very least two centuries. The tradition has largely been an oral one until very recently, and despite claims that the dance never changes, an "Aztec-ization" of certain aspects has been ongoing for some time. This has, however, occurred more openly and extensively in the last four decades and been carried to extremes by those who call themselves the Mexica. The Mexica have brought many changes to the Concheros' dance, although just as many appear to be linked to the deaths of an older generation of dancers. The decline of orality and the upsurge of a more inscribed approach are beginning to lead to practices being externally imposed rather than emerging from experience. The book offers new insights into the experience of dancing as a Conchero, of how the

Concheros manifest their religiosity by means of the dance whilst also exploring their organization and practices.

The many groups of Concheros vary in the type of dancers they attract, but this book reflects my experience of dancing with one group—Santo Niño de Atocha. This group (or *mesa*) had more middle-class and professional dancers than any other, whilst still attracting many *gente humilde* (humble people), most of whom are mestizos (although some are of clear indigenous descent). This mesa and the many others with which I had loose affiliations shared similar feelings about the Mexica, whom they considered not to be a part of the Concheros' association. But the Mexica's influence on the Concheros has continued to grow in the last two decades as the latter have become ever-more interested in the Aztec past. Most in the group of Santo Niño de Atocha now strongly believe that the dance is Aztec in origin, despite an ongoing foundation myth that indicates it started much later and elsewhere in Mexico.

The project had its genesis when I stopped briefly in Mexico City en route eastward. I was going to Chiapas to carry out postdoctoral fieldwork in an indigenous community on religious change involving escalating affiliation to so-called protestant sects. In Mexico City, I had been asked to contact a friend of a friend, which led to my first encounter with Concheros (and I am grateful to Chloe Sayer for this initial introduction). Some time later I returned to Mexico City with a small grant. The project, as it turned out, was not only anthropologically extremely wide-ranging but also had, for me, a personal element. I had lived in Mexico in my twenties—before I became an anthropologist—in the village of Tepoztlan, Morelos (studied by both Redfield and Oscar Lewis, although I was not aware of that at the time). I lived as a painter among other painters, both Mexicans and foreigners, and went occasionally to Mexico City to find a gallery to sell my paintings, with the help of friends, and to broaden my horizons. When I returned to Mexico City to realize this project, I initially met a large number of people, most of whom danced in the group of Santo Niño de Atocha and some of whom I had known of or had come across me when I had lived in Tepoztlan. Although such coincidences came thick and fast at first, some five years later they were still happening. I had chosen to study an organization or association of people whom I had thought would be completely *other* but which I quickly found linked with this earlier phase of my life. The period as a painter had been a significant one for me, and now, on an anthropological path that I had never imagined, would lead me back; the dance had done just that, at least tangentially. This was then a project in which I was both an outsider but also something of an insider as the *other* was not quite as *other* to me as I had anticipated. The idea that the self may be discovered in the other and the other in the self has recently become much more a part of anthropological currency, for what we have now are "multiple interconnected sites of representation" or, as Taylor has put it, "multiple authorial and spectatorial imbrications."[1] Although many of the people I danced with and talked to were in certain respects as *other* as my indigenous friends in Chiapas, many were middle-class and/or professional—only other in the sense that I am not Mexican and come from a different country (which provides grants to study others), whereas most of them, lacking such funding, are as interested in studying themselves.

I immersed myself in the dancing with an enthusiasm that paralleled that of most Concheros, in part because that was the only way that I could experience and hence begin to be able to understand what dancing under particular conditions can do for and to the mind-body. As Geertz has cogently put it, there is a need to have "actually penetrated (or if you prefer, been penetrated by) another form of life, of having, one way or another truly 'been there.'" Favret Saada pushes this just a bit further: "[T]here is no other solution but to practice it oneself, to become one's own informant."[2] I was indeed my own informant but I also received a vast amount of help from various dancers, particularly in the group of Santo Niño de Atocha.

I am particularly indebted to the now deceased *jefe* of the group, Compadre Ernesto (Ernesto Ortiz Ramirez), who accepted me as one of his dancers and gave me his time on numerous occasions to discuss at length his memories of the group during the middle decades of the twentieth century. I want also to mention Ricardo López Ortiz, his great-nephew, his inheritor, and jefe until, despite his youth, he too died in 2008.

I am extremely grateful to Angelica Ortiz de Zarate, who has been acting as a (non-academic) ethnographer of the dance for years. She devoted hours of her time to me, often over lunch, to discuss aspects of the dance—elucidating events a few days after they had happened, explaining terms, indicating what was to be expected, what was new and unusual, and generally helping me to find my feet, both as a dancer and as an analyst of the dance. I have also received assistance from Ernesto Garcia Cabral, who has supported this project throughout its gestation, more recently communicating by e-mail, reading drafts of the chapters (despite being in English), and passing documents on to me. Antonia Guerrero found time in her very busy schedule to discuss points of complexity or contention and entertained me at her house, as did others, such as Eduardo Aguilar, who demonstrated some of the more difficult dance steps and elucidated some of the language (particularly that of the prayers). Alfredo Ponce but more particularly his wife, Linda, who comes from a family of dancers, helped me to see other aspects of the dance, whereas Margarita Montalva gave support when it was most needed. I am also extremely grateful to those other jefes who assisted me on various occasions: Guadalupe Hernandez, Soledad Ruiz, Andres Segura, Jesus Leon, Guadalupe Jimenez Sanabria (Nanita), Teresa Mejia, Conchita Aranda, and Herman. I too thank the dancers: Carlos Piña, Federico Sanchez Ventura, Felipe Gutierrez, the Kamfer brothers (Cuauhtemoc and Marcos), Rosa Elia (the latter's wife and one of the Correa sisters), Miguel Gutierrez, Compadre Jesus, Roberto Partido (better known as Pando), and Berenice Garmendia. Also the many dancers whose first names are the only names I have recorded: Alberto, Daniel, Doroteo, Elvira, Francisco, Milagros, Nacho, Nanacatzin, Olga, Ollinkin, Oscar, Pera, Sonora, Susana, Teo, Tita, Tonahuitzin; the writers: Velasco Piña and Carlos Jimenez; the politicos: Margarito Ruiz Hernandez and Bernadina Green (although I am not sure she would agree with being so labelled). Thanks, too, to Enrique Figueras and Edwin Rojas; to the academics: Carlos Garma Navarro, Guillermo Bonfil Batalla, Andres Medina, Gabriel Moedano, Francisco de la Peña, Lina Odena Güemes, and Phyllis Correa. I mention also Anthony Shelton, who filled me in on the background to Mexicanidad at an early stage; William Beezley, who gave me early encouragement; Ruth Lechuga in Mexico City, who provided me with photos of the dance from the 1960s; Nigel Gallop, who loaned me a copy of *Mexican Folkways* by Frances Toor (when it was out of print); and David Maclagan, who gave me an invaluable copy of Kuruth and Marti's book on Anáhuac dances.

Fieldwork for this project was made possible by means of a number of small grants from the British Academy (for a period initially of a few months but extended to six in 1989–90 and for shorter periods in 1993 and 2002) and twice from the Nuffield Foundation. I received a Grant-in-Aid of Research from the Leverhulme Foundation from 1995–1997 to assist part-time in the initial writing of this book.

In the field, at least at first, I went to as many dances as possible, stayed up for numerous all-night vigils (when invited to attend), and listened to, participated in, and when appropriate initiated conversations with dancers about the dance. I carried out semi-structured interviews only during the later phases of the project (from 1995 onward) with some of the jefes and dancers who are acknowledged above. Once I felt that I had a good understanding of what was going on, these interviews assisted me in ascertaining whether my intuitions were supported by the dancers' own accounts and enabled me to put on record how the dancers themselves described the experience of dancing. I have tried where possible to obtain my information from more than one dancer: assertions that I make that are not referenced are of that type. The majority of the unattributed quotations are from Angelica. Where dancers are mentioned by name, this usually means that what was said was very much that dancer's personal opinion or that I was unable to talk to more than one person about that particular aspect—or that I wish to highlight the differing views of a range of dancers.

Hiccups had to be overcome while writing this book. The initial tension was between my personal reluctance to write in detail about people who had become my friends and the demands of academicism, which required me to reveal the details of a tradition that has until recently been predominantly oral, hidden from public scrutiny, and passed on predominantly by word of mouth from father to son.[3] However, in the past ten years or so, the Concheros themselves have made many more of their practices easily accessible. Several before me have set out to study the Concheros but have usually become dancers rather than writing about the dance itself. I too felt that pressure. What the dance seemed to be telling me was that I should stay in Mexico and dance and paint for a living, but I came back to England and carried on my work as an academic anthropologist.

I am grateful to all those who read the book outline and/or some or all of the chapters and gave me constructive comments, amongst whom were Nurit Stadler, Andrea Stockle, Harriet Bradley, Ben Smith, Marta Eugenia García Ugarte, Vicki Cremona, Barbara Bodenhorn, Piers Vitebski, Graham Harvey, and Susan Thompson. I am grateful too for the support given me by the Department of Social Anthropology, the Centre for Latin American Studies and the Computer Centre, Cambridge University. I am also very appreciative of all those at the University Press of Colorado who have undertaken most of the work of getting the book ready for publication: particularly, Laura Furney and Daniel Pratt. My thanks also go to the director, Darrin Pratt. Lastly, I thank my immediate family and those friends (and especially Ruscha Schorrkon, Susan Sellers, and Jeremy Thurlow) who have supported me in one way or another during the book's gestation. Any inaccuracies are mine and mine alone. The photographs were taken predominantly by myself in 1989–1990 except where otherwise stated. I was never permitted into the circle to photograph nor could I take photographs as I danced.

**0.1.** The sergeant of a group of Concheros at Los Remedios in 1995.

"The notion of 'belief' as a proposition to which the individual assents does not catch the quality of lived faith, where 'belief' has as much to do with affect, emotional, moral and aesthetic as with propositions. I therefore prefer to look to action, and its concomitant experience, to seek 'religion' in observances. The strategy requires rituals to be understood as performances devised to lead participant men and women through particular experiences: choreographed sequences of sculpted emotions developed out of a repertoire of prescribed actions which open a particular way to the sacred."

—CLENDINNEN, talking about Aztec dance (1990:110)

# CARRYING
# THE WORD

**1.1.** The flower form constructed during a vigil held in a house on the northern outskirts of Mexico City 1993.

# INCONGRUOUS BEGINNINGS

Those occasions when we come across the incongruous are comparatively rare. In Mexico City in the early 1990s, however, I encountered just that: groups of dancers who, calling themselves Concheros, enacted a sacred dance, circular in form and sometimes preceded by an all-night vigil. In one of the largest cities in the world, a religious tradition that claims to have indigenous rural roots was still flourishing as unchangingly as it could, despite the pressures and complexities of everyday life at the end of the twentieth century.

My first encounter with the Concheros was at a *velación* (all-night vigil). Usually held some nine days after a death, this particular vigil was for a man whose sons were dancers. The deceased was quite well-known in the Mexico City art and media worlds as he directed films and was also a dealer in antiquities. The occasion was thus supported not only by Concheros, a heterogeneous group of people who come literally from all walks of life, but also, at least during the earlier part of the night, by the luminaries of cinema, theater, and dance. In marked contrast to the professional middle-class aspect of the gathering was the ritual that slowly unfolded and took on more significance as the evening wore on. By midnight, most of the party attendees had departed and those remaining were fully involved in the rite to honor not only the dead man's soul (*anima*) but also those of the Concheros' antecedents. What struck me most forcibly at the time was how contradiction-laden the occasion seemed. Here were apparently sophisticated urbanites in one of the biggest cities in the world

I

performing the various rites of an all-night vigil with the care, dedication, and love usually found in Mexico in the rituals of rural peoples: the kind of religious devotion predominantly associated with those living in small face-to-face communities of a few thousand. In such communities people come together, from a sense of obligation as much as commitment, to celebrate a way of being by contacting one or more superhuman agents, a religion in the sense of a re-joining (*re-ligio*) with each other as much as the deity.[1]

Although this particular vigil was not followed by a dance, a few days later I witnessed thousands of Concheros dancing at one of their major obligations in the small town of Chalma. The narrow, congested streets were filled with numerous stalls selling candles, small statues of saints, devotions, pamphlets, and the other bits and pieces associated with the kind of religiosity found in a pilgrimage town. As I got closer to the church, the sound became louder until suddenly, nearing the gates of its precinct, out in the open space of the atrium I was hit by the full force of the drums mingled with the sounds of various types of rattles and the fainter melodic music of various stringed instruments. The energy in the air was palpable. The courtyard was completely filled with what at first sight appeared to be a multitude of undifferentiated dancers who from a proximate high point could be seen to be dancing in circle formations. Each circle's movements was constricted by those adjacent, each focused inward around its own upheld standard that, combined with the columns of smoke rising from the incense burners, gave a sense of extending inward and upward. The dancers were dressed in a wide variety of costumes, some with their bodies completely covered, others freer to move in more minimal accoutrements decorated with plastic silver and gold that caught the light as the sun descended toward the hills behind the church.

This was the end of the second day (Thursday) of one of the Concheros' biggest dances. That particular obligation is held in a place that is not so much a town as a large shrine dedicated to the incursions of large numbers of people, where every other house seems to be an inexpensive hotel. Many large crosses stand on the steep, cliff-like protrusions of rock that rise steeply from the fast-flowing river. Some had already been brought down and decorated with flowers, to be followed by candlelit vigils held all night in their vicinity. Pilgrims unconnected with the Concheros had been arriving throughout the day on their knees, having placed on their heads small crowns of fragile orchids obtained at the Ahuehuete, a huge tree probably dating back to before the Spanish Conquest situated in a village a few kilometers above.

As I watched the dancing, I realized that despite the spatial restrictions, the Concheros do not touch each other, that their movements are predominantly in their feet and torsos, leaving the hands free to play various musical instruments.

2

Facing inward, they dance in circle formation, enclosing their *jefe* (leader) and others who hold named positions. The dance is not performed for an audience, although on many if not most occasions there will be people watching. If the dance is a small one, locals will be present, people visiting the nearby church to pray, and curious passersby; at a large dance such as this one, people have come especially for the fiesta, to make offerings of flowers and prayers, and incidentally also to watch, and of course the omnipresent tourists. Predominantly, however, dancers enact for the sake of dancing, largely unaware of the image of their bodies in the eyes of other dancers in the circle, let alone in those of the bystanders, although the rich variety of their costumes may seem to belie this (Chapter 6).

A dancer never enacts alone but is part of a group (*mesa*). Each needs to work with the other members for necessarily they dance together and yet are apart, and this is of significance. The Concheros are backed by neither a formally endorsed institution (as are most churches) nor a prescribed organization (as are most religions). Rather they form a complex associative network of long-standing interpersonal connections and often affective relationships framed by the discipline of their tradition. Respectfully by means of the dance combined with their ritual prayers, the singing, and the music, the group as a whole aims according to the precepts of this oral tradition for "union" and "conformity" while each more individually may be moving toward the attainment of an impersonal and transcendent state of consciousness. The Concheros manifest a way of being that has become rare and certainly very different from the self-conscious and increasingly secular nature of everyday urban life.

To become a Conchero gives people the chance not so much to join an already existing organization (the Association of Concheros), although that is partly the case, but to be instrumental in an ongoing experiential process of a kind that particularly appeals to them.[2] As a multilayered phenomenon, the dance can be (and is) different for everyone, hence its appeal. No two dancers will necessarily give the same explanation as to what the dance signifies, and although most aspects of it display not only strong Catholic but also some indigenous influences, and increasingly those from other forms of spirituality, in the end each has his or her individual explanation. There is no one dogma: the metaphors deployed resonate differently for each (Chapter 5). Robertson Smith suggested a century ago that the practice of ritual is much more stable than the beliefs related to it.[3] What matters to the dancers most is the experience of participating rather than speculating as to what their dancing means.

There is also not just one way of enacting. Each group has its own style, yet each group guards the forms of the dances and attempts to keep them as unchanging as possible. Perhaps somewhat contradictorily, although it is expected that celebrants exert strict conformity to the dance's tenets, the dance can and does give agency to those who participate in a way that their everyday lives may not. This is especially significant for those who are frustrated by their lack of personal opportunities. To dance and follow the other practices too can provide that *something* that is otherwise missing in a person's life and for many being a Conchero becomes of central importance. What that *something* is, is one of the questions that this book attempts to answer. The book does not catalog the dances per se but rather focuses on the practice of dancing: of what is going on as a dancer enacts (Chapters 4 and 5). It looks too at what some of the Concheros—with whom I danced and talked to at length—believe themselves to be doing while they dance and what their experiences of the dance were, which is different for each (Chapters 5 and 7).

## EXPERIENCE AND THE EMBODIED SELF

Experience is notoriously hard to get at. People are either reluctant to talk about what they have experienced during a dance and/or have difficulty putting it into words: it is interior, individual, and above all a private matter. Although two dancers may execute the form of a dance in a very similar manner, what they experience and how they interpret that may be quite different.[4]

What the dance offers is the opportunity to re-member the body: to attain anew, by means of the "body-as-experiencer," another kind of embodied state.[5] It enables dancers to achieve a sense of connectedness and of intersubjectivity by means of a reawakening of all the senses, numbed by the doings of everyday life, and a rejoining (or re-ligio) with the earth by means of the feet: a form of unmediated experience.

For those involved in a full-time, routine job, five days a week in Mexico City, the daily round is often typified by a certain "disembodied" style of life, but the desire to try to compensate for this is strong, especially among the more self-conscious middle classes. Many of them cultivate their mind-body in various ways: a theme familiar throughout much of the so-called developed world.[6] For some (and not necessarily those from the middle classes) the way chosen is to dance as a Conchero at the weekend, which provides an opportunity to turn a mere physical (and spiritually deadened) body (*Korper*) into an energized and alive one: a reanimated body (*Leib*).[7] To dance is a way for the person who, in the Maussian sense, plays a role in everyday life to become reconnected with her inner sense of self and for that self to be opened to new experience. To put it concisely, the Concheros' dance enables a rejoining, an opening up, and sometimes the attainment of at-one-ment (atonement).

**4**

How does the dancer's bodily state change? The body has been investigated in the last few decades from a variety of theoretical stances.[8] To analyze
the Concheros' dance, a phenomenological approach that looks at the reanimated emergent body (the *Leib*) and sees the body as the "existential ground of
culture" seems most appropriate.[9] I am not primarily concerned here with the
symbolism of the body nor with the body as a representation (although this is
important) but rather with the body as a "crucial site or nexus in the construction of subjectivities" by means of embodiment, and in particular of what happens to the body during the activity of dancing.[10] Dancing in a circle creates
necessarily a sense of intersubjectivity, for dancers not only can see each other
across the circle but also need to respond to the dancers on either side of them.
What a Conchero experiences during a dance is a "heightening and intensifi-
cation . . . an altered awareness of his or her" self.[11] The dancer becomes less
immersed in the preoccupations of her everyday life, less the bounded individual self constrained by her body, so characteristic of Western society, and more
open not just to others but also to the world of the numinous; the world of
the animas—the spirits of the Conchero's ancestors. A dancer becomes a more
"diffuse, fluid self—a self that is multiple and permeable, and infused with the
presence of others."[12] The circle as a form implies an interacting sodality that
when in action with the dancers facing into the center as they do is effectively
closed off from and largely unaffected by the outside physical world. This for
the Concheros can occur even in the heart of downtown Mexico City in a place
such as the Zocalo, the square outside the cathedral.

Embodiment is, however, a mediated state that is in flux and that, when
dancing, is changing from moment to moment. As Csordas has put it, the
essential characteristic of embodiment is its existential indeterminacy.[13] To aid
in understanding this, I use two processual terms, the "ritualized" (or ritualization) and the "performative" (or performativity), that at a subtle level can
account for much (but by no means all) of what is occurring as the Concheros
dance. I use these concepts to develop a paradigm of practice or activity
grounded in "the socially informed body."[14]

## THE ACTION OF THE DANCE

Much has been written in recent decades on so-called practice theory.[15] Bourdieu's compelling notion of habitus endeavors to explain how practices are
generated, how we do what we do as we do it: that is of how dispositions and
values are embodied.[16] An actor's activity is objectively determined by his habitus and excludes the possibility of creativity.[17] Bourdieu takes up this position at the expense of human motivation: his sense of agency lacks subjective

empowerment. As Comaroff has indicated, "Bourdieu's formulation leads . . . so far into the domain of implicit meanings that the role of consciousness is almost totally eclipsed." In Bourdieu's effort to counter a subjectivist bias, he has gone "so far in the other direction that his actors seem doomed to reproduce their world mindlessly."[18] Jackson has pointed out that any theory of the "habitus or lifeworld must include some account of those moments in social life when the customary, given, habitual, and normal is disrupted, flouted, suspended, and negated."[19] As actors, we are both of the world and in the world: it constitutes us but we also constantly constitute it.

Humphrey and Laidlaw have developed a theory of ritual action that is a particularly appropriate tool for analyzing both the dance and a vigil because it allows for motivation or choice. Their concept of ritualization emphasizes "action" rather than "practice" and thus uses a different language.[20] Action in their terms is "intrinsically directed . . . so that action and purpose are ontologically inseparable."[21] This then is a "qualitative view" of action that does not see action as being opposed to thought.[22] Ritualization is then a process whereby the relation between intention and action is subtly transformed: a form of action that can be chosen. It pinpoints the means by which any action can come to have those special qualities that emerge when a particular modification of consciousness is made, namely, when the celebrant's awareness of his or her action is "preceded and accompanied by a conception of the action as a thing, encountered and perceived from outside."[23] Ritual is thus different from everyday action. Although the celebrant is still an agent in that he or she enacts the ritual act, the "act itself appears as already formed, almost like an object, something from which the actor might 'receive.'"[24]

When a dancer starts to dance on any particular occasion, the dance activities that have become habitual to the body through time, that (following Bourdieu) we might call the dance habitus, are called up. The Conchero aims to add as little that is new to them as possible. She attempts to curb her more usual everyday agency: her imagination and her desire to innovate. She endeavors to re-member them with her physical body and re-present them in her dance in the way (and this will inevitably be different for each) that she has always danced in the past: that is, to reproduce the conventional steps. This I too have called "ritualization" or ritualized action.[25] But ritualization is not easy to achieve: it is a quality that action "can come to have," providing the dancer is able to put aside her desires and ambitions or the thoughts that are running through her mind, so that she can focus her body/mind totally on her dedicated goal. Ritualization is effectively action that is intentionally made nonintentional.

Against this will be the actuality of enactment. No one can, or even necessarily desires to, reproduce only what has been inculcated time after time.

Although the dance is enacted under conditions that demand tight framing and re-presentation, this is not a professional or theatrical setting with the training that that implies. Inevitably, something of the personal is added each time, if not to the dance steps themselves then to bodily gestures, for example, how the shoulders or the hands are held. In the circumstances under which the Concheros enact, a dance that is repeated in its kinaesthetic totality in exactly the same way, occasion after occasion, would become stale and be unstimulating not only to those who might be watching but more importantly to the dancers themselves. Although the dancers should be aiming for nothing other than the "anonymous" movements of the dance, inevitably dancers express aspects of themselves and their desires when they enact.[26]

Moods such as happiness, exuberance, or sadness may inform their actions. These expressive aspects become apparent when a dancer is either unable to suppress the manifestation of certain emotions or, more significantly for this book, actually permits herself to express something of herself in her dance, whether this be a desire to enact more flamboyantly than usual or to try out something different. It is the latter that I have subsumed under the performative, and most dancers are involved in both ritualized action and the more performative; that is, they aim to carry out the dance as habitually as possible while at times expressing with their bodily movements something that is unique to that occasion.

In everyday life, embodied memory is brought into play for many of the activities we engage in, and analysts have tended to be more concerned with the habitual, with what is considered to be customary, than with the exceptional. Dance is enacted under rather different circumstances. What is exceptional on however small a scale—perhaps unique and attention grabbing—also needs to be taken into account. The non-habitual activities of daily life have a goal and are usually instrumental, intentional endeavours (on a physical level), and the actors have agency. When dancing, the enactors have a different kind of agency; they have what Hastrup has called "double agency."[27]

As individual dancers endeavor to enact conventionally, they may be thinking about "how" to achieve these nonintentional actions by trying to decide "what" needs to be added to them in order to get them right. They will thus also be caught up in trying to "get it right" in a subconscious way, whether this is by means of extra movements, unusual gestures, or facial expressions—a smile, a grimace, or an expressive twinkle in their eyes that can act as a sign to other dancers. This activity is produced in relation to and in addition to ritualization's intentional conventionality and is contingent and context dependent. Such performative actions can be communicative and are a not inconsiderable aspect of the dance. The performative then is that part of the action that is added (predominantly more, rather than less, consciously) to the ritualized action of the dance and emanates from practices or actions that are not necessarily dance specific.

Dance could perhaps be viewed crudely in terms of a division between opposites, between two types of experiential activity whose qualities differ. Put simply, from similarity of enactment to difference, or from repetition of the anonymous habitual forms to the new and one off. As already indicated, the actual situation is more complex than this: the ritualized and the performative are not a dichotomy but rather a result of the dancer's double agency. Any part of what appears to be continuous dance will consist of ritualized activity with respect to some performativity and of everyday movements and gestures. Ritualization and performativity are then differing but linked modes of activity with which to capture "the immanent logic" of a dance's instantiation.[28] They designate the type of activity in which the dancer involves her body-as-experiencer (see Chapter 4). The dancer can also focus on the kinaesthetic, on feeling or sensing what is going on in the body—that is, on her inner experience—which is much less easily controlled.

When dancers can be persuaded to talk about their dancing, it is clear that many urban Concheros conceive of it as a search for states of being beyond those of the everyday, for when some time into the dance ritualization aided by the performative begin to act together and the latter begins to augment the former, the state of consciousness of the dancer changes. Through time, the movements carried out with devotion, dedication, and increasingly the forgetting of the self can induce "an exaltation," which Deren refers to as "the province of divinity."[29]

A wide range of terms is used to encapsulate such states and the dancers themselves talk about them in a variety of different ways. The attainment of "sacred" experience, or at least the approach to it, I have loosely called "transcendence." Such a state emerges when the awareness of the physical world and of what a dancer is actually involved in decreases, and the dancer brings herself ever closer to the extreme of subjectivity. I have preferred "transcendence" to "exaltation" or "ecstacy" as its verbal quality emphasizes the processual nature of what is occurring—a state that is always in the making—rather than the substantive quality that the latter two give with their implications of a state attained that has static resonances (see Chapter 7).

## THE LOCUS OF ATTAINMENT

In a transcendent state, dancers loose much of their awareness of their surroundings, but locations are nevertheless of the greatest importance to the

Concheros. The Concheros do not just dance anywhere. Many people first come across them in the main Zocalo in Mexico City. Most mesas dance there occasionally, mainly for obligations that are distinct from their more usual dances, such as those linked to political events or historico-civic occasions like those that glorify Aztec culture heroes. Since the early 1990s the Zocalo has also become the location where would-be dancers congregate in the evenings to learn the steps of the various dances by mimesis in a non-ritual situation. Although dances are predominantly held in smaller locations, the Zocalo provides the exemplar par excellence of the kind of relationship that the Concheros have with the places in which they dance and is too the location that is central to many Mexicans' sense of identity.

## THE ZOCALO AS PALIMPSEST[30]

Although all cities, most towns, and even villages in Mexico have a Zocalo, the one in Mexico City is more significant than most because it is the site where Mexico as a nation-state is symbolically instantiated. Every morning and evening soldiers in formation accompanied by a brass band ceremonially raise the nation's flag. This is also the place where Mexicans from all over the country come to feel at the heart of both Mexico City and Mexico as a modern nation-state. In addition to this, it is one of the principal localities in the city where links with the pre-colonial past can be regenerated, for the Zocalo was part of the open space of the Aztec *teocalli*, or sacred precinct, at the center of the city of Tenochtitlan. The National Palace was built over the temple to Tezcatlipoca and the cathedral on an adjacent side covered, among other constructions, the skull rack (*tzompantli*) and possibly part of the ball court (or the temple to Quetzalcoatl).[31]

The area of the Zocalo can thus be seen as a palimpsest consisting of the overlying layers of previous cultures, each not quite obliterating the former and evocative of the changing history of Mexico, from being the center of the Aztec (Mexica) empire to Spanish colony to modern nation-state.[32]

To the foreign tourist this history is just one of many, of interest for the moment but probably soon to be relegated to the status of memento. For the Mexican visitor, on the other hand, it has until recently been part of an erased past, the memory of which has largely been suppressed and relegated to insignificance at a popular level.[33] The Zocalo has been predominantly a mere *lieux de mémoire*, a site "in which only a residual sense of continuity" remained, clearly European in architectural style as is the whole historic center.[34]

For the Concheros, however, both the Zocalo and the many other places in which they more habitually dance, some of which are not even in Mexico

9

City, have a different significance.[35] They are locations that concentrate "experiences and histories, even languages and thoughts," places with embodied potential, both political and spiritual.[36] As such they are *milieux de mémoires*, settings "in which memory is a real part of everyday life" and which can act as mnemonics to the past.[37] Nora has argued that such places predominantly no longer exist (at least in France) but for an oral tradition in Mexico, such as that of the Concheros. The places where they dance are infused with or permeated by cultural memory, albeit in some cases refashioned from historical sources during the nineteenth and early twentieth centuries but continuously regenerated since then.

## AN ORAL TRADITION

There has been a tendency in social anthropology to assume that specific places are not of significance: locations have often been seen less as figure than as ground.[38] Sometimes they have even been fictionalized in the interests of universally valid assertions. But the ways in which notions of belonging and attachment to particular localities emerge, are mobilized, maintained, and modified through time are increasingly being explored.[39] Locations can no more be taken for granted than can practices for they are relational, contextual, and by necessity "remade" on each occasion, just as the practices themselves need to be regularly re-enacted, particularly when they are part of an oral tradition. Locations can not only stir up memories linked to beliefs but can at the same time act as a familiar backdrop and mnemonic for bodily practices.

The many places where the Concheros dance are the loci of cultural or historical memory and these form a nexus with embodied memory and lived experience. Before they start to dance, the Concheros add another dimension to a *milieux de mémoire*. By calling on the deity and their ancestors, they ritually enact a cleansing of the space, thus bringing their past into the present and creating a coeval space-time context.[40] No full annotation of the steps of the various dances has yet been made, and until 1992 there was no complete record of the many songs and accompanying music or the prayers, all of which have been passed on predominantly by word of mouth. The verbal and musical can be easily annotated and become an inscribed and fixed form, but this is much less easily accomplished for dance (Chapter 7). Dance is probably more deeply embodied than other oral forms. As Connerton has remarked, "every group will . . . entrust to bodily automatisms, the values and categories which they are most anxious to conserve." They know "well [that] the past can be kept in mind by a habitual memory sedimented in the body."[41] There is some evidence to show that the steps and the overall forms of the dances do indeed change much less rapidly than other aspects of the practices, such as the clothing, which by its variety can give a very good indication of the changing beliefs held about the origins of the dance (Chapter 6).

Many who see the Concheros dancing in the Zocalo assume that they are witnessing a folkloric presentation, perhaps part of a comparatively new tourist attraction. For them, the dance is seen primarily as a leisure activity carried out in people's spare time or a personal fad, as a manifestation of popular culture that with time will lose its significance and disappear. This belief is reinforced occasionally by the fact that some dancers elicit donations; however, these dancers, known as *chimaleros*, are not considered part of the Association of Concheros. The Concheros never dance for money; as already indicated, the purpose of their dance is a spiritual one.

The Concheros' practices are not new but have been a tradition in some families for generations and passed on from father to son. In the nineteenth century, dancers performed in close collaboration with Catholic confraternities in many of the small towns and villages of central Mexico and still do so in many today. At present, however, dancers are found predominantly in the larger towns and cities, the dance (at least in its present form) having been brought to Mexico City by migrants toward the end of the nineteenth century (Chapter 9). Additionally, for some time now the Concheros have permitted people from non-Conchero families to join their ranks and have danced more publicly and on non-ritual occasions, effectively coming out into the open.

In the last two decades or so, dancers who call themselves "the Mexica" have emerged who appear to threaten many of the Concheros practices. The Mexica were omnipresent as I did my initial fieldwork. In this book I focus predominantly on the Concheros, but I discuss the Mexica too because of their ever-growing influence on the Concheros' practices. Further, the presence of the Mexica helped me to formulate my theoretical position more clearly as their mode of dance was so different from that of the Concheros. An observer at any of the large dance obligations would clearly notice the differences between the various dance groups. The Concheros enact sedately, with the male and female dancers placed alternately in a well-ordered circle. Most of the men will be dressed in similar costumes that cover much of their bodies, decorated with a plenitude of plastic silver and gold, with headdresses made from brightly dyed ostrich feathers. The leader of the group will be obvious, as he dances in the middle with several of his personnel. Some of the other dancers play the stringed *concha*, which they strum as they dance. This musical instrument, formed from the carapace of an armadillo, is unique to the Concheros and probably gave them their name. A drum and other percussive instruments usually back up the conchas, giving rhythm to the dance. Between sets of dances, there are occasional peregrinations into the church and the dancing may cease completely for a while as the dancers stop to sing. If our observer stays long enough, she will also see that the dancers sing and pray as the overall dance obligation finishes, for it ends as it begins, in a highly ritualized way (Chapter 3).

The Mexica, however, go through no elaborate procedures of ritualization and do not visit the church. Although the Mexica dance the same dances, there are no stringed conchas and their music is predominantly percussive provided by a variety of drums. Their clothing, too, is much more minimal with the men often wearing mere loincloths (topped occasionally by capes) and made only from natural materials with definitely no plastic silver or gold. The onlooker may find it difficult to determine exactly which dancer is the jefe, and the dances are enacted more performatively, much faster and more flamboyantly with what appear to be a plenitude of extra steps and ostentatious flourishes. Most put as much effort into their dancing as they can muster. For these enactors the dance is primarily a form of spectacle. They are noticeably younger, predominantly male, and clearly very aware of their bodies. Female dancers in such groups are rare and those who do participate are often unable to keep up with the speed of the dancing.

The observer might then ask, as indeed did a number of priests whose monastery sponsored one dance that I attended, "Is there anything to this dance other than show?" Such a comment is unlikely to be made about the first group described above, a very traditional mesa of Concheros whose spirituality is palpable. The Mexica are eager to differentiate themselves from the Concheros and have been vociferously intent on making radical changes. Although they have not altered the actual forms of the dances, the manner in which they enact them and the organization that supports them are different (Chapter 10).

Whereas the Concheros aim to move in harmony in their circle, each taking cognizance of the dancers immediately to their right and left, and invoke the deity, however this may be conceived, the Mexica have a very consciously formulated agenda. Each dancer enacts egotistically and in competition with every other, primarily concerned, it seems, with drawing attention to himself by his difference, whether by means of his complex foot movements or by his eye-catching attire.

Those who insist on calling themselves Mexica are peripheral to the tradition and are not recognized as members of the Association of Concheros. For the Concheros, continuity is of the utmost importance and many dancers claim that no aspect of the dance ever changes, that their tradition is part of an existential way of being. Innovation and conscious creativity are strongly discouraged. The Mexica, on the other hand, are determined to rid the dance of any Spanish elements and to "restore" it to its pre-Colombian form. Mexica groups are seen dancing throughout the week, as they performatively assert "Mexicanidad" in and around the Zocalo, which, as they are very aware, was the heart of the Aztec capital of Tenochtitlan.[42] For the Mexica the meanings attributed to the dance are as important as, if not more important than, the dance itself.

There are thus significant contradictions in the dance, which are exemplified at their most obvious level in the contrast between the Concheros and the Mexica; the former consciously attempting to ensure the preservation of the ritual forms, whereas the latter have a performative attitude linked to their desire for change. But this dialectic, as already indicated, is also found in the practice of most Conchero dancers, in the tension between memory and experience, between the habitual (the so-called traditional) and how the dances are actually enacted. The Concheros seek again the embodied forms of the practice and attempt to enact only those. However, it is difficult to do so even if the desire to innovate and add something new and expressive of the individual is kept to a minimum. The dancers are not actors on a stage but the inhabitants of a city, and Mexico City can be seen as an ever-changing backdrop to the dance, the theater of its enactment.

## THE CITY AS EXPERIENTIAL CONTEXT

In general, as Mexico becomes part of the First World, the many autochthonous practices that have in part given its inhabitants their identity, and hence for so long their values, are gradually being masked, if not subsumed, by modernity. As the ethos of capitalism gets ever stronger, everyday life in many parts of Mexico, as elsewhere on the globe, is increasingly characterized by "transnational flows of people, information, money and things," and Mexico City itself is a site of myriad transactions.[43] Mexico City has both the size and character of a global city, combining international innovative enterprise where finance and commerce are articulated with a multicultural population consisting not only of Mexican immigrants but also many from other countries. With its high "concentration of artistic and scientific elites and a large volume of international tourism," it is a dynamic place with enormous creative potential.[44] Although it is a creolized and hybrid space, at another level it is a localized, even autochthonous place with its own ongoing traditions.[45] For Mexico City dwellers, the city is predominantly a space of habitual practice.

As with most rapidly expanding cities, it seems overcrowded and impermanent, even precarious, and is a place of shifting immigrant populations. Mexico City is made up of a conglomeration of former towns or villages now linked to the older central city district and to each other by urban infill. There are many betwixt and between zones, some of which are considered violent, no-go slum or squatter areas where the middle classes seldom venture, but in some of which Concheros live and vigils and/or dances are held.

Much of the city's vibrant cultural life occurs on the streets. Each *colonia* (district) has a distinct character and still-strong sense of community engendered by its civic organization, its market, church, and festivities. Mexicans tend to be gregarious, and at weekends many venture to the city center or the outlying areas. Mexico still has a powerful Catholic culture, but one that is often synergistic and place specific. Religious practices are very much a part of everyday life; many still go to church and religiosity spills ineluctably out onto the streets with processions seen on the streets at all hours of the day and night. With the rise in consumerism, there has tended to be an ever-increasing disenchantment of the world, but in many places in Mexico and even in Mexico City spirituality still flourishes. The overall sense of the Concheros' practices is of a long-term retention of an oral rural tradition that has taken from Catholicism while maintaining itself as distinct and separate.

The Concheros make a significant contribution to the cultural life of Mexico City. They are frequently referred to in the media—in television interviews, in articles about the dance that appear in the popular glossy press, or seen dancing in photographs in the national daily newspapers. They have been exoticized in television films at home and abroad and described as a "living" aspect of the Aztec past. A number of their dances form part of the repertoire of the well-established Ballet Folklorico, a long-running entertainment at the theater of the Belles Artes, to which many better-heeled visitors, both foreigners and nationals, are drawn. But, as indicated, many will have noticed them dancing perhaps in their home colonia, by the side of the road as they travel through the city or beside the cathedral in the main Zocalo.

## THE CHAPTERS

This volume is in a way a book within a book. I begin by contextualizing the dance to understand why the dancers enact and what it is about the dance that draws them. My aim is to situate the dancers "within the system of signs and relations of power and meaning that animate them," although my overall view of the dance can only be partial, capturing "fragments" of the cultural field.[46] Chapters 2 and 3 are ethnographic and set out details of the context in which each dancer gains her experience of the dance in the sense of knowing what is expected of her. In Chapter 2, I outline the organization of the overall Association of Concheros and of a mesa, and in Chapter 3, I detail the activities that the Concheros perform during a vigil and a dance.

After providing an idea of what being a Conchero involves in terms of external practice, I turn in the second part, "The Experiential Nexus," to aspects of the dance itself. There I am less concerned with the physical context in which the dancers enact than with the internal state of the dancers. I focus on the buildup of experience and the various elements that contribute to that and explore the relationship that a dancer develops with the dance and with others by means of their shared experience and various external markers integral to the dance.

In Chapter 4, I explore the activity of the dance, examining in more detail than I have so far how dancers aim for ritualization tempered with a degree of the performative, the very basis of their experience of the dance. Chapter 5 looks at how the desired ethos of the dance, which develops through time as each obligation unfolds, is indicated by various verbal mnemonics. The words carried on the banners held aloft during the dance help to direct that experience, for they indicate the various phases that the body-mind should go through in the overall obligation and what it is that the dancers are seeking, although this is often difficult for them to put into words. I look too at the various tenets used to talk about the dance and in particular the phrase "carrying the word," which is how they tend to verbalize their embodiment of the dance. This tenet resonates with what they see themselves as doing as they dance. The emphasis in this chapter is strongly on ritualization and the denial of personal agency.

In Chapter 6, however, I show how clothing is one aspect of the dance over which each Conchero can openly assert a degree of individual preference. Although each mesa usually has an overall idea of how dancers should costume themselves, some more uniform-like than others, it is in the details of their dress (and, more rarely, the overall style) that dancers are permitted a measure of creativity. In this aspect, they can express realizations that have come to them during its enactment or at other times. The clothing worn can give the outside observer and other dancers an indication of the degree of experience or attainment of a dancer.

In Chapter 7, I ask the question, Why dance? to draw together the various threads of this experiential "commission" (a term the Concheros themselves use) in which the dancers are involved and how it lifts them out of their everyday selves. Although I begin by discussing briefly the significance of the other media used and of the music in particular, overall in this section of the book I focus on the processes of inner empowerment, that is, how the dance acts upon its enactors to change states of mind and achieve contact with the deity.

The third part, "Power Concerns," shifts the focus to analyze a different kind of power: the kind of empowerment that at the extreme becomes the egocentric pursuit by some of external prepotency by means of identity politics (which is touched on briefly in the discussion of clothing, for what should be the external representation of inner realizations are at times ego driven). Despite the claims that the dance must always be about denial of the self, in Chapter 8 I discuss the power struggles that have shaped the dance's organization and, more importantly, how dance groups form and segment through time. In Chapter 9, I look at these processes in a historical perspective. Here the dance is placed in the context of a long-term overview built up from the few known historical traces. Despite attempts to suppress most of the spiritual aspects of Aztec life after the Spanish Conquest, dance practices as oral traditions continued for centuries, particularly in rural areas such as the region of the Bajio, where the Concheros' origin myth claims their dances began. Dance, when mentioned in colonial documents and especially those related to the indigenous subaltern population, is usually described in negative terms. In the second part of the chapter, I reconstruct the history of the dance during the twentieth century by means of oral histories—an analysis that begins in Chapter 6 when I look at how the clothing worn has changed during the twentieth century.

Chapter 9 also provides the foundation for understanding the position taken by the breakaway Mexica, whom I discuss in Chapter 10. For them the dance is not so much an ontological necessity as part of a political stance, one of the many arrows that can be deployed in the bow of Mexicanidad. Although in the early 1990s, the Concheros strongly rejected any Mexica-ization of their practices, they have gradually adopted some of the Mexica's aspirations, ideas, and modifications. In effect, since 1992, the Concheros' dance has become increasingly Nahuatl-ized, and that of the Mexica, although still largely political, has become more concerned with the spiritual.

## TITLES AND WORD USAGE

"Carrying the word," one of the Concheros' main precepts, should be understood metaphorically, implying the forms of the dances, the words of the songs, and the music. The dance practices in particular, once embodied, enable the dancer to enact in a ritualized way, giving up at least in part her self-conscious self as she aims devotedly to recreate the ritual movements.

The "Forming the Self" of Part 2, on the other hand, cogently sums up what many dancers realize as they dance and why I believe they are prepared to dedicate themselves to "carrying the word." But if the dancing body (following what some dancers have said to me) is seen as a crucial "medium of self-development,"[47] "performing" rather than "forming" the self is by implication different. In performing, the dancer, rather than being open to inner experience, is presenting his (but less often her) self, at least in part, as a pre-formed being that is seen as complete or finished and not available to the kinds of ontological changes that transcendence can and does bring. In performing the self, the dancer chooses to assert intentionally. In Part 3, the book looks at power concerns and identity politics and touches once again on the difference between the Concheros' approach to the dance and that of the Mexica. Where for the Concheros there is a sense in which the dance is a means for them to open themselves up to it, as a fount of experience, and learn from it (which for some is seen as "work-on-the-self"). To the Mexica, the dance is much more a flaunting of a self that has already been formed; the Mexica have no personal existential doubts or uncertainties. They tend to describe their achievement in the dance as a "high," by which they mean an endorphin high, a form of physical "catharsis." The idea that this could (or, in the Concheros' terms, will) be connected to spiritual experience is mostly absent; for them the dance is less a form of communal devotion and more a performance backed by their ideology: a nativist and restorationist doctrine (Chapter 10).

Finally, as the perspicacious reader will by now have noticed, I have used "she" rather than "he" or "he and she" when I am talking generally about both genders. I have too used "Mexica" for both the singular and the plural. Because I frequently use "ritualized activity" linked to the "performative" to analyze the kind of activity in which the dancers are involved, I have on the whole avoided using "perform" as a verb and have wherever possible employed "enact." This is partly because perform has the everyday sense of "to do" or "carry out" and is used for a whole range of activities, but more particularly because I have given the "performative" or "performativity" a very specific sense.[48] "Enact" is a neutral term that does not imply any particular mode or way of acting but rather action carried out in a framed situation. The framing of the dance is important as the discussion on ritualization has already implied, and it is to this that I turn in Chapter 2 and even more specifically in Chapter 3.[49]

# PART ONE

# THE EXPERIENTIAL CONTEXT

**2.1.** Dancers moving into formation before a dance at Chalma.

# THE CONCHEROS

A book on the Concheros faces the challenge of how to do justice to the many dimensions of their tradition while keeping the larger cultural context in which it is situated in mind. Of how to portray as much as possible about the dances as collective enactments while also attending to the diversity of the enactors' experiences of them. I turn first to particulars of the wider organization and the prescribed dances whose significance each dancer learns about early on. I look next at a particular *mesa,* Santo Niño de Atocha, with which I danced, and at the positions that can be attained by dancers or that need to be allocated. But although the Concheros form an Association with a big A (at least in their own minds), theirs is not a form of organization with a big O; their order, if indeed there can be said to be any overall order, has only partially been inscribed and is not regulated by law. Phenomenologically, perhaps the best way to summarize the Concheros' organization is as "ordered anarchy" for it is fluid and contingent.[1] Aspects of the dance can disappear from one year to the next, and indeed certain occurrences, such as a meeting of the *jefes,* convened in 1989, may not be held for several decades (see Chapter 8).

To the novice, initially, there is no apparent overall organizational control, only a loose conglomeration of mesas.[2] Clearer is the fact that one dance event leads to the next, which rather than seeming to be part of an imposed external order is more like an emerging progression based on memory. The organization of each mesa is, however, clearly rigid; each is hierarchical and uses a

nomenclature borrowed from the military. A leader who is high up in the hierarchy is known as a general but more usually as a jefe, those immediately below
him as captains, the bearer of the standard as a lieutenant (or *alferez*), and
the dancers as soldiers. Importantly, however, there is more fluidity than the
militaristic terminology may at first indicate. There are few overall ordinances
and no absolute prohibitions, at least initially, but when a dancer is received
(initiated), she commits herself to the dance for life and promises that her
practice will comply with the traditions of that mesa.[3] This, of course, does not
mean that the tradition is unchanging, although the dancer should always bear
continuity in mind. In fact, those involved find change difficult to measure; it
is more obvious to those not participating continuously, such as the dancers
that come and go (or the anthropologist). Inevitably, traditions that are not
inscribed change, altering imperceptibly and contingently, because one person
or the group as a whole propels them in a new direction.

As several (more Catholic) dancers told me, the dancers are seen as soldiers for Christ and the conquest of which many often speak is a spiritual one.
The military terminology reveals a hierarchy that corresponds to the level
achieved in the dance and can be seen as a metaphor for the degree of spirituality attained: the dancers form a sacred army and the dance is their combat.
Dancers who reside in the countryside and those who have migrated to the
city but still see themselves as *gente humilde* tend to be more clearly practicing
Catholics. Others, and especially those more middle-class dancers who have
thought about their religiosity in greater depth, are often less overtly so. Thus,
the language used in the dance, although universal, has differing resonances.
For some its apparent esotericism is strongly Catholic (see Chapter 5), whereas
for others it is more indigenous and, at the extreme, related to New Age beliefs
(see Chapter 10).

## THE ASSOCIATION AND ITS PALABRAS

The dance of the Concheros has until comparatively recently been confined
to central Mexico where the overall ordering consists of three large associations. In relation to Mexico City, one association is in the region to the northwest known as the Bajio, in the States of Guanajuato, Queretero, and Jalisco.
Another is in the northeast in the States of Puebla and Tlaxcala, and the third
has members who live in the State of Hidalgo, in the State and City of Mexico
and to the south in the States of Morelos and Guerrero.

The adepts of the third association, known as La Gran Tenochtitlan, are
today predominantly concentrated in Mexico City. Overall, the other two associations tend to be more conservative in their practices, beliefs, and apparel

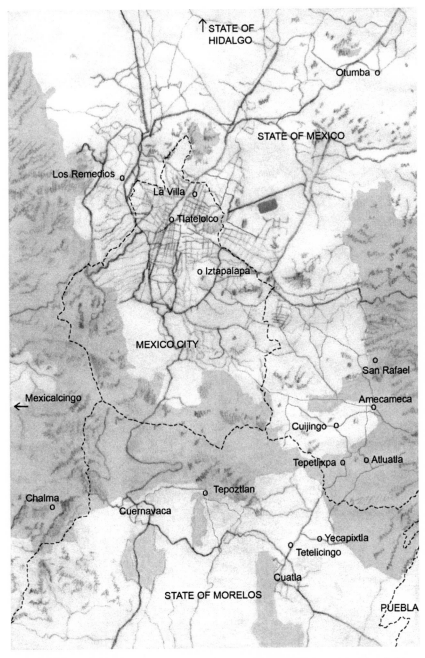

**2.2.** Mexico City and the various places with which the dance has close associations.

with more dancers who are still rural laborers. It was suggested to me that if I really wanted to study the dance, to know what the tradition used to be like, I should go to the Bajio, because what takes place in Mexico City is but a pale imitation of the dance elsewhere, a very hybrid form. However, as several trips to the Bajio confirmed, much of what is enacted in Mexico City, despite years of urban practice, is still close in many respects to the rural forms. Nevertheless, the mesas of La Gran Tenochtitlan do tend to be more socially heterogeneous, even though few dancers in the countryside are now rural (or indigenous) peasants. Many work as semiskilled or unskilled laborers, whereas those who have recently moved to the city have similar jobs or work in factories or hospitals or as drivers. Most dancers are mestizo and have lived in the city for some time, earning a living as secretaries, schoolteachers, shop assistants, and a wide variety of other occupations. Some mesas, such as Santo Niño de Atocha, attract professionals like solicitors and doctors; people involved in the arts such as painters, potters, professional dancers, and musicians; as well as academics and well-to-do housewives with time to spare. At the other end of the social scale are those who operate in the black economy. The dance also attracts people who are or see themselves as outsiders or social misfits. In the 1960s, Santo Niño de Atocha was one of the first groups to open up and attract people who were not direct descendents of country dancers but had been born in the city, known popularly as *gente de banqueta* (literally, "people of the sidewalk"). Some groups are still closed to outsiders but most today permit anyone who is interested to join their dance.

A number of mesas make up a *palabra* and several palabras constitute an association (or *conformidad*), such as that of La Gran Tenochtitlan. That association, also sometimes called the Union General or the Mesa Central, consists of two main palabras: Santiago Tlatelolco, comprising about eight mesas and associated with the location of Tlatelolco, and the Reliquia General, comprising about seventeen.

Each mesa is autonomous and under the command (*mando*) of its leader. It has a name and a banner indicating when it came into being, rules (which may or may not be written down), personnel, and its program of events. It also decides what the dancers should wear, but the dances performed, the songs sung, the prayers said, and the music played will predominantly be the same as those of all the other mesas in that palabra and even conformidad. The structure is thus primarily hierarchical and pyramidical but there are also crosscutting ties of alliance (see Chapter 8). However, a mesa does not need such alliances to survive: each is essentially autonomous and independent and aims to fulfil its range of obligations during the course of the year.

## THE PRINCIPAL DANCE EVENTS

The four principal dances are convened for different saints in locations of both Catholic and indigenous significance. The dance at La Villa is the largest and possibly the most important. Held in December, it is said to complete the sequence of the principal obligations, or to "close the circle."[4] La Villa is so spacious that all the groups can dance together at the same time.

The dance at Chalma tends to be spread over four days.[5] This place has been a pilgrimage site for at least two millennia. Located to the southwest in the State of Mexico, it was sufficiently difficult to access from Mexico City that it was not immediately conquered by the Spaniards. The church contains a black Christ and the crucifix includes portions of a miraculous image found in a cave behind the present church in 1537 where effigies of pre-Colombian deities had been worshipped for centuries. Amecameca is a country town in the eastern part of the State of Mexico and the dance there is usually smaller. This area was densely populated at the time of the Aztecs and, despite centuries of Spanish influence, is still dominated by place-names that are Nahuat (Nahuatl was the language spoken by the Aztecs). Its Christ figure, the Senor del Sacramonte enshrined in a cave, is considered to be a brother of the "Father" at Chalma. Los Remedios is also a pilgrimage center and the place of the Virgin of the Remedies. The image itself, clearly of Spanish origin, is tiny with a crescent moon at her feet.[6] When portrayed in popular imagery, however, she usually stands on a maguey from which pulque (a fermented drink made from maguey juice) is brewed and drunk in quantity at Los Remedios, enabling her to be seen as Mexican.[7] Today Los Remedios is just outside the boundaries of Mexico City but La Villa is within them. It was in the latter location that the dark-skinned Virgin of Guadalupe was said to have miraculously appeared to Juan Diego in the late sixteenth century. The Virgin has through the centuries become an icon and the national religious symbol.[8] La Villa is today the most important Catholic shrine in Mexico; its first church was constructed over an Aztec temple on the adjacent hill of Tepeyac and has been superceded by two located immediately below it.

The four prescribed dances are the biggest of the year; all the mesas dance together and the entire membership of participating mesas are expected to attend. The locations, known as the birthplaces of the four winds, form a conceptual cross in relation to the center, Santiago Tlatleloco (located in Mexico City). Santiago is believed to be the *correo de los cuatro vientos* ("the courier of the four winds"). As one female dancer put it, he is the animator: "[T]he mesas go out to dance, to do their work at the four winds but come to the center," where the fifth most important dance is held in late July.[9]

## THE SACRED GEOGRAPHY OF THE FOUR WINDS

The conception of the four winds, linked to the four directions (and usually assumed today to be the cardinal points), is of great significance to the Concheros. They dance "to honor the four winds," which are linked to "the way of the cross" (*el camino de la cruz*), the arms of which (the Santa Cruz) communicate with each other symbolically as segments of the year. The mountains were once of as much importance to this sacred geography as the towns; for example, the Cerro de Sacromonte above Amecameca and the Cerro de Tepeyac above La Villa are both mentioned in the song the "Santissima Cruz." Of even more significance is the Cerro de Sangremal, located in the Bajio, which marks the place where the Concheros are said to have originated (Chapter 9). It seems that some of the locations of the principal obligations have shifted during the course of the century as the arrangements for the dance have become more focused on Mexico City, as, for example, with those groups who dance at Iztapalapa rather than Amecameca.

## A MESA AND ITS ORGANIZATION

Despite the importance of the large dances, each mesa is primarily concerned with its own traditions. Each has its own annual obligations that may occur as often as once a week (and sometimes midweek) in addition to the four or five major dances. Many are smaller dances linked to fiestas in diverse locations that may be secular and religious, and some may be special onetime events initiated by invitation, perhaps a dance for a cultural occasion such as one I attended in Valle de Bravo in the State of Mexico. It was organized by the town authorities linked to the Casa de la Cultura (the Cultural Center).[10] As previously mentioned, mesas also appear at celebrations held to honor Aztec heroes or deities or at political events linked to indigenous rallies, such as to celebrate Dia de la Raza (Race Day) in October. These are events that take place in the central Zocalo.

## THE JEFE AND HIS ORATORY

The jefe as head of the mesa orchestrates the group's activities and mores. He (but less usually she) coordinates the annual events and decides which new invitations to accept for dances and vigils. Many leaders have the status of captain but are known more simply as *jefe*, or more informally still as *compadre*, as was Ernesto Ortiz (of Santo Niño de Atocha). The jefe is also responsible for the moral and, in some groups, physical welfare of the personnel and for overall discipline. He should carry out all his activities and responsibilities in a way that is "respectful and caring" of the dancers and of others in his mesa.[11]

**2.3.** Santo Niño de Atocha dancing on the outskirts of Mexico City (Colonia Arenal 1-A Seccion). Unusually, a circle has been painted on the ground with *"DANZA"* inscribed at its center.

Each establishes an oratory (*oratorio*), which acts as the headquarters of the mesa and where the jefe should be prepared to welcome dancers at any time. Its altar is usually decorated with flowers and supplied with candles, nightlights, and tapers. It is here too that the standard, held during the dance by the alferez, is stored (often with older ones that are no longer used) with extra musical instruments (particularly *conchas*) that can be loaned to dancers.

Above the altar will be images of various saints, especially the ones that the group particularly venerates; for Compadre Ernesto's group, they were the Santo Niño de Atocha, San Juan de los Lagos, and the Virgen de San Juan. In addition, more ubiquitous images may also be displayed, such as the Virgin of Guadalupe, Christ on the Cross, the Santa Cruz de Chalma, La Divina Providencia, and the Anima Sola. Others may be from sacred locations of significance to that mesa that it has visited in the past. A jefe can store his memorabilia here too: certificates of honors that he has been awarded, mementos from trips made, statuses conferred, and, more recently, photos of the dance and of himself. It should ideally provide space enough to hold the mesa's annual vigil and the vigil for the *animas* (souls) on November 1 (the Day of the Dead).

**2.4.** One corner of Compadre Ernesto's altar arrangements.

Compadre Ernesto's oratory was, however, a room in the house where he lived, which was delightfully ad hoc and so small that all the dancers of the mesa could have filled it many times over.[12] Other mesas have larger oratorios: the oratory of the Corporación (a group currently outside the two main palabras) is highly ordered and its altar more like that found in a Catholic church.

Compadre Ernesto held the position of jefe from 1922 until his death in 1997. Although he had ceased to dance by the late 1980s, he was always seated at the center of the circle, overseeing the progress of the dance by seeking a balance between non-coercive leadership and the need to fulfil the group's obligations; he felt strongly that these should be as unchanging as possible. He considered that in many other groups the discipline was being lost, which in part, he claimed, came from Catholicism. Although not a staunch Catholic, he was born and bred as such and this was the basis of his beliefs. He had little patience for New Age ideas and "energies" and even less for so-called pre-Colombian beliefs or practices; as a mestizo, from his point of view the dance was a post-conquest phenomenon.

Compadre Ernesto came from a family of *gente humilde* who were also dancers; he had danced all his life, never had a permanent job, and always been poor. He had little interest in literacy, but his considerable musical skills had been promoted at times by professionals. For some years after his wife's death in 1979, he had lived a hand-to-mouth existence. In the late 1980s, however,

**2.5.** Compadre Ernesto with his niece Carmela, his great-niece, and great-nephew Ricardo, whom he later made his inheritor.

he installed himself in the simple house of his niece, whom he had just rediscovered, in the colonia (neighborhood) of La Laguna in Tlalnepantla. La Laguna is one of the many poor areas on the outskirts to the north of Mexico City consisting at that time of patches of countryside interspersed with sprawling squatter settlements. Although La Laguna was quite urban with a few shops selling bread and other basics, its houses were less durable than they appeared at first: the street walls made from concrete block often masked much less robust structures within. The colonia is flanked in the west by one of the busiest six-lane highways into Mexico City, crossed only by a high footbridge, and on the south by the river of Los Remedios, a polluted and stinking waterway that moves sluggishly eastward, carrying sewage.

Ernesto Ortiz was humble, nonjudgmental, and known to be compassionate and generous toward his dancers. His words were simple and, as one dancer said, he always displayed a touch of humor. Her sense was that his "simplicity was much more transcendent" than that of many more pretentious jefes. He had no interest in imposing his will on his dancers. In his view, the dance was not about the militaristic, punitive discipline imposed by many jefes in the past and by some still today. As he once said of his leadership, "we are living in glory" for if thirty years ago the *sahumadora*, the jefe's principal assistant, had done something remiss in the center of the circle, she would have been instantly replaced and then punished afterward with three whippings. Today this kind of external discipline is infrequent. Some claimed that his mesa best maintained the old traditions and was by implication one of the most disciplined, but this was not immediately apparent to me, for the dancers did not move their feet in exactly the same way nor did they dress in similar clothing. Rather, for this group, it was the dancer's internal state that was most important.

Not surprisingly, Jefe Ernesto was not interested in power, although he was prepared to talk about it. To him it was of little significance as to whether he was seen as a general or not because, as he said, titles are unimportant. He had raised (started) many mesas in the States of Mexico and Hidalgo as well as in Mexico City and the dancers of these mesas were his followers. This kind of achievement usually brings with it the recognition of generalship, but he was denied this honor until just before he died. What interested him was imposing discipline by practice in order to conserve the tradition. One of the maxims of his mesa was that nobody could be prevented from entering it; other mesas that are more closed may not give permission to dance. A new dancer in his circle was not told how to dance but was left to learn by trial and error. Novices were rarely stopped from doing something differently; instead, he hoped that they would discover over time that what they were doing was inappropriate. As one dancer said, "my jefe doesn't prohibit anything."

Overall, Compadre Ernesto preferred that his group dance on its own at the big dances rather than being hemmed in by other groups. At Los Remedios, for example, he chose to dance the weekend before the official date or one week later to avoid congestion. He did this so that his dancers could concentrate on the obligation and avoid the competitiveness that can develop between groups, such as over the place chosen or the amount of space used. He was in his quiet way innovative: he kept to the traditions yet bent certain aspects to suit himself and allowed his dancers to do likewise. Because of this, linked to his personality, he was able to retain his dancers.

As for all mesas, the numbers who appear for any dance fluctuates: at a small dance as few as fifteen to twenty might turn up whereas for any of the major dances as many as a hundred dancers usually appear. Some of these dancers only go to La Villa or Tlatelolco (as the more regular dancers know from years of experience). Some stay for the entire dance, others for only a short while. The varying levels of attendance indicate the other demands on people's time and their other interests. In the past such behavior was punished (it was claimed) but such admonitions today would only cause a jefe to lose his dancers.

It is difficult to assess the overall number of Concheros. I estimate that there may be about sixty mesas and hence about 6,000 dancers in the Association of Tenochtitlan alone, and only some of these belong to one of the two main palabras. There certainly seem to be more mesas, and smaller ones, in the Mexico City area than in the more conservative Bajio, where groups often still have up to 300 dancers.[13]

More important, however, than actual numbers is the strength of the message that the dancers impart to those who see them dancing. The city-based groups dance at various locations and sacred sites in and around the city and in small towns nearby in the States of Mexico, Guerrero, Hidalgo, and Puebla and sometimes even further afield, such as in the States of Oaxaca, Chiapas, and Yucatan.

A jefe aims to sustain his group of dancers to maintain the tradition. He constantly needs to find new adepts, although some are more choosey about their dancers and some are more successful. Compadre Ernesto's group was open and encouraged people to join. Both he and they then could ascertain whether they were cut out to dance in the longer term. As the leader of the group, the jefe is the one who during an obligation usually determines the order of events and who is said to "have the government" (*tiene el gobierno*). The jefe takes overall responsibility for each dance obligation and oversees its development from the center of the circle.

## THE SAHUMADORA

According to some, the sahumadora is also part of the "gobierno," especially when the jefe is a man and she is his wife.[14] As such, she is responsible for the incense burner (*sahumador*), which before the dance gets underway she lights and keeps burning throughout the dance. Whereas the jefe is usually concerned with overseeing the external development of the dance, the sahumadora is largely preoccupied with internal matters, such as balancing the personalities and energies of those in the mesa. She ensures that any difficulties or tensions between dancers are resolved as the dance gets underway by effectively equilibrating and harmonizing the ambience of the dance and keeping nefarious influences at bay. Concerned with the more sacred part, she is said to be "the light, the center" of a dance or vigil, and her incense "cleanses and opens the road," enabling contact to be made with the deity and the *animas*. As one non-Catholic jefe also indicated, by "carrying the fire, that is, the incense burner, she convokes the four elements (water, air, earth, and fire) and the physical force of the four winds and with these, she invokes the deities." On a more mundane level, the sahumadora is responsible for ensuring that charcoal, the *ocote* with which to light it, matches, and the copal for the burner are provided. The incense burner must be given full attention at all times and should never be allowed to go out.[15]

**2.6.** Angelica censing a new pair of leg rattles during a dance at La Villa.

Each mesa usually has two sahumadoras, often known as the *malinches*; the second backs up the first and may ring a small bell during a vigil or before a dance begins (*malinche de campaña*). One female jefe suggested that the sahumadora is more important than the jefe, and others commented that a jefe is considered of little value if he does not have a "grande malinche."[16] But the jefe's position is the only one that is permanent.

Angelica has been first sahumadora for Santo Niño de Atocha since 1979. She established a footing in the group quite quickly, even though her family had not previously danced in Mexico. Acting as backup to the jefe's wife, Maria, she carried Maria's bag of incense at every dance and became her replacement when she died in 1974. Although her entry was easy and her rise fast, it was still some eleven years before she was received (in 1983). To be received implies that the dancer has made a commitment to dedicate herself to the dance for the rest of her days. It is not really an initiation into new knowledge but rather an acceptance of the responsibility of upholding the dance. During a special vigil, the incumbent is draped in the mesa's standard.[17] As Angelica put it, dancers take this step when they are prepared to dance "until God cuts off their steps": they make a commitment to God and *las animas de los muertos* (the spirits of the dead ancestors). Angelica asked for them and received them in the dance. Many dancers are frightened of the commitment and some dance for years without taking this step. On the other hand, no dancer will be received until the jefe is sure he or she is ready. Once received, a dancer is obliged to come to the four big dances.[18]

Angelica has worked through the years at various occupations. She particularly remembers her stint on the metro as a ticket seller before being dismissed in 1970, an injustice for which she hoped for a long time to receive compensation. Before and during that period, she had been involved in various theater projects as an actress and a mime and had even worked in a travelling circus for a while. She had also had a son, but as an unmarried mother "before the time," as she put it, "when that was really acceptable" she had a difficult time finding work. In the early 1970s, Angelica was going through a period of insecurity: she was "dying inside" and it was during this moment of crisis that she encountered the dance.

When I met her, she was working as a secretary in a middle-class area (Colonia del Valle) but lived in the historic center, where she had a set of rooms on a street in the seventeenth-century College of Vizcainas. Her accommodation was simple but spacious. A large windowless room divided horizontally, somewhat precariously, was used as a living space below with a bedroom and workroom above. A flight of stairs led to a pleasant, light upper room. Here her son, her nephew (whom she looked after some of the time), and her mother (when she came to visit) slept.

Water had to be fetched in buckets from a neighboring *vecindad* (communal tenement), and as she did not have a kitchen, she always ate out at one or another of the innumerable eating places in the city center.[19] When her job ended and money became scarce, she put together a kitchen. From late 1989 onward, neither Angelica nor her son, then in his early twenties, had any clear source of income; he was usually trying out some rash scheme or another. Although they had no immediate neighbors in the building—the units on either side had been boarded up for years—there was usually a constant flow of his friends and accomplices, as well as Angelica's *compadres* and *comadres*—Concheros who dropped in to visit her when in the area. She dreamed of one day running a restaurant on a piece of land that she owned on the southern edge of the city given to her by her mother. By the early 1990s, Angelica was finding it increasingly difficult to combine earning a little money with her activity as a sahumadora and was devoting most of her time to the dance.

Angelica remained loyal when in the late 1980s many of Compadre Ernesto's most dedicated dancers became involved with the Sufis. Although the Sufi rituals impressed her, she indicated that she did not feel them in her "bones": Sufism did not pull her in the same way as the Concheros dance.

She talked about it as "catching" you: "You don't look for it, it entraps you. It opens a path for you that you have to travel and the longer you are on it the more you understand. For all dancers are always learning; when you think you've got there, there is always further to go." As she put it, to dance is to be, and being leads to becoming. Little by little, it awakens an understanding. Dancing for her is not only a way of being with God but also leads to being better able to be with one's self.

## THE CAPTAINS: CABECERAS TO PALABRAS

Aside from the sahumadora and jefe, there are a number of other posts. Most mesas have up to four captains, although often these are only appointed just before a jefe's death. Compadre Ernesto's mesa in the early 1990s had four named positions—two *cabeceras de la derecha* and two *cabeceras de la izquierda* (heads or concheros of the right and left, respectively)—held by dancers who knew the procedures thoroughly because of their years of experience in the dance. As an obligation began, it was from these dancers that the three *palabras*, who actually take responsibility during each dance, were usually chosen. The work of the palabras is to encourage and look after the dancers, "to ensure that the obligations are carried out as they should be according to tradition and that harmony is achieved" (see Chapter 3).

The cabeceras in this group were different from many of the dancers in other groups. Because of his musical abilities and lack of chauvinism, Compadre Ernesto had attracted to his circle through the years dancers who were middle class or professional and who were more assertive than he himself was. Antonia, first conchera of the left, had joined the mesa a little after Angelica in the mid-1970s. Antonia is a successful painter, has had one-person exhibitions in Mexico City and New York, and in the 1990s was taking professional dance classes. During that decade, among other achievements, she put on a performance of "La Malinche" in Mexico City. Partly of Irish descent, she had been brought up as a Catholic and will without doubt stick with the dance for the rest of her life. She dressed for it with style and expected discipline from the dancers, not only with regard to how they danced but also in how they attired themselves. Antonia came without fail to all the important dances.

Margarita's story was rather different. The second conchera of the left, she had also been with the mesa since the 1970s. In the 1990s, she taught Arabic studies part-time at UNAM and edited a small journal called *Cuatro Vientos* (the "Four Winds"). She had become involved quite extensively with the Sufis as a dervish and that had taken her away from the dance for long periods of time and on occasional visits to New York. She is an excellent musician and

**2.7.** Compadre Ernesto taking refreshment during a dance in Valle de Bravo.

plays the concha very well. By the 1990s, she tended to come only to the principal obligations.

Of similar longevity in the dance was Alfredo, second conchero of the right. He had studied in London, supporting himself precariously by making music, which he still does to this day. Married to Linda, who comes from a family of dancers, he lives with her, their children, and her grandmother in a small flat east of the center; they are far from well off. It is hard for Linda to come to most dances because of her various responsibilities, but Alfredo attends with more regularity. He too joined the Sufis and was not seen much for some time but eventually returned.

Eduardo, first conchero of the left, had travelled to Santiago de Compostela in 1978 with the Compadre. Trained as a lawyer, he was in a more secure situation economically than many of the others. In the 1990s, he lived outside Mexico City near Amecameca, where he ran the family business.

## OTHER POSITIONS: THE SERGEANT AND ALFEREZ

The more arduous cargos of sergeant and *alferez* are not permanent, although they have no fixed periods of office (at least today). The positions are generally reassigned when the incumbent begins to find the task too burdensome, usually because he has become tired and thus less than meticulous in the performance of his duties. The sergeant's work is to ensure the order of the dance. Rather than submitting to its exigencies, he polices it, keeping an eye on all the dancers and disciplining them when necessary. He tries to prevent them from eating or drinking alcohol surreptitiously between dances and, as the dance begins again, orders them back into place. In the past he applied a whip when all else failed. In some groups, the sergeant still carries a symbolic whip and in others he dons a mask or a bear costume.[20] For Santo Niño de Atocha, the sergeant usually placed himself inside the circle.

The work of the alferez, or standard-bearer, is to dance carrying the group's banner. This is not a much sought-after position because the standard is extremely heavy and its bearer is expected to dance with it continuously either in the center of the circle or with the other dancers. During a vigil, however, the alferez' role is negligible, although the banner may be present. Federico had held the position for a while but it was passed on to Pando in the early 1990s.

Pando had had a tough life. Previously married with four children, he was living quite close to the house of the jefe in another rough area in the north of the City in the early 1990s. On one occasion when I offered to buy him a beer, he declined because of a promise (promesa) he had made to the Virgin. The original promesa dated from the time he had lost the use of one eye in a brawl. He had never been able to afford surgery, constantly had to dab at it, and wore a patch, which he believed strongly affected his ability to find another woman.

He began dancing late in life, having often watched the dance at Chalma but never participated himself. On one occasion, in the church he battled between "God and the Devil" as to whether or not to rob someone who had produced a wad of banknotes. Subsequently, he was searched on the riverbank by police, who failed to find the juanita (marijuana) that he had hidden in his clothing. So grateful was he for this miraculous deliverance that when a compadre suggested he should join the dance in thanks, he did so.

His life clearly took on a new focus thereafter. He drank and smoked less but found that a little of one or the other before a dance helped him to bear the heavy weight of the standard. He danced barefoot in order to be in touch with the ground and said he often felt as though he were flying. He had clearly been empowered personally by this responsibility, but after seven years he had begun to find the cargo too onerous. He wanted to pass it on to someone else or, at the very least, share it, but no one offered. Nonetheless, Pando still performed his duties assiduously; he had only not turned up three times (even before he held this cargo). He too had been received.

Pando's is very much a Catholic viewpoint, although he became a Jehovah's Witness when young in order to reject his childhood conditioning. He dances for the Virgin above all else and, as already indicated, is still involved in Catholic promesas. He abhors all the changes that he sees dancers "making egotistically to the dance." When asked why he danced, Pando was clear that to dance is to "adore your God," whoever or whatever that may be, and in the Catholic pantheon, as he admits, there are many saints. For him the dance was not a search for self (this was not part of his conceptual universe), but he did admit that it changed his outlook, cleared his conscience, and made him a better person.

Although it was the middle-class dancers who predominantly led the dance and formed the core of the mesa when I first encountered it, its continuity in the longer term was provided by those less involved in such a lifestyle, people such as Pando, the jefe himself, and others such as Doroteo (a dancer who should have raised his own mesa), but above all else by the many soldiers.

## THE SOLDIERS

Important though the named positions are, to hold an obligation a mesa needs soldiers, for without them there can be no dance. A good jefe will be able to keep his soldiers because they will have been drawn to the mesa in the first place by his/her personal qualities and feel that their efforts are appreciated. Some soldiers act as occasional palabras but many will never have the opportunity to do so. Predominantly, they are people who have been with the dance for less time than the cabeceras. One occasional palabra was Felipe, who by the late 1980s had already been a dancer for a decade but who did not yet (according to some) have the kind of understanding that warranted a cargo. While I was in Mexico City, he participated in every obligation. His singing was superb. He also made it clear that the dance was for him not something to be talked about but rather sensed. He worked as an events organizer at a bookshop and only had a restricted number of hours available to give to the dance. In the early 1990s, he decided to set up a business washing cars with his brother, who also dances. He is a considerate individual and does not push for power. He likes the equality to be found among Concheros, the freedom that associating gives to work things through, and having worked things through still be friends as Concheros.

Rosa-Elia, on the other hand, had danced since she was quite young. Her family is well-known in the dance and her many sisters are also dancers. In the 1990s, she married Marcos (who earlier had been the standard-bearer) in a ceremony held at Teotihuacan. She had a gruelling full-time job as a secretary and despite her many years of experience was often just too exhausted to come and dance. The jefe would have liked to have given her more responsibility and often called on her to lead the "Vibora" (the Viper), a dance of recent innovation appropriated because of its therapeutic effect and very different from the others.

In addition are the many that never "carry the word." Some will have joined quite recently and may change their status with time whereas others only come from time to time. Miguel was dedicated, had a lot of free time, and came to many obligations. He achieved increasing significance in the group, although he had danced for less time than Felipe and no one seemed to know what he did with the rest of his life. Carlos, who had danced for decades, had still not perfected many of the steps or the playing of the concha. Although he was one of the "old guard," he did not dance by focusing his attention on achieving ritualization and his steps were often not in time with those of others. At one point, it was suggested that he should be made alferez of the standard but he lacked the requisite discipline. He tended to arrive when he wanted and was always keen to get away before the final ritual had finished. As he drove a car and other dancers often relied on him for lifts, he often took them away before they were ready to leave. He had worked in a bullring, the theater, and many other occupations. When I first met him (by then he was in his late fifties), he lived in his brother's house in Mexico City. By the mid 1990s, he had settled in the town of Valle de Bravo where he made pots. He turned up to dance quite frequently for, as he once remarked, the dance is a wonderful place to meet women. Alberto studied film in the early 1970s, but rather than making movies in Europe (as he put it), he ended up in an open prison in Nayarit on a drugs charge, where he was able to read extensively. By 2000, he was back making films, but for much of the 1990s, he had made his living in a hand-to-mouth manner, selling *artesanias* (handicrafts), clever mirrors, or whatever seemed appropriate or came his way.

Of some of the women, Payata had been a professional dancer but by the 1990s only danced with the Concheros. She was married to an academic scientist and escaped from her family on weekend mornings to come to the dance. She took me once to a school of dance where I caught a glimpse of the link between professional dance and the Concheros as we watched a group of middle-class children dressed in pink ballet shoes performing Conchero dances to music played on a tape recorder. Berenice is an artist whereas Olga used to be a successful actress when younger but now runs an antiques business. Olga dresses exquisitely with great attention to detail (see Chapter 6). She was very close to the Compadre for a number of years, as was Tita, who for a while was the backup sahumadora. Tita made artwork from feathers, at the time, which she exhibited in Mexico and the southern United States.

The dancers mentioned so far in this section were the core who came to dance regularly when I first encountered it. These dancers, other than Rosa-Elia (see below), never danced with a mesa other than that of Compadre Ernesto, for they were loyal to him and most had been received. To begin with, however, a neophyte often moves from one group to another in search of the right mesa, or later by invitation or inclination or simply dissatisfaction with their jefe.

Susana, for example, who was apparently without a job, had time not only to fulfil obligations with Compadre Ernesto's group but to dance with others as well, such as the mesa in Tepetlixpa to which her *compañero* Herman belonged. During one rather busy week she danced twice and went to three vigils.[21] She was one of those dancers who clearly was involved with many mesas. She came from the same family of dancers as Linda and had not yet made up her mind as to where her loyalties would lie in the longer term.

There were others also during that period who came to all of Compadre Ernesto's obligations but who (like Susana) were not totally loyal and attended those of other mesas too. Dancers sometimes change groups temporarily (or more permanently), whereas others have more complex obligations. For example, Rosa-Elia, because of her strong family connections with other mesas, sometimes danced with them. In 1989, her sisters—Maria Luisa, Teresa, and Nancy—although also members of Compadre Ernesto's group, were dancing primarily with the jefe Felipe Aranda. At Los Remedios in early September, they danced with his mesa, not a week later with Compadre Ernesto. These choices, however, were not necessarily based on loyalty; the final decisions were often determined by other considerations, such as the need to attend school. Dancing with other groups is acceptable, provided permission has been obtained from your jefe.

A rather different example is that of Teonahuiltzin (or Teo for short). In 1989 she had no links at all with Compadre Ernesto's mesa but danced mainly with Mexica groups. She came from the Sierra Norte of Puebla, was of Totonac origin, and had apparently danced during her childhood. While studying in the city, she was drawn to the Concheros but eschewed their syncretism. In the community of Pantepec, where she was born, she claimed that practices still existed that were "pure and uncontaminated by Christianity." By 1993, she was acting as second sahumadora to Angelica but openly admitted that she danced with other mesas. Both she and her companion, Daniel, had been received by Compadre Ernesto on the understanding, apparently, that as long as it did not conflict with an obligation of his group, they could continue to dance elsewhere, *but* as his dancers. Teo's beliefs were an interesting combination of a veneer of Christianity with a predisposition toward anything that seemed more indigenous. She commented to me once about the lack of a unified philosophy among the Concheros but had her own well-developed views about what the dance meant (which she would have liked others to share). She danced, she said, for the *madrecita*, for Tonantzin or Mother Earth, but then went on to say in "the name of the Father."

In general, at any moment in time, there is usually a core of dancers who appear with regularity at every dance. A dancer comes for a while with enthusiasm, meets new people, and counts on seeing them at the mesa's various obligations, but then other interests may begin to dominate or responsibilities get in the way and that dancer may disappear for a year or more. With time some loose interest. As one dancer commented, "after about ten years the magic begins to wear off and the overpowering need to dance becomes less"; she was one of the dancers who became involved with the Sufis. Many of the more mature dancers are married and lead more settled lives, but for younger dancers whose lifestyle may be less fixed, their affiliations are often less clear-cut. There is therefore always a certain fluidity of personnel.

Many of Compadre Ernesto's dancers are still *gente humilde*, in the sense that they are not upwardly mobile (although they have grown up in the city). But as already indicated, Compadre Ernesto had drawn middle-class dancers to his mesa for decades and this continued through the 1990s. Most of the neophytes were people who were middle class, had or had had at some point a career, and liked to spend some or all of their free time dancing. There were also occasional foreigners who stayed long-term, usually in order to "find" themselves. For a time Compadre Ernesto's mesa was considered by other more traditional jefes to be overly heterogeneous. Overall, however, the dance is far from a middle-class phenomenon. Other mesas consist predominantly of *gente humilde* and do not particularly welcome middle-class or professional people as dancers. My acceptance as a dancer by Santo Niño de Atocha was, comparatively speaking, easily achieved but to have been accepted by other mesas would probably have been somewhat more difficult.

So how do outsiders join the dance? People become dancers by a variety of means. Some are invited by friends, whereas others become involved when as bystanders they are invited to join in and, having done so, decide to come again. According to one of the older jefes Don Camacho, in the past, a jefe investigated carefully those who came to join a group, but this no longer occurs partly because mesas are now much more open and there is not the time.

Also because of time constraints, rehearsals (*ensayos*) before an important obligation now seem to be rare, although in theory they are supposed to occur. In the past, apparently, a group practiced quite extensively in the run-up to a dance.[22] Today the speed and complexity of life in Mexico City is such that there is little opportunity and, as the General Gaudalupe Hernandez also pointed out, there are now so many obligations. His mesa, however, still holds a few, the one before the dance at La Villa in December being particularly important. A rehearsal can only ever be a practice session for the next dance because what occurs on each occasion is spontaneous. As Angelica frequently emphasized, the dance is always changing, it is always accommodating to the place where the dance is being held, to who has turned up to dance and what is happening in the group itself, and to the palabra, the association, and the world at large. No one can know in advance the order in which the dances will be carried out.

**3.1.** The flower form on completion in a Catholic home.

# THREE

# THE OBLIGATIONS:
# FRAMING THE CONTEXT

"At a Vigil . . . you will sense what it is that gives harmony . . . for it is the
discipline that produces this sense of harmony and a very strong energy."

—ANGELICA

Vigils and dances as events are closely interrelated and both are built up spatially
and temporally by means of ritual framing. Whereas the last chapter looked at
the personnel of the dance, in this chapter I want to detail the Conchero's
obligations by looking first at a vigil (*velación*) and then at a dance. Although
each dance is inevitably somewhat different from any other and one vigil differs
from the next, I will give an idea of the overall form of each. To begin with, not
every vigil is followed by a dance just as not all dances are preceded by a vigil.
A vigil held after a death will not have an accompanying dance as that would
be inappropriate. If a *mesa* is invited to dance for a cultural event or a town's
fiesta, these more secular one-time dances will not be preceded by a vigil. In
general, a dance follows a vigil only for well-established Catholic festivals and
the four major obligations (although for the latter, the associated vigils tend
to be quite small). A vigil usually has a powerful effect on the quality of the
subsequent dance: those who have been awake all night will already be in a
heightened state of awareness, which leads easily into the ritualized state for
which the dance aims. The vigils are immensely important to the dance and are
a prerequisite of it. In the opinion of many dancers, the dance would be lost if
the vigils ceased.

**43**

## A VIGIL IN PUENTE NEGRO

Vigils are held indoors in the house of one of the mesa's dancers or the jefe's oratorio. A more private and informal affair than a dance, attendance is usually restricted to members of that mesa. Special clothing is never worn, although those involved usually dress warmly in preparation for the long hours of work constructing a flower form which is laid out on the ground usually in the form of a cross and takes most of the night to assemble. On special occasions, such as a vigil carried out after the death of someone of importance to the group or to one of its members, outsiders do attend, such as relatives of the dead person, the owner of the house, friends, and colleagues.

The jefe is usually the first to arrive, as was the case for a vigil held in Puente Negro in the house of Roberto Partido (Pando).[1] Angelica appeared a little later than usual. Holding up her lit incense burner, she begged forgiveness of the jefe for her late arrival, which, she explained, had been caused by her uncertainty as to whether she was well enough to act as sahumadora. Staying up all night can be hard on the physical body, although vigils are usually cleansing and spiritually uplifting.

During the next couple of hours, other participants arrived, bringing with them large candles, nightlights, incense (and their incense burners), packets of cigarettes, and, more especially, bunches of flowers of all types and colors—carnations and pinks, lilies, gardenias, stocks, chrysanthemums, daisies, gladioli, and, if in season, marigolds. Closed flowers are considered particularly appropriate for the Virgin (the focus of the vigil), but in general they should be fresh and new. One early anxiety is whether there will be enough flowers for the construction of the form, but by the time the ritual itself gets underway there are usually plenty.

In this house, the altar was a simple table covered with a cloth and adorned with prized draperies. The furniture had been moved back, and the room transformed into an oratory for the duration of the vigil. As the vigil, to be followed by a dance on the next day, was part of the fiesta of the Virgin de la Merced, an image from the local church of Nuestra Madre de la Concepción was present. In addition, there were a stout wooden cross about four feet high (with a figure of Christ's head placed at the intersection of the arms) and a couple of banners.[2]

As the celebrants arrived, they presented themselves on their knees to the four winds and offered candles (or nightlights) to Angelica. With her incense burner, she made the sign of the cross above, below, and on each side of the candle before kissing the base of the incense burner and holding it out to be kissed by the celebrant. The latter then accepted the very hot burner and, holding it firmly at its base, made the sign of the cross to the four winds above, below, and to each side of the candle before returning it to Angelica, who repeated these same motions. This type of complex ritual sequence is part of the framing for both vigils and dances.

Angelica also censed the flowers and other gifts received and then the musical instruments proffered. Between arrivals, she placed the large flowers (such as the gladioli) in vases lining both sides of the altar for use in the final stages of the vigil. In preparation for the construction of the form, the remaining flowers had their stems cut short and the heads placed on various trays near the altar according to color or type. On this occasion, Angelica placed a bucket of red roses at the center front of the altar, which was surrounded by numerous nightlights, packets of cigarettes, a bottle of rum, and a large collecting box for the Virgin.

During the preparations, attendees mill around, talking to each other about the impending vigil or catching up on gossip. Others from the neighborhood came in and out of the house or simply leaned in through the open window to comment on what was happening. The sergeant, who oversees the catering arrangements, will see to it that the celebrants are usually offered coffee or herb tea and *pan dulces* (sweet bread).[3] At this time the *conchas* will be tuned, which for Santo Niño de Atocha only the jefe could do; snatches of music are played; serious discussions (or even minor disputes) about procedure are going on. But conversation, which is usually rife, should stop as the first invocation is sung, followed by various *alabanzas*.[4]

"Alabanza" is the collective name for the songs sung by the Concheros that are predominantly in praise of God. An alabanza may last for as long as twenty minutes. Each begins with what is known as the *planta*, effectively the refrain (or base), which is sung by the Conchero who initiates it accompanied by the concha. This is repeated by everyone after the various verses, of which there are many: "Panal divina" (Divine honeycomb), for example, has sixteen, each of which is sung twice, as is the chorus. Once the final verse is reached, a brief musical interpolation may follow before the chorus is sung once again by its instigator in an attenuated manner at half speed and subsequently repeated slowly and with greatly heightened emotion by all those assembled.[5]

The real work can then begin with the jefe saying a few words about the occasion, followed by the "Pasion" (Passion), a piece of music played on the concha that is simple, extremely powerful, and considered to be of "divine inspiration."[6] This moves directly into the *petición de permiso* (the petition for permission), which seeks to solicit aid and protection from the four winds and to render present various saints, the Holy Spirit, and, most importantly, the *animas conquistadoras* (the conquering spirits). As the petición is sung, two large candles placed earlier on either side of the altar are carefully lit.[7] Known as the *cabeceras* (heads), they are said to "open the way" and to represent duality.

| | |
|---|---|
| *Que viva Jesus,* | Long live Jesus |
| *Que viva Maria,* | Long live Mary, |
| *Que vivan las animas conquistadoras* | Long live the conquering souls of |
| *de los cuatro vientos,* | the four winds, |
| *Y el alma de "quienquiera" que nos da su* | And the spirit of "whoever" who gives us her |
| *Santa Luz.* | sacred light. |

As the last words are reached, the rest of the candles lined up in front are also lit. These are said to be the *cuenta* or *planta des animas*, believed to provide a direct link with the spiritual realm of the animas and which must be carefully scrutinized at all times during the vigil.[8]

The calling up of the various saints and the animas is followed by prayers (such as the Lord's Prayer at more Catholic vigils) and then more alabanzas. At this vigil, just before the permiso a clean cloth was placed over the trays of flower heads and they too were presented to the four winds and censed. The cloth was then carefully laid out on the floor directly in front of the altar in preparation for the construction of the flower form. This work is supervised by the sahumadora, who chooses two helpers (and these are usually female) to assist her in its construction. The work has two parts, the *tendido*, the laying out on the ground, followed by the *levantamiento*, the raising of the flowers.[9]

The sahumadora is responsible for the form's overall appearance, which will depend on the flowers available and the inspiration of the moment. As Rosa-Elia indicated, "The work of the vigil must come from the heart. Because you don't know what flowers you will have or what candles, which personnel will be present or what hour you will begin or end . . . you do it from the heart and it comes out as it should at that moment. To make the cross is a creation, and the force that you feel at the time of its manifestation is what is important."

She stated further that "you must not have a predetermined idea in mind as to how you will assemble the form" She placed particular emphasis on this because in the early 1990s, on various occasions flower forms had been shaped to predefined forms. An Aztec symbol, such as a nahui ollin (which takes the form of a diagonal cross), drawn on a piece of paper had been laid out on the cloth beforehand. Those involved had decided that they were going to make it "with five white flowers here, five red flowers there and so on when they had no idea who was going to do the work or what flowers there would be." Introduced by some dancers who had assumed a knowledge they did not yet possess as they were comparative newcomers to the dance, this idea had apparently been ridiculed by celebrants from other groups with whom Santo Niño had held vigils.

Often a simple cross with equal arms will be appropriate, sometimes with four smaller arms in its interstices. On other occasions, the arm farthest

**3.2.** The flower form under construction at the vigil in Puente Negro.

from the altar may be slightly longer than the rest (thus, giving it a distinctly Christian form, as was the case at this vigil).

The placing of each flower of the tendido takes time. After each has been chosen, the sahumadora offers it to the four winds by passing it over the incense burner and then hands it to her helper who also censes it. Each flower is said to be a soul linked either to the animas called up at the beginning of the vigil or to ones of importance to the helper. However, it is the sahumadora who "knows" what flowers should be laid where and thus determines the mix and color scheme.[10]

Making the tendido takes time because the work is only carried out while an alabanza is being sung. The ones considered most appropriate for this part of the vigil (on this occasion) were those that concerned the Virgin, many of which are recorded in a small printed book.[11] There are however a number of alabanzas that are still passed on orally such as the following one:

| | |
|---|---|
| *Santa Rosita,* | Saint Rosita, |
| *Santa Romero,* | Saint Rosemary, |
| *Vamos cantando a dios,* | Let us go singing to God, |
| *Vamos cantando,* | Let us going singing, |
| *Vamos rezando,* | Let us go praying, |
| *Vamos diciendo "El es."* | Let us go saying "He is." |

This alabanza refers to various herbs (*romero*, "rosemary") and includes, according to some, marijuana.[12]

As the celebrants settle into the work of laying out the form, the distinction between those who are Concheros and those whose house it is becomes clearer as many of the latter may disappear and go to bed. The work for this concentrated and painstaking first phase is usually done kneeling. As the work proceeds there are brief breaks during which celebrants can stretch themselves, talk, and get something to drink or eat; but as the music begins again, work should be resumed. Alabanzas considered appropriate to that phase are then sung as those present focus their attention on the cross being laid out on the ground, a space lit predominantly by candles. Once complete, thanks are offered to the assembled company in the form of short impromptu prayers about the work and how it was carried out, followed by an alabanza that marks the time of night reached, such as "Seria la una" (It could be one [in the morning]). A break in the proceedings usually then follows when everyone moves elsewhere to eat a meal, perhaps chorizo and beans with chili or tamales, and to drink coffee or pozole, and often to down alcohol or smoke surreptitiously.

The next phase, the levantamiento, consists of the slow taking apart of the form and the tying of these same flower heads to two wooden sticks known as

**3.3.** An alabanza being sung during a vigil. Note Compadre Ernesto playing the concha on the extreme right.

*bastónes*. The name is probably linked to the *bastón de mando* that all jefes are said to have. This phase is accompanied by singing and new helpers are appointed. At this particular vigil, each of the bastónes was begun with a bunch of white uncut flowers tied at the base and five roses at the top, and then the red, yellow, and mauve flowers from the tenidido were carefully secured by pieces of string to its length after each flower head had been censed once or twice more. The two helpers (and on this particular occasion I was one) worked together, each taking a bloom at the same time in consultation with Angelica. The alabanza sung near the end of this stage was "Recibe Maria las flores."

> *Recibe estas flores, con gusto y anhelo, que son escaleras que suben al cielo.*
>
> [Receive these flowers, with pleasure and yearning, for they are ladders that ascend to heaven.]

When completed, prayers are said and thanks offered, especially to the four winds, as the helpers kneel in turn and slowly direct themselves to each of the winds, on their knees with an incense burner in one hand and one of the bastónes in the other. The bastónes are then laid out on the ground, placed one over the other either in front of the altar or on other occasions on the altar itself.[13] The "Agradecimiento" (Thanks) is sung and prayers to the Virgin ("Ave Maria") and the Lord's Prayer are offered up and further thanks proffered to the animas. By this stage it is usually almost dawn (ca. 4:30 AM), and at that particular vigil everyone settled down to sleep perched on the edge of a chair or across two or more or lying on the floor wrapped in blankets.

## THE LIMPIA

More often at this time a *limpia* (cleansing) is initiated to purify each celebrant. Introduced by further prayers and alabanzas, extra bastónes are made up from the flowers not used for the main form. Sometimes the sahumadora carries out this cleansing, at other times it is the jefe or one of the palabras. At one vigil, held especially for a family who had predominantly absented themselves for much of the night, the room suddenly filled once again as all sleepily lined up as the cleansing started. The bastón is passed over the head, down the back, and then down both arms of each. Cleansed first were those members of the family who had been at the vigil, followed by those who had just reappeared, and then the Concheros. Angelica tended to move the bastón with so much force that the flowers were crushed and scores of petals fell to the floor, which is where eventually the bastónes end up too. The reason for this, as Felipe explained to me, is that the flowers have absorbed all the negative energy and need to be discarded. Usually at this point the petals from any remaining flowers will be thrown confetti-like over those present. As dawn breaks, the floor of the room is often covered in a multicolored carpet of flower petals; many Concheros commented to me on their beauty.

---

Vigils are occasions when people can mix and mingle in a way not possible at a dance. It gives celebrants a chance to talk informally and begin to get to know each other better. Although talking should stop while work is in progress, there is plenty of time to pursue conversations already started, broach new ones, exchange addresses and telephone numbers, catch up with the news about others, or philosophize about the Concheros and the nature of God. At a dance, this is more difficult because it is held in an open and public place and is more demanding physically.

The atmosphere of each vigil differs partly because each is organized for different reasons. Some are more Catholic, others much less so, some quite party-like and informal, others more restrained. Because the one described here was for the patron saint of the local church (most mesas probably celebrate several vigils each year for various saints in different locations), it was both Catholic and subdued, although the latter does not necessarily presuppose the former. It was restrained partly because we were in a very Catholic household and for the first time, but mainly because early in the night the assembled com-

**3.4.** A cleansing being carried out at the end of the vigil held for All Souls Day (Day of the Dead).

pany had processed with the image of the Virgin and the cross plus the banners of the mesa to the house of a man whose son had recently committed suicide. His house was not yet fully completed but by the standards of the area was not only large but extremely luxurious. Downstairs, horses were stalled, which we passed as we ascended a narrow concrete staircase to a large marble-floored central space decorated with many gold-plated fixtures. Here the images were placed, prayers offered, and several alabanzas sung before coffee and pan dulces were served. Shortly thereafter the group returned to the main vigil with donations of additional bunches of red roses for the altar. This was an unusual occurrence, although as Angelica often said, you never know what will happen next or what you will be asked to do.

It is common practice after the death of someone of significance to the dance or of importance to a particular mesa to hold a special vigil nine days later. The body is usually buried or cremated before the vigil and prayers (the Misterios de Rosario) are said every evening for eight days;[14] on the ninth night, a vigil is held when the *sombra* (literally, "shadow" but also spiritual protector) of the deceased is celebrated. At these vigils, the *animas conquistadoras de los cuatro vientos* will be specifically invoked by name, particularly those of importance to that mesa. For Compadre Ernesto's group, the animas of particular significance are those of former jefes in his palabra. The vigil aids the spirit of the dead person to leave the house. As one Conchera said, "all that's left of you is 'dressed' in flowers, watched over [in the sense of opened up to the spiritual domain] and then rises up. Nothing is left that ties you to the earth." Usually a year later another vigil is held (*cabo de año*) when according to the same Conchera, the cross is said to be raised. The deceased's friends usually come to both, some only dropping in for a brief period but others staying for the duration of the night. The altar is typically decorated with photographs and various mementos of importance to the deceased.

Vigils of mourning are different from those held for saints at which the personal animas are of almost secondary importance. Distinctive is the most important vigil of all, held on All Souls or *Día de los Muertos* (Day of the Dead) on November 2, to which all those who have been received into a mesa should come even if they only appear at five in the morning after another party or working a night shift. Those with children, however small, usually bring them for a while.

This is the moment in the year when households throughout Mexico build an altar adorned with fruit and flowers and decorated with paper cutouts of skeletons and colored pan dulces in the form of skulls.[15] At this vigil a more complex flower form known as the *santa xuchil* is laid out. Materially, the santa xuchil is a wooden structure with twelve arms, described by Angelica as the *santo sacramento* and in form rather like a monstrance in the Catholic church.[16] To this, the identically formed tendido of flowers is attached after having been set out on the floor. Extra bastónes may be made up to cleanse those present using other flowers but the santa xuchil is left intact. I was told that for Santo Niño de Atocha, the flowers are left to dry and then burnt and scattered to the four winds, possibly in February, when according to General Guadalupe Hernandez (from a different mesa), they are replaced by other flowers.[17]

At this vigil, the animas of all the previous jefes of a group and other important dancers are summoned. Initially called up were Maria Graciana and Juan Minero, well-known animas not just to the Concheros but in Mexican popular religion generally, to establish contact with the rest. Some thirty-six captains of La Gran Tenochtitlan were then summoned by name, followed by the names of the dead known personally to those at the vigil; all present (including myself) were asked to offer the names of five or six animas to the first palabra.

Each is called out in the form of a prayer.

*Anima de Ignacio Gutierrez, que en purgatorio esta, fue conquistador de la Gan Technochtitlan.*

[The soul of Ignacio Gutierrez that is in purgatory, he was a conqueror of Great Tenochtitlan.]

Those assembled then respond with "rogamos para el" (we supplicate for him). Compadre Ernesto indicated that previously each rogation was sung, which must have taken much longer.

As each anima is named, a candle (or nightlight) should be lit. According to some, this should be done not by holding a flame to the wick but by letting burning wax drop from a candle held above onto the wick of the candle below.[18] If the wick lights easily, the anima is said to have descended and shown that it wants to be present, but if not, this tells those who know how to read the candles that it may be "sentida" (sensitive or touchy) or "atorada" (obstructed) in some way. Only someone with expertise should do this, for reading the candles can indicate how the vigil is developing; it is said that from the sparking or spluttering, "everything can be seen." Effectively, the candle stands in a metonymic relationship to the anima, and for its duration (and one can be replaced if it burns down completely) can communicate to those who can read the signs. As one Conchero once commented, the candles are like a screen that lets you see how things are going: "We say things like, did you see how serene Compadre Faustino was tonight?"

At this particular vigil there were more than 100 nightlights and these were lit as the permiso was sung, each celebrant going forward and taking from her predecessor a small candle to light the next. Set out in the form of an open (Christian) cross directly in front of the altar, the candles enclosed a space that was filled later with marigold heads (cempasuchil). The form of the xuchil was laid out further away from the altar and also predominantly formed from marigolds, for they are associated with death and considered the most appropriate flower for the Day of the Dead.

The alabanzas during this type of vigil are different: much less Catholic, more specifically Conchero, and celebratory. Each concha player is given a chance to lead his or her preferred alabanza. That the atmosphere can be quite intense and not always easy to deal with was shown on this occasion, for there had been tensions beforehand.[19] The house where it was held was that of the then-second conchera of the left, who had not been appearing regularly. There were various mutterings about this throughout the night. The physical santa xuchil had not been brought and another had to be found, which appeared after considerable delay and much consternation. I was scolded for taking photographs, causing further mutterings of disapproval. Other anxieties were prevalent too; there was some upset about who had been chosen to do the cleansings and that someone had failed to kiss the cross on the altar afterward. Wrangles ensued later about transport to the next obligation, and in addition a lot of alcohol was being drunk. I had not been feeling completely well beforehand, but by the end I could hardly wait to escape—although probably the lack of air

**3.5.** The flower form at the vigil for All Souls.

in the concrete-frame house with small, crowded rooms was partly to blame. My reaction was, however, unusual for after previous vigils I had felt elated. To stay up all night may seem potentially quite exhausting. (Some jefes, but not Compadre Ernesto, allow celebrants to go to sleep.) In fact, a vigil can and usually does energize; the combination of singing all night combined with the lack of sleep (being *desvelada*) puts the celebrant into a liminal state and helps induce a heightened awareness and a new sense of self (see Chapter 7).

I have so far described the vigils that involve celebrants from just one mesa but this is not always the situation. Some vigils bring together dancers from more than one mesa, particularly those held before the four major dances. Mesas, however, find it easier to dance together than to hold vigils. It was at one such joint vigil that the critical comments about the drawing intended to predetermine (and radically alter) the flower form were made. The vigils held before large dances comprise several different mesas from an association and are usually much less private. One I attended before the dance at Los Remedios was held outside and the groups joined together not to build a flower form but to venerate a cross. Through the night, the celebrants kept watch over a large Cruz de Perdon (under the *mando* of jefe Miguel Luna from Tlatelolco), which had been brought in from the hillside to the church earlier and was to be returned at the end of the fiesta.[20] The vigil was held on Saturday night before the large dance on Sunday.[21] Very striking was the preponderance of brown skins, for most of those present were from country mesas. Their sense of what the religiosity of a vigil should be was different: the whole was much less self-consciously ritualized, the participants did not "stand on ceremony," and the hum of conversation did not necessarily stop as an alabanza was sung.[22] By about 10:00 PM, the number of standards indicated the presence of five mesas. One that arrived later began by singing urgently and passionately, as is usual in such a situation, "Llege, llege, llege . . ." (We've arrived, arrived, arrived . . .), and another gave as their greeting the following alabanza:

> *Buenas noches Señór General, buenas noches al pie de tu altar* (×2)
> *Con el Ave Maria, el Ave Maria, al Ave Maria hemos de llegar.*

> [Good evening Senor General, good evening at the foot of your altar
> With the Ave Maria, the Ave Maria, the Ave Maria, we have just arrived.]

This alabanza indicates their recognition of the presence of the general Guadalupe Hernandez, by whom they were then received.

The alabanzas sung were more varied than at other vigils because every mesa present sang different ones. Most had loose-leaf books containing the words that acted as an initial mnemonic. As a previously unknown alabanza began, Concheros from other mesas quickly picked up the tune on their conchas and the words of the refrain. Consisting of about forty-five people, the assembled company spent the next few hours singing (with a break around midnight and again at 2:30 AM for coffee and pan dulces).[23] The night had a very good feel to it. Many people were enjoying themselves together, playing their conchas and mandolins.[24] Listening to them was more like a jam session than a ritual; everybody was playing together, picking up the tune as they began and slowing down (often a little late) as the alabanza drew to an end and changed mode. The large cross lay on supports close to the ground, a vase of red flowers on one side and a candle placed at its intersection (brought by me) among various other flowers (brought by me and some others) that had not been ritually cleansed at the beginning.[25] Satin drapes were placed over the cross during the night but otherwise it was largely ignored until about 4:00 AM when it was ceremoniously lifted up, carried over to the church, and placed outside (the church was locked, although a service had been going on inside until 2:00 AM). Columns of dancers then formed, headed by the sahumadoras and the standard-bearers, who rocked gently from foot to foot. More alabanzas were sung, at first standing and then kneeling ("a powerful and painful experience"), culminating in the petición de permiso led by the general, followed by short invocations from those present. These brought the obligation to an end at about 5:00 AM.

Vigils are the less visible part of the Concheros' work, because they occur at night, usually indoors, and often in private houses and also because they concern internal states rather than external forms. During the watchful hours of the night, the significance of the animas becomes clearer. The Concheros believe that the "animas conquistadoras bequeathed" them "these obligations." This is a frequently reiterated phrase used as people begin to speak during a vigil or a dance. It is at a vigil too that the beliefs and sensibilities that give the dance its ethos are made most apparent. As one dancer indicated "it is the vigils that give the dance its center" and they are the more important form spiritually. The older and more powerful a dancer is the more animas he or she will be connected to and the greater will be his or her powers of invocation. It is from the animas that the *fuerza* (force) comes and it is their power that protects the celebrants. But their protection is also important during a dance.

## THE DANCE

The Concheros, as already indicated, are generally better known for their dances. Whereas the vigils enable a more spiritual empowerment as attention is given to inner processes, the external activity of dancing can engender an additional and different sort of power.

**3.6.** En route to the church in the early morning after the vigil in Puente Negro with one of the bastónes and bunches of flowers for the saint.

A vigil may lead straight into a dance; if so, the celebrants will be awakened by the jefe at about 6:00 AM (possibly to the sounds of a conch shell being blown). After a sustaining breakfast, in the early morning sunlight the dancers will slowly dress for the dance. This often takes time but gradually the new apparel transforms the faces of the night before as the dancers carefully arrange the feathers in their headdresses and help each other with their clothing (and some of the women put on makeup). Dancers who have not attended the vigil will start arriving, and by 11:00 AM—at the latest—it is time to dance. Forming themselves into two lines, the celebrants move with slow dance steps (*pasos de camino*) as they traverse the streets headed by the palabras. In Puente Negro, the palabras were followed by the sergeant and the jefe, flanked by the standards, and the sahumadora moved between the lines.

On arrival at the church, they received a blessing from the priest and were engulfed by crowds of people attending a mass (followed by communion) accompanied by rock-style music played on guitars. Simultaneously, the sounds of Las Mañanitas drifted in, played loudly outside by a brass band where too the Nuestra Madre de la Concepcion in her box awaited them. Accompanied by huge bunches of flowers, she had been taken to the church by a small procession just after dawn to ask permission to dance there. Now she was positioned outside in the place where the dance would later take place.

**57**

**3.7.** Preparing to dance outside the church in Puente Negro. Note the cross of the patron saint on the right.

If there has been no vigil the night before, preparations for the dance are carried out at the location of the dance. The dancers change their clothes as discreetly as possible in the open air, present their musical instruments to the sahumadora to be cleansed, and are received by the jefe or, if not taking an active role, by the first palabra. The first, second, and third palabras will have already been chosen for that obligation. After singing the alabanza "Al la batalla, mi General, que lleva su santa luz" (To the battle, my General, you who carry your sacred light), the dancers then congregate into two lines headed by the second and third palabras and enter the church. Although the first carries the responsibility for the dance—that is, he carries the word—it is important that the second and third not only collaborate with the first but work together as protectors and supporters in order to develop the potential of the dance. Throughout the obligation, the second will decide which alabanzas to sing and the third (the regidor de danzas) will decide who is to dance next.

Once inside the church, the permiso is sung to gain consent from God and the Virgin. As the dancers leave, they move out backward, still in ritual formation, and sing *Nos vamos de tu presencia, nos vamos a caminar* ("We leave your presence, to take the path"—literally, "walk"). Whether a dance is preceded by a vigil or held on its own those involved are now ready to ask permission to dance from the four winds. This is done with a series of complex but continu-

**3.8.** Dancers in Aztec-style costumes enacting in the Zocalo while being watched by passersby.

ous maneuvers in which they present themselves in two columns to the four winds, moving from the north to the east wind, then to the west wind, then to the south, and then to north again. This frames and demarcates the extent of the space in which they are to dance. The two lines subsequently fan out into a circle and the sahumadora, the jefe, and the standard-bearer take up their positions in the center with the drum.[26] The space within the circle is then further ritually cleansed by the sahumadora, bringing the dancers into an ever-more liminal space. This she does by presenting her incense burner once again to the four winds as alabanzas of thanks are sung and prayers (including the Lord's Prayer) intoned. Minor adjustments may then be made as some celebrants change their positions such that each dancer has someone of the other gender on either side, if possible. The moment to dance has almost arrived.

Another process of framing is then undergone as all ask permission with their feet, initiated by the shouting out of "El es Dios." This permiso is repeated before every single dance and ideally (at this early stage) accompanied by the music of the pasión. The first dance is always led by the jefe or by the first palabra and the leader sets the pace and style from the center where all the other dancers can see him. This is followed once again by the permiso, the dance of the second palabra, the permiso again, and then that of the sergeant. The third

**59**

palabra completes the initial set of dances, and by then, the tempo and tone of the obligation will have been set. The next to dance in the center will usually be any honored older dancers or visitors to the group. Participating visitors will have gone through a separate ritual with their standard earlier as the space was being cleansed.

Throughout the obligation, the dancers with positions will dance together in a loose inner circle, many of them playing conchas; the outer circle will be made up of the soldiers. In the center too will be the drums, the sahumadora, and the sergeant. For very large dances, however, there may be as many as three circles, the first consisting of the palabras and guests, the second those with conchas and other musical instruments, and the outer the soldiers. Children are usually accommodated within the circle or the space between circles.

It is then up to the regidor de danzas (the third palabra) to decide who will lead from the center. By placing himself in front of his chosen dancer and gesturing with his concha, he invites that dancer to come into the center to enact the next dance. The dance chosen is usually one that that dancer feels particularly comfortable with and is able to perform with confidence. This is important, as all the other dancers will be taking their cues from him or her and trying to follow as best as they can. A second dancer can sometimes be chosen to support one who is unsure of him- or herself.

No specific dances are enacted during this phase, although some obligations start with a dance that is linked to the location or occasion. At Los Remedios, for example, "El Pulquita" (referring to the drink pulque) should be performed ideally by the first or second palabra. Thereafter, there is no preset order either of alabanzas or dancers. A particular named dance may be danced once, not at all, or as many as three or four times.

Few know the total number of dances. Some indicated that there were as many as twenty-five but others estimated as few as fifteen (which roughly accords with an assessment I made in 1990). If superficially classified by what they are named after, most can be categorized as follows: Aztec deities, animals (in Spanish), natural entities or elements, agricultural practices, and those that are most apposite for particular occasions or locations as mentioned above.[27] But there are also plenty that defy a simple classification, such as "El Pólvora" (the explosive or the lively) and "La Cruz" (the cross).[28] One dance normally follows quickly after another and the circle may dance for up to four hours without a break. If any dance is performed most often, it is "El Sol" (the sun), which is frequently danced several times during any one obligation, closely followed by "La Cruz," a dance that has a more clearly Christian form. In the opening sequence (planta), each dancer first takes three danced steps to his or her left, stamping with the right foot after the first two and after the third

**3.9.** A dancer in the 1960s. This may be a one-off performance. (Photograph Ruth Lechuga)

marking out a cross on the ground. This is followed by three steps to the right, stamping with the left foot and again marking out a cross on the ground.

For every dance, the planta is danced twice, followed by a variation, which is also danced twice, before the planta is once again enacted twice over. All dances have a similar structure but the number of variations differs, with some having as many as eight. Which of these variations is chosen will depend on the knowledge of the dancer in the center and what she senses is appropriate. The variations are slightly more complex than the planta. The circle of dancers will know when that dance is about to end because the initial sequence will be danced more slowly and in a marked way.

The movement of the dances is primarily in the feet, consisting of turns, stamps, twists, crouchings, leg crossings, and small jumps. While dancing, the dancers do not touch, although in "La Paloma" they cross legs fleetingly as they move and in "El Venado" the dancers go down onto their knees briefly. "Aguila blanca" has an intermediary part that is sometimes enacted during which the dancer in the center, on his knees, bends slowly backward until his head touches the ground, usually still playing his concha. A small group of female dancers form a circle around him, each placing a foot on his stomach. This is quite unlike any of the other dances (and I never saw it performed), although one visiting dancer from Apaxco did apparently sometimes enact it with Santo Niño de Atocha.[29]

A better idea of the overall unanimity of the dance can be gained by an analogy with the solar system: the dancer in the center is like the sun surrounded by its planets, with the sun marking the rhythm and the planets dedicated to following the sun. The dancers must be aware to an extent of how their personal "orchestration" of the dance is blending in with that of their neighbors on either side.[30] And indeed another analogy used by some dancers was that of an orchestra. The dancers in the circle know their steps (more or less well, depending on their experience) but gain their sense of the timing not just from the music but also from the way in which the dancer in the center (the conductor) executes it. They are facing into the center, focusing their attention on the person dancing, not facing outward to the onlookers; the dance (as it were) turns its back on those watching.

Until comparatively recently, throughout the association the discipline inside the circle has been tough. Once the circle had formed and the dancing had begun, it was unacceptable to leave the circle for the entire duration of the obligation; indeed, dancers were not supposed to ask to leave even to relieve themselves. Today, people enter and leave the circle between dances with a freedom that was inconceivable fifty years ago. In Compadre Ernesto's group, it was even possible to rest in the center for a dance or two, although dancers who did this were considered to have little fortitude. Dancers who arrive late wait until there is a gap between dances when they can then enter the circle, present themselves and their musical instrument to the sahumadora, and ask permission to dance from the first and other palabras. Predominantly, they then move around the circle, presenting their "arms" to each and every dancer.

A dance obligation as a whole usually lasts about seven hours with a break for *comida corrida* (the main meal of the day for Mexicans) at about 2:00 PM. If there has been a vigil the night before, however, the dancing may finish at that time. Sometimes the mesa itself provides the food: a simple repast of beans and chicharrón (crackling) as at Los Remedios. At the bigger dance at La Villa, however, dancers more usually fend for themselves; those with money to spare eat in the numerous family-run eating places in the market adjacent to the atrium. In Puente Negro, at the dance following the vigil, the dancers were invited (by the priest) to eat in a hall behind the church. On other less Catholic occasions, they may be invited to eat in private houses often located some distance from where they have been dancing. After the meal, as they depart, the dancers will offer thanks, may perform a few dances, and sing the following:

| *Muy agradecidos* | Very gratefully |
| *De esa casa vamos* | We leave this house |
| *Pues con tu licencia* | And with your permission |
| *Ya nos retiramos.* | We will now withdraw. |

Alabanzas are as important to the dance as they are to a vigil. Some, such as the one above, mark transitions, but the majority sung before, during breaks, and after a dance are more likely to be about aspects of the conquest of Mexico, which the dance both confronts and challenges. Often sung early on, "Cuando nuestra America," for example, tells the military and spiritual conquest of Mexico and in the refrain refers back to the pre-Colombian city of Tenochtitlan. "Estrella del Oriente," in contrast, tells the story from a more indigenous point of view and mentions the resistance of Cuauhtémoc, the beginnings of the Concheros (at Tlaxcala) and the raising of the first banner at Dolores Hidalgo. It also celebrates the continuing use of indigenous musical instruments.

Concha players can and do improvise during the singing of an alabanza and may indicate this by shouting out "El es Dios" if the mode is about to change after a verse. This interjection is, in fact, heard frequently throughout dances (and vigils) as it can also indicate thanks. On occasion, the dancing and music stops as the dancers sing the "Guadalupana," one of their most moving songs:

| *Del Cielo Bajo* | From heaven she came down |
| *Triumfante y ufana* (×2) | Triumphant and proud |
| *A favorece Nos* | Favor us |
| *La Guadalupana.* (×2) | The Guadalupana. |

As the dancers come back from having eaten and before they return to their positions in the circle, all surround the jefe, sahumadora, and palabras to sing one or more alabanzas. "Estrella del Oriente" can often be suitable for this moment for it mentions that it is time again to "pursue the path":

*Estrella del oriente que nos dio su santa luz* (×2)
*Es hora que sigamos el camino de la cruz.*

[Star of the east that gives us your sacred light
The time has come to pursue the path of the cross.]

This can also be sung as the last dance is being enacted. At one obligation, at La Villa, facing west into the setting sun as it gave an ever-more penetrating light, all gathered together once again. Just as the various permissions at the beginning had created the appropriate spiritual context for the dance as the dancers moved through the stages of the framing, so now at the dance's end there was perforce a complex ritual of separation. Initiated by singing part

**3.10.** Dancers at Los Remedios.

of the permiso very sedately, the assembled dancers then gave thanks for the occasion with "Gracias a la Gran Senor, alabamos tu grand poder" (Thanks to the Lord, we praise your great power) while standing very still. At the same time, the sahumadoras moved their well-filled incense burners through the four winds more or less in time to the music, and the now stationary standards fluttered in the evening breeze. This was followed by words of thanks from the jefe linked to information about the next dance and any other matters of importance.

During this extremely elaborate ritual, clouds of incense rose upward and bells were rung in time to the alabanza, giving the ritual moves a more precise timing. The rest of the dancers, some by now obviously tired, then stood together and sang:

*Es hora que sigamos el camino de la cruz.*

[It's the hour that we follow the path of the cross.]

And so ended the dance that day.[31]

# PART TWO

# THE EXPERIENTIAL NEXUS:
# FORMING THE SELF

**4.1.** Two dancers singing as they play their *conchas* as the *permiso* is enacted before the dance at La Villa.

# FOUR

# AGENCY AND THE DANCE:
# RITUALIZATION AND THE PERFORMATIVE

Whereas the first part of this book was concerned with the context of the dance, with its organization and practice, in this part I look at the experiential nexus. Here, I develop further the theoretical position I outlined in the introduction and aim to analyze what dancers are doing while they dance and how they experience it. In Chapter 3, I showed that a vigil as a ritual has certain aspects that are open-ended and performative whereas a dance, although it can be seen as a performance, has many heavily ritualized episodes. In general, ritual and performance have been conceptualized as disparate entities but the Concheros' practices indicate that this distinction need not be made. Here I look at both a dance and a vigil within the same analytical framework. Although these two terms may continue to be reified and used as descriptive categories, such an analysis says little about agency or intention. By employing the terms "ritualization" and the "performative" (or performativity), a great deal more can be said about the activity observed.

## ANALYZING RITUAL AND PERFORMANCE

Turner was perhaps the first to consider performance seriously. For decades, his work on ritual, which he defined as "formal behavior for occasions not given over to technological routine, having reference to beliefs in mystical beings or powers" with its suggested stages and the dichotomy of structure and anti-structure, dominated the work of many anthropologists. Later Turner explored with Schechner the possible continuities between the rituals that he had observed in Africa and the performances of the theatrical world.[1]

As an interest in performance grew, it became part of an attempt to look at the unfolding of events of all kinds in a more actor-centered and political mode, a means to assess what gave events life and to offer, as Bell later noted, a "solution to the way in which theory fails to grasp action" (and, I would add, contingency).[2] However, to foreground performance at the expense of ritual is often to use the term "performance" in a very wide way. This recent overuse begins to replicate the history of the earlier wide deployment of the term "ritual."[3] For if "beliefs in mystical beings" is excluded from Turner's definition, we have a term that covers a range of activities that have sometimes been called "secular ritual." Moore and Myerhoff stake out a continuum for this: at one end they place those practices with a prescribed formality; at the other, those that are more open and spontaneous.[4] Nevertheless, any one so-called secular ritual may have a range of activities that lie at different points on the continuum; for some of the activity may be more heavily rule bound than others. As Goody has pointed out, however, the category of secular ritual results in a series of possible actions that is so wide-ranging that it could include—and here he is quoting Bocock—"handshaking, teeth cleaning, [and] taking medicines."[5] It becomes, in effect, a category so broad that it lacks analytical power. An overemphasis on performance leads to similar difficulties, for just about anything can be seen as performance: getting dressed, eating a meal, or travelling on the subway, but so too can teeth cleaning and taking medicine. As Roach has noted, "[w]hat once was an event has become a critical category, now applied to everything from a play to a war to a meal."[6] And, as Bell has indicated, a "focus on the performative aspects of ritual leads easily to the difficulty of being unable to distinguish how ritual is not the same as dramatic theater or spectator sports."[7]

As much of the activity in preliterate societies was ritualized (or had ritualized elements to it), it is surprising that ritual as a rigid category, set aside from the activity of everyday life, became as important to anthropology as it did. Tambiah commented that "anthropologists cannot in any *absolute* way separate ritual from non-ritual in the societies they study" but was talking about form rather than activity per se.[8] Gerholm suggested a different perspective. Instead of looking at form, he looked at the activity and at the qualities and/or characteristics manifested by such activity, a mode of analysis that can take account of more fragmented and divided forms.[9] Today we are more aware that most enactments are composite, made up from bits and pieces taken from here and there, formed through a process of bricolage while constantly undergoing change. Following Gerholm, I look at how ritual and performance are intermingled; ritual does after all have to be performed. What I will argue here is that ritualization rarely occurs alone but is usually linked to the performative, which brings it to life. Thus, rather than establishing a continuum just for "secular ritual," if one is imagined for enactments in general, the discussion can be put on a stronger analytical footing. At one end can be placed those acts that are tightly prescribed both physically and mentally—the heavily ritualized—and at the other, those that are more open and allow an increasingly expressive, possibly individual or emotive element (which may be more or less consciously orchestrated)—the highly performative. Tambiah pointed out long ago that some rituals were more performative than others and that the performative side of ritual could be distinguished from the more formalized dimension, which he saw as the repetition of invariant and stereotyped sequences. He emphasized too that no performance of any ritual is ever the same as any other, a point also made by Bauman: "performance always manifests an emergent dimension."[10] Humphrey and Laidlaw explore in considerable depth in *The Archetypal Actions of Ritual* the more prescribed aspect of enactments but give much less attention to the expressive and communicative, the divergent element that differentiates one enactment from the other.[11]

Although I too foreground ritualization, I have developed a paradigm for the Concheros' dance that also enables the performative aspect to be taken into account and that ultimately combines both. Each celebrant's enactments will be more or less ritualized, depending on the context, but also more or less performative, depending on the circumstances.

Humphrey and Laidlaw have argued convincingly that ritualized action is qualitatively different from non-ritualized activity.[12] But if we dissolve the notion that as a form, ritual is dissimilar to performance (and the examples from everyday life given above suggest that this is not the case), then we need a way of looking at enactments that encompasses both these qualities, which are usually present together to a greater or lesser degree. What is called for is a way to define how action that is ritualized is different from normal everyday activity (or practice) on the one hand and, on the other, to pinpoint and detail that other important aspect—or mode of enactment—that can be used to create distinction, contrast, and vitality: the performative.

## TOWARD RITUALIZATION

"Cultural elaboration of codes consists in the distancing from such spontaneous and intentional expressions [as the emotions and states of mind of individuals] because spontaneity and intentionality are, or can be (perhaps even should be), contingent, labile, circumstantial, even incoherent or disordered."

—S. J. TAMBIAH[13]

When ritual activity is taken to the extreme and carried out conventionally and without innovation, it can be described as "ritualistic." As Tambiah suggests, extreme "distancing" occurs when ritual can seem "to repeat certain sequences and actions to the point of compulsive tedium," becoming completely without meaning and hence ritualistic.[14] Ritualization might then be used to describe the process whereby an action that once had intention and could be given meaning has now become empty. That is not how I will be using the term "ritualization," although ritualized action does have something in common with ritualistic activity but is not as extreme. Rather, ritualization has to do with the special way in which any act may be performed and the quality that any action can come to have. It does not depend on the agent's intentions other than the actor's intent to act conventionally.

To an extent the action is (or is increasingly becoming) part of the habitus.[15] Ritualization involves more, however, than simply the activation of the dispositions of the habitus. If it were simply habitual action, it would be quotidian and unremarkable like everyday activity. However, precisely because actions that might in someway be similar to these are carried out by someone adopting "a particular attitude to his or her action, and enacting what s/he does therefore, in a particular, qualitatively transformed way," the acts or actions become ritualized.[16]

Ritualization does not describe the actions per se but the way that any act may be carried out; the modification (when required) of that intrinsic feature of action is its intentionality.[17] It is the attempt to carry out the action in a particular way, as it should be done or as it has always been done before, that makes the act a ritual act.

Ritual action is stipulated and not necessarily accomplished by processes of intentional understanding. It does not imply that any particular beliefs, ideas, or values are held by the actors as to the meaning of the action.[18] It is the quality of the ritualized action itself that should be looked at rather than the purposes that those who perform ritual may or may not have. This is because the relation between intention and action is transformed by taking a particular attitude toward the action. Various ways of describing this have been used in the literature: the adoption of the "ritual ruling," adopting a "ritual stance," or making a "ritual commitment."[19]

As indicated in the previous chapter, as a dance obligation starts, the "ritual stance" is entered as the overall space is framed and cleansed and later on as each dancer performs the *permiso* with her feet. This occurs before the first dance can be enacted and is subsequently repeated before every dance as each dancer enacts that particular set of steps as exactly as she can while also adopting the "ritual commitment" (an attitude that, as some dancers put it, enables them to "offer themselves to the deity").

The adoption of the ritual stance is an indicator of the quality of ritual action; it is prescribed, rule bound, and restricted by convention rather than the result of consciously formulated strategies. Dancers who are following in the family footsteps will feel a sense of duty, an obligation of a spiritual kind, to carry on the tradition and enter into the ritualization of the dance as fully as they can.

Ritualization is not in itself contingent. The impulse behind ritual action is to get it right, to do it as it should be done, and to add as little of the self as possible. At the beginning of a dance there may well be an element of contingency (the everyday or the performative) but every attempt is made to eliminate the fortuitous and to carry out the actions as stereotypically as possible. As one dancer put it, "one has to have the humility not to do anything creative inside the dance; one has to care for the tradition."

The action is prescribed; it is ready made and precedes the conduct of those who come to enact it. In other words, the steps a dancer may want to perform are not at issue. To dance as a Conchero, a dancer has to accept the constrained quality of the movement and attempt to dance in as rule-bound a way as possible. As she enacts, she will consciously be attempting to dance in the same way as previously. However, how she actually dances may not be the same and attempts may be made on future occasions to rectify this. By choosing to adopt the "ritual stance" the actor accepts that she will not, in a sense, be the author of her actions (that they will not be creative), although she is carrying them out. Thus, in my terms, she attempts to deny her personal desires or intentions or, as Tambiah put it (following Suzanne Langer), psychic distancing occurs as the enactor adopts conventionalized gestures. In Humphrey and Laidlaw's formulation the dancer "removes the sovereignty of herself as agent" for in ritual "you both are and are not the author of your acts." The degree of ritualization will depend on the extent to which the actions or dance steps to be enacted are felt to be stipulated and "therefore separated from the enactors' intentions in acting."[20] As Linda said, "you have to leave your personality at home." You must come to the dance obligation as a dancer, as a professional, in the sense that the you, you profess or offer as you dance is not your personal self, but a non-self, a non-intentional self or, as Tambiah put it, a simulated self, distanced from its private emotions. You have to "behave like a dancer. You live your private life in the house, and you don't bring your personal problems to the circle." The longer a Conchero dances, the more ritualized her dance is likely to become and the more competent she will be at adopting the "right attitude." The rule-bound quality of the activity provides the "identity" for ritual acts in the absence of intention.[21] As Irvine has noted, formal occasions (should) invoke positional and public rather than personal identities, a process that Geertz, for Bali, has called the anonymization of individuals.[22] Ritualization, in sum, involves a modification of the normal intentionality of human action; it effects a "subtle and yet pivotal transformation . . . in the relation between intention and action."[23]

There may seem to be a danger here of reifying intentional and non-intentional (or even conventional action), of ignoring the aspect of interaction with others.[24] Can we really distinguish them from each other? Are not most forms of everyday action a combination of some intentionality at one level and some unintentional activity at another? In everyday activity, there is usually a goal—the need to get something done—but in ritual, the enactor has no material goal; it is not instrumental action. Rather, as she enters the ritual commitment, the dancer needs to aim for a metaphysical one of being with the deity. To ensure that this happens requires that the actor intentionally acts non-intentionally.[25] In most everyday activity this is not the case. Although many activities are carried out in a habitual fashion, there is always an aspect that is contingent and usually there are no overall constraining rules for how the activity should be performed (unless the person sets them herself), whereas for ritual or for a dance there are. So the dancer enacts only those movements that she has learned in the past to be part of the dance. If the dancer has been enacting for years, these will probably have become inculcated dispositions and part of her dance habitus. The aim of the ritual stance is to rescue these unmodified from the habitus and to make them manifest, thereby achieving ritualization.

Most analysts have assumed that ritual communicates and is expressive. Mary Douglas, for example, has said that "ritual is pre-eminently a form of communication." Tambiah too affirms this when he points out that "ritual is a culturally constructed system of symbolic communication." He qualifies this statement, however, when he says that it has "little to do with the transmission of new information and everything to do with interpersonal orchestration and social integration and continuity." What I have tried to show so far is that ritualization does not entail the intention to communicate but rather involves the need for the dancer to "distance herself from her own subjectivity" and to enact altruistically. Tambiah points to this when he says that the formalization of ritual "is linked to ritual's being conventionalized action and that this conventionality in turn psychically distances the participants from the ritual enactment," thus putting "in jeopardy the usefulness of the intentionality theory of meaning for understanding ritual."[26]

In the case of the Concheros, what the dance communicates to neophytes initially are either external meanings provided by other dancers, ones they may have read about, or those they have thought of themselves. Only much later do these become inner realizations that come to them while they are dancing. Ritual is not about communication but it can be a vehicle for it. When a dancer enters ritualization by denying her ego and making contact with the deity, she enables a one-to-one inner communicative experience that excludes the other enactors with whom she is dancing. Interpersonal communication, however, belongs to the performative and involves a different manifestation of the self: in Battaglia's words, a "different rhetorics of self-making."[27] The performative aspect of a dancer's enactment communicates something of herself to other dancers, such as her state of mind or her energy level. It is by means of the performative that a dancer sends out bodily messages that can be read by other dancers or by an observer who is already familiar with the dance, for, as Battaglia has suggested, there can be no selfhood "apart from the collaborative practice of its [con]figuration."[28]

## THE PERFORMATIVE (OR PERFORMATIVITY)

"The one-sidedness of the approach which insists upon the invention of tradition results from an inability to see the performativity of ritual."

—P. CONNERTON[29]

I want here to explore and clarify what I mean by the performative. Ritualization, at least as I discuss it here, is carried by the performative: it cannot be maintained without performative effort, for each enactment of a ritual will be dissimilar. The degree of performativity can be used as a measure of difference between enactments or parts of an enactment. The performative is that aspect that gives vivacity, divergence, or difference and can be communicative. Like ritualization it is qualitative, but the performative consists of features that are, if anything, diametrically opposed to those of ritualization.

The performative is the more self-expressive side of the activity that dancers show as they dance, separate from but linked to ritualization's conventional action and that later in an enactment can be manifested in relation to ritualization. If ritualization implies a state where you are not the author of your actions, the performative is rather the opposite. If entering into ritualization acts to constrain the actor, the performative is that aspect of enacting in which the dancer can express something of herself that can be more or less consciously manifested, depending on the circumstances and the context. A vigil of the Concheros could perhaps be analyzed purely in terms of ritualization because it consists predominantly of constrained activity. For a dance, however, which has to be performed in a much stronger sense, it is clearly important to look not only at the ritualized aspects but also at the more performative.

Although I am primarily concerned analytically with what is happening to the individual during a dance, the state of intersubjectivity that develops between enactors is also extremely important, because to dance demands an awareness of other enactors and a certain level of nonverbal communication between them. For much of the time, the awareness of what the dancers on either side in the circle are doing is of an everyday kinaesthetic kind. Dancers manifest a "somatic mode of attention" that is culturally elaborated in all of us of "attending to and with one's body in surroundings that include the embodied presence of others," which is achieved by semiconscious or embodied mechanisms.[30] Dancers are aware of each other and attend to each other as they keep out of each other's way by using the same somatic mode of attention that we all use in everyday life. If one dancer gets too close, the other takes cognizance and seamlessly moves out of the way.

Ritualization and performativity are mediated by the body (both emotionally and somatically), and the performative aspect of enactment can often be a spontaneous response to the contingency of the situation. Before I discuss the performative any further, however, I will look at how it relates to performance.

## FROM PERFORMANCE TO THE PERFORMATIVE

"The concern is with performance . . . as something creative, realized, achieved, even transcendent of the ordinary course of events."

—D. HYMES[31]

Ritual has largely been the preserve of religious studies and anthropology, but performance has been the concern of a wider range of disciplines.[32] The way performance, the performative, and indeed performativity have been defined differs from discipline to discipline and from writer to writer.

There are probably as many definitions of performance as there are of ritual. As one writer has remarked, performance is an "essentially contested concept."[33] If anthropology has had a predominant working definition of performance, it has been that of "cultural performance," which is similar to the event approach to ritual. Performances can, in this sense, be seen as "bounded, intentionally produced [expressive] enactments which are (usually) marked and set off from ordinary activities, which call attention to themselves as particular productions with special purposes or qualities for the people who observe or perform them."[34] Schieffelin has suggested that they partake in "the social construction of reality," and Csordas observes that cultural performances have the power to alter or "transform both experience and social relations" and are "arenas not for representation, but for the active constitution of religious forms of life."[35] To an extent, our everyday lives are performative. There is "something fundamentally performative about human being-in-the world[ness], for how we perform can change our lives."[36] We need to look then not at performance as a form but rather as a process.

Turner has pointed out that the etymology of performance derives from the Old English *parfournir*, "to complete" or "carry out thoroughly," which had nothing to do with form.[37] Its range of meanings has changed over time from one predominantly located in the everyday (1500s) to one that foregrounds the special occasion, at first the more sacred (1611) and later the secular (1709). The former does not necessarily communicate, but the latter must. Thus, the overall sense has changed from performance as activity to performance as event.[38]

There is, however, a clear difference between "a performance" and "performance," which enables us to shift our understanding of the term from the idea of a framed space-time event back to seeing performance as part of the process of life. Geertz, in distinguishing between "an experience" and "experience," suggested that "an experience stands out like a rock in a Zen sand garden."[39] That is "an" experience is worthy of being commented on and can be startling and different, whereas experience is part of the flow of life: older people have more experience because they have lived longer than those younger than themselves. Likewise, "a performance" has the sense of unique activity, a special event carried out in a framed space that is separated from the flow of normal life, whereas "performance" can be seen as a processual aspect of everyday practice—actions have to be performed—and in certain circumstances can be used as a measure of the effectiveness (or even productivity) of activity.

In Goffman's writings on how the self is presented, the emphasis is on performance as an expressive process of impression control or management and strategic maneuvering by means of which human beings normally articulate their purposes, situations, and relationships in everyday social life with respect to other people. What Goffman's use of the term clearly indicates is that although performance is a part of everyday life, the measuring of it causes it to become a more consciously formulated aspect of action that needs to have (conscious) effort or work put into it. Currently, analysts (in fields such as management and business) measure the desired output of individuals in their work and this is often linked to a demand for performance maximization. This sense implies self-conscious activity, the activity of performing to reach a particular goal, which is clearly communicative and includes Bauman's idea of a "consciousness of doubleness"— the enacting of an action being compared mentally to a "potential, ideal, or a remembered original model."[40]

Thus, the two senses of performance are not as disparate as at first they may appear. A performance in a theater is clearly an event that is separate from the usual but so too is the assessment of someone else in everyday life. If people are being appraised, they know that they will have an audience assessing what they are doing and that this can be seen as distinct from other everyday activity, as it is framed separately.

A further way of analyzing the performative is the socio-linguistic approach, which shifts the focus from event or genre and looks instead at the verbal performative act itself. This seems at first sight to be much closer to the way in which I want to use the term "performativity." Utilizing the performative utterance approach, from the work of Searle and Austin, the "illocutionary force" of the speech act can be analyzed wherein, in the Austinian sense, "saying something is also doing something."[41] In this sense, ritual speech acts (and presumably the bodily acts associated with them) can be seen to be performative. However, the use of speech act theory appears to have little relevance for dance itself, unless we switch the equation around, wherein doing something (or enacting certain steps or gestures) could be said also to be saying something. Thus, the performativity of a dancer's enactment might be said to communicate something, but this does not assist us much unless we develop a metalanguage of the dance per se.[42]

Concentrating on the performative allows the analyst to look not at the "subjective or symbolic meaning of symbols" but rather at the conditions under which "symbolic acts [may become] meaningful."[43] What the enactor does may be meaningful to herself but will not necessarily have meaning or the same meaning for others; in other words, ritualization does not and performativity will not necessarily convey "information," but the latter may well have referential, propositional, or analogical meanings,[44] for, as Tambiah has pointed out, the way meaning has been conceived in anthropology has been "a deadly source of confusion."[45]

A recent trend has been the growing interest in the ethnography of the performing arts. Much of this work was strongly influenced by Turner and his work with Schechner.[46] Here experience as much as meaning is of significance, and this effectively brings the argument back again to cultural performance.

In conventional theater, the performance of a play consists of the presentation of a form that is separate from everyday reality: the viewer observes the action on the stage and is not in any way a participant. It is carried out under certain conditions in a specially designed space and is a heavily framed situation. There is a text to be followed and the actors have to learn their lines so that they can repeat them night after night. They must not speak with their own words, although the play may change slightly during rehearsals. In fact, they need to mould themselves into a character who is other; the words, the actions, the dance steps, if there are any, and even the gestures need to conform or be true to their idea and embodiment of their characters and repeatable night after night. Thus, the part, once learned, becomes to an extent habitual for the actor, for when she begins to act she falls into the part. Schechner has called this "restored behavior."[47]

However, if acting were but mere repetition and lacked renewal and creativity, it would be dull and tedious and the overall play would become moribund. Such a production could be termed "ritualistic," a manifestation of what Peter Brooke has called "deadly theatre."[48] The actor needs to challenge the other actors at each performance, communicate with them, and give life to the part. She is, after all, involved in dialogue. As Tambiah has remarked, art forms are prevented from "deterioration into degenerate banality by controlled modulation."[49] How the actor builds up the character on each occasion will have become largely habitual, but over and above that, what the actor puts into the character or how she finally makes the character must be different in every performance. The words must be enunciated afresh on each occasion, otherwise the play will not work; in certain productions new words may even be added. Exact repetition is neither possible nor desirable, for "no action or sequence of actions may be performed exactly the same way twice; they must be reinvented or recreated at each appearance."[50] Roach has called this the transformation of experience through renewal or "repetition with revision." The actor in the theater aims to produce the habitual form of the action but also adds something new or different: the performative.[51] Inevitably, the actor acts slightly differently, thereby inadvertently adding something of his or her own, a form of improvisation in a weak sense.

That extra something is expected (and permitted) and more vital to the theater than to the dance of the Concheros, because a theatrical performance is just that, "a performance" of its characters who are enmeshed in the plot. As Hymes has pointed out, "some performances are desultory [and] perfunctionary . . . , while others are authoritative, authentic." He has described this quality as the key to assessment.[52] A dance of the Concheros, however, is different, because it has a spiritual aspect and is not enacted primarily for an audience. Some groups express little externally as they dance, appearing to move with a minimum of effort or intent, whereas others are more energetic and apparently express more, wanting to communicate with other dancers through the intensity of their participation. Regardless of the differences, both achieve ritualization.[53]

If we take into account the "shift[s] of expressive orientation," we can look at the extreme of everyday behavior when someone puts much more into an activity than is strictly necessary.[54] If they overdo it (from the observer's point of view) to sublimate an emotion—that is, less than consciously—or in a somewhat more self-conscious way, we have an even clearer sense of what performativity is.[55] This behavior might then be called a "breakthrough into performance."[56] Further, we might describe some everyday activity as "quite a performance" and realize that the performers may be trying to communicate something by the way they enacted.

The performative is then that something that is added to intentionally conventional action. It is the expressive, spontaneous playfulness or work of the body over and above that which is required to do the activity, whether this is riding a bicycle, acting in a play, or dancing as a Conchero. Performance is potentially able to communicate, whether it is intended to do so or not.

The sense in which I am using the term "performative" then has to do with how the dancer, while distancing herself from her everyday state of subjectivity, can also express something of other states of her being-in-the-worldness. The performative aspect of an action or enactment captures how the self is manifested, an individual way-of-being in the world that is distinct from but intermingled with the depersonalization of ritualization. Performativity is, crudely put, that which makes each enactment for a dancer different from every other, even if that difference is slight. Ritualization ensures that by the taking up of the ritual stance, each dancer's enactment is as much like that of every other dancer's as possible: that the enactor has "got it right." The performative, however, is less a ruling than an inevitable or unavoidable occurrence that may be out of the enactor's control; that is, it may be a spontaneous response to other dancers. Or it may even become a consciously formulated intention over and above the ritualized. With regard to the performative, the enactor might ask himself or herself, Has it worked? This can be related to an often subconscious desire to make it work. On the other hand, the enactor might have the desire to make a difference by communicating something.[57]

The ritualized aspect is there, stored up in the somatic memory, to be called out at any moment, whereas the performative differs in kind and is both more temporal and more transient. As Phelan has pointed out (talking of the theater), "performance's only life is in the present." It cannot "be saved, recorded, documented, or otherwise participate in the circulation of representations: once it does so, it becomes something other than performance."[58] The performative, as an aspect of representation aids representation but is not itself a representation. Performers have a bodily presence but are also able to bring forth a new presence in the sense of something novel, fresh, or even enthralling.[59] Presentation is clearly closely linked to a sense of presence, which has always been hard to characterize theoretically but is found in the link between competence and expressivity.[60]

Finally, the performative will be communicative if sufficiently different so that other dancers pick up on this difference. It can even be political if by enacting performatively the enactor succeeds in changing the ritualized form in the longer term or, more usually, during a particular dance simply fails to take account that her (but more usually his) performance is disruptive. The latter may occur when a dancer who is a visitor is asked to perform *his* dance in the center and moves in such a way and so rapidly that the usual ritual stance of the group is disrupted. What is usual for that dancer (and probably others in his own group) is experienced by those in the circle not as a ritualized form that they can follow (animated by a measure of performativity) but as purely performative. The visitor thus draws the body of dancers out of their state of ritualization and into a self-conscious state of mimesis, a "tangled state" where they are trying desperately to do something new without the benefit of practice or embodied knowledge. A breakdown of the dance may then occur and it will often terminate in disorder.[61]

From this it can be seen that ritualization and performativity are not absolute terms but relative ones; what is perceived as mere performativity by one group could in fact be another group's usual state of ritualization. Some groups (from another group's perspective) have added extra flourishes or mannerisms to their steps, which seem like vulgar performatives to a group that dances much more staidly. This is particularly true of some dancers' views on the Mexica's way of dancing (see Chapter 10). The above situation, however, can be remedied by the first *palabra* asking a dancer who is known from experience to be easy for all to follow to enact the next dance. In addition to this, the desired state of ritualization can also be restored by the permiso.

In the longer-term perspective of the disrupted mesa, once a novel gesture is repeated numerous times, it becomes less performative and more a part of the dancers' ritualization. A dancer will know when something she has done is completely new, perhaps because she did it intentionally or it just slipped out, or she was following by mimesis the person leading in the center. If she does it again the next time she dances and then again on subsequent occasions, the new and different will cease to be so, at least for her, and will begin to be part of her embodied practice. To the observer this may not be quite so clear and the interpretation will of necessity be relative: what is seen as performativity will thus depend very much on the observer's point of view.

## MIMESIS: LEARNING TO "CARRY THE WORD"

"Practice has always a double effect. It makes him, on the one hand, more able to do whatever it is he is attempting; and, on the other hand, by the phenomenon of habit formation, it makes him less aware of how he does it."

—G. BATESON[62]

"By exercise the body comes to co-ordinate an increasing range of muscular activities in an increasingly automatic way, until awareness retreats, the movement flows 'involuntarily,' and there occurs a firm and practiced sequence of acts which take their fluent course."

—P. CONNERTON[63]

How is the embodiment of a set of movements attained? How is ritualization achieved? I suggest initially by copying for as the dancer learns to dance, each time she begins to enact, her movements become increasingly less consciously sought and more embodied or habitual. At first, the ritual commitment is simply not there. Gradually, however, as the dance steps come more easily, the dancer can begin to concentrate on taking up the ritual stance. Later, as she begins to dance, she can easily ensure that her activity is predominantly non-intentional.

A ritual practice, such as dancing, is a way of acting and being that has to be inculcated. People learning ritual acts start by copying, but to do this they have to exert the "conscious will . . . to choose each of the successive events that make up the action from a number of wrong alternatives."[64] That is, the ability to reproduce what they are watching others do (or have been taught by others) requires thought about what is actually being done; they need to learn the templates of the activity and the rules that interconnect them by a process of mimesis.[65] That is, when people are learning to dance, they have to make a self-conscious effort to produce the steps for they do not know intuitively yet which step follows which. But with sufficient time—and the amount of time taken varies from person to person—what the enactor does can be described as the "making manifest" of what have become embodied activities.[66]

By adopting the ritual stance, the dancer can reenact the practices without thought about the details in the appropriate setting. That is, when instead of having to think about which step follows in the permiso and what the feet and torso should be doing, the body moves into dance mode and takes over. It is only when dance (or any ritual activity) has become thoroughly embodied, when it can be carried out with an ease or facility that seemed at first impossible, that ritualization can be said to be in place and (re)achievable.[67]

However, there is more to ritualization initially than this. When it can be achieved physically—when the body is enacting the steps as they have been carefully learned and carried out before—if the action is to transcend normal everyday action, the mind too has to be stilled. The mind needs to be released from the flux of everyday agitation, at least in part focused on the spiritual side of the activity, and turned toward the deity for this is part of the ritual commitment. In the learning process, once the actor can manifest the physical part of the activity, assuming a particular attitude toward it also becomes easier. Ritualization thus has to be constantly regenerated inwardly if the dancing is not to become quotidian and mundane. In other words, the dancer has to ensure that she continues to commit herself to the ritual stance and thereby uphold it.

But how is ritualization reaffirmed or renewed as dancers get tired after hours of dancing? What is it that gives life to an enactment? How is the dancing physically energized? How is transcendence achieved? This is where ritualization and performativity are closely interrelated and it is to these questions that I now turn.

## THE RELATIONSHIP BETWEEN RITUALIZATION AND PERFORMATIVITY

"[Ritual is performative in the sense that it has] something to do with the production of a heightened sense and intensified and fused communication."

—S. J. TAMBIAH[68]

"[There is the] tension between rhetorics of an individuated, autonomous self and rhetorics of a collective or relational self. [T]hese rhetorics sometimes, but . . . not invariably, oppose each other as the grounds of social action (as well as that action itself). That is, some situations produce the action of tacking between the two as incompatible positions, others of tacking between them as complimentary positions, still others of appropriating one rhetoric to the cause of the other."

—D. BATTAGLIA[69]

I have so far largely disaggregated ritualization from performativity as though they were discrete processes. This has, however, been an analytical exercise rather than the reality of the dance. When enacting, they are difficult to separate from each other. At times the distinction may be a matter of the viewer's perspective, much like the color of a fabric woven from two different colored threads where the overall color from one viewpoint appears to differ from that from another.

This distinction is not then a dichotomy; rather it is closely linked to Hastrup's idea of double agency where the actor as agent both "is" and "is not." The training (of an actor or dancer) permits the self to enact between identities as a double agent, making it possible to work on "being" and "becoming" simultaneously.[70] The Concheros enact with ritualized restraint (being) and also performative expressiveness (becoming) at the same time. Ritualization and performativity can perhaps be seen as forces that are part of a dialectical process and that act in different dimensions (or opposing directions), rather like phenomenological vectors, which Leder defines as "a structure of experience that makes possible and encourages the subject in certain practical or interpretive directions, while never mandating them as invariants."[71] The idea of a vector helps to emphasize the complex nature of dancing. The various vectors take the dancer somewhere qualitatively—for some of the time, especially at the beginning of a dance, in different "directions" or into disparate modes of consciousness. Another way to look at the two is that at any moment in the dance, the celebrant's enactments emerge from her incorporated knowledge and experience of the dance in the past (which has become ritualized) coupled with what she expresses of her desires in relation to the contingencies of the present moment (the performative).

Taking a slightly different approach, Barba has suggested that there is a physical tension between opposing forces in the body that develops during activity and that this is especially the case for certain forms in the Orient. He suggests that the body is charged with energy because established within it are "differences of potential which render the body alive [and] strongly present." He uses a trope: "The dance of oppositions is danced *in* the body before being danced *with* the body." The way that a Noh actor walks, for example, means that his "energy . . . is the consequence of the tension between opposing forces."[72]

I want to utilize Barba's suggestion as a metaphor for what I see happening in the Concheros dance. The Conchero dancers do not have the training of Noh dancers and what they aim for is different, but this suggestion gives materiality to Leder's notion of phenomenological vectors. I explore this further in the following more ethnographic section.

At the beginning of an obligation, as the space is framed and cleansed involving ritualized activity, much of a dancer's attention will still be predominantly in the everyday world (see Chapter 3). At the beginning of each individual dance, the permiso is enacted, pulling all the dancers back into a more ritualized state after the previous dance. During any one dance, there may be a high degree of performativity in the enactments of a few dancers as variations emerge that enable them to express something of themselves. To an onlooker, there will probably have been a perceived difference between the various dancers' overall enactments. The permiso brings the dance back to order and can also act as a bridge back into ritualization after a break of more than a few minutes between dances when normal everyday activity will have recommenced.

The relation between performativity and ritualization is thus event dependent and could be said to turn on the "moment of improvisation." Performativity "embodies the *expressive dimension of the strategic articulation of practice.*"[73] Performativity can thus come in at that point in time after the propensities of the (ritual) habitus have become activated and will be located at its creative, improvisatory edge in the moment that it is carried out "though everything that comes across is not necessarily consciously intended."[74]

Performativity and ritualization thus continue to manifest and act in relation to one another throughout a dance. When a dancer is asked to come from the periphery of the circle to enact his or her dance in the center, it is up to that dancer to animate the others in the circle who will be inspired to follow her example by giving as much of themselves as possible to the dance. The way the dancer in the center enacts may be strongly influenced by performativity or it may be her normal ritualization. However, I will perceive the overall difference between my dance and her dance as performative. This may encourage me, and the other dancers around me, to put more energy into our dance and even to attempt to dance in a way similar to the dancer in the center.

When the dancers are tired and the quality of the dance is becoming lackluster, the performative can be consciously deployed by the jefe or first palabra of a group to revitalize a dance. The palabra may then invite a dancer to come into the circle who will, when permitted, really let go. Rosa Elia described a dancer who could do this and who many thought of as conceited. The implication was that his dance was overly expressive, thus more performative than ritualized, at least from the point of view of the rest of the group. She added that a time comes in the dance when although you are beginning to feel exhausted, "it is necessary . . . to tap another level, to generate a further source of energy." If a dancer such as the one described is invited into the center, he aids such a transformation. His dance, which appears to be predominantly performative to others, may for him in large part be ritualized. His enacting inspires the others to dance more animatedly. By enacting close to those most depleted, the dancer in the center "lifts them up," enabling a transformation of their energy to occur.

Therefore, the dancer does not just let herself be danced, letting her body flow with the dance, although when that is happening she both is and is not the author of her acts. She is involved in an activity that she is more or less conscious of doing, responding to embodied knowledge while not consciously directing it—a state of "being" (in Hastrup's terms). But she can, at the same time, have the conscious intention of putting something more of herself into it, of pushing herself as far as she has pushed herself in the past, to the limits (or beyond) of her more normal state of ritualization—that is, she enters into a state of "becoming."

There is thus a tension between creativity and restraint, the desire to be expressive and to innovate or improvise, while at the same time needing to keep this within the boundaries of what is considered acceptable (or traditional). One of the aims of the dance for the Concheros (if the dance can be said to have an aim) is to achieve the two together: a successful dance is when ritualization and performativity (and much else besides) enhance each other. Any dance enactment then is a complex of several types of activity. The oscillation between ritualization and performativity may be slow or rapid. In fact, this is a changeover or movement that occurs repeatedly, even continuously, throughout a vigil and a dance. Later, however, at another level, both can and do act together and this is particularly the case as an enactment proceeds and slowly builds after many hours of sustained dancing. Thus, when the ability to act according to their dance habitus comes easily to a dancer (after years of experience), a further state comes into play that emanates from that earlier ritualized state and overlays or merges with it. This occurs when the dancer is much less aware of what she is doing for she acts with total involvement and what Turner has called "flow" occurs.[75]

As the dance builds up, as an event it begins to have emergent qualities: the whole becoming greater than the sum of its parts. At its start, the circle is made up of a number of individualized dancers, each enacting according to their ritualized propensities while ensuring that they do not collide with each other as they move to the right or left, each trying to "get it right" while possibly also adding their own performative extras. As time passes the overall dance develops as each dancer begins to adjust, shaping her dance to that of everyone else. The dancer enacting in the center shows the way and all those in the circle can or should modify the way their ritualized steps and gestures are actually enacted. Theoretically, once all the dancers in the circle have had their chance to dance in the center, each dancer will have responded to and been influenced by all the other dancers. Each will have begun to enact a form that is a hybrid of the moment. This is, however, an idealistic scenario. In reality, some dancers exert more influence than others and some are not easily persuaded to respond.

As time goes on, however, the experienced dancer can be said to begin to have a feeling of a heightened, "intensified and fused communication."[76] This is a sense of well-being with herself, of being in direct sensory contact or "flow" with those around her.[77] A sense of "normative communitas" develops and the dancers experience a state "of euphoric communion with . . . [their] fellow beings."[78] This differs from "existential communitas," a "direct unmediated [state often] ephemeral in duration" when dancers can be said to transcend.[79] In other words, as the dance develops, as a state of flow is achieved, dancers can then begin to be transported into what has been called "a supranormal, transcendental, 'antistructural,' 'numinous,' or 'altered' state of consciousness."[80]

This state is higher than the earlier state of flow and is one during which what the adept experiences is again individual. I discuss the experience of transcendence in more detail in Chapter 7.

**5.1.** The various alferezes from the *mesas* who have been dancing together ritually disengaging at the end of the obligation at La Villa.

# CONCHERO SPEAK:
# CARRYING THE WORD

In Chapter 3, I gave an overall idea of the structure and content of both a vigil and a dance as an outsider might observe these activities. Here I want to look at the words of the Concheros' leitmotif—union, conformity, and conquest—which appear on all their standards and are used in their various interjections, as is the expression "El es Dios." These verbal expressions aid dancers in knowing what it is they are aiming for, of how metaphorically they should set about "carrying the word," that is, embodying the dance and its various practices. As expressions, they are less contingent and more deep-seated than the words of the alabanzas and will mean little to an outsider, at least initially. But they direct a dancer's action-thought and aid in the development of the ethos of the dance. First, however, I want to look at the expression "carrying the word" (*llevando la palabra*).

In Chapter 2, I showed that the Concheros' names for the positions that can be achieved in the dance are militaristic and hence hierarchical. For the dance itself, however, *palabra* is the name given to those who are allocated named positions as the obligation starts. Their work of overseeing the development of the dance and taking responsibility for it is known as "carrying" or "bearing the word." Simply, *palabra* means "word." When linked to *dar* (to give) it has the meaning of "to give" in the sense of "to offer." If a dancer is "offered the word" (and to give the word to someone is an expression used in Spanish as it is in English), this grants them the permission for whatever act they may then instigate. However, the dancer who can give the word is also in most cases the one who is able to take responsibility—to carry it. At the end of an obligation, for example, as the dancers gather around their *jefe* to be told when and where they will next dance, that too is *dar la palabra*, and the jefe is empowered to make this promise because he is a jefe and because as first palabra he "carries the word." Those who act as palabras for the duration of an obligation are given these positions precisely because they have many years of experience and know what should be done.[1]

As already mentioned, when a dancer leads her dance from the center, she carries the word and is empowered, even if only for a short time. Palabra refers both to the person and their ability to communicate, although this is often nonverbal in nature, such as the nod and gesture with his *concha* that the third palabra gives to a dancer to indicate that she can lead the next dance from the center.

On a different scale, the many mesas that make up the grouping known as Santiago Tlatelolco can be referred to as La Palabra de Santiago Tlatelolco, as indeed can every mesa within that palabra. Each mesa, although in conformity with the larger grouping, has a voice and character of its own and its procedures will be somewhat different from those of the other mesas in that palabra. As a group, each can and usually does communicate something different with its dancing, although at the same time it has much in common with the larger conformity (La Palabra de Santiago Tlatelolco) of which it is a part, sometimes also called "La Palabra General."

One dancer described Ignacio Gutierrez, the most powerful jefe the Concheros have ever had, as the jefe of all jefes. She said that he was the one who *llevó la palabra general de todos las palabras*. Verbatim, this glosses as "he carried the general word of all the words," which makes little sense in English. One exegesis given to me was that of all the palabras in the dance and certainly of all those who came under his leadership, his palabra was the most powerful, that is the most *general*, because his was able to subsume all the others. In a sense, this is the complete opposite of what "general" usually means; general knowledge is something everyone knows and therefore might be considered the least powerful. This apparent contradiction touches on the paradox of the dance. The dance itself is open to anyone who wants to join and learn the procedures. As I understand it, there is no complex body of esoteric know-how associated with it. Rather, experientially embodied knowledge builds through time as a Conchero dances. The knowledge that a general has is the same as—but at the same time much more than—that of an ordinary dancer; it may appear to be secret but can be attained by anyone, provided they have the time, patience, and aptitude to slowly rise through the ranks.

The term "palabra" has a particularly powerful resonance because until recently the tradition has been an oral one. To experience the procedures is not to learn a form of inscribed knowledge but rather to learn a somatic one acquired through time that, especially in the case of the dances themselves, cannot be obtained from a broadsheet or a book. Further, the ethos of the dance is easily as important as its forms and can only be attained by doing. There is the adage that knowledge is power; in a sense, those who have oral knowledge are perhaps more powerful than those who have acquired it by literary means, for anyone who can read can gain knowledge from a book and many others can know the same thing. Those who have oral knowledge can choose with whom they share it and sanction the conditions under which this may occur. Those who want to acquire Conchero know-how have to conform to the tenets of the association and set up a personal relation with a palabra—the one who knows—and they show by how they enact that they are worthy of this. The skills and knowledge of the palabra are in a sense hidden and felt to be powerful. Oral knowledge encourages continuity because it is embodied but must be shared with others for the tradition to continue.

Many who dance as soldiers never attain sufficient know-how to be received, and those who have been received may only perform duties such as that of a lieutenant. Others may be made captains and act as palabras for the dance. Some of those who have wide experience of the dance that is *general* knowledge, which is both organizational and spiritual, become jefes or even generals.[2]

"General" thus carries a double meaning. Metaphorically, the role of the dancer, who is a general, is the leader of the troops. That person is, however, also one whose knowledge is *generally* acceptable to all; he (or she) is often charismatic, with the added qualities of being able to give spiritual leadership and guidance, and able to submit his (or her) ego to the powers above. To be recognized as a general, a dancer needs to be seen as such by those at a high level in the hierarchy rather than by the mere foot soldiers (who can be easily taken in). A general is someone whose knowledge of the practices of the dance is impeccable and is also spiritually empowered.[3]

The designation of palabra as used by the dancers to name apparently diverse positions hierarchically within the dance reveals a side of the dance that is not otherwise immediately apparent, that is, its overall egalitarian and inclusive tendencies. As one Conchero has written, "we are all equal inside the circle."[4] Anyone can aspire to become a palabra, and their tenure may last only for the duration of one dance or for a much longer time if they hold office, beginning as a captain and possibly through time accumulating more knowledge and rising to become a jefe and then perhaps even a general.

Carrying the word is often heard as reported speech and could be said to summarize what the Concheros see themselves as doing as they dance. It is given greater depth, however, and reinforced by the terms "union," "conformidad," and "conquista" that appear on the banners. These are a crucial part of "Conchero speak," as is the invocation "El es Dios" uttered before, during, and after dances and vigils.

## THE RITUAL LANGUAGE OF THE CONCHEROS

Ritual language is clearly an important element in the process of entering a ritualized state; prayers are said before the dance begins, and the verbal *permiso* enunciated as the dancers take their positions. As the dancing commences, however, the verbal is predominantly replaced by the nonverbal, with the exception of "El es Dios" and the three precepts. The precepts are not actually uttered during a dance but are seen on the banners and are certainly kept in mind. However, just as ritual actions do not necessarily carry particular meanings, I argue here that neither do the ritual precepts and invocations. "El es Dios," for example, is not necessarily enunciated for its meaning and is independent of the speaker's intentions. These invocations are "verbal gestures with immanent" potential for meaning rather than representations of thought. Following Merleau-Ponty, these are words that are used in terms of their particularity and resonance "as one of the possible uses of our bodies."[5] They are conventional phonetic gestures, just as the dance steps are standardized movements with which the dancers can take up an existential position, whose meanings are partly obscure at a semantic level.[6] Like the dance steps, they too have become embodied and are manifested or uttered when appropriate. In fact, their use is often ambiguous as a result of language's "iterability."[7] Although what is communicated is not informational, the terms may still have referential, propositional, or analogical meanings.[8] This special verbal language associated with the dance will probably mean little to a dancer until she has danced for some time. Nevertheless, as her dancing improves and she gains experience, the terminology used by others will begin to acquire a particular sense for her.

One of the aims of this chapter is to show that language is another way of constructing experience and gaining access to that world. As Csordas has suggested, "language can give access to a world of experience in so far as experience comes to, or is brought to, language."[9] What exactly is meant by "El es Dios," for example, is not clear. Although easily memorized, the expression is not immediately understandable; a literal gloss is "He is God." "Union," "conformity," and "conquest," however, appear to be more transparent. These are the tenets of practice. They are the maxims that the Concheros carry in their heads as they dance and aim toward a ritualized state. They indicate the type of work that, although mental, is linked to the physical (the "body-self") that everyone in the circle aims to attain during a dance to ensure a good outcome.[10] In what is otherwise a largely oral tradition, these three precepts have gained a rather different significance from their everyday usage. Emblazoned iconically on the banners, they are words that are literally carried. They act, at least for the neophyte, as performative injunctions that encourage the dancer to push her dance toward a more ritualized state. For more seasoned dancers the terms have long since become incorporated.

The dancers do not think of themselves as carrying these words as reifications, rather they act as mnemonics with which to conceptualize the dance when they are dancing and to discuss it with other dancers or the anthropologist afterward.[11] Precisely because these aphorisms are present on the banners, they have become not exactly "indefinable" (for the words have not changed in form) but are used in a particular way by each dancer.[12] The exegesis of "union," "conformity," and "conquest" is verbal and ongoing: the interpretation of these terms varies from group to group and among individuals.

## THE BANNER

On the front face of each banner, almost invariably there is an image of that group's saint, such as Santo Niño de Atocha, often framed by the three precepts. Each standard is of great significance to the well-being of a mesa. As Eduardo rather baldly put it, "if you don't understand the concept of the standard, you won't understand the dance." He continued, "[I]t may appear to be just a flag, a little bit of material nailed to a pole, but it is the *santo arbol* [the saintly tree or stave] whose *sombra* [spiritual protection] covers the group from the moment when the arbol is raised [i.e., the group is initiated] at a spiritual level."[13] In a sense, it roots a mesa to the particular place where that standard was raised (say, Amecameca) and a particular time, the date of its raising. "The spirit of the arbol covers and protects you, it needs to be venerated, looked after, censed, and a candle burnt for it (*prende su luz*). The standard gains power through time and represents the power of the mesa and must at all costs be respected." In the words of another dancer, it is "the palabra."

The precepts on the banner are presented in a linear relation to one another: union, conformity, and conquest. Union refers to the coming together of all the dancers, the attempt that each dancer makes to unify herself with others in the dance. Conformidad takes this a stage further and implies a state of being that conforms to the tenets of practice, the need for each dancer to restrain her impulses and desires. Whereas conquest refers in part to the need for each

**5.2.** Three banners leaning against the wall as a dancer and his family dress for the dance at Tlatelolco.

dancer to conquer herself, to change the body-self of everyday life, but also to conquer others, whether they are dancing or watching. The precepts are also said by many to indicate temporal causality: union is achieved as the dancers congregate, conformity as they follow the danced permission, and conquest later by means of the dancing. They thus appear to relate to the sequential stages of ritualization, but just as ritualization is intermixed with the perfor-

**5.3.** Miguel Gutierrez with the banner of the mesa of his father (Alberto Gutierrez), also Santo Niño de Atocha.

mative and other forms of activity, union may be important at certain times later on in the dance, when, for example, conformity has broken down and the unanimity of the dance is threatened.

Initially I was confused by these terms; each seemed to mean something different but, at the same time, the same thing. I therefore look in detail at each in turn.[14]

## UNION

Union in the first instance is used to refer to those people who are part of an organization who join together in a common cause. As jefe Teresa Mejia said, "to be at Chalma at four in the afternoon, dressed [i.e., uniformed] and ready to dance . . . that is unification." However, it is also employed in the sense of comm-union, the sharing in common, of participation in a spiritual community, and can also be used at a more abstract level in the sense of re-union to mean the achieving of a former state of union. As Soledad Ruiz put it, union needs to be achieved so "that the rite can be carried out, or accomplished without obstacles or hitches. You must try to unify yourself with the others; you must be prepared to work collectively. In other words, the conditions for participation need to be created. For me, union is the disposition to participate in the event, the need to attain a union of intention."

## CONFORMIDAD

Conformity implies the need to conform to the tenets of practice, to dance according to tradition; it indicates that the dance is rule-bound activity. On a practical level, it indicates the need for a dancer to dress, as Linda put it, "according to the dictates of the group and the level of knowledge that she has achieved in the dance." In terms of an obligation, this means to carry out the dance as it should be enacted; for example, when the dance begins, the first palabra should dance the first dance. If an announcement is made the dancers will be asked if they agree, that is, if they are in conformity: *¿Estan conformes compadritos?* Conformity thus also has the implication of a state of being that is harmonious, of a psycho-political union. On this level, a conformity consists of mesas that are either part of the same association or in alliance with one another. According to Compadre Ernesto, ensuring that you have sent dancers to other groups to fulfil your obligations is also a part of conformity. On a slightly more abstract level, conformity refers to the type of harmonious enactment achieved by the circle as a whole when no dancer enacts in a way that "belittles the dancing of others." As Soledad pointed out, "conformity means that you relinquish or divest yourself of your ego so that you can be obedient, for the dance is based on this principle. You cannot agree to lay out a cross or move into the center of the circle if you do not accept completely this commission, this work that has been yielded up to you."

## CONQUISTA

Conquest is in its more abstract sense "the conquest of yourself more than anything; to be able to control your impulses [and] beautify yourself, to control the human inclinations of egoism, ambition for power, prepotency . . . all of that." As Soledad indicated, "it is to accept the dance as work on yourself, on your defects, on your negative inclinations. This is conquest of your self."

However, it also refers to what it may communicate, for to "conquer others, in the sense of attracting to the dance those people who you think can be converted into adepts," is part of its denotation. Although in principal the dance is not enacted to be watched, those doing so (if there are any) may in the future want to come and join the dance. It is used also to refer to the corralling of dancers from other groups or to the forming of an alliance with another group. In this sense, it is less processual and more about attainment. If a dance has been successful in a new location, it will be described as a conquest, especially if the dancers of the group sense that they will be invited back the following year (as happened when Santo Niño de Atocha danced in Valle de Bravo, a town in the State of Michoacan). Some describe the obligations in general as conquests, and at present an increasing number of Concheros are calling their dances "Danzas de Conquista," their name until the early twentieth century according to some.[15]

Soledad Ruiz pushes the concept further when she claims that conquest also has esoteric resonances. "Those who are not concerned with the esoteric or with attaining ecstasy but with the more mundane aspects of the dance will call themselves Concheros, while those who are aware of the invisible potentialities which the dance aims to tap will name themselves dancers of conquest."[16] Conquest can also refer to the association, for one document clearly states that all who are inside the general order of the conquest should respect it.[17]

"Union," "conformity," and "conquest" as propositions are used loosely in discussions about the dance. At one level, they form an esoteric language with which to talk about the dance and, consequently, have a certain felt power. A neophyte will probably not immediately incorporate them into her verbal exchanges for they will still have an edge to them. The more a neophyte dances and the dance grows on her, however, the more likely she is to use the terms in discussions about the dance and also in her daily discourse, although she may never consciously define them. But the longer she has danced, the less she will need them to remind her of what she is trying to do, and these external maxims will become incorporated and linked to the embodied mode of the dance's actualization.

There is then no consensus as to the meanings of "union," "conformity," and "conquest." In a way, the ideology of the dance is encapsulated by these terms, but as everyone defines them slightly differently, therein lies the freedom of the dance and also its spiritual framing. Above, I predominantly quoted one dancer's definitions and used other dancers' to expand on those. In reality, there is a great deal of slippage between the terms. Soledad, for example, tends to use "conformity" and "conquest" with a degree of overlap: for her, "conformity" means "you relinquish your ego," and "conquest" enables "the dancer to control the human impulse of egoism." Sometimes dancers imply that it is through conformity that union ensues and the required outcome of conquest is achieved. However, perhaps in something of a contradiction, conquest can also be a route to union and is used at times to refer to creating union: *a conquistar la unificacion*.

Like the uses of "palabra," analyzed at the beginning of this chapter, these precepts can refer to units of the organization: conquest can refer to the group, to the dance, or to the association, as indeed can "union." The general, Guadalupe Hernandez, talked about the need to ask permission to dance elsewhere outside "this union." "Conformity" likewise can be employed to refer to an entity (*este conformidad*) or a way of acting (*un asunto de conformidad*). Finally, "conquest" is often equated with "palabra." One jefe named himself as Captain, Fundador y Conquista at the end of a letter. The association of "palabra" with "conquest" is probably stronger than with the other two, although there are instances when "palabra" is used in place of "union" or "conformity."

Although there is a great deal of latitude in the interpretation of these precepts, they clearly encapsulate how the dance should be thought about, talked about, organized, and above all experienced. Together, the terms have many of the nuances of ritualization linked to the performative but there is also a sense in which the three terms can be used interchangeably. Any one can perform the work of any other and act as an index of what it is that the Concheros aim to do both physically and spiritually. Teresa Mejia, one of the more traditional jefes, elucidated this when she said that "the three things are a single word: it's a joining of the three things." Later in the same conversation, she described the dance as being like "a flower that is always flowering. You take hold of it alive, alive, alive . . . and you have to spread [*contagiar*] this to the person next to you. This spreading is conformity, conquest, union in one word."

The length of the communication on the reverse side of a banner is extremely variable. The one illustrated in Figure 5.4 has a quite complex message:

> Union, Conformity and Conquest, Danza Azteca of La Gran Tenochtitlan. This standard was raised on the day 17 of February 1988, under the order and protection of the Jefe Faustino Rodriguez and the Jefes Mariano Zavala and Ernesto Ortiz, under the patronage of the Generals Florencio Gutierrez and Andres Segura. It stands thus as the first wind of the dances of the Conquest, naming Gabriel Hernandez Captain of this oratory. The witnesses were Jefa Guadalupe Jimenez and the Captains, Emilio Alvarado, Salvador Contreras, Vicente de la Rosa, Justino Rodriguez and German Tecoapa.

The banner of Teresa Osorio, one of Compadre Ernesto's allies, is much simpler:

> This standard was raised by the Mesa of Santo Niño de Atocha, by the Capitana Ma Teresa Osorio Mtz, in memory of her Father, Cap Gral, Gabrial Osorio, y, Dolores Ortiz.

This is not intended to be read while dancing but between dances. On the front there is an image of the Santo Niño de Atocha, above which, curved around the image, are the words "Union, Conformidad y Conquista," and the date and place: "Mayo 3 1975, Mexico, D.F." The banner of Compadre Ernesto's

**5.4.** The standard of the mesa from Amecameca, one of Ernesto Ortiz's more important allies.

**5.5.** The images on Compadre Ernesto's banner.

mesa is also simple. On the front are five small images: at top left, the Señor de Sacremento; below, the Virgen de los Remedios; on the right, the Señor de Chalma; below, Santo Niño de Atocha; and in the middle, el Señor Santiago.

## EL ES DIOS

The three precepts, as already indicated, together constitute the words that are carried—bearing the word—but this can also be stated another way. Emblazoned on the banners they are less veiled than those words that are only passed on orally. Linked to union, conformity, and more particularly conquest is "El es Dios," which implies a shift from the process of dancing and what this should entail, of being (a state that dancers will have known previously), to a more abstract sacred level of becoming. "El es Dios" is frequently enunciated as an invocation rather than an injunction and has enormous significance for the Concheros. "El es Dios" may imply transcendence, when "one becomes all and all is God."[18] There is thus the implication that once a dancer can begin to carry the words "union" and "conformity"—that is, achieve ritualization—she has become a proficient dancer and can then work on herself (conquest) and begin to become more godlike.

This might seem heretical to Catholics who believe that no person can become God (although plenty have become saints), but there are vestiges here of indigenous and even pre-Colombian beliefs. For many indigenes, the images to which they gave their attention (whether we call this praying to or communing with) are believed not to represent the deity but rather to *be* the deities.[19] In the origin myth, the Santa Cruz appears to the indigenous dancers, who afterward danced around a stone cross they had requested for a whole week, kissing and venerating it and shouting "El es Dios," thereby indicating their belief that the cross was a deity.[20] In Tenochtitlan, prior to the Conquest, people acted as deities (*ixiptlas*) for a one-year period and received honors before being sacrificed. "El es Dios" may refer to this practice.[21]

The phrase comes into the permission sung before the dance begins and is completed there by *Padre, Hijo*, or *Un solo Dios y el Espiritu Santo*.[22] At a vigil during the singing of an alabanza it is frequently added in an exclamatory manner after a solo verse, before everyone else comes in with the chorus. During a dance, ordinary conversation should not and mostly does not occur and few words will be heard other than this invocation. The dancer in the center petitioned to lead the next dance, for example, will shout "El es Dios" before she takes the dancers through the danced permiso, to which the other dancers will reply with the same words. It is also uttered at times during the dance and as a dance terminates. The invocation reminds each dancer (and instructs the neophyte when necessary) at many stages of the dance to be aware that she is dancing not for herself but for the deity. It reminds her that she must keep up her ritual stance by following the dictates of union, conformity, and conquest and let her ritualized state, aided by the performativity of the moment, take her further. The invocation is much more than a bridge between normal activity and the dance, much more than a command to enter ritualization again; rather, it is linked to transcendence. The phrase when spoken indicates that the speaker is not speaking on his or her own behalf but is empowered and speaking impersonally, even divinely.

Stripped to its essentials, "El es Dios" has a heightened sense.[23] He (*El*) is a linguistic sign for God (*Dios*) and the one is connected to the other by metonymy. However, where the words "union," "conformity," and "conquest" are linked metonymically as each actualizes the dance, the meaning of "El es Dios" is more metaphoric: each dancer is aspiring to be godlike.[24] A jefe, it is believed, is closer to being godlike than are his dancers; the dancer in the center whom the others are following is more godlike than they are (especially for the duration of her dance as she carries the word). The invocation implies that each dancer aspires to make that metaphorical leap, desires to *endiosarse* (to be godlike or to deify oneself); as one dancer put it, "it is my work, my vigilance, my faith, that enables me to become godlike."[25]

Another dancer put it differently. She implied that "El es Dios" is an invitation to the deity to enter each dancer, indicating that what is about to happen is occurring by consensus and not according to the dictates of one person's will.[26] Indeed, in the dance itself, the expression is used to mark a transition from normal everyday interaction to an interaction that is achieved by non-discursive means that may become transcendent. I have tried to let "El es Dios" resonate rather than gloss it too closely; it is quite clear that it means different things to different dancers. I return to it in Chapter 7, when I look more closely at transcendence.[27]

The invocation can be used at other times too. When a celebrant wants to speak during a vigil (and/or a dance), she always begins with "El es Dios" and ends in similar fashion. In the past, I gather there was usually a meeting after a dance during which the dancers expressed their opinions about the obligation that had just occurred, each comment framed by "El es Dios." At the formal meeting of jefes that I attended (see Chapter 8), "El es Dios" was used both to open and to close what amounted to speeches. Although those attending the meeting were certainly considered to be more godlike than the ordinary foot soldiers, the meeting itself was about the political problems within the association and often seemed to be less than divinely inspired. It can thus be used in a much more parochial way, as an almost formulaic interjection—an indication that someone is moved to speak or desires to carry the word: "Conchero-speak" par excellence.

## CARRYING THE WORD

Many of the invocations used during ritual are more significant for the sounds they produce—their musical qualities—than for their illocutionary meaning. As analysts we are often overly interested in elucidating what is meant by such utterances. Linguists have often "imprisoned sound in the hermetically sealed vault of referential meaning," and I could perhaps be accused of that here.[28] For the participants, "union," "conformity," and "conquest" are more like performative aids to ritualization than illocutionary (or even perlocutionary) acts. They, like the military terminology, are metaphorical.

When these terms crop up in discussions about the dance, however, both in everyday life and on more special occasions, they have a significance that goes beyond the everyday. In Conchero discourse they are often repeated one after another: *Yo creo que a estar acceptado nuestra union, nuestra conformidad, [nuestra conquista] yo creo que . . .* ("I believe that to be accepted our union, our conformity [our conquest], I believe that . . ."). This parallelism increases the force or heat of the argument and also enables the speaker to draw out a thought and embellish it.[29] Although these three injunctions are conventional, they are believed to have physical potency, whereas "El es Dios" appears to have a more spiritual power, even a magical resonance. The latter has the mnemonic ability to assist in taking the dancer from one state to another because of the associations, desires, and feelings that it sets up when uttered in the right circumstances (somewhat like "abracadabra" or "open sesame"). As "each dancer fulfils his own part in the circle and cleanses his naked singularity in the collective catharsis of the cosmic movement," it enables the transformation from an embodied being to one much less aware of its body-self.[30]

In this chapter, the analysis has shifted to the Concheros' own terminology and the expressions they use to think about and discuss the dance with each other. They are adjunct to a mode of action in the Malinowskian sense.[31] If "union" and "conformity" can be equated with ritualization to an extent, "El es Dios," like "conquest," is linked to transcendence and indicates where a state of ritualization linked to performativity can take a dancer.

This sparse vocabulary linked to the dancing frames the situation in a non-physical way, giving a special feel to the dance. It is usually anticipated that dance will create a sense of difference, but that this effect in part can be achieved by means of language is perhaps less usual. These expressions are "attention-demanding" in the sense that they focus people's concentration and indicate to the dancers what they should be attempting to do; that is, they act as external mnemonics for what any dancer is trying to achieve as she dances.[32]

Ritual language brings experience to the celebrant not, as might be supposed, in terms of meaning but rather because these few, frequently repeated words are perceived as having performative potency irrespective of their predictability and lack of clear definition.[33] They communicate as one of the many elements of the interpersonal orchestration that occurs in the process of the buildup of the dance, its social integration, and its continuity. They aid in the overall process of the "convergence" of the various media—the songs, the music of both the conchas and the drums, and the dances themselves, which all clearly also have their own nonverbal language (Chapter 7)—as ordinary level interrelations are transformed into what has been described as higher-level ones when "total experiences" can be produced.[34] These ritualized injunctions and invocations can act to focus attention perhaps more potently than the other media, at least initially, for the very reason that language is usually expected to carry meaning in the semantic or referential sense rather than as mnemonic force.

Finally, the expression "carrying the word" has for the Concheros a rather special connotation. The use of this phrase implies not only a complex process of embodiment but one of social interaction essential to the dance. The implication is that each dancer is trying to give her self to the dance while molding her enactment to that of other dancers and she must also communicate—or as Teresa Mejia put it, "spread" (*contagiar*)—what she experiences. In the following chapter, I discuss one of the other ways in which the Concheros can carry and spread the word.

# CLOTHING MATTERS

So far I have been concerned with the dancers as subjects who by their "mode of presence and engagement in the world" actively embody the dance through time and re-present it. This chapter moves from an analysis of the dancers' experience of what is happening to and within the body, over which the dancers have only a certain amount of conscious control, to look at what is displayed on the body, at how dancers dress themselves. As Csordas has recently argued, the body is best understood as a subject that is "necessary to be" rather than an object that is "good to think," but when it comes to sartorial preferences, the latter is more clearly the case.[1]

The verbal expressions used during a dance follow a restricted code (as indicated in Chapter 5), but the clothing worn is much less constrained and is an aspect over which the dancers have much more individual say in the signifying process. A dancer's clothing is usually a combination of both the conventional and the individualistic: on the one hand, it speaks to the general sartorial views of that dancer's *mesa*, but it can also express a dancer's ontological sense of self and say something about what the dancer considers the dance to mean. It is indicative of the self the dancer professes and has invested in and this self can be re-presented to those she dances with as well as act as a self-reflecting mirror. In what they wear, the dancers have more freedom to improvise, to follow inspiration, or to act as bricoleurs; their clothing giving them an opportunity to be creative within the broad rules laid down by their *jefe*.

**6.1.** A woman dancer at Tlatelolco.

The importance of dress to the dance is that it is eye-catching and can act as a strong signifier. Overall, it is festive, exuberant, and often ostentatious; much is highly decorated, brilliantly and diversely colored, as well as lustrous or glittering, with a great variety of textures and finishes. Even if the observer's eye is not captivated by the dance itself, the costumes worn usually excite comment and speculation. Because they can be seen as texts to be read and interpreted, it is also an aspect of the dance that takes up a lot of time and attention. Clothing matters.

Clothing in general has received much more anthropological consideration recently.[2] Everyday clothing can make statements about social and cultural values. Tarlo indicates how in India, a person's ethnicity and social status (or caste) can be assessed from what he or she wears. It is one of the first things that can be read about other people, often before we have even spoken to them. What they wear addresses us and demands our attention.[3]

In many cultures, however, people often wear special apparel for particular occasions, such as for a ritual or ceremony. This tends to be a marked form to which more care and attention is usually given: a bride wears an elaborate dress for her wedding just as a Conchero dresses in special clothing for the dance. It is a form of active rather than passive dressing.[4]

In other situations, in Latin America, for example, indigenous men in particular are increasingly adopting standard Western clothing when they want to pass as mestizos for work purposes.[5] Within such communities, dress can be used to signal certain political affiliations; to dress in indigenous clothing (or *traje*) can bring political and/or economic benefits when dignitaries visit a community. For dealing with tourists too, a conscious decision can be taken to dress up in the very clothing that has in the past tended to perpetuate the group's marginalization.[6] In such communities, this is a clear example of the growth of a self-consciousness about what is worn. But is this switching clothes to other *clothing* or to a *costume*? Indigenous men who have worn trousers for years may feel that when they don their traditional traje for a particular reason, they are now dressing up, putting on a costume.

In societies where individuals tend to have a variety of clothes, what is worn on a daily basis can be changed in a different way. The wearer can express her taste by means of what she chooses to buy from the heterogeneity available in the consumer clothing market. She can then decide what to wear from her wardrobe (or *"personalia"*) to express her sartorial affiliations.[7] On any particular day, the individual may chose to signify or represent one aspect of their personal identity or social self instead of another. This is clearly a process of clothes changing rather than costuming. But when it is necessary to dress up for an occasion when, for example, black-tie is obligatory, such vestments may be so unusual as to feel more like a costume than normal clothing, in other words, a change that has been caused by circumstance rather than choice.

The more often a set of clothes is worn, the less it feels like a costume and the more like clothing. There are many situations in daily life when uniforms (the clothing worn by associations of persons) are required for particular roles: police officers and nurses wear "occupational dress."[8] Clearly, these garments will feel initially like a costume, but the wearers presumably soon get used to them and wear them as a matter of course. Although a uniform aims to mask personal identities, taste, and social position, it acts also as a cultural marker of a different identity, a professional one.

In many societies, people have few clothes; therefore, when they dress up for occasions that are extra to their everyday activity—the marked case—they put on the same type of clothing but their newest and best garments. Dressing up can, however, have different connotations. For us it may signify the preadult activity of putting on the discarded clothing of our elders, of bricolage and choice, of costuming ourselves in an attempt to playfully create a different persona.

The clothing of the Concheros aims to do both: the dancers are not only dressing up for the dance but also putting on a set of garments that transforms their identities. The distinction between clothing and costuming can thus also be concerned with consciously changing or presenting a different self. This distinction is a fine-grained one and is sometimes difficult to make. For the purposes of this chapter, I have used "clothing" for those vestments that are predominantly everyday clothes, and I have used "costume" for those that clearly bear no relation to what dancers wear on an everyday basis. In some groups, the dancers all dress in similar fashion according to their gender, and for these groups what they wear can more clearly be seen as a uniform (*uniforme* being the term used by many). The ideological origins of the uniform are usually unknown, but nevertheless, each dancer suppresses her personal predilections to re-present the group's identity. However, after a while the visual effect for the onlooker can become one of a semiotic blandness with intimations of the folkloric. The sameness—uniformity—of the costuming turns the surface of the body into a passive object of "ideological representation" rather than allowing it to be the focus of attention of each dancer's embodied "being-in-the-world."[9] In many groups, however, the garments can vary widely between dancers. For most, there is some expectation of the need to conform to an overall style but there are immense possibilities for personal expression in the lesser garments and the details of them all. In this, dancers are often very creative indeed.

Although my concern is primarily with Santo Niño de Atocha, whose dancers' garments are as heterogeneous as their backgrounds, I will look at what is worn more generally by the Concheros. Although most are in many ways traditional—certain types of materials are used and certain styles are followed—they are very much an investment in a dancer's sense of her dance-self at the time when he or she fabricated the outfit and, therefore, should perhaps be called vestments. This is the aspect of the dance in which the dancers have most agency. By what they wear, dancers can say something about their identities, their ontological predilections, or their personal taste and aesthetic, as well as what they have learned through the dance, all of which can be intermixed with or overlaid onto what is considered the appropriate style.

What follows is an analysis of the range of styles and their related aesthetics. Although the range of garments worn ultimately defies classification, some clear overall tendencies can tell the viewer a good deal about a mesa's beliefs before any dancers have even been spoken to. The following is both an etic and an emic codification of garment style. Dancers pointed out the differences to me initially, but these also quickly became apparent (although not all dancers would necessarily agree where one style ends and the next begins). Following this, I discuss the clothing of women and briefly that of particular post holders before looking at how one dancer describes how she determines what designs to use for her costume.

## STYLE AND AESTHETICS

Very loosely, two overall styles are interrelated in a fairly complex way with various aesthetics. The members of country groups and older, more indigenous dancers tend to wear garments that completely cover the body, which I have called Chichimeca style, a catchall category for all clothing that extensively circumscribes the body. I have so named it because many of the dancers who wear this type are from country mesas, some of whom still call their dance "Danza Chichimeca." City dancers and many younger dancers (even from the countryside) tend to wear an Aztec style, which is more minimal. Both are frequently enhanced with silver and gold decorations made from plastic. The Chichimeca style clearly predates the Aztec.

## THE CHICHIMECA BACKGROUND

For both male and female dancers the Chichimeca style is characterized by full skirts that go down to the ankles or just below the knee.[10] A plain white top is usually worn and the shoulders are covered by a large collar or a chasuble (a sleeveless tunic open at the sides), which is put on over the head and comes down to below the waist. For men, a full-length cloak and decorated wrist protectors can be added to this. All these garments, including the wrist protectors, may be made from the same cloth, although the materials deployed have changed considerably through the decades according to their availability and a changing aesthetic. Each dancer will also wear a headdress usually made from dyed ostrich feathers, leg rattles tied around the ankles, and *huaraches* (sandals) on the feet.

In its simplest form, this style dates from the end of the nineteenth century or earlier and is indicative of the influence of the Catholic Church, for the sacred body is both a socially controlled body and a well "wrapped" one.[11] Historically, the Chichimeca consisted of numerous groups who were hunters and gatherers and occupied the arid dessert-like areas to the north. They proved difficult to conquer and made numerous raids into Hispanicized domains and particularly the Bajio during the ensuing centuries (see Chapter 9). They are frequently represented by mainstream Mexican culture as archetypically rough and bellicose.[12]

This style, however, is not the sort of clothing that Chichimeca indigenes wore. It is clearly not appropriate for a hot climate and is in this sense a misno-

**6.2.** General Guadalupe Hernandez dressed in Chichimeca/Azteca style.

mer. I have, however, adhered to this classification because it is dance groups from the countryside whose older celebrants predominantly still wear such costumes and call their dance "Danza Chichimeca" (and some of whom may not be Concheros although plenty of Concheros dress in this style). This style too can be seen to be a costume variation of the typical clothing of rural peasants—consisting of a shirt and loose white trousers (*calzones*) made from manta—that some still wear today as a basis for their dance attire. Dancers who dress in Chichimeca style are predominantly those who still have a Catholic agenda and take it for granted that the dance has Catholic origins and originated in the Bajio (see Chapter 9).

Early Aztec-style costumes, quite similar to those still worn today, were already appearing in the 1960s. Typically, those consisted of stiff satin-like or velvet materials in predominantly plain colors and were decorated with a profusion of motifs, the most recurrent being Aztec in style but others had *grecas* (a Grecian fret), circles, and/or large *V*s. Such decorations were often in contrasting colors bordered by silver or gold fabrics or made from the latter, but the color of the cloth tended to be the dominant one in the costume's overall appearance. Each article of clothing was also edged with a dense trimming of small feathers, usually dyed one color, which contrasted or set off the skirt

**6.3.** Dancers dressed in Chichimeca style at La Villa. Note the Grecian fret on the costume of the dancer on the left, facing the camera.

and/or chasuble, for example, bright pink with blue or turquoise with red.[13] On their heads the dancers wore a diadem of similar materials variously shaped to support a profusion of large ostrich plumes pushed in at the back and dyed in bright primary colors. They wore huaraches on their feet, sometimes made from colored leather and with similar decorative motifs. (Indeed, these motifs were found too on the shields that some dancers carried.)

Although any one costume differs from any other—often considerably in terms of the small-scale patterning, use of color, and the distribution of materials—each in its own terms amounts to a set piece with little internal variation. The overall effect is of showy near uniformity and of a predetermined staginess. The dancers of a particular mesa knew that their uniforms should hold together as a preconceived whole that on the larger scale should express as few personal predilections as possible. How had this particular aesthetic developed?

## THE PRECURSORS

Two earlier descriptions of Conchero attire—one from the town of San Miguel de Allende (in the Bajío) and the other from Mexico City, and both from the late 1930s—show somewhat different apparel.[14]

More individual creativity or bricolage is suggested by what was worn in San Miguel. A man's costume consisted of a brightly colored skirt, often embroidered with spangles, gold, lace, or openwork of some sort, with the hems just below the knees. Colored stockings and huaraches of "plaited leather often with little bells attached," the bells also were sometimes worn around their ankles. The captains "wore cloaks, and whether large or small these were always richly decorated with drawings and symbols which were often very curious," such as a depiction of the word "Jehova" or the image of a bird—probably a turkey—with two hearts and a leaf frond.[15]

The headdresses were finer in detail and showed a great deal of variety. They were decorated with hen or occasionally dyed ostrich feathers "placed around a . . . crown richly embroidered with polychrome beads, mirrors and images of Christ, the Virgin or the Saints." The crown circled the head or "took the shape of an arc, high in front and falling at the sides of the face, while others fell behind the ears."[16]

Many of the more decorative aspects found in San Miguel had mostly disappeared by the mid-twentieth century, such as the strings of beads that "fell on the face in such lengths that they obscured it, often leaving only the nose and mouth uncovered," and the decorations on the skirts (as described above). Absent too were the "wigs of artificial hair, which hung loose to the shoulders." Round shields were still in evidence later on, but gone were the wooden sabers edged with flint.[17]

Some of the women's attire was similar. They "too wore feathers like the men's or straw hats decorated with colored ribbons and mirrors or images of the Saints."[18] They wore their hair loose and "adorned themselves with kerchiefs [*paliacates*], necklaces, earrings and rings." The overall effect was one of variety, for they used a mix of colors and decorations "without distinction" and "*colgajo*[s] [hanging pieces of cloth], . . . ribbons, mirrors, bells, images especially of San Miguel or the Virgin of Guadalupe, shining beads, in fact anything that glitters and is of brilliant color that would give a festive air to the person." The implication is that personal bricolage, at least at the small scale, was much encouraged and that the makers gained a great deal of satisfaction from the complexity and the craftsmanship that went into the making of the various pieces of paraphernalia, which were often added to their best clothing.[19]

The costuming of this mesa, however, may have been different from others in the region. Chichimeca-style costumes, described as "regional" and "from the Bajio," were already being worn by some dancers in a mesa in Mexico City by the 1930s.[20] The costumes worn in this mesa, La Gran Tenochtitlan, show further an interest in Mexico as a nation and are also beginning to emphasize "indianity."

The headdresses, for example, were made from canvas, corona-like in form, decorated with a multitude of small beads (*chaquira*) sewn in greca patterns or depicting "flowers, faces and other figures" in vivid strong contrasting colors. At the side of the face and covering the ears were hangings of the same material ornamented in similar fashion. The whole was topped by dyed feathers of swan, pheasant, and ostrich; the feathers were few in number and small in size, comparatively, giving the overall impression of green, white, and red—the colors of the national flag.[21]

The material from which the men's costumes were fashioned was primarily chamois leather, whether jackets, large neck collars, chasubles, skirts, trousers, or even their capes. The *manguillos* (armbands), worn just below the elbows, were made from coyote skin and decorated with designs applied in oil paint or burnt into the leather.[22] Solorzano and Guerrero make it clear that some wore white shirts and that although some men wore leather trousers, most chose skirts.

It is probable that these dancers in Mexico City were in a different position both financially and socially from those in the Bajio. The use of leather and leather fringing on their trouser legs and skirts, for example, was seen as archetypically Chichimeca, because it was known that they wore leather for their dances. In fact, the photos show costumes that bear a strong resemblance to the clothing worn by stereotypical "red Indians" as depicted in U.S. films.[23] Leather was undoubtedly more readily available than it is now, and it is rarely used today. Other aspects of this mode of dress have also disappeared, such as the scarf of red or yellow silk decorated with embroidered flower designs, which often included the dancer's initials or name, and the decorated huaraches sometimes painted with gold or silver.

However, an awareness of the Aztec past is clear in the name of the mesa and the designs on some of the chasubles and skirts are in fact figurative images of Aztec warriors, be-feathered and with shield in hand (although these dancers did not carry shields). Thus, by the 1930s, the influence of an "Indian," even Aztec, ideology was beginning to be evident in Mexico City.[24]

## AZTECQUISMO

A general interest in Aztec iconography as a source of imagery dates back much earlier to the period of the Porfiriato (1876–1911), when the construction of Mexico as a nation was undertaken by and for creoles. However, the interest was a superficial one, seen simply as a source of symbolism for the propagation of nationalism.[25] After the revolution of 1910, there was more awareness generally of Mexico's indigenous past as archaeological investigations began

**6.4.** Dancers at Santiago Tlatelolco in 1958. (Photograph by Ruth Lechuga)

at Teotihuacan (the capital during the earlier Classic period). More enlight-ened scholars went further and began to think that Mexico's current indigenous population should no longer be perceived as a race, which it had been hoped was on the verge of extinction after centuries of enforced poverty, isolation, and an assumed incapacity to confront technical change. Instead, the indigenes began to be conceptualized as the ideal material for mestizaje to be achieved by a process of miscegenation and education.[26] Gamio suggested that those aspects

**6.5.** A dancer at La Villa in 1964. (Photograph by Ruth Lechuga)

of indigenous culture that related to the arts could be brought into national culture and that music and dances, for example, should be folklorized and propagated. This became a real possibility with the establishment of the Secretary of Public Education (SEP) in 1921 and the instigation of the cultural missions.[27] The folk dances collected were taught in schools and performed at festivals and, by the mid-1930s, at the Belles Artes in Mexico City in a program known as Danzas Auténticas Mexicanas. The wife of the then-president Lázaro Cárdenas sponsored these performances, which included Conchero dances enacted by professionals.[28]

In the creative arts, a synthesis between European and indigenous ideas had begun to take off, with official encouragement, as clearly evidenced by the murals by Diego Rivera in the National Palace (1929–1930) and the earlier cycle at the Secretariat of Public Education (1923–1924).[29] He, his wife (the painter Frida Kahlo), and many others became interested in things indigenous, such as mythology, clothing and handicrafts, and music, dance, and songs—in effect, in *Mexicanidad* ("Mexicaness").[30] Mexicanidad diffused from the avant-garde into the wider culture of Mexico City as the use of Aztec-influenced nick-names and Aztec names for clubs, restaurants, and products became popular, as did the use of Aztec iconography.[31]

As already indicated, the renewed interest in the past had already trickled down to some Conchero mesas in Mexico City by the 1930s even though most dance groups were still closed and not yet openly celebrating Aztec origins. Dancers from the mesa of La Gran Tenochtitlan, for example, hinted that at La Villa they danced for Tonantzin rather than the Virgin of Guadalupe (although this was forbidden by the government at the time) and that the dance at Chalma was for Huitzilopochtli. They claimed that their headdresses were like that of Cuauhtémoc, the last Aztec emperor. They also emphasized that their ancestors had probably performed the same dances.[32] Solorzano and Guerrero's persistent questioning of the group's jefe, however, culminated in their being told that if they wanted to know about the origins of the dance, they need only look in "la Historia," meaning published accounts of the Aztecs. The dance tradition ran in the jefe's family but no indication is given of its longevity. He may have been better educated and in touch with a more professional world, although it seems that few of his dancers had passed more than the second grade in primary school. The authors reveal too the then ongoing paternalistic attitude toward such people for they describe the dancers as "our" indigenes and of limited "culture."[33]

By the middle of the century the fashion for Aztecquismo had become more widespread. At that time, although many urban costumes were more theatrical in style than the earlier ones, many male dancers were no longer wearing a skirt and top but rather a loincloth. It is important, however, to distinguish between the inclusion of Aztec decoration and imagery and the Aztec style proper, which really took off in the 1950s.

## AZTEC STYLE

For the inhabitants of Mexico City, the Aztecs, besides having a more acceptable image than the war-mongering Chichimeca, are conceptually if not actually their direct forebears. Some groups did (and often still do) call their dance

"Danza Azteca-Chichimeca." The same type of fabrics and feathers used for a skirt and chasuble by one dancer may be used by another for an extensive loin-cloth that tapers off just above the knees, a collar hung around the neck that sometimes covers part of the chest, ankle protectors, and a long cloak.

By the late 1950s there was also a transition in the use of materials. Increasingly, the appliquéd decoration of beadwork or of many colored satin ribbons began to be replaced by more industrialized fabrics, such as plastic silver and gold. It is clear too that the materials used depended on their avail-ability. Imported and then dyed ostrich feathers replaced indigenous white tur-key and eagle plumes as these became more difficult to obtain.[34] Whereas the costumes of the 1930s and 1940s were made predominantly from more natural materials such as leather or from fabric that was more gently flowing, those from the 1960s are characterized by the increased availability of more artificial, stiffer fabrics.

The growing interest in the origins of the dance also led to a greater aware-ness of the sartorial aspect. At least in the city mesas, it was not enough to modify everyday clothing, as the dancers in San Miguel in the 1940s had done, whose vestments had a homemade feel. A separate costume was increasingly becoming de rigueur. By the 1960s, what was worn for the dance, at least by many groups in the city, seems to have become increasingly staged and less personally detailed, to have become without a shadow of doubt costuming rather than clothing.

This is clearly also linked to economics. Dancers in the city have usually had more money at their disposal than do their country counterparts, who are more likely to have a simpler lifestyle. The city dancers too have been able to take advantage of a much wider range of materials, such as manufactured fab-rics, dyed feathers of various kinds, and artificial and plastic silver and gold fab-rics. They can also afford to change their apparel more frequently. Today some dancers still dress in theatrical accoutrements similar to those of the 1960s. A shop in the old center of Mexico City called El Faron sells costumes for danc-ers to equip themselves, if they so desire. Overall, however, dancers prefer to fabricate their own or call on the expertise of a member of their mesa.

More recently, the designs employed have shown the strong influence of Aztec iconography and have tended to be much finer grained. In the 1960s, the imagery on the front of an Aztec headdress would have been indicated by a very stylized representation in plastic silver of, for example, the great calendar stone—the huge Aztec carving unearthed in Mexico City in the late nineteenth century and frequently reproduced on tourist bric-a-brac. As the search for authenticity has increased and as reproductions of the codices have become more widely available, dancers have begun to be more discerning about the

**6.6.** Dancer dressed à la Aztec. Note the detail in the headdress.

**6.7.** Male dancers displaying their headdresses between dances.

imagery they employ, although many of these costumes continue to be deco-rated with artificial materials. Headdresses are more likely to use natural pheas-ant feathers than dyed ostrich plumes. Some have serpents rising above their heads, out of which spring feathers, depicting the mythological plumed serpent Quetzalcoatl; others go further, deploying real stuffed birds. In addition to deities, conceptual symbols are used, such as the calendrical glyph *ollin* (which signifies movement) and glyphs for water, rain, fire, and wind. The aesthetic is still theatrical but is beginning to move from a "fake" one toward one that is more natural.

There is also evidence that Aztec-style costuming became more promi-nent as attitudes to the body changed. A dancer who wanted to dance in an Aztec-style loincloth—but "without his sweatshirt" in San Miguel de Allende in the 1940s because "our ancestors danced with their upper bodies bare"—was severely reprimanded by his jefe because dancing bare-chested was considered "uncivilized."[35] The Church also did not approve of unclothed bodies in its environs, although gradually many more danced with bare torsos without incurring displeasure. The Aztecization of the costumes may thus have been held in check in the past by fear of how the Church might react to what could be perceived as an indication of a dancer's belief in the indigenous as opposed to Catholic origins of the dance.

It was during this period too that dancers from non-Conchero families were permitted entry to the dance for the first time. They may have felt at greater liberty to re-create aspects of the Aztec past than did the more traditional dancers. Although overall the dance was still Catholic, dancers were beginning to challenge the supremacy of the Christian God by invoking pre-Colombian deities. Aztec costumes, for example, often have either a skull design or a small replica of a skull on the headdress or pectoral, and this is an even more frequent and powerful signifier for the so-called Mexica.

## THE MEXICA AESTHETIC

The Mexica aesthetic, which appears currently to be threatening the long-term durability of the Aztec, is much stricter. The Mexica never employ plastic silver or gold; they only utilize natural materials, preferably those that were available before the Spanish Conquest. Their aesthetic depends on a closer reading of the Aztec past and is considerably less theatrical

Their loincloths are made from skins—such as snake or even leopard skin but more usually leather or suede—rather than manufactured materials. The headdresses are adorned with natural rather than dyed feathers and include not just pheasant and hen feathers. Dancers often search for tropical bird plumes— such as those of the hummingbird, macaw and other parrots, and in rare cases the quetzal. These introduce richness and subtlety to the colorings. Additionally, many have decorated earpieces hanging from their headdresses made from colored beads, leather, and/or feathers redolent of those from the late 1930s. They adorn their chests with necklaces of leather strips or beads, and their collars and armbands, both at the wrist and higher up, are also of leather, suede, or fine beadwork (*chaquira*) and again frequently decorated with feathers. In addition, they often wear knee pieces and prefer to dance barefoot.

Mexica costuming is very concerned with detail. It has adopted the practice of hanging beads over the eyes and wearing long, flowing wigs of real hair, both of which, it is claimed, have been culled from the codices (rather than the earlier dancers of the 1930s). Some of the older jefes I talked to remembered the practice having to do with wearing wigs, and certainly Diego Durán, in his chronicle, talks of Aztec dancers wearing false hair.[36] The Mexica assert that they do so because the inhabitants of Tenochtitlan mostly had long hair.[37] When not wearing a headdress, their hair is controlled with a red band (*ixcuamecatl*). They also carry shields, as did the dancers in San Miguel in the 1930s, but not swords.

There are similarities in how the Mexica put together their garments to those described by Solorzano and Guerrero for the Concheros. To the Mexica, bricolage is also important. However, these are not costumes but carefully and individually crafted vestments. A Mexica dancer does not talk about his attire as a "uniform" because by wearing it he wants to express not conformity but above all his individuality. A Mexica dancer assembles bits and pieces, which to him are sacred, precious, or exquisite and worthy of being included, restricted only by the need to be natural and the means at his disposal. Typically, a Mexica dancer puts hours of work into creating the beadwork or making his headdress, pectoral, and shield.

---

Although today many Chichimeca costumes are decorated with Aztec motifs and as most Aztec-style costumes have become increasingly individualistic in recent decades (and the Mexica wear a very similar style), the classificatory categories I have employed—as should be clear by now—are for the purposes of analysis only. In practice, there is a considerable degree of overlap, for style and aesthetic do not necessarily change together.

The difference between Chichimeca dancers and Aztec dancers is linked to the latter's awareness of the Aztec past, even if this link is superficial, although the materials deployed for both styles for some time have been quite similar. The Mexica's vestments, despite appearing to create a clear break, are in part a continuation of the Aztec style and linked to a return to some of the practices of the 1930s. The biggest disjunction that the Mexica have created is their ideological rejection of much Conchero practice and their emphasis on a reinterpretation of the Aztec past reflected in their desire to use natural materials. Where the Aztec style is effectively a pastiche of Aztec clothing, the Mexica aim to re-create the actual clothing of the Aztecs to the extent that they can and to build a philosophy by which they can both dance and live (see Chapter 10). Whereas the dancers in San Miguel in the 1930s could be classified as Catholic peasants or ex-peasants (some of whom were more indigenous than others), the Mexica in general are New Agers who have rejected the Catholic Church altogether and Christian beliefs in general.

This tripartite classification is made too at the expense of eliding the enormous variation within each of these categories, particularly within the Chichimeca and the Aztec styles. As indicated, the attire in San Miguel de Allende in the 1930s used markedly different materials from the coeval costumes displayed by the group in Mexico City, and both were more varied, amateur, and ad hoc than the costumes found in the 1960s and still in use today.

## WOMEN'S VESTMENTS

What women wear for the dance is even more difficult to classify. Women need to cover the upper part of their bodies and wear dresses or skirts no matter what

**6.8.** Sahumadoras between dances at La Villa.

type of mesa they belong to and what their beliefs and personal inclinations are. This leads to a less obvious difference in style. For women, the difference between the Chichimeca and Aztec aesthetic is signaled most strongly by the decoration: the Chichimeca style uses small feathers like fur trim (as opposed to the Aztec's practice of using none at all) and dyed ostrich feathers in the head-dress instead of the Aztec's undyed pheasant feathers. The distinction between the two groups may also be indicated by the cut of the costume—Aztec-style dresses are often very straight with side slits to permit some movement whereas Chichimeca skirts are much fuller. It is not as easy for a woman to dress in Mexica style; a whole snakeskin outfit would be prohibitively expensive. Also, the Mexica have far fewer female dancers. On the other hand, Chichimeca cos-tuming for women looks much more like that of the men in their group, for their long skirts and chasubles are very similar, whereas women in groups who wear Aztec-style attire find it difficult to mirror the men's minimal loincloths. Some, in an attempt to do so, wear a skirt that stops well above the knees, but I only saw a few examples of this in and around Mexico City. If the group is Mexica, women wear a top made from cloth of some sort, despite their reluc-tance to wear fabrics, and perhaps, at the extreme, a loincloth similar to that of the male dancers, leaving the legs bare.

In some Aztec groups, the differences between the attire of the individual women will be much more striking than that of the men partly because the area

**6.9.** A young dancer wearing a tight Aztec-style dress.

of the body that needs to be covered is larger (although men's cloaks some-what counter this). Sometimes, when the male dancers of a particular mesa are clearly dressed à la Azteca-Chichimeca, each in a fairly distinctive loincloth decorated in plastic silver and gold with heavy chasubles, the women of that group may be wearing dresses that are quite different from each other's. One might be made from pale blue fabric decorated with white feathers and extend down to the ankles with an open back, and another might have a long dark red velvet dress decorated with Aztec symbols in plastic silver.

The women's vestments indicate that they have more freedom to dress according to their inclinations, but overall the men's often reveal greater creative exuberance. Some female dancers do dress to the extremes, but on the whole it is the men who sport the most different or flamboyant costumes, such as the one whose headdress was made up of feathers almost two meters long. Many women sidestep the problem of how to dress by wearing a hand-woven indigenous *huipil*; these are usually decorated with woven or embroidered motifs in a wide range of colors on a white background. Like recent Mexica male garments, women's indigenous huipils are often similar to those seen in the codices, but they are also paying homage to contemporary indigenous women. Many combine a huipil with a plain cotton skirt and indicate their preferences, beliefs, or interests by the images and motifs used in their headdresses and the use of scarves or hanging cloths, ribbons, belts, small bags, necklaces, and other adornments.

In this analysis, I may have given the impression that the majority of male dancers in most groups will be dressed in a similar style, but this is not necessarily the case. Often many may be wearing Aztec-style attire but some will be clothed in Chichimeca-style costumes and others will be dressed in garments that very much follow their own aesthetic. Dancers quite often have several costumes. The general Guadalupe Hernandez, for example, has a Chichimeca costume that he wears most frequently but also an Aztec one that he puts on if there are two dances in rapid succession. A dancer may also don a costume that is a hybrid, for example, part Azteca-Chichimeca (perhaps a cloak covered in plastic silver and gold Aztec designs) and part Mexica (the loincloth), although this is rare. Some defy classification and it is also impossible to catch every variation. In Santo Niño de Atocha there has never been an overall style for men or women. The dancers' attire was heterogeneous because Compadre Ernesto encouraged individual expression in this area. One male dancer occasionally wore a monk's habit, which he said was his way of getting back at the Catholic Church. The only way to tell that all the dancers came from the same group was that they danced together regularly.

**6.10.** A sergeant from Los Remedios wearing a wig of black hair, a red kerchief, a mask, and white *manta* trousers. Note the images of Christ. He has a whip tucked under his left arm and a stick in his right hand. His appearance was unusually compelling and he clearly came from a rural community.

## THE SHOWING OF POSITION

As discussed in Chapter 2, aside from the regular dancers, each group also has named personnel, such as the sergeant, who is concerned with keeping order within the group and protecting it from outsiders. Today such personnel rarely dress differently from the other dancers, but in the 1930s "various of them wore masks . . . represent[ing] the devil" or "they were known as the 'madmen' who frightened off those watching and kept them at a good distance."[38] They introduced a playful element into the dance and could also keep spectators amused between dances. In Mexico City there were typically four: the devil, the old man, the old woman, and a hermit.[39] Rural mesas in particular often still have sergeants who wear animal costumes, but today it is rare to see the sergeant actually chastising the watching crowds, although this was not the case in the past.

## INSPIRATION, COMPETENCE, AND PROTECTION

Various dancers told me that the details of a dancer's attire should reflect the "state of conquest" that the dancer has achieved in the dance. Ideally, a dancer should begin with a white costume and very few feathers—essentially, a blank canvas—and add symbols and feathers as competence is achieved or gained and recognized by her jefe. Compadre Ernesto talked of beginning with one feather, gaining a second the following year, and only ever using six. Today it is rare for dancers to use so few, and I saw Compadre Ernesto with as many as eighteen. Conversely, I was once reprimanded for dressing too simply but saw little evidence of a precise sumptuary code, at least for Santo Niño de Atocha.[40]

In general, as each dancer starts, she slowly feels out what she should wear according to the often fairly loose tenets of the group and her own inclinations. Many wear ordinary clothing at first. One way to add designs to your garments is according to the symbols associated with your Aztec birth sign as found in the Tonalamatl (the Aubin codex), which might suggest, for example, a deer with a flower. As a dancer gains in experience, insight will come as to how these initial symbols should be altered or further elaborated.

The dancer in-vests in her garments her inner self, thereby building up her protection, for the garment is a manifestation of that dancer's personal power. As Rosa-Elia put it,

> [f]rom the beginning I always wanted to manifest what is traditional, to combine the four elements and the four points or winds.[41] My clothing has always focused on these, and the majority of the designs I have employed have been based on them. The teaching has been that you look for symbols

that you most identify with and elaborate your costume accordingly; then you look for your feathers, your sandals, and make your leg rattles, for your costume is your protection. You put your energy into it and at any moment in time, it can protect you.

You make and use your costume and then you change it, because you can't go on using it after it begins to deteriorate. When you make a new one, you keep the old one. I'm using the one I made for my wedding because the previous one is too old. I haven't begun to make the next one yet as I've not found the symbols that at this moment . . . I feel most affinity with. Normally the symbols come from the codices in the anthropology museum, which also has collections from archaeological zones. The tradition is not only documented there, but there is also oral knowledge passed on from father to son, from the captains to dancers, and from dancer to dancer. We are obliged to study and further our knowledge, as well as look for documents to be sure about what we are doing. My next costume will have new symbols. Sometimes I keep one or two symbols from one costume to the next but not always: the designs are always changing.

The implication here is that Rosa-Elia makes new garments as the old ones wear out. However, even if for many the idea has begun to disappear that their achieved competence should be reflected in their vestments, it is still not appropriate to make exactly the same outfit twice. The new dress is indicative of a dancer's awareness that what is or should be appropriate has changed. As a dancer gains insight, this should be mirrored externally by what she wears. A new outfit will reflect too what is considered to be fashionable at any particular point in time—sometimes it is simple dyed cotton, at other times more elaborate materials—for as Sapir's dictum indicates, "fashion is custom in the guise of a departure from custom."[42]

Elaborating a new outfit may take a considerable amount of time and money. Some dancers told me that a dancer should, if she can afford to do so, make a new one every year to wear to Chalma or La Villa. Indeed, a large dance can act as a challenging deadline: Olga mentioned to me in October that she was making a new outfit for La Villa in December. Sewing it oneself is considered important by many women. Once a new garment has been elaborated, the old one should be kept respectfully but not worn. As Rosa-Elia put it, "we are accustomed (or rather the captains have shown us) that when you stop using one, you keep it. You use the new one until that too is too old to use."

Some dancers are clearly more interested in their appearance than are others. They are probably more aware of the statement that is made by what they are wearing, although it may be that they simply have more time and/or money available. Such dancers usually have several ongoing costumes at any one time. Some women dancers (and some men) seemed to treat these more like a wardrobe of dance costumes, wearing one for one dance, another for another obligation, according to some predetermined personal code. Guadalupe Hernandez's practices in this regard have already been mentioned. Antonia also had a range of vestments and headdresses, some more clearly based on Aztec iconography than others. One was a simple skirt and cape top made from manta; another was similar in style but made from a blue velvety material with colored ribbon appliqué. She clearly enjoyed designing and made her own everyday clothes as well as those for the dance, as did Olga (whose collection was displayed in the Zocalo metro station in 1993). Angelica too had several dance costumes at any moment in time. Some were fairly conventional but she also designed others with particular symbols, including one that signified that wars should end and peace begin, a message that she hoped other dancers and, more especially, those watching would notice.

A dancer's outfit is thought about, carefully made, and stored between obligations. It is not appropriate to lend it to another dancer. It is, after all, very personal, made for you and usually by you. Nor is it appropriate to wear it at any time other than for the dance. Early on during my fieldwork, I once suggested putting on leg rattles when a group of us were dancing socially after a Conchero dance. The suggestion was met with dismay, for these too are a protection worn only during the dance.

A dancer's paraphernalia is not just a repository of "virtuoso artistry" either but can also be one "of competitive aesthetic development."[43] Dancers who place a great deal of emphasis on their vestments are in a sense competing as to who can produce the garment that most clearly expresses not only their personal state but also the state of the dance as currently experienced. Men in particular compete in terms of manifesting their aesthetic, and this is particularly so among the Mexica in their attempts to each appear to be the most *chingon* (awesome). In some groups many have costumes made by one of the women dancers that may be fabricated to their specific requirements, or the maker may try to get a sense of what is most appropriate. Pando has one that is predominantly blue made by one woman dancer and a white one fabricated by another. He had been told that the colors white, yellow, blue, and red have particular meanings although he could not remember what their significance was. He was clear, however, that he preferred the white to the blue, but he did not explain why. If he danced twice in any one week, however, he wore the blue and then the white.

A dancer's garments also determine to an extent how she or he can move in the dance.[44] Rosa-Elia at one time had both a long and a shorter outfit. The long dress rather restricted the movement of her feet, as do the skirts of those who wear Chichimeca-style attire. She greatly appreciated the freedom of movement that a shorter skirt gave her, just as do the male Mexica dancers in their minimal loincloths. As one female captain said, "there are some that leap less and others more. Others mark [their steps] well while others do no more than run and jump." Although she obviously had a poor opinion of the latter mode of dancing, undoubtedly the shorter skirts of the women dancers and the more minimal loincloths of male dancers, especially Mexica ones, permit much more freedom of movement.

The costuming of the dancers in Compadre Ernesto's group was probably more varied than most other mesas, as already indicated. There were few stated prohibitions. One dancer did tell me that the compadre had not liked straight (i.e., tight) skirts, although I saw some key dancers wearing these. Few of his dancers came in fully fledged Chichimeca- or Aztec-style dress with a plenitude of plastic silver and gold decorations, but then again few believed that the dance is Catholic in origin. Some of the dancers' costumes were a hybrid of various styles, and most were carefully designed and especially elaborated.

## CLOTHING MATTERS

During the twentieth century, the attire worn has changed from garments with "a very primitive flavor"—that is, from those that were more individualistic and homemade—to costumes that were theatrical, each one similar to another and fashioned from artificial fabrics, to once again those that emphasize the individualistic and the natural.[45] These changes mirror some of the changing social categories of the dancers themselves, from rural peasants to more self-conscious town or city dwellers to those with more of a historical awareness (such as the Mexica) or ecological awareness (such as those mesas who make as much as possible of their costumes and especially their headdresses of cornstalks).

Costuming is clearly of great significance to the dance. The garments worn can be in part a re-presentation of a range of images taken from a predetermined semiotic code, of which most mesas have their version and attempt to impose more or less strongly on their dancers. In part also, each set of garments is a form of individual expression reflecting the taste, economic standing, and personal propensities of the enactor. The observer can know little of the inner bodily experience of the dancer, but her costume can reveal a certain amount about that part that she is prepared to make public, and often her costume reveals more of her inner self than is intended. A dancer's costuming is very much a way of circulating ideas about a dancer's identity in a semiotic form.[46]

Although the garments worn for the dance matter, they matter much more to some dancers than to others. For some it is the dance that counts and what is worn is relatively unimportant. Dancers may simply have put together their clothing as best they can, and this is particularly true of some men. Herman, the inheritor of the Tepetlixpa group (see Chapter 8), often danced in just a t-shirt and jeans, and even when dressed up clearly did not give much consideration to his costuming. I found dressing for the dance quite difficult. Although I daydreamed occasionally of making myself the sort of costume that could be compared to those of Antonia and Olga, what I actually wore was a huipil and a white manta skirt. It was challenging because I knew my costume should have significance but I did not want to claim a status that I did not have.

In Chapter 4, I suggested that ritualization is not intended to communicate. Although a dancer's clothing is clearly part of the ritual process, dress concedes to the performative in a much more permanent way than any other aspect of the dance. For some, the clothing worn may even be purely performative. "It may . . . quite simply embellish him and focus visual attention on him" even if this contradicts the unspoken tenets of the dance. Hollander has commented, "When characters utter no sounds, their clothes obviously speak more loudly."[47] This certainly is how the Mexica think about their costumes, although they are also garrulous. The semiotic code of costuming for the Concheros is much more easily deciphered than the dance itself, for what the dance means is much less clear-cut. It is to this that I turn in the following chapter.

# SEVEN

# WHY DANCE?

"[T]hese dances that some people call entertainment . . . are not amusements, we dance because it lightens the heart, because we are conquered by God Our Father."

— CAPITAN GENERAL in San Miguel de Allende[1]

"You close yourself. You don't look around you because you shut yourself into what you are doing. You are concentrating and dancing. You are making turns and taking steps but you don't know what or where you are."

— JEFA TERESA MEJIA

"Dance . . . is an ek-static movement which opens us to the wholeness and expansiveness of Being, and a movement which intensifies our grounding and our contact with the powers of the earth."

— D. M. LEVIN[2]

Only by dancing, by gaining know-how, can the enactor know the dance. In this chapter, I attend to the experience of the dancing itself. I look at why it is that people are drawn to and enter the dance and what it is about the enacting of it that catches them and keeps them coming. In Chapter 4, I looked at the process of ritualization that each enactor must perforce undergo as she enters into the spirit of the dance, focusing her attention on re-attaining its forms and on reproducing the steps and gestures in accord with their well-established patterns. I was concerned there with the relation between the inner self and the dancer's body. Here I begin by looking at the enactor's relation to the music

**7.1.** Dancer at Los Remedios in 1960. (Photograph by Ruth Lechuga)

played, the songs sung, and the incense burned. As the dance obligation builds over time, a state of intersubjectivity is created between dancers, achieved in part by the physical work put into the dancing by each dancer, by the media used, and more particularly by the surrender of the everyday self and the contact achieved with the *animas* (spirits)—or to put it in the Concheros own terms, the attainment of union and conformity that leads to conquest. Transcendence can and does sometimes occur and is a state in which the celebrant is once again on her own and gains insight into her own life. As a number of dancers indicated, the dance can teach a new way of being-in-the-world that can give added meaning to everyday life. The dances are never performed alone or, in the case of an accomplished dancer, in her spare time; it is what is achieved together that is important, for there is not only the discipline of the dance—its ritualization—but also the need to respond to others as a shared somatic state develops. "Transcendence" is a term best left to resonate, and when dancers did speak to me about it, I mostly have let them speak for themselves in this chapter.

## DANCE IN THEORY

There is no doubt that dance is a significantly different activity from other forms of movement, but anthropologists have often found it hard to define as something apart from other structured systems.[3] I have so far used the term "dance" as though as a form it is unproblematic. However, not all dancing has music, and not everything that appears to be dance is called dance.[4] On the other hand, in some cultures, forms that appear to Western eyes to be un-dance-like actually are or have been so classified.[5] But does a distinction need to be drawn?

Increasingly, analysts have been challenging such genre definitions. Ness uses the designation "choreographic phenomena" to analyze a range of patterned body movements that include those used in ritual practices, whereas Lowell Lewis has argued for the use of the term "movement" in place of "dance."[6] Although I sympathize with these approaches, I will not be following either suggestion. This is in part because the dancing of the Concheros is so much more clearly dance in Western terms than either the Brazilian capoeira or the Philippine sinalog.[7] Furthermore, the Concheros themselves use the term "dance" to describe some of their activities, and what is attained by means of this sacred activity clearly differs from the effects of everyday action or other specialized movement forms. What I explore in this chapter is precisely what this difference is by trying to understand why the Concheros dance.

It is only in the last few decades that anthropologists have really begun to look at dance. Early anthropologists on both sides of the Atlantic (such as Boas, Radcliffe-Brown, Evans-Pritchard, Bateson, and Mead) gave some attention to the dances they encountered, but a period followed thereafter during which dance was given only cursory mention. It was often dismissed with such statements as "and then they danced." As Kaeppler points out, "[i]t is commonplace to separate dance, along with music, from other forms of human behavior, and label it 'art.' Once it has been so separated, it is often felt that it need not be dealt with."[8] The interest in dance has expanded enormously in the last few decades.[9] Despite this, there is still a general tendency to trivialize, denigrate, and naturalize the significance of dance practices.[10]

Dance is difficult to write about not only for lack of an easily used or decipherable analytical language but more particularly because it is an experience that is visceral, synesthetic, and multisensory.[11] The look of a dancer's body is of significance for theatrical dance, but for more informal dancing, such as the dances of the Concheros, of more importance is what the dancer feels, senses, and experiences—and therefore what she gives to and gets out of the dance. Dance is perhaps even more difficult to write about if one is not a dancer by training, a position I share with Cowan.[12] However, I danced with the Concheros regularly for six months and have done so whenever possible subsequently; I can therefore say something about the experience of trying to learn how to dance, the dancing itself, and its effects. Writing about the politics of dance is always far easier than the poetics, for as Isadora Duncan said, "[i]f I could tell you what it meant, there would be no point in dancing it."[13]

## TO DANCE

Many of us are attracted by social dance, enjoy it, and, although we may not dance for months, wish perhaps that the opportunity arose more often. Frequently, we dance alone in a crowd of other dancers, or the steps performed by the person dancing "with" us bear little relation to our own, as we both respond in our individual ways to the rhythm of the music. Interpersonal communication is often restricted to eye contact, or even to shouting over the music, rather than by means of the body. Our ability or preparedness to respond to each other is often sadly lacking. The kinds of dances that encourage this type of interaction (e.g., the waltz or foxtrot) have recently been enacted little in the more developed parts of the world, although coupled dances are still common in Latin America, such as the tango or salsa (and both of these dances are currently quite fashionable in the West). Bodily conversation is essential for these dances, and at their best, the two bodies enacting are closely linked and perform as one—even when moving in opposing directions as in the tango—engendering a sense of synchronicity and intersubjectivity. This is the case even more so for dancing linked to a form of communal spirituality. When the dance of the Concheros really takes off something similar occurs, although as already mentioned the dancers rarely touch one another. This "taking off" only happens occasionally but perhaps can do so because in comparison to the tango, the steps of the dances are straightforward.

In general, dance as a form allures because it involves a response to music by means of movement. Those who dance as Concheros, however, do so for rather different reasons than those who go out to dance on a Friday night. The latter are enacting dance forms that are social and no more; these forms are there to be imitated and embodied but do not come with any form of wider organization (a concomitant association) or spiritual links. In this sense, the dances of the Concheros are distinct from other dances that are circular in form, such as those practiced by Westerners.[14] A Conchero can dance week after week, or even just occasionally, and find a community where the spiritual ambience, ethos, and practice remains predominantly unchanging.

The reason why the Concheros dance rather than just singing or playing music may ultimately be unanswerable in sociological terms. Nevertheless, I will make some suggestions toward that end.

## GETTING THE FEEL OF THE CONCHEROS' DANCE

The feel or experience of the dance will be different for every dancer but will begin for each in much the same way and is probably best described from my own point of view and what I saw of other beginners. As previously mentioned, the dancing takes a circular form and each dance is fairly simple, beginning with an opening phase performed by the feet that is then followed by a variation (see Chapter 3). The beginner's first hurdle to overcome is following the steps. To achieve this, I needed to look at the dancer in the center to get an overall visual image of the pattern I should be making with my feet while at the same time be aware of the dancers on either side of me. I quickly realized that if I did not pick up my feet quickly enough as the circle of dancers moved to the left, I would find myself in the way of the oncoming dancer on my immediate right. As Angelica put it, "the challenge lies in the feet." Initially, this felt less like dancing than an enforced scramble, an uncomfortable attempt to copy that often resulted in shuffling quickly out of the way. Parkin has called this a "tangled" state that can be seen as "dys-functional" and involves a "skewering" of corporeal awareness. In other words, a state in which the dancer is painfully aware of her body because what she is doing is new and difficult and may even hurt (whereas under normal conditions she is not conscious of it).[15] During any dance, the initial sequence is repeated again and again and, as it is learned, begins to become a form the body knows increasingly well and can enact in response to the music without consciously trying, with a lightness and alacrity very different from the earlier struggle. The dances are simple, easily memorized, and not difficult to recall as they become incorporated. As this occurs, the dancer's bodily state changes from one of acute bodily awareness to one in which she can once again take her body for granted.[16]

I have probably eclipsed several hours of dancing (or even several months for the less agile) into a few moments here. In reality, the process of poesis as opposed to mimesis, and the moving from the latter to the former, of "making not faking," takes place quite slowly.[17] With more practice on further occasions and as ritualization came, I had the increasing feeling that my body was doing something that freed the everyday me, allowing me to be elsewhere. Before I look at this state in more detail, however, I will discuss the effects of music.

## THE INTERACTION WITH MUSIC & THE OTHER MEDIA

The dancing is greatly aided by the accompanying music, and this is especially so for neophytes. Music has a physical effect on the dancer and is emotionally affective, thus enabling ritualization. Dancing consists not just of what the dancer does with her body by means of its embodied practices but also includes the body's involuntary response to the music. As Radcliffe Brown pointed out, "[a]ny marked rhythm exercises over those submitted to its influence a constraint, impelling them to yield to it and to permit it to direct and regulate the movements of the body and even those of the mind." If the dancer "does not yield to this constraining influence, it produces a state of restlessness that may become markedly unpleasant." The dancer who yields still feels the constraint

> but so far from being unpleasant it now produces a pleasure of a quite distinct quality . . . the pleasure of self-surrender. The peculiarity of the force in question is that it seems to act upon the individual both from without . . . (since it is the sight of his friends dancing and the sound of the singing and marking time that occasions it) and also from within (since the impulse to yield . . . to the constraining rhythm comes from his own organism).[18]

Music provides "a special way of organizing human bodies" that through the medium of social interaction "offers an intensity of feeling and quality of experience."[19] Music and song tend "to entrain activity rather than thought" and almost seem to compel individuals to "experience, participate in, and accept" liminality "rather than abstractly conceptualize or question it."[20] Feld has shown that sounds activate and stimulate deeply felt emotions. Sounds are, he suggests, socially organized to modulate "special categories of sentiment and action when brought forth and properly contexted [*sic*] by features of staging and performance."[21]

As already indicted, the Concheros' dance is accompanied by music played on the *concha* by some of the dancers in the circle and those in the center. Placed there too are one or more large drums. Every dancer also wears a pair of seed leg-rattles (*ayayotles*) tied around her ankles and most dancers hold a *sonaja* (rattle) in their right hands, both adding percussive resonance. The sound of the leg rattles in particular is integral to the dance as they clatter as the dancer moves. In effect, shaking the sonaja or playing the concha could perhaps be said to be the dance of the hands. In addition, some dancers play small pipes; others, notched sticks; and some, small Aztec-style two-tone slit drums (known as *teponaztli*), which they hold under their arms while they move. Although the concha leads with the melody, enabling enactors to know which dance it is and marking their place in it, often more dominant is the percussive combination of drums, rattles, leg rattles, and notched sticks, predominantly at a lower pitch.

The sounds from this collection of instruments adds up to a complex combination of the melodic, rhythmic, and timbrel. The slit drum produces two tones, a third apart, whereas the large drum, especially when it is a wooden reproduction of an Aztec *huehue* (rather than being made from an old oil drum), can produce a second tone a fifth higher if beaten at its edge. In time with the concha, the regular pulses of the drums also produce overtones and reverberations, causing each drumbeat from any one drum to overlap with the last. The other instruments tend to come in as they please (or can) with crisper sounds and often as echo-pulses to the booming drums. This combination is sonorously dense and there are no breaks or moments of quiet during any one dance. Ideally, the Concheros attempt to play in unison (as they also attempt to sing in tune) but often they do not achieve this. The music creates a sense that those drumming and others "are in synchrony or playing together precisely by being out of phase, that is, each at a different point from a hypothetical unison."[22] Curiously, the overall dissonance adds to the power of the music, to its affective impact, although to Western ears it may sound cacophonous. Bystanders may well try to follow the melody of the concha and ignore the rest, but to the Concheros the sonic redundancy enables ritualization and, later on during a dance, transcendence.

The incense is also enabling. The effect of olfactory substances is known to assist in synchronizing emotional and physical states, although for many the use of incense is as much a part of Roman Catholic worship as Conchero practice. Nonetheless, the familiarity of the incense does not lessen its effect as a stimulus that furthers ritualization by "obstructing discursive reason" and stimulating memory, among other effects.[23]

Just as the forms of the dance stabilize the vagaries of individual inclinations, the dominant rhythm of the music pulls those enacting into its ambience and overrides personal indecision.[24] Each dancer responds to the music with dance steps that are becoming or have become habitual, and each will do so according to the rhythm of the music that draws each dancer to attune their movements to a stimulus initially outside the self. The rhythms of the self are taken over by those of the music, although some dancers obstinately refuse to let this happen, such as Carlos, who rarely danced in time. Those who might instinctively move faster or more slowly are pulled (or entrained) bit by bit by the rhythm of the music (and the dancing of their co-enactors) into a state of intersubjectivity.[25] The rhythm of the music is easily picked up by the body, and this process enables a group of heterogeneous dancers who may not have enacted together previously to begin to act in harmony.

However, it is not quite as simple as this. The dancer who is leading the dance from the center will move in her own individual way in response to the music. By playing her concha at her own tempo, she is setting the rhythmic ambience within certain limits and those playing other instruments will respond to her. This is partly what makes it "her dance."

Thus, those in the circle dancing together are responding not only to the music but also to the visual bodily cues given by that dancer. She is frequently more experienced and therefore more open than those in the outer circle; she thus acts as the template for all those around her and is the source of engagement and inspiration. Those in the outer circle need to respond also to the less easily seen movements of those dancers on either side, which as the dance progresses are increasingly sensed by the body rather than seen with the eyes.

Each dance enacted is different from any other not only because the form of the dance itself changes but also because the dancer leading it is a different person. Each dancer's enactment is singular, each dances in a slightly different way from any other, for each person brings something of herself to the dance as each has a different bodily makeup. As Angelica put it, "the energy of each is unique and flows out to all the other dancers in the circle. What we aspire to in the circle is to impregnate ourselves with the energy of each and every dancer." Thus, the obligation is not unchanging in quality hour after hour as one dance follows another; for every dance, the dynamic alters as the enactor in the center changes. The circle experiences how each of these dancers experiences the dance: some can give much more physical energy to it than others, and some more spirituality as some are in altered or higher states of consciousness (and I will say more about this later). As Eduardo pointed out, the dance is democratic for "leading the dance at one moment is a jefe, at the next an *anciano*, the next again a woman and then perhaps a young person."

## DANCE AS WORK

The Concheros talk about both vigils and dances as work. To stay up all night is not only a sacrifice but also fatiguing and tough on the body. To a certain extent, dance is like exercise in that "you develop your body as your very own instrument," as Arnaldo put it. Music is produced by means of an instrument, but in dance "it's the body that's the instrument. The use of the body in the dance is an athletic one . . . but it's also an art." To dance for hours at a time unceasingly in harmony with other dancers requires discipline and effort; it is "hard work." Eduardo admits that the day after a dance his legs and his muscles usually ache.

Eduardo dances because it makes his "organism feel good. At the physical level something happens"—"you produce endorphins"—and it is the production of these during sporting activity that gives those participating a sense of well-being. He went on to say that dancing gives the participant so much more than, say, running and that this something is largely mental. When you dance, you feel better in yourself; "all is much simpler, you center yourself, you stimulate yourself. Leaving a dance . . . you leave more intelligent. The conversations are much better. You gain something . . . although it goes away again. You leave the dance more agile, brighter. Not just radiant or energized [*prendido*] as when you've exercised." Eduardo both exercised and danced and was very clear that there was a profound difference between their effects on him.[26]

Dance then is unlike sport in the effects (and affect) that it produces in and on the body-self. In part, this difference is because the Concheros' dance does not involve competition or have a physical goal. Most sports have an end in sight and continue until that end is achieved. The dance of the Concheros could carry on indefinitely and in the physical sense is more like running or swimming for pleasure, although neither of these have a spiritual side to them. Perhaps a better comparison is to one of the martial arts, such as Tai Chi.[27] The dance is work also in the sense of being efficacious in achieving not only personal well-being but also that of the larger community.[28]

Dance, along with other forms of ritual, differs from other types of group activity in the kind of social interaction that it entails. The dancer, although ultimately enacting alone, is moving her body rhythmically to the music and in relation to those of the other dancers in a communal endeavor. The ritualized side of the dance necessitates entering its preformed patterns, which requires energy initially, but after some time, these take over the body and the "anonymous movements" can then be repeated with ease.[29] Like any physical movement system, however, the positive effects on the body of the dancer diminish as time passes after the event.

## AS A SOURCE OF POWER

For those watching an individual dancing, a group of Concheros dancing, or a number of groups dancing (which is the situation at the bigger dances), it is immediately clear that dance has a potency and hence the potential to be political. It creates a sense of presence. There is an energy that can be felt; the ambience is charged by the activity of so many people moving in coordinated juxtaposition. Although a mass of people in proximity can loosely hold together for a period of time (e.g., for the duration of a demonstration), groups of people dancing can have a far greater unity of intent.[30] Dancing creates something that is extrasensory, not in the sense of the paranormal but rather the synthesthetic: the effect that is created when the various senses acting in unity create a harmony quite unlike that found in everyday interaction. The power inherent in dance probably accounts, in part, for why the Spaniards repressed the music and dances of the Aztecs soon after the Conquest.[31] Individual by individual, it is what dance can do to the boundaries of the self, it is the inner changes wrought by dance—and the accompanying music and song—"as the self evaporates," that are empowering and might make it seem threatening.[32] The Concheros certainly see the dance as being powerful in this sense. For many this power is closely linked to their alliance with the animas, and for some of them this is the "real work of the Concheros."[33]

This power is not political nor is it that of personal empowerment, although it can lead to that, but rather a type of power more like *mana*.[34] An example of the use of this energy is a cleansing carried out during a dance. As Eduardo indicated, this is not a procedure dancers know how to do with their conscious minds. If he were asked to do one at the beginning of a dance, he would, he claims, be unsure as to how to proceed. However, "at the end of a dance, if you ask me, I'll do it for you because I have the power [*la fuerza*] and the disposition [*la disposicion*]. I have my heart open, my mind free, so I can do it. However, it's not I but the dance, the circle of the dancers that can cleanse you." The vitality or power that the group dancing as a whole has gained (or that is coming through them) enables the cleansing. Eduardo, in this instance, has not only had his own energy transformed by the dance but his is now intermingled with all the other dancers' transformed energies, and he merely acts as a conduit for that substance. That is, while the cleansing is going on, the dancer who is performing is at the center of everyone's attention and becomes, it could be said, the "El" of "El es Dios."

The power of the dance thus stimulates and can change consciousness. As it works on the dancer's sense of self, it can engender an awareness that was not there previously. What happens to each dancer is individual, however, for as Angelica said, "in the dance, the dancer has to find herself; the Concheros don't predetermine."

## TO TRANSCEND

"And only then, as the self evaporated and the choreographed excitements
multiplied and the sensations came flooding in, did the god draw near."

—I. CLENDINNEN, talking about Aztec festivals[35]

Many analysts agree that the different media (the horizontal components or
dimensions) dynamically interact to aid in the enabling of "the vertical dimension by which higher-level integration is achieved." This occurs as "lower-level
units build up into or fuse into higher-level units and processes . . . to converge
. . . [as] total experiences are produced."[36] This has variously been called the
supranormal, transcendence, ecstasy, the numinous, or altered states of consciousness. As indicated in the introduction to the chapter, I prefer transcendence, partly because it clearly implies a change of level but also because it is a
processual term.

Many dancers claim that the way to "find God" and the self is to transcend.
But how do they achieve this? Is it the result of personal input or does it occur
because of the dancing? Music is clearly important. The sounds and reverberations produced by musical instruments have not only aesthetic but also pro-
prioceptive or bodily effects (e.g., on our inner ear, our sense of balance, and
muscular tension), which may be more or less consciously undergone or are
"unavoidable."[37]

Needham was concerned with the use of percussive instruments as a way
to "communicate with the other world." He suggested that although rhythm
and melody are important in processes of transition, it is the percussive impact
that is most significant. One of the difficulties here is the lack of clarity as to
what is considered percussion, an "extremely disputable category in musicology." However, it is not the percussive instrument per se but, as Needham
suggested, the rhythm, melody, or the repetition of a particular note or resonance—or, as Blacking has put it, the "carefully modulated pattern of sound"
in general that may be provided by other instruments—that may also be affective and enable transition. Blacking points out too that in the case of possession dances, "a metronomic rhythm on rattles and/or drums is simply a means
of coordinating body movements and it is the dancing rather than the noise,
which effects the transition." Drumming undoubtedly has a strong emotional
impact. The sounds produced are often loud and, as Rouget suggests, "dramatic or obsessive" and the vibrations frequently almost palpable. Music then is
not directly responsible for trance or possession, rather music "spurs [it] on."[38]
Most Concheros were certainly clear that they considered the dancing to be of
most significance; they said little about the link between dancing, the music,
and the other media used. At times during a dance, the music even stops and

the dancers continue to enact in almost complete silence without any change in their inner state.[39]

In part, the achievement of union and conformity (and subsequently conquest, which can be seen on one level as transcendence) has to do with the overall structure of the dances. Eduardo believes that as a discipline, and unlike other forms, the dance works on or exercises both sides of the brain. He indicates that all of the dances consist of "powerful, symbolically balanced structures, mathematically attuned to the cosmos." They have, he claims, been carefully honed through time, which is why dancers should have respect and not to do anything to change them.[40] For every step into the center, there is one out again. For every downward movement, an upward one follows. For every two steps to the left, there are two to the right. At the end of each sequence, the dancer should be more or less in the same location in the circle as she was when it began.

The other overall principle of the dance is that the dancer should always move to the left first, and the *permiso* that opens each dance apparently emphasizes the left side more than the right, although the dancer ends up on the spot where she began. When you are asking permission with your feet, "[y]ou move first to the side of the spirit [the left] with all your spirit and your substance to affirm that you, in the name of the Father, the Son, and the Holy Spirit are with the most Holy Trinity, the triangle of creation." You do this by turning completely, first to the left then to the right. You then trace out a cross on the ground with the toes of your right foot, subsequently stamping your left foot three times twice over, before repeating the sequence the other way round. This is followed by another three stamps with the left foot. There is a degree of variability in this sequence, with some marking out three points on the ground rather than tracing out the cross; the three points may also represent the Father, the Son, and the Holy Spirit. The fourth beat is then used to raise the foot upward, toward the heavens, before the three stamps with the other foot are enacted.

It is also a question of the sustained effort that the dancer puts into the movement. Like any other kinesthetic activity, the more you persevere, the more you get out of it, even if this pushing of the body is punishing. Eduardo noted that "the task [in the dance] is that you bear with it." You have to keep going. "Pain hurts; the dance hurts [too]. Sometimes you've got a sprained foot but you have to keep dancing. And if you overcome this . . . paaaaa!" This expression was Eduardo's way of indicating a change of consciousness. He asked if I had felt in the other forms of exercise I had taken the "retribution" that you feel in the dance. By this, he meant loosely the recompense that comes with the change of consciousness, the sense of freedom, of entering an apparently disembodied space without limits. He was clear that this was different from the "high" obtained from other pursuits, such as sport, because of the mental and bodily discipline—of ritualization—linked to the physical effort.[41] You have to "let yourself go with everything you've got . . . give your all. You have to overcome or jump over it [*brincar*], and then possibly you get a kind of ecstasy." Often after a number of hours of enacting, although the dancer feels tired and that he has already given everything to the dance, he then needs to push himself just a little further.

This also has to do with concentration. As a dance begins, the celebrants' minds are generally on many things. They will certainly be thinking about the dance itself and about initiating union and aiming for conformity. But their thoughts will also be on everyday matters, such as what they are going to do for the rest of the weekend or whether their belongings are safe where they have put them while they dance. Or they might be thinking about their personal problems or involvements, or what so-and-so thinks about them, or what they need to remember to ask when the next break occurs. But as Eduardo said, "The dancer needs to be alert and try to put all her attention into the dance. You can't be chattering and messing about," and this applies in particular to the *palabras* who are carrying the word. In fact, the palabras' attention (and that of other dancers too) is often split into several parts. With one part of his mind, the palabra needs to keep surveillance over the circle of dancers. "It's a matter of checking" with your eyes; "you have to have circular vision and see everything that is happening. You have to know when a dog's got into the circle, when a *compadrito* has fallen over, . . . at what time the sun comes up and at what time it goes down. It's work and you have to be alert!" Half the time, a palabra is concentrating on these signs and on the interpersonal power struggles between dancers (see Chapter 8).

Although Eduardo confirms that he is trying to be present with all his spirit and all his veneration, some time into the dance, a quarter of his thoughts are still on more mundane matters, such as his fears, his difficulties, and his dreams. His thoughts may be also "about eroticism and money and how good I look and that I dance well" and that he is catching the attention of other dancers. At this stage only a quarter of his thoughts are directed toward "the grand pyramid of the creation, from corn [at the bottom] to 'El' [at the top]. And you can pass by the angels, the saints, the beautiful, the clouds, and the water until suddenly you achieve a connection." The implication is that this combination of thoughts changes or should change as the dance proceeds and will be different on each occasion and for each dancer. As Angelica said, "it takes a long time to harmonize, to unite yourself with your companions, and the larger the circle is, the harder it is to harmonize yourself with all the others." Whatever its size, the longer the dance goes on, the more each dancer's attention will (or should) become focused on the spiritual, that is, on the animas. It is the work of the palabras to ensure that this happens and, as indicated in Chapter 4, particular dancers may be invited into the center of the circle to help raise the state of others. Sometimes Eduardo tries consciously to direct "two-fifths" of his attention to the animas, but even then, that occasion "when you succeed [*logras*] in a dance" is rare. Despite his years of experience in the dance, he only "gets there in one or two dances" but "it's for this that each dancer aims." Exactly what "succeeding," "the connection," or "getting there" is, is experienced by the self and is difficult to put into words.[42]

Thus, transcendence tends to occur, as Soledad indicated, after the dancers "are harmonized, and each dancer breaks away or separates herself [*se desprenda*] and offers up prayers or gives their thanks." She portrayed the dance as a goddess who "talks directly to you, to you alone, not to the group." As Soledad put it, "the jefe introduces you, presents you to the dance. It is the dance however [that] teaches you and adopts you as her apprentice. It is the dance 'who' chooses you, and the dance becomes your mistress." Rosa-Elia envisions the process differently. She indicated that as the dance goes on, "your spirit [*espíritu*] is rising, moving toward the nonmaterial world and most of the worries of the everyday world fall away. This is difficult. When you dance you are praying with the other dancers." She continued, "You forget your exhaustion, you forget about the outside world, as you dance you forget about being tired. Suddenly you are filled with good emotions; you want to smile, laugh, or shout something completely spontaneously, such as 'No, we're not alone, we're all together.'"

This state, which can be called "ecstasy," sometimes evolves slowly out of the earlier state, but at other times it is more like the sudden opening of a door. On some occasions, as Eduardo pointed out, he is dancing "and it suddenly happens and I start to cry and cry or I'm laughing. It provokes me." He adds that "it is at that limit, on that edge that the majority of things happen in the dance." Whereas for Teo, the experience seems to be more esoteric: "I don't feel as though I'm dancing in myself. It's another dimension, it's not to see, hear, or touch. It's something else. I dance to put myself in contact with nature and the cosmos. When you don't have this knowledge you are dancing without control. It's like going out in a boat without a compass to steer your rudder."

This then is a state beyond union and conformity (ritualization), in which everyone feels togetherness, and is rather a state where you are again on your own, over that edge, and what you experience is completely unique. To paraphrase Merleau-Ponty, we should remain aware that "primacy of perception" necessarily implies "privacy of perception."[43] This could be said to be a new psycho-mental state that is superimposed on an earlier physico-mental one. As already indicated, transcendence is part of what is meant by "conquest," the third term in the Concheros' leitmotif. However, as Angelica succinctly put it, "[t]he dance doesn't conquer, you conquer yourself; dancers are conquerors but as a dancer you are always free."[44]

## MEANING?

When I first began dancing with and talking to Concheros, I found myself trying to note what dancers claimed the different aspects of their practice meant. I had naïvely assumed that meaning was of great significance and that I would build a corpus of information about the dance that led to a generally accepted explanation as to what the dance signified. I presumed that the meanings indicated would be rather similar for all dancers and that I could collate or merge the various interpretations given into a single coherent strand. I soon realized that such a compromise would be not only unrepresentative but would posit closure where there is none.[45]

As the dance has been an oral tradition until recently, and because the dance itself is a fluid form where one movement flows into the next and its organization is comparatively loose and unstructured, the dance does not impose specific meanings on dancers.[46] Although all the *mesas* dance similarly named dances and follow similar steps, the Concheros do not hold identical beliefs as to what the dance means. Each dancer's idea about what the deity is may differ slightly or even substantially, and this is where the freedom of the dance lies.

I have in this chapter used as examples the views of three or four of the more vociferous, but not necessarily more formally educated dancers; however, the range of beliefs is far wider than represented here. Not all dancers will say that they dance to contact the animas, although the animas are important for everyone and are frequently mentioned in the prayers and benedictions (see Chapter 3). Only some will have the idea of the "grand pyramid of creation," reflecting the Aztec belief that the cosmos has many layers.[47] Country dancers are far less able to verbalize a cosmology, and their idea of the deity is more likely to be predominantly Roman Catholic. Regardless of beliefs, all the dancers are part of a community in that they are all working toward attaining contact with the deity through dance, but who or what the deity is, or what the dance means, can be quite different for each. It could be said that the dance is about individuation through community. A person becomes a "dividual," that is, inextricably connected to others, and is then divided off once again to become individuated.[48]

# WHY DANCE?

"All the world can dance, but not all are dancers."

—CAPTAIN SOLEDAD RUIZ

"Nobody, 'no-*body*' can learn an unfamiliar neuromuscular pattern without being willing to acquire a new and perhaps startling insight into who it is they actually are."

—S. A. NESS[49]

"The image [of unity] is created out of internal homogeneity, a process of de-pluralization, manifested less as the realization of generalized and integrative principles of organization itself and more as the realization of particular identities called into play through unique events and individual accomplishments."

—M. STRATHERN[50]

A dance event is multisensory, involving not only sound—the music and rhythm of the drums, the ayayotles tied round the dancers' ankles, and at times the singing of songs by the enactors—but also smell—the olfactory effect of the smoldering incense burner in the center of the circle. The visual (aesthetic) is involved too, for dancers put a great deal of time and attention into their clothing and are concerned about how they look. And the visceral and kinesthetic are also significant as a dancer experiences the dance both in and with the body.

In this chapter, I have looked briefly at what dance is without trying to define it specifically and discussed the difference between it and other physical movement forms. I have looked too in a certain amount of detail at one of the reasons why the more dedicated enactors dance—the desire to be "energized," to communicate with the animas, and possibly to transcend—and what this means to them. However, for many this is not the only reason why they are involved, at least initially, and it is clear that there is a wide range of different explanations as to why people join the Concheros. Every motive is valid; indeed, if there were not such a variety of discourses about the dance, especially today, many groups would not be as large as they are.

Some come to the dance because they like it as a social forum and as a way to meet people, and I certainly met an enormous number of people during my fieldwork. These participants enjoy dancing for its own sake. For them, the dancing acts as a stimulating diversion but does little in a spiritual or embodied-in-the-world sense, perhaps because they do not give it the right kind of attention. Half or more of their thoughts are probably always involved in interpersonal politics and socializing. They are in fact permanently in a state of normal, if not self-, consciousness. Others may not only really enjoy dancing but put a great deal of perfomativity into it through their "inventiveness, energy, and sheer acrobatic skill."[51] They aim to perfect their style and are sometimes seen

**144**

as pretentious, but it is an endorphin high rather than transcendence that they aim for. Others enjoy the excuse to dress up and, as Teo rather disparagingly put it, they "think it's very sophisticated to put on a headdress." For them, the dance is mainly about self-adornment or sartorial competition. Or they come because they feel frustrated with their everyday lives and the dance offers some form of compensation, but they are not really interested in the dancing as a spiritual form.

Others join because they want something to follow. They do not want to be told what to do but they do want a form that they can imitate. In other words, they want to be involved in something that is not thought about much at a conscious level but that can be learned by mimesis. These dancers may or may not experience more from the dance than they initially anticipated. Some dance because they do not have enough music in them to make life dance for them, as Celine put it. They are lacking at a psychological level and dancing gives them that extra something. For some it is a way to feel alive; they dance for affective reasons. Involved in a routine job, five days a week in Mexico City, to dance during the weekend provides an opportunity to turn a deadened body (*Korper*) into a living body (*Leib*).[52] I am not characterizing actual dancers here but rather aspects of why any one person might be drawn into the dance.

Some become Concheros for more conventional, spiritual reasons because it is a way of making *promesas* to the saints in a Roman Catholic manner. Pando (the alferez) joined the dance initially with exactly this intention (see Chapter 2). People may have particular problems that they are seeking to solve and join the dance for a while, but often they are so bound by their conventional beliefs that they do not "hear" the message of the dance. On the other hand, many come and try the dance for a while and then move on to other pursuits. "They decide that the dance is not for them, it doesn't teach them anything," or the dance tells them that "this is not your path," as Soledad put it.

For the more established dancers, those who have been Concheros for, say, five, ten, or even twenty years and to whom the dance has indicated that it is their path, there is far more to being a Conchero than the aforementioned reasons, although these may well be part of their original attraction to it and their ongoing concern early on. For this group, the dance holds a highly significant position in their lives; to dance has become a necessity, an activity that has to be carried out frequently—once a week or once a fortnight at the very least. Moreover, it is different from the habituation of something like swimming because it is more than an endorphin high. As Soledad said, "the dance teaches you what you need to know to dance if you are chosen; . . . it teaches you how to live and how to give meaning to your life. People stay if the dance teaches them something." From being nothing, you become something more, at least for a short time afterward. What I hope to have pointed to in this chapter is that the effects of dancing feed the self and thus feed daily life. Dance is "etched into the senses and graven into the muscles" of the body and this embodiment is registered in how the body manifests in daily life, as much in mental attitude as in physical comportment.[53]

For such dancers, as Soledad indicated, "to dance is first and foremost an ontological necessity not a social one, the dedicated dancer has a religious need, a spiritual need, for the true function of the dance is the fusion it produces between the cosmos and the individual. Being a dancer is a characteristic of the heart and [is] not just to do with ability." Most experienced dancers will achieve a transcendent state during the dance, even if only briefly, and will claim that if dancing has a goal, achieving transcendence is it.

Finally, dance entails a non-visual form of know-how that cannot simply be reproduced and understood by means of verbal description. Nor can it just be spoken about, it has to be done and the only way of doing it is to dance. The ethnographer, to study the Concheros, needs to attune her sensibilities to non-visual frequencies.[54] Dance is an embodied form of knowledge that can only be re-presented by the body that knows to another that desires to know by means of the body itself. Those who do not dance cannot know what dance is; they cannot experience what dancing, metaphorically described by the Concheros as "carrying the word," can reveal to the self that is opened to that pre-objective being-in-the-worldness.[55] As Deren has pointed out, "*exaltation results from participation*, it does not precede and compel it."[56] For the Concheros, knowledge is engendered by active engagement in the dance and it is for them a way of becoming. An investigator who was frequently to be seen at dances while I was doing fieldwork planned to write an authoritative book on the Concheros but had never danced. Many dancers told me that because of his lack of this particular experience, he was in no position to write the book. To have know-how of the dance and to learn from it, the dance has to be danced.

# PART THREE

# POWER CONCERNS:
# PERFORMING THE SELF

**8.1.** The various mesas who have danced together, singing at the end of the dance at La Villa.

# ALLIANCES AND IDENTITY POLITICS

*"Somos divinos cuando baillamos, per cuando hablamos, non."*

[We are divine when we dance, but when we talk much less so.]

—ERNESTO CABRAL, commenting on his fellow dancers

In Chapter 2, I looked at the overall organization of the *mesa* of Santo Niño de Atocha by placing the group in the context of the Reliquia, that part of the association to which it belongs. I said little, however, about the mesas with which it has close contact. Each dance group is devolved and autonomous but has a degree of interdependency with the other mesas in its part of the association. In terms of practice, a mesa will dance on a regular basis with certain groups but will also have a special relationship with other mesas, some of which may even be in other palabras. A group will enact with other mesas on a number of well-established occasions throughout the year, and sometimes less well-established ones too. Those mesas with which a group dances are its allies who lend it support, just as it lends them support for particular obligations. Alliances are an important aspect of the dance, for without these the association would not function at all. The strong relationships of loyalty and cooperation that exist between the mesas that dance together sustain the various parts of the association (or at least did so through the last two decades of the twentieth century).

Jackson has pointed out that our "preoccupation with order and structure may be seen as a form of wishful thinking [that] the systematic and objective order which the ethnographer 'uncovers' in the course of fieldwork may not mirror any external reality, but function as a magical defence against the unsystematic disorientating reality he or she encounters." We as analysts tend to deny or underrate contingency or chance, for, as Dewey has pointed out, we tend to look for mechanisms whereby an organization, the so-called objective order, reproduces itself according to rules that evolve from and reproduce tradition.[1]

In Chapter 2, I presented the association as though it had a clear-cut hierarchical structure, although in phenomenological terms the best way to summarize the Concheros' organization is "ordered anarchy."[2] There is no overall unanimity as to the association's organization other than the wide directives loosely laid down in the Reglamento de Conquista, which applies to all of La Gran Tenochtitlan. Its form is dynamic and depends on which alliances are strongest at any particular moment in time. This in turn depends on the personality of the *jefes mayores*. The representation of the dance as a circular form with the power at the center, Tlatelolco, and the four winds at the cardinal points (receiving equal emphasis) is the Concheros' own conceptual model. But the overall organization of La Gran Tenochtitlan is not a ritualized constant but is continuously shifting and has an evolving form—less a circle perhaps than a changing or broken spiral. This is because the importance of the winds changes as the balance of power alters and the significance of one location lessens as another rises. Although it is claimed by many that all the palabras and their mesas go to Amecameca on Ash Wednesday, in fact, at present many go to Iztapalapa, a *delegación* or borough in the southeast part of the city. Where dancers reside is one of the deciding factors. Those who are part of a rural group to the east of the city in a place such as Tepetlixpa (in the State of Mexico) give the sacred topography of the organization a different emphasis. Furthermore, not all groups in Mexico City have always been associated with Santiago Tlatelolco as their center; some who are part of the Reliquia have closer ties with Santiago Iztapalapa and some with the cathedral.[3] Nor is the significance of any one mesa fixed but depends on who is empowered.

Within the mesas themselves, there is no overall clear-cut and inflexible organization. No two groups have exactly the same named positions (*rangos*), and each has its individual forms and its own program. The power at the core too is far from constant. When an old jefe dies, an immediate shift in the balance occurs as the jefe of another mesa whose power may reside elsewhere or has previously been eclipsed gains ascendancy. Nor is there street consensus as to who are the generals. If a jefe is admired for his qualities of leadership by his dancers and others in allied mesas, they may refer to him as "my general" and not realize that their jefe is "without a crown" (*sin corona*) and that he may not have been initiated as a general by the association. Indeed, he may well not even be thought of in those terms by dancers in other non-allied groups.

Although most of those who dance claim that they dance for spiritual reasons and that the dance is about the denial of self, in fact the association is rife with power struggles, and these are another reason for why the overall form of the organization is not a ritualized constant and is continuously shifting. This chapter then looks at a different kind of power from that discussed in Chapter 7. Although the charismatic power of the leader is important, under certain circumstances this may become a form of power that is more political and egocentric, rather than spiritual. At the extreme this can become the willful manipulation by dancers who may claim that their activities are "God-directed" and that they are enacting in a ritualized way when they are in fact making performative ploys backed by consciously elaborated claims.

As Fabian has suggested, we tend to privilege affirmative behavior, the positive, and to look less at "action that denies, contests, . . . or simply dissimulates," which we will tend to "qualify as anything between curious and deviant." He argues that "negativity" needs to be incorporated into our basic conceptualizations of social praxis instead of being relegated to deviance or domesticated as drama.[4]

This chapter analyzes some of the power struggles that characterize the dance, including the problems associated with the rapid rise to power of some dancers and the inheritance of a group sometimes before but usually after the death of a jefe, which often involves dissent and occasionally fission. I discuss interpersonal struggles in general and how the association copes with these. The focus here is on identity politics and the ruptures that can occur at certain times in even fairly conservative groups, such as that of Compadre Ernesto. Before I look at the problem of identity politics, however, I want to discuss the alliances formed between groups, without which the dance could not flourish and would probably not continue.

## ALLIANCES

An alliance brings one mesa into ongoing contact with another. Alliances provide the rationale and means whereby a number of mesas dance together at an obligation, thus forming a larger circle. In fact, most dances on most occasions consist of several groups who are allies. Alliances are important because the number of ongoing relationships a mesa has is a measure of its ability and power to draw others to it. To be able to mobilize dancers from allied groups for an obligation is a sign of its strength and an indication of its leader's personal charisma.

Compadre Ernesto had a number of long-term allies, the most important of whom were Alberto Gutierrez (whose mesa was also called Santo Niño de Atocha) and Faustino Rodriguez of Tepetlixpa (whose mesa was Dulce Nombres de Jesus). All three men were contemporaries in age and had danced together for many years before first Alberto and then Faustino died in 1989. These were strong connections that had stood the test of time. The mesas had rather similar procedures; all wanted to conserve the dance forms, and the dance had a similar meaning for each of them. In the late 1980s, the three were some of the very few old jefes left in the Central Association.[5]

Although Compadre Ernesto has always danced in the city, he had also initiated groups in the countryside. Such groups remain under the power of the parent group, *bajo nuestra sombra* (under our influence), until they raise their own standard. Some groups, such as the one at Juamantla in Morelos, have maintained this intermediary status for years. They were happy to do so as Compadre Ernesto was always described as one of the "white" jefes whose work was entirely positive, as was Don Faustino, who was said also to have been a *granicera*.[6] Don Faustino was also an instigator, had always lived in the countryside at Tepetlixpa, and was described as a "conqueror," claiming people for his mesa in the State of Mexico.

Alberto Gutierrez it seems was different. Described as a renegade and nick-named "El Indio Jarrero," he was likened to Juan Minero, a well-known popular *anima* mentioned in the Concheros' and other prayers.[7] He was a healer, could do cleansings and resolve *brujerias* (witchcraft), but was also a medium. His curing powers were much in demand and attracted large numbers of dancers, both from his own and other groups, to whom he was also very supportive. He also attracted people who were not Concheros. He had a profound knowledge of the dance that he was able to impart to his dancers, and the dance named the "Vibora" (mentioned in Chapter 2) was his innovation. Although he had taken on the position of secretary of the Actas de la Reliquia General, he had not raised any groups, unlike the other two. All three held the traditional values of the dance in high esteem and wanted to see it continue as it had been practiced in the countryside. At important obligations, the three groups danced together joined also by others.[8] Thus the dance at Amecameca in January, during that period, was not just an important dance for one of the four winds (according to the typology) but also one convened by an important ally.[9]

Other alliances may be less close or long term. Dancers from Apaxco (in the State of Mexico) joined Compadre Ernesto's mesa in various locations in 1989, such as at Otumba (Hidalgo) for a dance held there annually on September 14 linked to the town's community festival. The dancers from the Apaxco group predominantly dress in Chichimeca-style costumes. Cresencio's long flowing skirt (*nahuilli*) was decorated with much plastic silver and gold, and his faster and more flamboyant dance meant that he stood out when dancing with Compadre Ernesto's group (see Chapter 4). Thus, although not as close an alliance because of some differences of opinion about the forms, it was still highly valued.

An alliance can involve even less frequent meetings than this. Two groups may perform a single obligation together, as, for example, the vigil held in the Zocalo on June 30, 1993. This brought together Compadre Ernesto's mesa and that of the Insignias Aztecas of Jesus Leon. In conversations afterward, the negative aspects of the collaboration rather than the positive side of the event tended to be emphasized; there had been disagreements about how the flower forms should have been built and laid out (see Chapter 3). This is an annual joint vigil held especially for the Aztec Tlatoani, Cuitlahuac that both groups had committed themselves to. The implication was that the experience, although not successful, would be repeated the following year.

Mesas also enter into alliances that may turn out to be short-term. For a while, they may go to each other's obligations although they have not danced together previously. Compadre Ernesto's group, for example, collaborated closely at one time with the Corporación de Concheros, a mesa independent of the two main palabras.[10] The Corporación was invited to attend certain dances and to join the mesa of Compadre Ernesto at obligations where the group had not danced previously. Santo Niño in its turn was invited to go to their obligations, such as a dance in Chalma in August 1993. This rapprochement was being undertaken, I gathered, in part because of the awareness that the old jefes who had brought their dance to Mexico City were dying. It was thus an attempt to consolidate the tradition of the dance.

This too was a tentative alliance as the two groups did not agree about *bases* (fundamentals). The dancers of the Corporación consider Compadre Ernesto's dancers not to be "real" Concheros and that the concha they play is not the true instrument. It should be made, they claim, from a gourd (*acocote* or *guaje*) rather than the shell of an armadillo. They also dress differently. The two groups thus have disagreements about the material forms but also as to the relative status of the two. In general, the decision as to which is the senior (or leader) and which the junior (or follower) in an alliance depends on the experience of the jefe: the older and more experienced, the greater the influence a jefe has. More generally, the question of seniority depends on the dancers' point of view unless one jefe is universally accepted as being particularly powerful. However, if one jefe has raised a mesa and the other has not, then there can be little doubt as to the interrelationship. The relationship of Compadre Ernesto, Don Faustino, and Alberto Gutierrez was different as they were considered to be on a par: each jefe was the senior at home but the follower when elsewhere.

Manifestations of amity or recognition are also made at a big dance when a mesa sends some of its soldiers to dance for a short period with the other groups present. This expression of conformity is much less common today. In earlier decades, a small number of dancers travelled great distances to join with the dancers of different mesas, even from different *conformidades*, to fulfil an obligation. Compadre Ernesto commented that "you might find dancers from Aguascalientes, Queretero, San Miguel de Allende, and San Francisco all dancing together," thereby regenerating and reinforcing both old and potential alliances.[11]

Small-scale alliances of a more personal kind are also to be found, such as when a dancer leaves his or her own group to join with one that is rather different. This was the case with Conchita Aranda. Her mesa by descent is that of her uncle, the general Felipe Aranda, who had raised many groups but none with the traditional discipline of the older ones in part because he was instrumental in furthering Mexicanidad (see Chapter 10). Conchita is a "traditionalist," dressing in Aztec-style silver and gold, and she much preferred Compadre Ernesto's forms. She had asked Compadre Ernesto's permission to come and dance, bringing the dancers of her mesa with her, and permission had been granted. Alliances help to reduce the isolation that a group may otherwise experience, although a network of interconnections is probably less important today. Groups in the countryside are now less dependent on actual contact by word of mouth to find out what is going on as instant communication can be achieved by mobile phone or e-mail. Nevertheless, disseminating information about future dances and other matters is very much a part of the end of an obligation. Moreover, the kind of trust and amity that is engendered when groups dance together and, more particularly, hold a joint vigil cannot be inculcated by other means. Alliances generate that network of interconnections so important to the welfare of the association, leading to friendships and often social mixing on occasions not related to the dance.

## THE MEETING OF JEFES

Alliances are important politically. A strong or charismatic leader draws not only dancers to his mesa but also other groups who want to dance with him. In fact, the power of the Reliquia comes in part from the seventeen or more member mesas that bring, in addition, their own allies. Contact between groups is occasionally made in a more expedient way as when a meeting of all the jefes was called in 1989. This was not just a matter of allies talking to allies but of all the jefes in the association of La Gran Tenochtitlan coming together for a day to reach agreement about certain aspects of the overall organization.

The meeting had been called by the general of the Reliquia, Guadalupe Hernandez, ostensibly because of problems about the inheritance at Tepetlixpa after the death of jefe Faustino Rodriguez. At the meeting, some eight jefes with the backing of some of their captains and other supporters congregated (the total present was about thirty-two people).[12] Typically, different mesas at obligations form separate circles and dance if not exactly in competition, at least not in union with each other—for the union achieved is within the circle and not between circles—but in this instance, they were gathered together in one space: the *oratorio* of the Luna family (of the Palabra of Santiago Tlatelolco). Old disagreements, although aired, were apparently put aside in the interest of coming to some sort of consensus on the matter to hand, which was a discussion of the problems involved in the inheritance of a group. This brings me to the second part of this chapter, which leads into a discussion on the more personal power struggles between certain dancers which are usually linked to a rapid rise to power.

## INHERITANCE

What dancers say should happen with regard to inheritance and what actually occurs seem to be different. According to many dancers, a group should pass from a father or mother to a son or daughter, although there are many cases of the leadership passing to spouses or brothers. During the lifetime of the jefe, he or she will usually choose one or more inheritors from his or her children and possibly also from other dancers prominent in the group and they will be made captains. As indicated in Chapter 2, these are usually four in number.

In the case of the inheritance of Tepetlixpa, Don Faustino had not really clarified the position before his death. He had never married but he had named two captains. One was Justino, who was his nephew but did not dance and was thus unknown to many in the mesa. The other was Herman, who danced and was married to Don Faustino's niece. Both, however, claimed the position of first captain and each was supported in his claim by some of the dancers from the mesa itself and by other allied mesas. The situation was complicated further by Salvador Contreras, who had been received into Don Faustino's mesa (as his godchild) and as such was one of Compadre Ernesto's allies.[13] He had apparently had his eye on the inheritance and backed Justino, but he also encouraged and drew in another contentious jefe, Andres Segura, leader of the mesa Xinachtli. On that side of the fray, canvassing was being carried out and mesas from as far away as the conformidad in the Bajio (some 125 miles from

Mexico City) were being pulled in. A serious rift threatened and the meeting had been called to attempt to calm the situation. A decision was reached after many hours of lengthy discussion and some argument. It was proposed that Herman, because he was a dancer and married to the late jefe's niece, should be recognized as the inheritor.

During the meeting, other matters were discussed, such as the overall organization of the association. In the past, it was claimed that the organization of the Concheros had been much more clear-cut and palabras and mesas had collaborated more closely with one another (see Chapter 8). As the tradition is predominantly an oral one, it is difficult to obtain details of past practice but the meeting proved to be a way of learning about the history of the Concheros in Mexico City (in an unsolicited form) and statements made by speakers about the past were substantiated or denied by other, often older jefes present.

Although the meeting appeared to succeed in reaching conformity over the proposed new jefe, in fact the lobbying continued over the next week with Andres Segura still pushing hard for the other candidate. He had decided, according to various people with whom I talked, to divide and rule, as he knew the inheritance was not yet secure. One dancer suggested that he had been interested in the region for some time and thought that this was a good way to begin to make conquests among the various groups near Tepetlixpa. He thus continued to back the breakaway faction of Justino whereas Herman's faction received the support of Ernesto Ortiz and the mesa of Santo Niño de Atocha, plus most of its and Don Faustino's joint allies.

Andres Segura was a maverick. He was able to conquer potential dancers easily and was said to be the "perfect initiator." However, he found it hard to keep dancers and most only tended to stay a short while before going elsewhere. Andres Segura explained this rapid turnover as the result of his tough discipline, but according to others his methods were bad and he could be a bully.[14]

Held in the mesa's usual oratory, the all-night vigil (*velacion de reconocimiento*) included the initiation of the inheritor, Herman , which seemed to indicate that he was the legitimate successor, or at least able to assert himself as such. Another vigil, however, was also held throughout the night in a nearby house for Justin, supported by Andres Segura and various other captains (such as Salvador Contreras and Jesus Leon). Carried out simultaneously throughout the night, both groups danced on the following day among many others in the large courtyard of the church in Tepetlixpa. For much of the time those dancers who supported Herman were worried about possible disruptive tactics from the other side, such as pushing against their circle or even trying to invade it, but this did not happen.

**156**

Did Justino, the nephew who did not dance, have a better claim than Herman, a nephew by marriage and a dedicated if not yet mature dancer? The tension caused by the inheritance passing to an experienced dancer rather than a member of a jefe's group by direct descent characterizes not only this case but also many others. Alliances often go counter to kinship considerations; it is precisely because there are strong alliances between dancers, loyalties to a group, and relationships that have become stronger than blood that difficulties can arise when it comes to inheritance. Don Faustino probably felt leanings toward those of his blood as he came closer to the end of his life. However, even when the inheritance is not contested at the time of death, there may be other problems. Often the children of a jefe are disinterested in the dance. While he or she is still alive, they appear not to value the tradition, having seen it since early childhood as something that may be thrust upon them. Often as they become teenagers, they cannot wait to get away. Alternatively, if they are interested, there are power struggles that take the form of disagreements with the parents long before the parents die. In this case, the children may well break away from the parental mesa and form mesas of their own or join others that already exist, and they will probably gain positions of authority quite quickly because of their knowledge of the dance. On the other hand, the children may adopt a different kind of group from that of their father. He may be in the Reliquia but his children might join the Corporación or a Mexica-style group. Such an occurrence can be threatening to the stability of the overall organization, as illustrated by the events following the death of Ignacio Gutierrez in the 1960s (see Chapter 9).

Sometimes an inheritor may simply not have the financial means or the capability, desire, or necessary experience of the dance to undertake the organization of a mesa. One such instance is that of Miguel Gutierrez, the son of Alberto Gutierrez. Miguel was in his thirties, and although he had danced as a child, he had subsequently evinced little or no interest in the dance, causing his father considerable concern about the inheritance. However, with the encouragement of Compadre Ernesto, and partly to please his father, Miguel had gone to a special obligation (at Caxuxi in Hidalgo). Within a year of this event, his father died, but at peace, knowing that his son had found the dance again and hoping that he would carry on the tradition. Miguel began to enjoy dancing and to come regularly to Compadre Ernesto's obligations. He talked to me about the dance not as something he had chosen to do but as something he had to do. Some ten years later, however (in 1995), Miguel had still not raised his own mesa. He continued to dance with Compadre Ernesto, gaining experience all the time, although he always brought his own banner with him. Most of his other paraphernalia was kept in storage in Apaxco, where his family used to live, including his antique Santo Niño. Decorated in gold and considered to be a particularly miraculous one, this figure had been taken out on many pilgrimages during his father's lifetime. By the mid-1990s, Miguel had gone to the United States to work with the hope that with the money he earned (and a wife) he could perhaps reinstate his own mesa.[15]

As already indicated, inheritance often presents a very real problem for a mesa. The vacuum left by children who do not accept the inheritance provides an opportunity for a power struggle among other possible incumbents who, even if named as captains before the jefe's death, can never be the "true" inheritors. From what various Concheros have said, only a general's son can become a general, although this calls into question the authenticity of the status of most generals. Many generals' sons are less effective as palabras than were their fathers, such as the inheritor of Felipe Aranda, for a general is someone who raises mesas and conquers and possibly takes dancers away from someone else. That is, generals are self-made persons, usually charismatic and with proven leadership powers. Equally, it is often felt that only the children by the most recent wife can really inherit a mesa.

## DIVISION/FISSION

In the case of Tepetlixpa, it became clear that the split that the meeting of jefes had hoped to prevent had nonetheless occurred when both Herman and Justino were given ceremonies of recognition. Although many groups appear to be quite stable, fission and subsequent separation are in fact common and almost a prerequisite for the continuity of the dance, and certainly one of the means by which it grows. If the number of mesas does not multiply, the organization of the dance becomes static, the size of groups unwieldy, and their internal dynamic dysfunctional and hence inoperable. The Tepetlixpa case was a matter of an internal battle between two sides, a case of fission and then separation that drew many other allied groups into the fray.

I turn now to a different case. In the mid-1990s as Compadre Ernesto's mesa grew after the celebrations for the "discovery" of the Americas 1992, a group of dancers left the mesa after an apparent quest for power by a comparative newcomer. The politicking for this split mostly happened within the group and primarily involved only the group itself, although those who broke away did seek the support of other jefes and in particular that of the generals, but their actions did not, to my knowledge, result in the calling of a meeting of jefes.

Ernesto Ortiz had no living children. His wife, Maria, died in 1979, and their adopted son sometime in the 1980s, and Ernesto had not married again.

**158**

There was thus no immediate inheritor of the group. The group had had four principal dancers, or cabeceras, for years. Known colloquially as the "jefe's pillars," the cabeceras performed the roles that the captains would have done had the jefe named them. He, however, put off the final commitment as to whom to give these positions, although Antonia, the first conchero of the left, was said to be the jefe's adopted daughter and was assumed by many to be the inheritor (see Chapter 2).

In 1989, the first conchero of the right was Eduardo. For most of the time, however, Eduardo was away from Mexico City in Cancun (Yucatan), where he was raising a new group; therefore, Antonia assumed the position of first palabra in preference to anyone else at any dance. Margarita (the second conchero of the left) was also often not present at dances because she had little free time, and partly too because both she and Alfredo (the second on the right) had recently been lured away from the dance by the Sufis, as had many long-term dancers in the mesa. The frequent absence of up to three of the pillars meant that the positions of the palabras had to be filled by other dancers.

In 1991, the jefe made all four of them captains, partly because of his age but more probably in response to a struggle for power that was beginning to develop in the group. In 1989, Juan had just returned from Cancun, where he had been in close contact with the Concheros through Eduardo and his new mesa. He and his friends found it easy to enter the group; they were all middle-class and if not actually affluent had the potential to be so. Juan often had short-term financial difficulties but was involved in television and thus earned substantial sums when he did work, and the jefe had always had a soft spot for those from the middle-class with a little more to spend. Moreover, the newcomers were friends or friendly with many who already danced in the group.

Juan's dancing was good and he learned fast; he also rapidly mastered the playing of the concha. He wrote alabanzas, made exquisite dance clothes for himself, and fashioned various artifacts, such as headdresses, conch-shell trumpets, and a staff, including one he made especially for the jefe. Whereas the attentions of the pillars had waned somewhat over the years, the new arrivals where available to help: they took the jefe to the doctor, paid for his medicines, gave him presents, and generally made themselves useful. Compadre Ernesto liked Juan and considered him gifted. A power struggle for position thus developed between the four long-term but frequently absent captains (the pillars) and Juan, who gained support from one of the sahumadoras, the mesa's second-most powerful position after that of jefe. Ernesto Ortiz had been suffering from ill health for some time and had been unable to dance with the group for a number of years. It seemed as though the jefe's strength and authority

**159**

diminished, as Juan's power grew. Few dances occurred when Juan did not take the position of first palabra, and if any of the pillars appeared, usually something of a standoff ensued as to who would take that role and there would be some disagreement as to how the obligation should be carried out.

For example, Eduardo was particularly put out on the occasion when he was dancing in Mexico City after a long break and Juan (as first palabra) should have gone through a particular sequence of words that Eduardo (as second palabra) would have then mirrored, singing them an octave higher (*en compas*). On this particular occasion, all was going well when suddenly Juan left out part of the ritual and "jumped from one to five," as Eduardo later put it. Another alteration that he noted was the tendency for a group of dancers to go into the center to lead a dance, rather than just a single dancer. The jefe was made uneasy by the situation, but the four pillars did not always appear and Juan did. This enthusiasm and dedication added to his advantage, and the more Juan took over, the more the four pillars stayed away.

This situation continued for some time and by 1992 a split had occurred. The four pillars decided to form their own mesa even though this involved a huge amount of work and they were not sure that they really had the time. They took with them many of the dancers who were their personal friends or followers, leaving the jefe without his usual means of support, not only in terms of the number of dancers but also psychologically and economically. This was probably the first mesa formed by predominantly middle-class adepts.[16] They made this decision with the support of the generals and others in the association, and jefe Ernesto gradually came round to it. He, however, was now in a weak position: his pillars had gone and been replaced by people who had much less experience of the dance. Juan tended to assume the position of first palabra and the second was taken by Felipe or Miguel, again both neophytes by comparison to the pillars but with more years of experience in the dance than Juan.

Juan often went in the place of the jefe when the mesa of Santo Niño de Atocha was asked to lend support to a new group or invited to some event. Despite his precarious health, however, the jefe was now more involved organizationally than previously. As a result of Juan's networking, the mesa now received more invitations and requests than it had for years and most of these were channelled through the compadre's house, where there was now a telephone. As these demands grew, the compadre asked Juan to carry out more of these duties for him.

In 1995, however, the question of the inheritance took an unexpected turn. At the annual vigil and meeting of the mesa in January, the jefe announced who his inheritor was to be. Much to most dancers' surprise, the jefe chose his great-nephew Ricardo, who had lived in the same house as the jefe for some years but had never shown much interest in the dance.[17] The decision showed clearly that the jefe was still capable of making decisions.

The jefe began the process of initiating Ricardo. He was received as a dancer in June at a mass for Corpus Christi in San Juan de los Lagos (Michoacan), and then days later a vigil was held at the Sanctuary of the Santo Niño and the Señor de los Plateros in Fresnillo, in the State of Zacatecas. This was followed by a ten-day pilgrimage to San Juan Nuevo de los Milagros and again to San Juan de los Lagos. His position was also ratified by the Luna family at Tlatelolco as his *padrinos* (godfathers). It had also been accepted by the generals Guadalupe Hernandez and Camillo Bársenas who had apparently been pressuring Compadre Ernesto into making Ricardo a captain for some time, but he had wanted him to learn the procedures before giving him the position. The jefe, who had looked terminally ill for years (and certainly since I first met him in 1989), was a changed man. Finally, he had as his inheritor a kinsman who lived not just in the same part of the city but in the same house.

Speculation was rife in the mesa as to what would happen upon Compadre Ernesto's death. Ricardo was already showing signs in 1996 that the glory of being inheritor of the mesa was beginning to wane; he did not always show up at obligations and on one occasion went off to "work" (i.e., apparently to dance or drink) rather than coming to an all-night vigil. Perhaps this is not surprising in a young man of twenty who has had authority suddenly thrust upon him, but it was a situation that did not augur well for the future. By the late 1990s, therefore, the future of the mesa was still not as secure as Compadre Ernesto might have hoped.

Whereas Ricardo had power thrust upon him as an insider, Juan's rapid rise to power was that of an outsider. The sudden empowerment of an outsider is not unusual but in this case was, as one long-term dancer pointed out, rather too rapid, too easy, and thus dangerous. He was received within a few years of joining the group, which is not often the case. Angelica pointed out that this is a process that can take up to twenty years; she was received after eleven. To be received is serious and is not so much an initiation into new knowledge as an acknowledgment that you accept the responsibility of dancing for the rest of your life without fail (at the very least, at the principal obligations). Juan, accustomed to directing in his working life, tended to apply the same techniques in the dance and was generally perceived as too controlling, but he also brought new alliances to the mesa as, for instance, with the Corporación.[18] Juan's next move might have been to form his own mesa and draw dancers to him, as many others had done before him, but he had the disadvantage of lacking the necessary status of captain. This might have been something that the jefe, in his generosity, could have bestowed upon him before his death, provided Juan kept dancing.

Many others have risen equally rapidly. Andres Segura, mentioned previously as active in the Tepetlixpa fray and who had been adjunct to the group of Santo Niño de Atocha in the 1960s, moved on to the mesa of the Virgen de los Dolores, whose jefe was Miguel Alvarado. Under its protection and as a captain, he later formed his own mesa, Grupo de Danza Azteca Xinachtli. Andres's rise was not considered as threatening as he came from an indigenous family, and in his grandparents' generation there had been dancers. Furthermore, he was himself a professional dancer. He had studied medicine for two years when young and then worked in the theater before training as a ballet dancer at Belles Artes. He subsequently taught choreography and modern dance. He attracted young dancers to his mesa in the early 1980s who while they were finding their feet professionally, tended to be bedazzled by the dance.[19] Andres Segura's mesa has, however, never grown in the same way as Compadre Ernesto's, which toward the end of the twentieth century probably had the highest number of adherents involved in the arts and the professions. Segura tended to call himself a general but was not generally accepted as such by the association.[20] He was a *hombre conquistador*, an initiator into the dance; what he most enjoyed was conquest and that was probably why he added fuel to the difficulties of the Tepetlixpa inheritance.[21]

I have so far talked about the rapid rise to power of some dancers and the question of inheritance in rather negative terms by looking at the drive of certain people and the reactions that they provoke in the dance. Juan undoubtedly began with the best of intentions. His interests initially were for the well-being of the mesa (and the jefe) but later he became involved in personal empowerment. The battle over Tepetlixpa could probably have been foreseen because the situation had not been clarified by the old jefe before he died. This often occurs but not all inheritances involve a "battle." When Guadalupe Jimenez Sanabria (Generala to some and not to others) of the Insignias Aztecas died (ca.1994), her son, Jesus Leon, took over as one of five inheritors, all of whom work together without any difficulties. Even if inheritance does involve fission initially, often there is a rapprochement later. The group formed by Compadre Ernesto's pillars, for example, came to dance with him at Chalma a few years after the initial breakup.

## IDENTITY POLITICS

The meeting of jefes in 1989 was the first to have been convened in eight or nine years; thus, many were in doubt about the details of the overall organization. The general opinion was that the guidelines of the tradition were being forgotten and that there was not enough interaction between groups. Many backed the suggestion that meetings of this kind should be held more often, possibly as frequently as once a month or at the very least several times a year. New forms of organization were suggested, such as Andres Segura's proposal to form a council of *ancianos* (like those of North American Indian groups). Segura pointed out that North American Indians were more conscious of the need to preserve their traditions than were the Concheros. A board of directors (*mesa directiva*) was proposed by his brother, Emilio; and Jefe Leon suggested a council of older guides (*consejo de guias mayores*). The overall response to these suggestions was not entirely unanimous: it is important to remember that each mesa is independent and autonomous and that the forms of each group are different and must be respected.

What was agreed, however, was that some type of guidance from the older jefes was acceptable if not essential to regenerate the smooth running of the association. General Guadalupe Hernandez then suggested that the Concheros needed to imitate the practices of fifty years ago and talked about forming a *gobierno* (government) (see Chapter 9). This suggestion tied in with others made, such as Soledad Ruiz's proposal that in the interests of strengthening the organization, the four generals (present at the meeting on that particular day) should be assigned a wind or cardinal point each, with Manuel Luna at the center (where he had been since the 1940s). It was stressed that this did not mean they were in charge of that dance but rather that each symbolized the event, for, according to Soledad, the dances would be "organized . . . by agreement and not according to orders." Guadalupe Hernandez thought that the association should be ready to receive outsiders and mentioned Ignacio Cortez (whose group is called Tenoch).

One group of mesas knows little of others, especially those outside their conformidad, hampering their understanding of the larger whole. A mesa sees how other mesas dance when they are invited to dance together and they appreciate the differences in their practices, especially if they perform a vigil together. In reality, aside from a few peripatetic dancers, outsiders (such as anthropologists) probably know more about the ways in which groups differ than does any insider who loyally supports one group over a period of years.[22]

The next meeting of jefes may have been held in May 1990 as planned but I had had to leave the country by then. It had taken many months to engineer the 1989 meeting, and unless another disaster threatened, future meetings would have had little to discuss. In the past, groups have pulled together when under the influence of a charismatic leader such as Ignacio Gutierrez (see Chapter 9). Neither of today's two most powerful generals, Guadalupe

Hernandez and Camillo Barsenas, is quite as charismatic. The desire for union at this higher level is generally overridden by the differences that exist between mesas. Holding a meeting is a measure that the wider organization can take when its harmony (conformity) is threatened by political acts that go just too far, for behind all this politicizing it has to be remembered that the dance should not be used as a tool in a search for power. As I hope I have shown, however, segmentation is healthy, for without it the dance cannot spread and grow.[23]

This chapter has moved the discussion from a concern with inner empowerment to one that looks at external empowerment. It has given an overview of the identity politics of the dance during a particular period. Groups get together as allies because they feel an affinity with one another and enjoy the experience of dancing together and lending each other support. Alliances bring strength to the dance and give it continuity. When studying the inheritance of a group, the analyst is challenged to bring into the open the mechanisms by which this occurs. Although claimed to be kin-linked, inheritance does not always occur along these lines and depends very much on the group itself. It is in this aspect of the dance that identity politics can become most fraught, and this chapter looked at some of the recent power struggles. The following chapter places this segment of Conchero history in a wider perspective.

# NINE

# ORAL TRADITION, MYTH, AND HISTORY

"I remember well December 12, 1946. I was present with Manuel Piñeda.
It was the first time that I knew that I could belong to a dance. For me
it was a marvelous experience . . . a thing never seen before although it's
repeated every year. I came from an origin, a very, very humble one. We
were orphans and lived with our grandmother. I had not brought with me
even ten centavos for the bus, its cost at the time. I went from the Colonia
Morelos on foot. I don't remember having a sip of water; I don't remember
buying anything to eat because I didn't have any change. Notwithstanding,
I passed that day marveling, running from group to group until the last
dance, until everybody gave thanks and I saw that it had ended [and] they
returned to their houses so happy and contented! I wasn't hungry or thirsty,
and had no need other than to give thanks to the great dancers of that time.
I entered by chance wondering whether I could belong. I thought it was a
traditional thing, that they carried their *palabras* from fathers to sons. And I,
with my family, had never known about it. For me this was an open door to
paradise."

—GENERAL CAMILLO BÁRECENAS, from a literal transcrip-
tion of a speech recorded during the Meeting of Jefes 1989

Until very recently, as indicated earlier, the tradition of the Concheros has been
predominantly an oral one. Entry to that "open door to paradise" achieved
by means of the dance has been passed down by embodied practice from one
generation to the next. The history of the dance is told in their *alabanzas* and
remembered in speeches; little has been preserved in written form as the dancers have been largely preliterate. Not much is known then about its organization

and if it existed in something like its present form before the early 1900s when the name Conchero appears to have been adopted. It is clear, however, that the dance gained momentum in Mexico City as it was brought in from the countryside, mainly from the Bajio, toward the end of the nineteenth century and that the migration of dancers continued into the twentieth. A few traces indicate that there might have been dancers in Mexico City during the nineteenth century; however, the Concheros' mythology places its origins firmly in the Bajio.

In this chapter, I provide a background against which to evaluate the history of the dance during the twentieth century. The latter part of this chapter pieces together the story of Santo Niño de Atocha based on the many conversations I had with the jefe Compadre Ernesto, who gave me details of how and when he established his group and of the role he played in the tradition of the dance. As in all oral traditions, memories of past occasions can be kept alive when linked mnemonically to specific events that highlight the remarkable and excise the nondescript. Those who have always relied on oral memory usually have remarkable recall and can provide a rich fund of detail. This history has been pieced together too from recollections that were brought up at the meeting of jefes (Chapter 8), and Angelica, the *sahumadora*, was able to fill in some of the gaps from her diaries on the dance that she has kept since 1978. It was, however, only in 1992 that she and some of the other dancers in Santo Niño de Atocha began to put together a chronology of the *mesa*'s significant events.[1] Until then the mesa had had no readily available written record of its history.

Oral traditions have no determinate historical depth; we cannot know when practices or beliefs were formulated or the date at which elements were added. As the embodied histories of subaltern peoples, they are usually not privileged in written accounts because such people's lives have been of little interest to hegemonic discourse and consequently there are few records from which historians can easily reconstruct their practices. Thus, the analyst needs to rely on traces, memories, sacred objects, and remnants. This is predominantly the case for the Concheros, although during the twentieth century the dance has not been without some documentation. When a dancer achieves a position, this status is usually affirmed with a certificate outlining the post attained and signed by witnesses. If the post is that of a jefe, other jefes must act as witnesses.[2] Such documents are displayed in a jefe's *oratorio*, and when access can be gained (which is sometimes difficult), they can give historical structure to the more fluid temporality of the recollections of the dancers.

I have framed the oral history of Santo Niño de Atocha very broadly in terms of the major political changes that occurred during the twentieth century, but I will first place it in a longer-term historical context. Although some claim that the dance dates back no further than the early 1800s, the first part of the chapter looks at what is known about dance in the Bajio from the sixteenth century onward, when myth indicates that its Christianized form originated. I look generally at other dances, such as those of the Moors and Christians enacted by or for confraternities. For many dancers, and especially for the recent generation of older, more conservative jefes (now mostly dead), the dance was clearly believed to be Christian and linked to the Franciscans. This belief remained largely unchallenged in many mesas until the recent so-called celebrations for the discovery of the Americas focused many dancers' awareness on the pre-Colombian past. Since the late 1980s, interest in that past and claims for a continuity of the dance from the time of the Aztecs have become much stronger.

Although many forms of dance clearly existed before the Conquest, it is an open and probably unanswerable question as to whether any of these are closely related to the Concheros' dances of today, for as Lockhart has so pertinently observed, dance leaves no tangible traces.[3] However, even if the giving of an all-embracing name (the Concheros) to the dancers is comparatively recent and the overall form of the dance has changed through time, circle dances were certainly important to the Aztecs.[4] Of that era, we know much more about dance in Tenochtitlan than in the countryside and much more about the dances of the higher orders than of the lower. However, although some versions of the myth attribute a Catholic origin to the organization of the dance, other sources indicate that the dances are pre-Christian. There is thus a tension between Indianism—the desire for the dance to have indigenous and possibly even pre-Colombian origins, which is particularly prevalent at present—and orthodoxy or Catholicism, the still-received belief held by many recent jefes that the dance is strongly linked to the Catholic Church and thus possibly Hispanic in origin. What I aim to show in the next section of this chapter is that neither of these two viewpoints tells the whole story; the evolution of the dance is considerably more complex than this.

## MYTHICAL ANTECEDENTS

According to the predominant (oral) version of the Concheros' origin myth, the autochthonous Chichimecs were in full battle in 1531[5] against the Spanish when Santa Cruz with Santiago (de Matamoros) miraculously appeared. They subsequently converted to Christianity and asked that a cross be erected to act as a marker. As they danced around it they shouted "El es Dios." The battle had taken place on a mountain that in memory of the bloodshed came to be called Sangremal ("bad blood"). These events are commemorated in one of the Concheros' core alabanzas:

| | |
|---|---|
| *Santísima Cruz, Santísima Cruz,* | Most holy Cross, Most Holy Cross, |
| *Del cerro de Sangremal,* ( × 2) | From the mountain of Sangremal, |
| *Dondé corrió la sangre,* ( × 2) | Where the blood flowed, |
| *Llegó hasta el arenal,* | That reached the sandy ground, |
| *En medio del encinal.*[6] | In the heart of the forest. |

A more detailed account probably based on that written by the cacique Don Nicolás de San Luis Montáñez has been the source for most of the more recent written versions. It relates how the Chichimecas were in the thick of a battle against Christians, most of whom were probably converted indigenes deployed by the Spaniards. This battle was being fought without arms when suddenly a shining cross was seen, suspended in the air, and at its side an image of Santiago.[7] Night was fast approaching, but Santiago miraculously held back the descent of the sun and the struggle slowly died down of its own accord. Seeing this marvel, the Chichimecas "shed many tears" and presented themselves to be evangelized. By this time, both sides were so bespattered with blood and roughed up that it was difficult to tell Christians from barbarians.[8] The battle, it is claimed, occurred on the day devoted to Santiago, July 25, and apparently the day of an eclipse of the sun, which might account for why the tussle is said to have stopped so suddenly and why too the Chichimecas were brought to Christianity in such large numbers.[9]

"Chichimeca" was the loosely used and pejorative name given to a number of different indigenous peoples who lived as nomadic hunters and gatherers in the vast expanses of arid land to the north of New Spain. Many continued to resist the Spaniards during the Chichimecan wars (from 1550 to 1600) and well into the eighteenth century, even after Christianization.[10] In fact, many of the more settled indigenes, such as the Otomís and, in particular, those of higher rank, had already become Christians and had been converting other indigenes for some time as the evangelizing army moved north.[11]

The text continues by describing how the day after the battle, the recently converted asked that a cross be put up (the Santa Cruz), but the first one was hidden (i.e., rejected) and a second requested made from stone. Even though a cross was provided, the Chichimecas were still not satisfied because it was not large or high enough. "To comply with their gods," they fetched the stones themselves to form a miraculous cross, which they danced around for a whole week, kissing and venerating it and proclaiming that "this is the cross that must serve as a marker for evermore" while still holding their bows and quivers of arrows.[12] The implication here is that they were already familiar with the dance but had begun to perform it for the cross, the Santa Cruz.

Devotion to the Santa Cruz grew year by year and spread widely, and it is still strong to this day. Fernandéz witnessed dancers in the Bajío in 1940 coming from the countryside in procession into San Miguel de Allende and bringing with them their Santa Cruz, which was erected in the church and around which they then danced. Comparing his description with a sixteenth-century Michoacan text, he noted that not much had changed.[13]

Warman's interpretation of this clearly Christian version of events is that the Chichimecas were so terrified by the appearance of the Santa Cruz, that as a sign of repentance they asked for a cross.[14] But would Chichimecs, as nomadic peoples, have been familiar with the cross as a symbol? They probably had few material images and instead deified aspects of nature such as the sun and the moon. Certainly, in their cosmology the Aztecs mapped the world into four spatial sections (oriented to the sun), which formed a conceptual cross that gave cohesion (or stability) to what was otherwise conceived of as an unstable and slippery earth. The four directions could easily be transformed into the European idea of the four winds—north, south, east, and west—which predates the precision of the compass and, as already indicated, is still employed by the Concheros today.[15] One of their alabanzas describes Santiago as the messenger of the four winds:

| | |
|---|---|
| *Que viva y que viva* | How alive, how alive is |
| *Senor Santiago,* (× 2) | Saint James, |
| *Porque el es el correo* (× 2) | For he is the courier |
| *De los cuatro vientos.* | Of the four winds. |

This version of the myth also claims that the indigenes danced before fighting and that the day of the battle was not the first time that they had danced in honor of the Christian God.

Indigenous dances were presumably Christianized (and vice versa) to a certain extent as the Spanish gradually moved north with their indigenous (Otomi) troops conquering the area that today is known as the Bajio. According to one oral version, one of the converted caciques who oversaw the fight was the great General Conín, who in the Montáñez version had insisted that the battle be fought without weapons. He "was sitting on his horse on the mountainside watching the battle [and on] the ground beside him stood a Chichimec with bow and arrow. . . . [I]n front of him stood a Conchero playing his concha. It is the truth. And so you can see, there were Concheros then." In this version, the various sides have clearly become fused, for we are told that Conín, although fighting a battle against the Chichimecs, actually had a Chichimec standing at his side who was playing a European-style stringed instrument.[16]

According to an earlier "official" version circulating in 1583 and now generally accepted by modern historiography, the battle never took place at all. It was unnecessary because Conín (who was a merchant) had already become a Christian and had taken the name Hernando de Tapia. He used not force but persuasion to bring "about the surrender and conversion of numerous Chichimeca groups." Other expeditions of pacification had also used promises and gifts of artifacts and foodstuffs. In fact, the term "conquest" may well refer to the distribution of clothing to Chichimec chiefs.[17]

Gruzinski suggests that the battle may have been invented "to explain the origins of the miraculous cross and satisfy the Franciscans' demands." He discusses yet another version, drafted originally in the mid-seventeenth century, which lays all the emphasis on Montáñez but otherwise plays down the role of the Spaniards.[18] By then, even those who were caciques and part of the colonial elite—which included the Tapia family—were increasingly excluded from dominant positions by the arrival of rich Spanish herders and traders.[19]

Most Concheros I talked to had heard the first and simplest version of this origin myth and, especially if country dancers, often know little else about the antecedents of their dance other than what the alabanzas can tell them. Some of these alabanzas recollect the Conquest; *Ya llegó la conquista a Mexico* (The Conquest has come to Mexico), for example, enumerates the different religious orders that came, from the Franciscans to the Carmelites, and another, *Cuando nuestra América* (When our America), relates the story of Hernán Cortés and the Conquest and the downfall of Cuauhtémoc. In *Gran inspirador Cuauhtémoc* (The great inspirer Cuauhtémoc), the last emperor's acceptance as a Christian is lauded, and in *Estrella del Oriente* (Star of the East), he is linked as a king (*rey*) to Charles V, the Holy Roman Emperor and King of Spain at the time.[20] The origins of aspects of the Concheros' organization are also mentioned in the last, such as the raising of the Palabra General in Tlaxcala and the Reliquia General in Dolores Hidalgo (Guanajuato).[21]

## DOCUMENTATION ON THE DANCE

A recent document produced in San Miguel de Allende in 1978 by the Confraternidad Tradicional de Danzas Chichimecas gives a better sense of how one mesa has chosen to conceptualize its history.[22] It outlines in a more pragmatic way than the myth the evangelization by the Franciscans. In the early 1500s, two Franciscan padres (Fray Francisco Doncel and Fray Diego Burgos) came from Valladolid (today Morelia) to the Bajio and managed to establish a monastery. In 1535 they were tortured and killed by the Chichimecs, guided by their leader Marcelíno Braulio and his second-in-command Nicanor Michiqui, who still believed in "idolatry."[23] In 1539, the (abandoned or hidden) figure of Christ that had been brought by the Franciscans was found by Otomi Indians who lived on the mountain, known as Palo Huerfano. They presented it in the name of the conqueror for they had already "inherited" the Catholic faith.

There is a large gap in the long-term history covered by this document. Nothing is said about how the confraternity came into existence, only that it has continued from "generation to generation of grand caciques until the generation of the General of Generals of the Chichimec Indians, J. Jesús Morales." The latter was "born in 1818 and died in 1905, leaving as inheritor of the group, J. Miguel Morales López, born in 1893," who received the generalship of the conquest in the *altos* and *bajíos* on May 3, 1916.[24]

This document mentions the complex tensions that still exist in the dance today between Catholicism and so-called pre-Hispanic religiosity (idolatry) and between resistance and submission. From the various versions of the myth we gather that in San Miguel it was the Otomí who were instrumental in establishing an enduring form of Christianity. It was they, according to this document, who resurrected the cross knocked down by the Chichimecs, and yet this particular confraternidad claims its general is a Chichimec Indian.[25]

As I indicated earlier, "Chichimeca" was the generic name given to a number of indigenous groups who inhabited a vast area of about 25,000 square kilometers.[26] An example of how these indigenous peoples were perceived is given on the dedication of a church to the Virgin of Guadalupe in Queretero in 1689, at which, apparently, there appeared a "disordered confusion of wild Chichimecs." They wore no clothes other than those that just "permitted decency," had a multitude of "ordinary" feathers in their disheveled hair, their bodies were painted in earth colors, and they "horrified everyone by their activity." The writer was a Spaniard or Creole and clearly shared the dominant preconception that the indigenes were barbaric. The Chichimecs continued, as previously mentioned, to attack Spanish settlements and especially cattle ranches well into the eighteenth century. Some Concheros who talked to Moedano about this period may have been referring to these events when they mentioned *levantamientos armados* (armed uprisings). It is not known, however, whether those who danced were directly involved in insurgency.[27]

For lack of other sources, this document must be taken at face value, but if it was rewritten from generation to generation, it may have been subject to creative reinvention. That the document never attempts to trace out the history of the group from the mid-sixteenth century probably indicates that this history was indeed an orally transmitted one until the early nineteenth century (and only the origins and the present day were considered to be of interest). Alternatively, it could be that this particular confraternity, at least in its present form, only came into existence at that time. This latter explanation would account for the emphasis on the Chichimecs, for by then they had become

171

something of a trope; I shall return to this later. The origins of this confraternity and that of other mesas too can be more easily understood in the light of the history of Catholic confraternities.

## CONFRATERNITIES

Confraternities in New Spain in the 1500s, as in Spain itself, were lay brotherhoods and initially restricted to indigenes. Organized by the friars or the secular clergy, they had written constitutions and aimed to evangelize and acquaint their members with the "obligations, sacraments, rites and devotions" of the newly imposed religion. Part of their work was to assist in social welfare, and they were often, at least in the early days of the Conquest, linked to hospitals and to the provision of funerals. During the late sixteenth century, as mining developed in the Bajio, indigenes (such as Tarascans, Mexicas, Otomis, and Mazahuas) who had been attracted to Guanajuato as workers helped establish chapels and hospitals (as part of the confraternities); the Mexicas' hospital, for example, was still extant at the end of the 1600s. Confraternities could give not just material help but also personal support to members, particularly during periods of crisis, such as the epidemics that killed many indigenes in the later half of the sixteenth and early seventeenth centuries; they continued to be the places in towns where indigenous migrants (*extravagantes*) could find assistance until the mid-eighteenth century. They offered a way for displaced indigenous peoples to create a new form of community apparently linked to the new faith, and for those who were spiritually confused (in a state of *nepantla*),[28] to establish a stable sense of identity often still founded on a more private form of indigenous religiosity.[29]

For most, their main work was to celebrate the fiesta of their particular saint. Understandably, however, confraternities whose members were still predominantly indigenes were rarely charged with the care of the patron saint of the community. In some places, the mayordomos (confraternity members) also held positions in other civic or even ecclesiastical establishments. To perform their work, confraternities usually established coffers to build up their wealth. They were partially funded by monthly subscriptions and later on by means of gifts of land to a virgin or for an effigy. In some areas, their assets also consisted of animals and cattle, which were usually seen as the property of their saint and slaughtered for fiestas, for which the confraternity was usually able also to produce the rest of the food and the drink. In more fertile areas, they grew corn, and in the Bajio, *tunas* (the fruit of the prickly pear cactus) and magueys were used to make alcohol.[30]

Charged initially in towns with organizing the Catholic processions, the confraternities' work soon extended to music, singing, and dancing. The alcoholic excesses during fiestas, however, were condemned by the Church as was the dancing not only inside churches but also in sequestered places. Only songs and old stories examined and approved by the priests were allowed. Prohibited too was the wearing of masks or other adornments that had any appearance of idolatry about them. The immediate effect of such measures was to force the indigenes into clandestine activity; they began holding their ritual dances in secret and at night, outside the ambit of the Catholic Church. Sahagún attests to this in 1576, when he reported that there had been a deplorable increase in the "*areitos* [dances] that secretly and at night they perform in honor of their idols."[31]

Song and dance were inextricably intertwined and deeply embodied aspects of pre-Conquest religiosity, as one of the early chroniclers, the Franciscan friar Pedro de Gante, realized after he arrived in New Spain in 1523. He commented, "All their worship of their gods consisted of singing and dancing in front of them." If they could not be fully converted, de Gante's attitude regarding these practices was to encourage the indigenes to use Christian symbols and to sing in Spanish. Sahagún took a different stance and composed Christian songs translated into Nahuatl and sung to pre-Colombian music. Another way to license or even incorporate indigenous ritual practices still in their pre-Christian form, such as the dances, was to permit them only at times designated by the Christian calendar and only outside the church; in rural areas such measures were more difficult to implement and probably many more pre-Christian practices were carried on inside.[32]

Although complaints continued well into the late seventeenth century, the Church increasingly began to tolerate, as part of the colorful pageant of Catholicism, practices that earlier it had tried to extirpate. By the late sixteenth century, Mexico seemed to be "overrun by Indian religious associations." By 1585 there were more than 300 cofradias, and the early seventeenth century was in fact the time of their "greatest vigor." Men, women, and children could join them and participate in the activities and, more importantly, the festivals. They offered a means of association that was accepted and even encouraged by the authorities for they appeared to offer a form of social control.[33]

As the power of the clergy declined and many parishes were secularized, however, the ecclesiastical establishment increasingly lost jurisdiction over the newly formed confraternities, some of which dispensed with the legal formalities in order to save money and to avoid creating formal ties with the Church. Many were virtually autonomous and were confraternities in name only. These continued to arouse the suspicion that pre-Hispanic practices were still rife, often with good reason. Essentially, the indigenes took an imposed form that should have been strictly regulated and modified it, thereby creating a means by which they could retain some autonomy. Confraternities gave the indigenes a degree of freedom from the scrutiny of the Church and from civic society (especially in the countryside) that would not otherwise have been possible. In sum, they gave "stability, continuity, cohesion and a collective identity" at a time when the indigenes most needed it.[34]

Despite early suggestions that the indigenous population needed to be drawn into the physical church and away from their house altars, their homes were usually comparatively free from scrutiny. In urban areas soon after the arrival of the Spaniards, the indigenes began to place Catholic saints on household altars in what came to be known as *santocalli*.[35] Predominantly, confraternity altars were furnished with the image of a Catholic saint from whom they gained their name. She or he was often surrounded by images of others saints, including, later on, the Virgin of Guadalupe.[36] Often of more importance in rural areas were sacred objects consisting of pre-Hispanic images, figurines (*idolos*), and "small jugs" on which the prosperity of the house was believed to depend. These could not be moved from their place or even touched. Seen as animate, they embodied the well-being of the lineage, were passed from father to son, and provided a source of continuity and solidarity. In addition, there were bundles of herbs and other plants used for curing and magical practices, such as marijuana, and hallucinogens, such as peyote and magic mushrooms. Catholic images also began to be seen not as mere representations of saints but rather as the saints themselves.[37]

Confraternities maintained a network of contacts with other sodalities in their own communities and frequently with others further afield. If a confraternity did not have sufficient sources of wealth or obtain enough money from its subscriptions, members, both men and women, were sent out to raise funds for their saint. Those from around Mexico City especially traveled to Toluca, Cuernavaca, undoubtedly the Bajio, and even to Michoacan. "Surrounded by musicians, the collectors carried the image in a reliquary; people gathered to welcome them, dances were organized, while holy images, rosaries and small jewels were sold by the collectors."[38]

By the late 1700s, however, many of these confraternities were under pressure from the Church. It began to try to curtail not only the freedom to collect money but even their very existence, as it tried to clamp down on those that did not have formal constitutions. District governors attempted to strengthen their own authority by taking away responsibility for the confraternities from the parish priests. Increasingly, many confraternities owned fewer cattle and much less land as both were sold off because of economic need or the actions of unscrupulous members. As a result, many began to be sponsored by individuals or became private associations.[39]

# THE DANCE OF THE MOORS AND THE CHRISTIANS

I now turn to the predominant form of dance that confraternities enacted. Part of the earlier description of the Chichimecas in Queretero indicates that they horrified onlookers because of the way that they "played with their bows and wooden sabers, causing fear with the barbaric tumult of their disordered and fainthearted fights." In fact, they were in the town to perform a ritualized battle between the Spaniards and the Chichimecas that had developed out of the dances of the Moors and the Christians introduced by the Spaniards in the late sixteenth century. Both dances were used as vehicles of evangelization. Warman has charted the ready acceptance of the Christian dance, at least in the Valley of Mexico where the population was accustomed to dances and to mock combat in the *guerras floridas* used to take captives. These were part of the "extravagant theatricalism" of the huge festivities that occurred regularly in accordance with the Aztec calendar.[40] Associated with the cult of the Santa Cruz, which with the assistance of the Franciscans spread rapidly from the Bajio, the fight had quickly transformed in many places into one between the infidel indigenes (the Chichimecs) and the Spaniards. Alonso de la Rea describes one such dance for the fiesta of the Santa Cruz in Michoacan in 1643 when "the military" skirmished with "the Chichimeca" in order to recapture the *árbol santo de la cruz*. The military personnel included a captain, *alférez*, and sergeant who were chosen to command the battle. On prior days, music played on clarions (or bugles) had been mixed with shots from harquebuses and the explosion of fireworks.[41]

Confraternities were clearly behind the organization of this mock fight for, as Rea puts it, such festivals only existed in communities that had sufficient means and personnel available. The positions listed are those typical of many other confraternities and of the Concheros' organization to this day. Rea's description of the dance itself indicates the dancers were moving in time with the military, and while the "soldiers" went inside the church, the dancers enacted in the patio outside.[42] Rea states, "This dance has been lessening as the Indians have wasted away" but was still found in Queretero and other towns (located in today's state of Morelia). It is clear from the above that the dance described was not an aggressive one between the Chichimecas and the Christians but was rather a more informal indigenous dance, known as a "mitote," whose enactment was permitted but not in the sacred space of the church.[43]

As to how the more harmonious mitote changed through time, I can only tentatively suggest some answers here. It seems quite likely that those forms of dance that had a strong spiritual side and called on supranatural entities, as the Concheros today call on the animas of their ancestors, were continued by indigenes and the less Hispanicized lower orders. It is likely that just as some dance confraternities who performed the dances of the Moors and Christians became so well-known in the late seventeenth century that they were invited from time to time to enact in other towns, other forms of dance may also have been performed. Clavijero, for example, talks about a *tocotín*, "an ancient dance . . . which is quite beautiful and so decent and sober that the Indians are permitted to have it in the churches," and which was still being danced as late as the 1770s.[44] Probably then some of the confraternities who traveled to other communities also performed harmonious dances more like the dances of today's Concheros (who incidentally also travel to diverse communities). It is recognized too that through time the dances of the Chichimecas against the Spaniards took other forms or became known by different names, such as the "Dance of the Santiagos" or the "Dance of the Plumes," or simply became known generically as "Danzas Chichimecas."[45] Today the mixing of different types of dances still occurs at the large obligations; at La Villa, there are both circular clog dancers and mock fights between the "French" or "Americans" and the "Mexicans" (none of which are Conchero groups).

## THE CHICHIMECA TROPE

I now turn to how the Chichimeca trope developed more positive connotations and how for subaltern peoples generally became iconic of the indigenous past. During the second half of the eighteenth century, the Creoles had shown a much greater interest in and appreciation of the Aztecs than previously.[46] This was, however, more of an ideological crusade to rid themselves of their colonial oppressors than any real interest in or concern for actual indigenes.

In painting, the image of the Indian clad only in feathers had been around since the early days of European contact. Such a figure was often depicted as representative of America, and Josefus de Ribera y Argomanis's 1788 painting of the Virgin of Guadalupe shows an indigene apparently dancing and dressed in feather headdress, collar, and skirt with bells tied around his ankles. The significance of this type of imagery had grown in the late eighteenth century as an interest in archaeology and ethnohistory increased among the more educated.

One early example from 1808 is a description of a pilgrimage that took place in 1616 written by Carillo y Perez and loosely based on earlier sources. It describes the processing of the Virgin of Los Remedios to Mexico City to intercede during a prolonged period of drought. The pilgrims carried arches made of bulrushes and large *xuchiles* (flower forms) while a continuous rain of flowers "poured down onto the image of the Saint carpeting the road in abundance." Indigenes dressed in their Indian clothing came from their villages

**9.1.** Josefus de Ribera y Argomanis, Our Lady of Guadalupe as Patron of New Spain, 1778.

to pay respects; men wore the *"Xuihtzolli"* on their heads, others the *"Queztal-piloni*, a plaited headdress," and they performed the *"Malacaquetzalli, Tlanque-choltontec and Aztatzontli."*[47]

By the early nineteenth century, these dances had already been renamed the Dances of the Plumes, as Carillo y Perez points out. He affirms that they had been linked in the seventeenth century to those that represented the Chichimecs. He was probably also in part describing a contemporary pilgrimage, for many of the elements (e.g., the *xuchiles*, the incense, the fireworks, the use of flowers) were—and still are—very much a part of indigenous processions in the Bajio. This passage clearly shows an iconic interest in the Chichimecs, although it also reflects the continuing perception of actual indigenes as primitive. Increasingly in the nineteenth century, the middle classes made excursions to La Villa, Los Remedios, and Chalma to see the "inditos" enact their various popular dances, such as those of the "reaper, the weaver, the mitote and . . . the conquest."[48]

Perhaps more importantly, the continuing deployment of a Chichimecan identity for the dance in the Bajio gave the confraternities a way of preserving an indigenous or increasingly syncretic socio-religious identity during a period of disequilibrium. If the confraternities in the sixteenth to the early eighteenth century had been in some ways more like guilds that aimed to protect and unify groups of native craftsmen, especially in towns, as Gibson has proposed, I would suggest that from the early nineteenth century onward, the organization of confraternities began to become more like secret societies, no longer controlled by or linked to the Church—and probably increasingly composed of close kin.[49]

## THE EIGHTEENTH TO THE LATE NINETEENTH CENTURIES

The late eighteenth century was the start of an unsettled period for Mexico. Its indigenous populations in particular suffered a loss of self-sufficiency linked to a worsening socio-economic situation. It was also a period of oppression for confraternities. Many were disbanded and reduced to the category of mayordomias or could only continue by admitting Spaniards. Once admitted, the Spaniards took over, reducing the autonomy of the indigenous members and bringing them closer to the Catholic Church. Although many had already lost much of their land, later state laws linked to the Ley de Lerdo of 1856—the reform laws instituted by Benito Juarez that demanded the sale of all Church property—further depleted the resources that they had managed to acquire by legally confiscating land and livestock. In general, the nineteenth century saw the beginning of forms of fraternity-like associations that were less ostensibly religious in character as the colonial order slowly disintegrated, and European and North American political intervention increased.[50]

The long-desired independence from Spain was finally gained not by indigenous insurgents but rather by the Creoles, who were strongly anti-Spanish, as previously mentioned. What had begun in 1810 as a religious protest led by Hidalgo, drawing in indigenes from a wide area and marching under the banner of Guadalupe, became a full-fledged revolt demanding the death of all Gauchupines (Spaniards). Although the rebels were eventually crushed, the Declaration of Independence at Chilpancingo, engineered by Morelos in 1813, suggested that New Spain should once again be known by its pre-Conquest name of Anahuac.

Freedom had been limited in New Spain during the second part of the eighteenth century; the Spaniards prohibited publications that praised the Aztec past for fear of provoking religious doubt and attacks against Spanish domination. Secret societies undoubtedly developed in Mexico during the early 1800s, despite the Inquisition's attempts to stamp them out.[51] Many, it seems, aimed to spread ideas about religious tolerance and secularization, although some were also undoubtedly Masonic. For example, the Yorkinos founded in 1826 an Indian-Aztec Lodge, dedicated to the Virgin of Guadalupe as the symbol of independence and Mexican-ness. Historians have suggested the possible existence of other types that had rather different agendas. Guzman has stressed "the syncretic form and lack of orthodoxy" of some of the Masonic lodges, and in particular of "those who organized fiestas and processions for saints."[52]

It is clear that those in power were worried about the rising number of associations and the increase in clandestine activity, although the concern was probably focused more on political than religious activities initially, as indicated by a decree passed by Congress in 1828. This decree prohibited clandestine meetings and established punishments ranging from suspension of a suspect's rights from one year to banishment from the Republic for life. The mid-nineteenth century was also an era when the authorities attempted to suppress public celebrations to halt what they perceived to be at the root of social disorder, such as Carnival on Shrove Tuesday in Mexico City, which for some time became an event celebrated indoors. Dancers then were not the only people who went underground.[53]

This period was also the beginning of the era of the document.[54] Rather than passing on traditions orally, written records began to be made. I now turn to two extant documents, an "Act" and a "Copy of the Plan of the Dance of Sangremal," apparently dated 1838 and 1839, respectively. The subject of these are Chichimeca dancers in the Bajio.[55] The Act contains references to the events that had recently occurred in Mexico and to Catholic practice yet also emphasizes the need to be "valiant Chichimecas." The document discusses the organization of a confraternity, which was headed by a hierarchy of a junta of seven individuals. Its instigator, Ignacio Teodoro Sanchez from Queretero, claims descent from the Christianized Otomis who came from Jilotepec. He indicates that he presented himself in 1814 to the *general mayor* and says that he "demonstrated . . . my rights and my titles of conqueror as indicated by several documents that have been stored so that . . . they will be available for presentation as ours . . . legal as they are."[56] The claim to have archived documents raises problems of authenticity, particularly since Sanchez admits to developing or reinventing the "Danza Chichimeca."[57] The Copy of the Plan of the Dance of Sangremal stipulates "that all the documents should be renewed, leaving the old ones to verify the truth and provide testimony, and the new ones so that they can be understood and endure."[58] The key here is undoubtedly the word "renewed."

The "Danza de los Sanchez" was apparently well-known in and around Queretero.[59] The document refers to an independent brotherhood and its continuation.[60] Warman classifies "the constitutive document" as clearly that "of an independent or self-sufficient religious association [or order] of a popular type" and likens this to the organization of the Concheros.[61] This junta or hermandad does not quite follow all the precepts typical of a secret society, but many are quite similar to those followed by the Concheros, although the names of the positions are different.[62] It is also clearly Catholic.

Interest in a probably largely reinvented and specifically Aztec past was at a high point in the early decades of the nineteenth century, as the documents discussed above indicate. A full-fledged revival of pre-Colombian religiosity would not have been tolerated by the Church nor would it have been socioculturally possible. Catholicism became the only legal religion despite strong anticlerical feeling toward Spanish priests and the Church in general, possibly forcing many indigenes or those of indigenous descent to give, at least outwardly, a more Catholic appearance to the forms of their religious practice.

Then in 1857, the liberal constitution moved strongly against religion and effectively disestablished the Catholic Church. Federal authorities were awarded "unspecified powers to regulate religion and its external discipline," which must have further affected the confraternities.[63] Some dancers today maintain that the dance had strong Masonic links but it is unclear whether these are claimed for the middle of the century or during the Porfiriato.[64] During this period, confraternities became ever more secretive as they tried not to publish their existence to the general public or to the established order. Miguel, the son of General Alberto Gutierrez, who had died in the late 1980s, had often been told about the period during which the dance was hidden and of its reemergence toward the end of the nineteenth century.[65]

Travelers interested in finding untouched customs or even traces of them in central Mexico were frequently disappointed, although Tylor was told about "solemn dances in the church" performed by indigenes in Chalma.[66] The Confraternidad Tradicional de Danzas Chichimecas probably managed to survive throughout the nineteenth century by means of its informal networks, much like those in existence today.

The mid-nineteenth century was also a turbulent period politically. The United States, backed by the Freemasons, invaded in 1847, and from 1857 to 1860 Mexico was torn apart by a civil war, which was followed by external interventions that led to a European emperor, Maximillian, from 1864 to 1867.[67] During this period, the indigenous population was considered a problem, although Maximilian is recorded as receiving delegations of "*salvajes*" accompanied by one Galicia Chimalpopoca; the group that made the most impact were the Kikapoo.[68] The country eventually settled down into "a grave-like peace" for the last third of the century (1876–1911) under Porfirio Díaz, becoming increasingly stable, but it also moved rapidly to the right.[69]

If much religious practice became more locally orientated or even individual and private during the middle years of the nineteenth century, as Beezley has suggested, the Church, which had begun to slowly reorganize itself, began to regain some of its former status during the Porfiriato. By the 1880s, a measure of reconciliation between church and state had been negotiated. New dioceses were created and bishops ordained as young and newly trained priests arrived back from Rome in an attempt to give new impetus to Roman Catholicism. Pilgrimages to Tepeyac and the shrine of the Virgin of Guadalupe were reinstated and the Virgin was "crowned" in 1895. These developments enabled the dance to come out into the open once again and its practitioners to renew obligations that had not been possible for many years, although there was clearly still anti-Indian feeling in Mexico City.[70] Jefe Manuel Luna told of a Conchero jefe from Guanajuato who came to Mexico City with his dancers to pray in the cathedral. Accused of witchcraft, he was jailed for fifteen days while his supporters waited for him in a park situated in the Zocalo. Miraculously, he was released looking better than when he had entered as the "Virgencita" had given him succor in the form of food and drink. Manuel Luna described this event as having been "many years ago," before he was born, probably during the Porfiriato. He indicated also that the jefe had come to the capital to get permission from the Palabra General to raise a second palabra in the Bajio, which suggests an ongoing collaboration between dancers in the Bajio and in the city of Mexico in the late nineteenth century.[71]

Although the Porfiriato was a period of national consolidation, it was also a period of rapid social change linked to technological development: railways and bridges were constructed and large civic buildings and monuments built. A statue to Cuauhtémoc, located on the lavishly laid out Paseo de la Reforma, was unveiled in 1887 and thirty-four other statues followed, mostly of independence- or reform-era heroes. Tramways crossed the city, electric lights were put up, and the first electric tortilla machine began operation. Mexico City became during Porfirio Diaz's regime the alluring capital city of a modern industrializing nation, at least at its center, while on its peripheries a rapidly growing migrant population was settling. The city more than doubled in size between 1877 and 1910, growing from 300,000 to 700,000, and this population further increased during the Mexican Revolution. Many lived in close quarters, the lucky ones in the tenements (or *vecindades*) in the center, but more often in simple dwellings they constructed themselves further out. The migrants were attracted to the city's possibilities and most worked long hours for low wages.[72] It is from this time too that the testimony of the dancers themselves begins.

## THE TESTIMONY OF COMPADRE ERNESTO

Ernesto Ortiz Ramirez, jefe of Santo Niño de Atocha, came from a family of dancers, his father from Queretero and his mother from Guanajuato, where she had been born.[73] The couple moved to Mexico City just before their son's birth—on November 2, 1902—and settled in the Colonia Morelos, where Ernesto started to dance at about the age of ten. Other dancers who had also come from the Bajio (from Queretero, Guanajuato, and San Miguel de Allende) began their city lives in the same colonia. Now an inner-city district, it was at that time on the periphery and the land was "up for grabs." Ernesto remembered, "One oratorio was in front, another to one side, another two blocks away." In the early twentieth century there were still relatively few dancers from the Bajio, their dance activities were concentrated predominantly in that colonia and the neighboring one of Guerrero. Once more dancers had settled there and the groups became better established, however, their dances became more widely dispersed. In general, today no one part of the city has a greater concentration of dancers than any other; oratorios are widespread and found in many districts.

Ernesto's parents were not conquerors; they had not "opened the way" in the city. The right to dance there had been established by the Gutierrez family, who had come in the late nineteenth century. Before I say more about Ernesto Ortiz, I will outline the conquest by that mesa, which today still leads one of the predominant palabras in Mexico City and with which Santo Niño de Atocha is associated.

## THE RELIQUIA (RE)ESTABLISHES THE
## DANCE IN MEXICO CITY

The Reliquia General raised its banner in Mexico City in 1876.[74] It is said that Jesus Gutierrez "came conquering from the Bajio" with the standard (the *reliquia* or physical relic) and a document and assumed the position of Captain General de las Danzas de Tenochtitlan during the last decades of the nineteenth century.[75] The physical standard, the Reliquia, is seen as marking the moment when the dance came out into the open again. Apparently, it still exists and has many more images on it than most do now and, although in tatters, is jealously guarded; no photos have ever been permitted.[76] After the death of Jesus Gutierrez, his palabra passed to his wife, Andrea Rodriguez, and her brothers, who acted as captains. Thereafter, Andrea's son, Ignacio Gutierrez Rodriguez, inherited the position probably in the late 1920s and became a powerful and effective general from the 1930s onward.[77]

The years of the Revolution had been hard ones for the dance and it more or less disappeared completely. Many were killed, oratorios destroyed, and the dancers "arms" stolen or "burnt."[78] In 1919, dances in public places were banned.[79] During the anticlerical, right-wing presidency of Calles (1924–1934), church education was curtailed (especially at primary level), manifestations of Catholic ritual were banned (such as processions and open-air services), and priests were required to register with the government. In 1926, the bishops in response suspended the holding of mass and Semana Santa was not celebrated in 1927. Many churches were closed and the one at Tlatelolco was converted into an archive. It was even suggested that the church at La Villa that housed the Virgin of Guadalupe be turned into a museum celebrating the revolution. The actions of Calles caused bitter conflict between church and state, culminating in the war of the Cristeros (1926–1929) but did little to further the Revolution's goals of emancipation and enlightenment.[80]

As early as 1922, Vicente Marquez apparently instigated the Corporación de Concheros, an alternative form of confraternity that was less clearly Catholic. He called together "all those who had been Captains before the Revolution" to form his Corporación, which Stone describes as being a unique kind of group.[81] The Corporación (or Cooperación) de Concheros is still going strong today but, along with several other mesas, has always remained outside the Union General, formed by the Reliquia and Santiago Tlatelolco (see Chapter 8).[82]

The revolution also triggered a period of fervent ideological activity. Many intellectuals felt that it was of the utmost importance to forge a meaningful national identity: Gamio called his 1916 book *Forging the Nation*. Although the revolutionaries' project had some Porfirian antecedents (described as "a pallid cerebral and arty indigenismo"), the Indigenismo of the 1920s predominantly had social aspirations and a more genuine concern for and interest in the indigenes and their cultures. Under Vasconcelos, as minister of education, the building of schools was undertaken and the arts encouraged. With time these schools became the principal propagators of nationalism (children saluted the national flag often daily). Many during this period saw the Aztec past not only as *the* source for building the Mexican nation but also wanted to see a connection between it and living indigenes, particularly in the 1930s.[83] A vast project was begun to document and promote indigenous cultures.[84] For some, such as Vasconcelos, who identified himself as a mestizo rather than a Creole, the indigenes were seen as superior national "stock" to be "grafted" in, and others described them as "brave, faithful, frugal, virtuous" and "moral in character" with an "ability to change" because of their "latent energies."[85] Although indigenes were seen to be just as capable as (if not more so than) mestizos, much of the discourse still had racist overtones. Even Vasconcelos implied that indigenes lacked historical agency, and to the majority, they continued to be seen as degenerate, miserable, and languishing in ignorance.[86] The predominant aim was to turn the indigenes into mestizos by means of education. As the left-wing president Cardenas stated, he wanted not to "Indianize Mexico but to Mexicanize the Indigenes."[87]

The Cardenas sexennial (1934–1940) helped to improve the lot of Mexico's indigenous people considerably. He established close contact with many and convened the first of a series of Indigenous Congresses in 1936. Attitudes toward the indigines were changing in the city too. What had been an unmistakable and pernicious racism in the nineteenth century and the early decades of the twentieth century was gradually disappearing. The clear-cut demarcation between the mestizo who had some white blood and the indigene who had none was being replaced by a more sophisticated cultural model that masked the racist element, at least in the minds of those in the higher echelons. Migrants who came to the cities were seen as part of a class rather than a separate race and culturally mestizo even if they still practiced many of their rural (indigenous) practices in the home.

But the process of rapid urban growth and subsequent proletarianization of those who had migrated was not linked to secularization. The Cristiada (or Cristero war) had demonstrated how strong Roman Catholicism was in Mexico. Dioceses were divided up and more parishes created as the churches reopened, which became increasingly easy to do after 1940, when Camacho as president declared himself a believer and chose not to apply those articles in the constitution that were anticlerical. The image of the Virgin of Guadalupe was brought out from her hiding place and reinstalled in a newly renovated church at Tepeyac, where in 1933 she was pronounced patron of all Latin America.[88]

After the churches reopened and renewed the possibility of holding processions and other religious rituals in public places once again, the dance recovered under the generalship of Ignacio Gutierrez (Tata Nacho).[89] He had many jefes and "many troops" under his command (*mando*) in the Reliquia General.[90] The dance gradually renewed itself under his leadership and he also gave it a firm organization. He probably also established during the 1930s and 1940s a greater degree of independence from the Bajio. His sons, known as the brothers Gutierrez, danced for a while but then disappeared. One, Florencio, went to Guadalajara and lost contact with his father for many years. When Tata Nacho died in 1960, his wife, Felipa Sanchez, became the generala for a while. Because his sons were not around, Guadalupe Hernandez, who had been one of Tata Nacho's captains, was named as inheritor but was unable to assume the position for quite some time for his claim was not supported by some of the more significant dancers (such as Gabriel Osorio, Felipe Aranda, and Manuel Luna). Eventually, however, he was recognized as the general "representing" the Reliquia.[91]

Guadalupe Hernandez's own mesa is that of the Virgen de San Juan de los Lagos and the cross of Santa Cruz de Catedral in Chalma is in his care. He has also raised several mesas.[92] Guadalupe Hernandez is still dancing today, is comparatively young, and was one of the generals with whom Compadre Ernesto as a member of the Reliquia was closely associated. Guadalupe Hernandez's power base became stronger still after the death in 1993 of General Manuel Luna, who came from the other paramount palabra in the city, that of Santiago Tlatelolco.

## THE PALABRA OF SANTIAGO TLATELOLCO

The Palabra of Santiago Tlatelolco was raised in Mexico City in 1883 in Calle Mina, located in the Colonia Industrial, by Maximino Tellez.[93] It was passed to Ignacio Becerra (probably in the early decades of this century), whose daughter, Ester, became the wife of Manual Luna. There is a certain amount of dispute as to whether Tlatelolco or the Reliquia raised its banner first in the city, but as has been shown earlier, these are the kinds of internecine disagreements that still go on to this day.[94]

The Palabra of Santiago Tlatelolco certainly achieved ascendancy in the city in the early twentieth century but the Reliquia challenged this position during the lifetime of Ignacio Gutierrez. In the latter part of the century, Manuel Luna became the most important general, while Guadalupe Hernandez, as inheritor of the Reliquia, had to bide his time. The Reliquia may well once again achieve the paramount position, although in the late 1980s the various generals were striving to achieve a *gobierno* (government) in which all would cooperate, as had been the case in the middle of the century.

## THE GOBIERNO

In the early 1940s, the first priest in charge of Santiago Tlatelolco after its return to the Catholic Church suggested that the dancers of Santiago Tlatelolco call themselves the "Association of Religious Dancers that pertains to the Church of Santiago de Tlatelolco." This association or alliance was to include all the mesas of that palabra and those of the Reliquia too. He also offered the use of the church as the *cuartel general* (headquarters), an arrangement that carries on to this day. During this period, the dance was linked quite strongly to the Church and most jefes were devout Roman Catholics.[95]

Within this union, there were two clear-cut governments. General Manuel Luna led one, allied with groups such as that of Fidel Morales and Guadalupe Alvarez, whereas General Ignacio Gutierrez led the other with the brothers Barrera and Felix Hernandez. During that time, at any one dance one of the jefes from the Reliquia played the role of the jefe superior, assigning the dance spaces to all the groups who were present. According to Guadalupe Hernandez's recollections, it was Felix Hernandez at Chalma, the Barrera brothers at Los Remedios, and General Ignacio Gutierrez at La Villa on December 12. From the other gobierno, Manuel Luna with Fidel Morales led the dance at Tlatelolco. This division of responsibilities clearly indicates that the Reliquia was at that time the more powerful of the two.

By the mid-1950s, the strong alliance between the two governments had begun to decline, although at Chalma in 1958, Ignacio Gutierrez and Manuel Luna came together once again. The new alliance and hence its re-empowerment did not to last long, however, for in the 1960s Ignacio Gutierrez died and as Guadalupe Hernandez was not immediately able to assert himself as general, an erosion of the organization occurred, enabling Santiago Tlatelolco to begin to regain ascendancy.[96] Thereafter, for some years each group in the Reliquia went its own way (including that of Compadre Ernesto).

Guadalupe Hernandez suggested that this breakdown was triggered by Ignacio Gutierrez's death. It is clear that Tata Nacho, as he is still fondly referred to by many dancers, was extremely charismatic and that without his powerful personality, a vacuum was created in which the carefully structured supportive organization that he had built up for the dance rapidly began to disintegrate. Compadre Ernesto recalled how prior to that time the various mesas had cooperated over matters of health (just as confraternities had done in the past). Money was collected in a wooden box at a dance by a sergeant who visited the various oratorios to attend to and care for those dancers with health problems.[97] Gradually, the dance lost much of its discipline and drive, as the rehearsals before dances, which were de rigueur during Tata Nacho's lifetime, became less common and conformity within the circle of the dance was not enforced as strongly.

The changes were probably also related in part to the opening up of the dance when, from the point of view of some jefes, the tradition began to loose its integrity, for during this period the dance was drawn into an external arena that was secular rather then religious. Stone mentions the differences of opinion about whether the dances should have become part of a "government section called 'National Dances.'"[98] Certainly, as the dance became more widely known, many city groups opened up to *banqueteros* or *gente de la banqueta*, that is, people from the city who did not come from dance families. This was in part necessary as many had become too small or introverted and were badly in need of new blood.

The transformation was also the result of the socio-cultural climate. By the 1960s, the focus of interest in and acceptance of Mexico's indigenous peoples with their still-distinctive cultures had changed once again. The previous program of desired assimilation was gradually changing into one of acceptance of indigenous difference. The indigenes were not quite yet citizens (and many indigenes did not get the vote until the 1980s), but they were at least seen as part of the nation. The indigenes began to have a more active voice by the 1970s, and many started to demand from the very body that had educated them full citizenship and the *reinvindicacion* of their ethnic rights.[99] The Instituto Nacional Indigenista (INI) was increasingly criticized for its earlier role of incorporation, and in the late 1970s redoubled its efforts to aid the dissemination of indigenous languages rather than seeking their demise. This period marked the beginning of the rise in "Indianity," which allowed for the emergence of the Mexica movement in the late 1980s. By that time, Compadre Ernesto had finally reestablished his own mesa of Santa Niño de Atocha. I will now trace his path to this position.

## ERNESTO ORTIZ AND HIS MESAS

Although the family of Ernesto Ortiz did not conquer in the city, they were of standing in the Bajio. His mother, Dominga Ramirez, had had a mesa, which she may have founded, called the Mesa de San Juan de los Lagos, associated with the place of that name in Jalisco that recognized the Reliquia. After her death, the inheritance passed to Ernesto and he became captain of the mesa and headed it from 1922 onward. Meanwhile his sister, Dolores (Lola), had married Gabriel (or Graviel) Osorio, whose mesa was that of Santo Niño de Atocha. When Compadre Ernesto's oratory burned down in 1942, he decided some years later to join his sister and her husband and to dance with Santo Nino de Atocha as an adjunct (*adjunto*) (see Appendix 5).

Gabriel Osorio died in about 1958 and Dolores became the jefa of the group. Ernesto stayed on to give her support as her *sombra* (literally, shadow or protector). The children of Dolores (the most recent of Gabriel Osorio's wives and thus those most eligible for inheritance), Remedios and Ramon, were very young at the time of his death and were not then interested in (or capable of) inheriting the group. Some time later, Dolores installed four captains for the mesa, as is traditional, before she died in 1973. Two of these captains, Cruz Hernandez and Guadalupe Torres, departed, each to form his own mesa, both called Santo Niño de Atocha, leaving the other two captains, Pedro Rodriguez and Teresa Osorio (known as Mejia). Teresa was the daughter of Gabriel by an earlier wife and the *compañera* (partner) of Pedro Rodriguez.

Although not a captain of that mesa, Ernesto Ortiz and his wife, Maria Robles, a Yaqui indigene whom he had married in 1924, supported his sister's mesa throughout this period (and were at times economically dependent on her). Another person linked to the mesa at this time was Andres Segura, also an adjunct. Together, Ernesto and Andres Segura collaborated in the transmission of the tradition in various ways, including appearances in the film *El es Dios* (directed by Guillermo Bonfil) and a record "Danzas de la Conquista."[100] The film shows Compadre Ernesto living simply (without running water and sanitary facilities) still on the outskirts of Mexico City but by then some considerable distance from its center: by 1960 the city had more than 5 million inhabitants. He had previously worked as a builder and occasionally as a factory worker, and he also had fabricated *artesanias*. By the time of the film, he was making ends meet by means of the dance itself and went every Sunday to perform outside the cathedral. There, dressed in more minimal (Aztec-style) clothing than that usually worn for an obligation, he and a handful of younger dancers aimed to attract the public by their Conchero dancing, which included acrobatic embellishments, such as doing the splits.[101]

The film (and other documentation from this period) also shows the Concheros carrying the national flag, although this is never seen today. In 1978, most members of the mesa—together with Don Faustino Rodriguez from Tepetlixpa, Compadre Ernesto's spiritual brother (see Chapter 8), and Teresa Mejia—went on a pilgrimage to Santiago de Compostela in Spain. However, there were personal tensions. On their return Andres Segura left the group and

Teresa Mejia also separated from the family mesa after she was left by her companion in 1976.[102] Teresa's brother, Florencio Osorio, had formed his own mesa some time previously. He is professionally a *voceador* (town crier). Voceadors are usually the first to arrive in Chalma and are said to "open the road." One of the large crosses at Chalma, the Santa Cruz del Perdon de Penetencias, is in the charge of his mesa. According to Angelica, six mesas, all called Santo Niño de Atocha, have come out of Gabriel Osorio's original mesa.[103]

It is not clear where the finances for the trip to Spain came from, although the filmmakers had a wide range of contacts in professional and more moneyed circles and may well have secured funds for the mesa. No dancer ever wants to admit that any funding for the dance has been received from an outside source, although it is clear that there are individuals who are happy to act as sponsors. Most Concheros highly value their self-sufficiency and independence. Occasionally, money may have been channeled their way by the INI and they may even have been co-opted for spectacular occasions.[104] Nonetheless, the way in which one group can best insult another is by implying that its continuing existence depends on subventions from outsiders, whether from the INI or the PRI (Institutional Revolutionary Party).[105]

By the late 1970s, Ernesto Ortiz was left with the few dancers of the original mesa of Santo Niño de Atocha who had not gone elsewhere. Because of his long association with Santo Niño while serving as his sister's sombra, he adopted the group as his own, allying it (or reaching conformity with) his original group of San Juan de los Lagos, his true mesa of inheritance. Although he has no clear right to be jefe of Santo Niño de Atocha, as the brother-in-law of a former jefe he can be seen as an inheritor. As Angelica put it, "he has on one side San Juan de los Lagos and on the other Santo Niña de Atocha." This situation never sat well with Teresa (Osorio) Mejia.

Compadre Ernesto had already begun to draw in people born in the city who had come across the dance but who had no previous connection to it, such as Antonia and Angelica. Many, however, unlike these two, did not have the long-term dedication brought to the dance by those whose families had been dancers for decades. Some—such as Andres Segura, who formed his own group, Xinachtli (Chapter 8)—showed that he had little respect for the tradition and was seduced early on by Mexicanidad (Chapter 10).

Mexico was once again changing rapidly, as was the mesa. By the 1970s, the population of Mexico City had reached 9 million and by 1980 it was 14 million. The year 1968, which had brought the killing of hundreds of students at Tlatelolco, also saw students demonstrating in many other parts of the world against government repression. The following decade was a time of growing internationalism. Increasingly, the compadre and his mesa (and that of Andres Segura as well) gained cultural recognition elsewhere as the Indian *reivindicación* movement took off in the United States. Santo Niño de Atocha was invited twice in 1976 by the Mohawks to tour the United States, visiting indigenous reservations, Chicano communities, cultural centers, and universities. The following year the group visited Guatemala after the earthquake. As already indicated, an initial visit had been made to Santiago de Compostela in Spain in 1978. A second trip was made in 1992 "in conformity" with the mesa Insignias Aztecas, resulting in that group raising a mesa in Spain: Santa Cruz Espiral del Senor Santiago de Compostela.

In 1988, the mesa visited New York City, invited by Nur, the leader of the Sufi group Neredin.[106] The number of cultural occasions and visits abroad, particularly to the United States, continued to grow during the next decade as awareness of Mexico's indigenous past increased both before and immediately after the celebrations for the 500-year anniversary of the discovery of the Americas held in 1992.

Finally in 1995, Compadre Ernesto received the long overdue acknowledgement of his position in the dance and was officially named a general. In the same year, the interpersonal jostling for the succession of his group, which had been going on since the early 1990s (Chapter 8), finally ended when Ernesto Ortiz named his great-nephew (Ricardo López Ortiz) as his inheritor. Compadre Ernesto died—or as the Concheros say, was *llamadó a cuentas*—in June 1997.

# TEN

# THE MEXICA AND MEXICANIDAD

In this penultimate chapter, I look at those dancers who call themselves Mexica and identify with the movement loosely known as Mexicanidad. Although some Concheros become involved in identity politics, as indicated in the previous chapter, to the temporary detriment of the harmony of the dance, the Mexica tend to be involved far more frequently in interpersonal power struggles. The Mexica dance the same dances as the Concheros but give them a different ethos, have a somewhat different perspective on their origins and raison d'être, and are much less interested in spiritual attainment. By the articulation of often-invented meanings, the Mexica are seeking to create new identities for themselves.[1] Mexicanidad is, in effect, concerned with proto-nationalism, "a kind of radical nationalism with millenarian tendencies."[2]

The aim of this chapter is to give a synopsis of the ideology of Mexicanidad in order to provide the context for assessing in the final chapter the longer-term influence of the Mexica on the Concheros. The Mexica participate in a wide range of activities of which dancing, although important, is but one strand of a larger project. They see themselves as the carriers of Aztec knowledge, which by the twentieth century had become predominantly vestigial. Their prime concern is with *reivindicación*, that is, the re-creation of the pre-Hispanic past. They aim to reawaken the Mexican people to the significance of the Aztec era. In some ways, the Mexica have no place in this book as they do not consider themselves to be Concheros and the Concheros do not recognize Mexica

10.1. Mexica dancer playing a drum.

groups as part of their association. However, the notion that the forms of today's dances are directly descended from those of the Aztecs is an idea now shared by many Concheros. During my early fieldwork, I mixed and mingled

192

with many Mexica dancers and some of the leaders of Mexicanidad but they did not welcome me or encourage me to spend time, let alone dance, with them. I assumed this was because I was a woman and apparently a "gringa." However, Lauro Ayala Serrano, a Mexican anthropologist, indicates that he was also kept at arm's length and that many leaders refused to be interviewed by him.[3]

As far as the Concheros are concerned, the Mexica have brought unacceptable changes to the dance: they are accused not only of failing to maintain but also of politicizing the tradition. They dress distinctively and play different musical instruments, choosing pre-Hispanic drums rather than the stringed *concha* as they are aware of its European origin. They also dance more individualistically and much faster. They have rejected many of the Concheros' ritual practices, such as holding all-night vigils, singing *alabanzas*, and saying prayers. The Concheros' leitmotif—union, conformity, and conquest—is never seen on their standards and "El es Dios" is never heard during a dance. Instead, the more political exclamation "Mexica tiahui" (Mexica onward) is usually exclaimed, particularly at a dance's end. Whereas the Concheros use few words and prefer to let the dance speak for itself, the Mexica tend to talk incessantly, have multiple explanations about it and prefer not to listen (even to each other). Their dance is, from the Concheros' point of view, a "detraditionalized" form.[4] Their significance to this book lies in the influence that they have exerted over the Concheros in the last decade or so.

One of the aims of Mexicanidad is to rid Mexico of the Gauchupines (a derogatory term for the Spanish and their descendants) and their imported and imposed cultural practices. The Catholic Church and Catholicism are anathema to them and they aim to restore Aztec religiosity. They talk not of God but of *teotl*, but not as a theistic equivalent of the Christian God. The *teteoh* (plural of "teotl") "refers not to anthropomorphized deities but rather to the elements of life (fire, earth, sun, moon, water)," that is, to depersonalized manifestations of energy, although some claim these represent aspects of humanity—"appreciated, fine, intense, marvelous, magnificent."[5] The teteoh are some of the various manifestations of Ometeotl, the Aztec's supreme deity.[6] It is important to stress that all Mexica without fail are firmly committed to the belief that the Aztecs did not commit human sacrifice, despite strong archaeological evidence to the contrary.[7]

Rather than mesas, the Mexica have *kalpultin*, the Aztec term for small self-governing communities.[8] Unlike a mesa, a *kalpulli* is not primarily a ritual grouping but rather a more political organization whose purpose is to structure the lives of its members in an all-embracing manner. Some Mexica live communally and most claim (or at least attempt in part) to conduct their daily lives in as Aztec a way as possible. Each kalpulli has a leader, usually the founder, who makes most of the decisions and decides on the practices of the group and, more importantly, its precise ideology. There are much greater differences among kalpultin than there are among mesas. Many do not endure for long because the frequent struggles for power, linked to disagreements among members over ideology, can usually only be resolved by dissolution or by splits and regroupings. Despite these huge differences, kalpultin share the core philosophy of Mexicayotl, which asserts an all-embracing revindication of the Aztec past. A brief historical overview of Mexicayotl's development is essential to understand both Mexicanidad (as the movement is called today) and the Mexica themselves.[9]

## MEXICAYOTL

Aztec sources provide fertile opportunities for a reinvention of the past for much of the information we have is pictographic or complied by friars, such as Sahagún, shortly after the Conquest and far from complete. The Mexica consider some of this evidence to be specious and have rejected many of the historical facts while fabricating others, thereby putting themselves in a powerful position to reimagine that past.[10] Mexicanidad, then, has not emerged from an ongoing oral tradition but is rather an invented tradition that is literature based.

Mexicayotl as an ideology was first expounded in a book of that name published in 1969. Characterized by a strident nationalist and messianic message, it depends predominantly on spurious scholarship. It confounds historical time, mixing the various high cultures of Mexico, such as that of the Mayas, Olmecs, and Toltecs (which were powerful at different places and times from 1500 BC to AD 1500), and makes no distinction between Aztec culture and the earlier cultures in Teotihuacan. All, it is claimed, spoke Nahuatl. The idea that the Aztecs did not commit human sacrifice is also found in this volume.[11] Rodolfo Nieva is undoubtedly the author of *Mexicayotl* (although the book is published in his sister's name, Maria del Carmen Nieva), but it was he who masterminded and gave cohesion to this pro-cultural movement. A lawyer who also worked as a journalist, he claimed in the 1930s to be of Creole descent for he was by birth part of Mexico City's elite.

Unions, social organizations, and movements of all types flourished at that time. Some had the welfare of the country's indigenous population at heart,[12] but many more were as reactionary as the one started by Nieva.[13] Others were cultural, such as the Indigenous Confederation of Mexico, founded in the 1930s by Juan Luna Cardenas.[14] Cardenas claimed descent from a noble line of Aztecs and his alias was Juan Metzli. He organized various rituals in the village of Hueyapan (in Morelos) and a school (*calmecac*) in Mexico City, where he taught classes in Nahuatl and on the Aztec calendar. This renewed interest in the Aztec past reflected a trend among intellectuals and artists (see Chapter 6).

Nieva had become loosely involved with his group in the early 1950s. By then, he had already begun to develop a double identity: on the one hand, he was very much part of the hegemonic world of the professional mestizo. He worked in the offices of the Federal District in Mexico City, a position he desired to better, and was involved with predominantly mainstream organizations (such as the National Civic Association). At the same time, he was becoming seriously involved in a politics of Indianity that was very different from the state's model of Indigenismo. He no longer called himself a Creole but declared himself an indigene and by 1959 had established the Confederated Movement for the Restoration of Anahuac (MCRA). Through this organization he could direct his nationalist inclinations toward glorifying the imperial Aztec past. He had taken too the significant step of renouncing Catholicism, as the movement became the means whereby he sought to overcome his identity crisis.[15]

Membership of the MCRA was predominantly middle class and professional; some were Freemasons and most resided in Mexico City. The activities of this network were many and varied and involved the publication of the newspaper *Izkalotl* (Resurgence). This first appeared in 1960 and contained articles on the Aztec past and a variety of ideas about how that past might be re-created; it is still published sporadically today. Cultural and commemorative gatherings were organized for Aztec culture heroes, such as Cuauhtémoc (the last Aztec tlatoani, who was killed by the Spaniards), whereas Spanish heroes, such as Cortés, were belittled.[16]

In 1967, Nieva went further when he founded the political party El Partido de la Mexicanidad, by means of which he aimed to compete for the presidency in the elections of 1968.[17] However, he died suddenly and his demise was linked to various otherworldly causes: that it was not yet the moment for the Fifth Sun (which I discuss below) or that the indigenous *sacerdotes* (sages) of Texcoco, although consulted regularly about the activities of all the groups involved in Mexicayotl, did not approve of this latest move.[18] This was, however, also the beginning of a time of repression—marked by the massacre of students at Tlatelolco in 1968—as Mexico faced not only an economic crisis as growing pauperization caused migration to the cities but also one of values and identity.

After Nieva's death, his sister, Maria del Carmen, took over the movement, severing it from mainstream politics. With the term "culture" added to its name, the MCRCA (the Movimiento Confedorado Restaurador de la Cultura de Anahuac) still existed in the early 1990s, albeit in a rather residual form. Maria del Carmen put most of her energies into teaching Nahuatl, although she had never fully mastered that language.[19] She elaborated cultural ceremonies and dances, such as the "Autochthonous Dance of Happiness," which was an Aztec-style marriage known as the "creating of duality" (or the binding of the *tilmatl*). She also held beauty contests for which she dressed in floor-length Spanish lace dresses.[20]

By the late 1970s, the MCRCA had started some ten kalpultin in and around Mexico City.[21] Eventually, a number of independent organizations appeared, such as Zem Anauk Tlamachtiloyan (ZAT; Center for Preamerican Culture). Formed in 1977, it was a cultural association for "the defense, investigation, teaching, and recovery of 'our' old cultures."[22] Among those involved was Maria del Carmen, by then known by the Aztec name of Izcalotzin.[23]

The MCRA had little interest in rural indigenous people nor in the ordinary people who lived at the height of Tenochtitlan's ascendancy. Rather, it aimed to restore the urban imperial Aztec past but without such aspects as the frequent payment of tribute dues, the extremes of stratification, and human sacrifice. Nieva and his sister traveled frequently in their Mercedes Benz to visit indigenous men of knowledge in various communities around Mexico City. One in Xochimilco, who some claim had started the M.R.C.A., initiated Nieva into the Consejo des Ancianos in his community and supported Nieva's view that he was of indigenous descent. Although they took the time to consult with these indigenes, they thought of these people as being from a very different world and never saw them as social equals, or even potentially so.

Revelations were important too in the search for the past. Of great significance was the so-called *consigna* (order or instruction) that the last tlatoani Cuauhtémoc was said to have left just before the capitulation of Tenochtitlan. Many claim to have received this mandate and the accounts of when and where this occurred are numerous.[24] The importance of Cuauhtémoc had increased throughout the nineteenth century and his appropriation as a cult figure became increasingly frequent by mutualist societies and Masonic lodges; the Aztec Lodge held a wake for him in 1890.[25] In a spectacular "discovery" in 1949, his bones were unearthed in the church of Ixcateopan (in Guerrero). According to the oral tradition of the community, ten generations of "secret guardians" had been established to protect the mandate of Cuauhtémoc and the secret of his tomb. These were revealed in 1949 because of a prophecy that Cuauhtémoc would return at the time of "the value five" (the Fifth Sun).[26] The finds were endorsed by the then-governor of the state and published by the newspaper *El Universal* (for which Nieva wrote a column), and Eulalia Guzmán, a historian with strong Mexicoyotl leanings, was sent to investigate.[27] Her opinion was that the bones were bona fide, a supposition that found support with many, including the painter Diego Rivera. After public outcry, however, two further investigations decided otherwise and confirmed that the bones were the remains of several women and a child.

## THE FIFTH SUN

The Suns were distinct eras in Aztec thought.[28] The end of the fourth and the arrival of the fifth had been imminent for a while. Many claimed that it occurred in 1985, when the Age of Aquarius began—according to Western astrology, whose origins are Indo-European but which can be related to astrological calculations based on the Aztec Calendar Stone—whereas Maria del Carmen picked September 21, 1999. Overall, this temporal confusion can be read in two ways: as a failure to sever Aztecquismo from European thought (a frequent occurrence for many Mexica) or as an attempt to show that Aztec thought predates that of Europe or at the very least is global in its nature. Interestingly, the date is always given according to the Gregorian calendar.

## MEXICANIDAD TODAY: NAHUI MITL

According to Tlakaelel, who claims direct descent from the Texcocan poet Netzahualcoyotl, the Fifth Sun began in 1975.[29] He published his autobiography *Nahui Mitl* (1992), written with the assistance of at least one anthropologist, by means of which he aimed to perpetuate the culture of Anahuac by unifying the indigenous peoples of all America. According to myth, the Chichimeca (see Chapter 9), after they had arrived in the Valley of Mexico in the thirteenth century, ritually threw four arrows (the nahui mitl) to bring together the indigenous peoples from the four directions. Tlakaelel had previously traveled extensively to the "four directions" and revived vanishing traditions.[30] He founded his own kalpulli, known as Koakalco, and started others with the same name in the United States and Canada. His kalpulli is probably best known for its sun dance, taken directly from a Sioux Lakota tradition and quite different in both form and content from the Concheros' dance of the sun. The four-day ritual involves fasting and abstinence (even from water), self-sacrifice in the form of bloodletting from the chest and arms, and (men only) being strung up from the branches of trees by maguey ropes pushed through the skin of their shoulders.[31] Despite the nature of this ritual, Tlakaelel has drawn a large number of followers. This ritual usually takes place in the indigenous community of Ocuilan near Chalma. Its residents gain neither benefit nor admission, and a good number of the celebrants are best characterized by their blond hair and expensive cars.[32]

Tlakaelel claims to have "trained" and to have strong connections with some of the less extreme proponents of Mexicanidad.[33]

## NEW OR COSMOPOLITAN MEXICANIDAD

In contrast to the Mexicanidad of Tlakaelel, which is highly nationalistic despite the inclusion of a Sioux ritual, New Mexicanidad is much less overtly so. Its discourse is more cosmopolitan, spiritual, esoteric, and New Age and much less xenophobic. As a predominantly middle-class subculture, it is better able to accept or tolerate difference.[34] The person most closely associated with it is the popular writer Antonio Velasco Piña. His best-selling novels have looked sometimes at the Aztec past (e.g., *Tlacaélel*) but more usually at what he believes should be happening in Mexico at present. He is one of the many now involved in various Eastern and esoteric traditions (Buddhism, Hinduism, and the Hermetic Tradition) and their forms, (e.g., Tai Chi, transcendental meditation, and yoga). Those drawn to his writings are enthused by his suggestion that Mexico has an important part to play in the spiritual future of the world as its center moves westward from Tibet.[35]

Nevertheless, his fiction demonstrates the very same supremacist and messianic tendencies as did the pronouncements of the MCRA, albeit in a more sophisticated and less acerbic form. It also points to the national sense of inferiority explored earlier by others.[36] A movement has come out of Velasco Piña's writing known as the Reginas, based on a fictional character of that name, whose followers celebrate encounters with ritual representatives from various sacred traditions.[37] They travel to the different chakras of planet Earth and cleanse and purify the sacred places of power, both elsewhere and in and around Mexico City, such as Amátlan in Morelos.[38] Most of Velasco Piña's followers are middle- or upper middle-class Mexicans, many of them female with money and time to spare. They usually wear red headbands (*izcoahuecatl*), which effectively is the uniform of the more spiritual Mexicanistas. Velasco Piña has introduced his own form of dance, known as Citlalmina, that combines Tibetan dances with elements from those of the Concheros.[39] He has had close contact with many mesas for years. For him, his fictional Regina actually lived and, it is claimed, he asked Don Faustino to help bury the remains of Regina near the volcano of Iztaccíhuatl, close to Tepetlixpla where Don Faustino's mesa was based.[40]

## A NATIVIST SPIRITUALITY?

The cosmopolitan Mexicanidad of Velasco Piña is more clearly spiritual than other forms. It has culled beliefs and practices from many global traditions, some more esoteric or mystical than others. However since Nieva's rejection of Catholicism and the publication of *Mexicayotl* in 1969, one of the aims has always been to regenerate the cosmological beliefs of the Aztecs, an objective that today's Mexica take very seriously.

Tlakaelel recently provided a clear statement on his position. He has with age become less xenophobic and confrontational and more interested in the mystical and spiritual side of "his inheritance." In 1993 he registered his organization In Katonal (House of the Sun) as a church, for which he submitted documents that laid out his beliefs. These included a list of Aztec deities and their powers, although he stated, "effectively we do not worship different gods but rather venerate the expression of the Great Spirit in both nature and ourselves."[41] His spirituality enables devotees to draw closer to the "Great Spirit," the "Universal Creator," but surprisingly by means of practices that are apparently North American in origin—such as the stringing up of the body and the smoking of the sacred pipe.[42]

Tlakaelel's prescriptions appear to combine a form of polytheism (of which the various saints in the Catholic Church are also an example) with a pantheism in which there lurks an apparent monotheism (thus, possibly pleasing to the authorities, as would be the almost Christian emphasis on all "human beings" being "brothers").[43] Ometoetl is usually considered the supreme deity of the Aztecs, but Tlakaelel describes Ometoetl instead as the principle of duality and plays up the significance of Mexicayotl as *the* way or the supreme organizing force at the expense of Ometeotl.[44]

The various entities usually classified as deities, such as Huitzilopochtli, Quetzalcoatl, and Ometeotl, are seen by Tlakaelel and many Mexica as representations of energies. Some of these are elemental to life itself, such as the sun (Tonal Teotl). Others represent aspects of humanity or the self; Quetzalcoatl signifies cosmic intelligence and Tezcatlipoca, memory) Huehueteotl, the deity of fire, is seen as fire itself and as ancestral energy.[45] Importantly, to the Mexica Huitzilopochtli is not the deity who at the time of the Aztecs demanded frequent human sacrifice to assist the sun to rise every day, but rather he is an abstract and powerful energy described by some as the sun itself.

Most Mexica do not want to call this religiosity for in their minds the term is coterminous with European hegemony, repression, and manipulation (in other words, Catholicism). They are in the position of having no ongoing Aztec or even indigenous practices on which to base their rituals and have mostly (re)invented their own—such as the New Year Ritual or the "seeding" (choosing) of names—which may account for why Tlakaelel felt the need to incorporate long-standing rituals from North America.

For most, Mexicanidad is not a re-ligio, a re-joining with the kinds of tangible spiritual entities normally associated with big and little religions traditions, but represents rather an ideological position.[46] At the very least, it provides an array of entities or energies that its followers can not only identify with but also manipulate (as if they were Aztecs), and these have carefully been kept abstract. Many Mexica believe that religiosity resides in nature, not in man, and that there should be no anthropomorphic or zoomorphic figures of deities such as the Aztecs had, although I did see some plaster casts of the deity Coatlicue used for a dance. The energies or forces are those of the natural world said to be found in the ether (even in the polluted air of a city the size of Mexico City) and must be revered and respected.

As a form of religiosity, Mexicanidad would have been rejected by the authorities in Mexico a few decades ago[47]—who would have seen it as parareligion—but will now possibly become more acceptable. The Catholic Church is under increasing pressure to be more inclusive as both Protestantism and sectarianism have grown rapidly in the last few decades. And although the many followers of Mexicanidad have convinced themselves that by taking on a set of beliefs and practices (such as those propounded by Tlakaelel) they are in some way re-creating the past, many of their practices, such as the dance of the sun, have little to do with those that existed at the time of the Aztecs. Rather, a hybrid "indigenous mystical spirituality" is being developed and applied to a completely different way of life.

## NEW AGERS?

It has been suggested that New Ageism implies a freedom from previous brainwashing and the baggage of the ego, that by means of rituals or others processes the development of a self-realization or spirituality is achieved whereby authority comes from the inner or higher self by means of experience.[48] Certainly, most Mexica do not want to be followers (even of someone like Tlakaelel); they place great emphasis on the individual self-realization that comes from the inner self, not from some outside agent. The various manifestations of teotl—or "representations," as most Mexica label them—are defined more in terms of characteristics of the self than are Tlakaelel's categories and are more about solipsistic self-fulfillment. They have perhaps more in common with the terminology associated with the self-awareness of psychoanalysis than with manifestations of the cosmos. The Mexica's beliefs tend to lack an overall ethical code; there is no shared moral code between groups and sometimes not even within a group. The path of each is often in conflict with that of others, which seems to indicate that they have not distanced themselves from the baggage of the ego. They use their self-empowerment for identity politics rather than for the building of a spiritual community.[49]

The Reginas, for example, have an altogether lighter touch when talking to outsiders and much closer ties with New Age religiosity. Their beliefs and practices meld with its many strands and tend generally to be holistic, that is, able to discern the not immediately apparent connections between things; and to be mystical, inspired by spiritism and esotericism generally. They are concerned with the ecology of planet earth and with the cosmos, with extrasensory travel and the paranormal.[50]

## EARLY MEXICA INFLUENCES ON THE CONCHEROS

As mentioned in Chapter 8, as early as the 1970s General Felipe Aranda is known to have been sympathetic to the ideas of the MCRCA. He claimed descent from Moctezuma, and it has been said that his mesa dates from 1731 (in Mexico City). Although he had become an evangelist for a while, he later joined forces with the maverick Andres Segura. Together they provided a bridge between the Concheros and Mexicanidad and effectively brought the dance to the Mexica. Many of the early Mexica kalpultin were formed as offshoots of their two mesas. Even as late as the early 1990s, however, the Mexica's ideology was predominantly unacceptable to most Concheros. If Compadre Ernesto and Jefe Faustino of Tepetlixpla were invited to take part in one of the Mexica's events, they did so, such as for the ceremony for the commemoration of Velasco Piña's Regina, but their participation did not mean that they were sympathetic to Mexicanidad.

## THE MEXICA TODAY

Many have been strongly influenced by Mexicayotl although few know about Nieva or have seen the book; it has been out of print for years although xerox copies are in circulation. Tlakaelel has influenced many who see him as the living archetypal embodiment of the "indigenous warrior," and most have read the novels of Velasco Piña, the books of Carlos Castañeda, the various journals, and the vast secondary literature on Mexicayotl.

Ce-Acatl, started by long-standing supporters of the movement in 1992, is the most professionally produced of the journals.[51] It aims to unite the various groups and is concerned with the "research, diffusion and assimilation" of history "rigorously studied" without "fanaticism."[52] Published every twenty days (monthly according to the Aztec calendar), it quickly became the means by which the various kalpultin both proselytized to gain new adherents

**10.2.** Mexica dancers blowing their conch shells at Tlatelolco.

and advertised courses on the Nahuat language, philosophy, calendars, cosmic vision, astronomy and mathematics, and of course dance (*chitontiquiza*). It also disseminated information about the various Nahuat universities and meetings, such as the Annual Congress of Anahuac in Chilpancingo (first held in the late 1980s).

After the rebellion in Chiapas in 1994, however, *Ce-Acatl* changed its agenda and became more concerned with the problems and rights of today's indigenous peoples, thereby appealing to a wider audience. But its new focus was of little interest to most Mexica. In fact, when its editor suggested that some of them might be interested in helping the many indigenous people living in dire poverty on the outskirts of Mexico City, this idea was met by indifference.[53]

Overall, the Mexica are apolitical and not concerned with the city's future except where it concerns them personally. They have no interest in increasing the rights of the country's 10 million autochthones. If anything, they have a fear of the countryside and do not want to think about how such people live. Whereas the early proponents of Mexicayotl were mainly middle-class professionals with politico-cultural interests, the followers of Mexicanidad today consist of people of humbler origins but with New Age tendencies.

Predominantly, they come from non-advantaged backgrounds (urban lower middle- or working-class families). They are young and have yet to establish themselves in life and mostly operate outside the dominant economy. Indeed, many make only a precarious living (as indeed do many Concheros). In the early 1990s, I came across only a few Mexica dancers who had full-time jobs and very few professionals: one had his own business printing business cards, one trained dogs, one was an actor, and another worked for a computer company. Many often made money by means of interpersonal exchanges, such as selling artifacts for the dance to other dancers and fabricating handicrafts.[54]

Most Mexica assume a Nahuat name as part of the process of adopting a new identity, as did many of the earlier advocates of Mexicayotl. Names may be chosen intuitively or found by means of the Tonalamatl, an Aztec astrological device used to predict an individual's fate according to their date of birth. Most use these names all the time, but some keep a dual identity, using their birth names (e.g., Juan Gomez Sanchez) for the wider world and their Aztec names (e.g., Izcoatzin) for Mexica activities. The renaming ceremony is said to be free but usually involves a quite large "contribution." Reciprocal exchange is still strong among the Concheros but is not part of the Mexica's conceptual universe. Potential adherents are expected to pay not only for this ceremony but also for the practice dance classes they are asked to attend as part of their training to join a kalpulli.[55]

After the renaming ceremony, a Mexica can begin to fabricate his costume. The Mexica wear clothing based only on the Aztec codices. Men wear a loincloth (*maxtlatl*), a pectoral (*cozcapetlatl*), and sometimes a cloak (*tilmatli*).[56] Women dancers tend to call the garment that covers their chests and genitals a *quechquemitl*.[57] The headdresses (*copilli*) are often highly elaborated with long feathers in order to "better capture the energies from above," as one dancer informed me. Leg rattles (*coyoltin*) are both percussive musical instruments and articles of clothing. They usually dance with a shield (*chimalli*), which is possible because they do not play conchas. They deploy a wider range of pre-Colombian musical instruments than do the Concheros, but the percussive nature of their music makes singing difficult, and since they consider the *alabanzas* to be Spanish in origin, this is not considered a limitation.[58] Unsurprisingly, most of the dances have also been renamed: the dance of the sun is known as Tonatiuh; the cross (*la cruz*), as Centeotl; and *corazón santo* as Ehécatl (see Appendix 3). These new names are direct translations into Nahuatl of the names of the Concheros' dances rather than a reintroduction of names used by the Aztecs.

In Tenochtitlan (and elsewhere), dancing was an extremely important part of the staged dramatic rituals, and it was less a ludic and aesthetic activity than a veritable "mise-en-scène of their cosmovision."[59] As dance was strongly linked to singing and music, *in xochi, in cuicatl* (literally, the flower, the song) was a metaphor used for the singing (especially the verbal composition) linked to music, which also included dancing.[60] The dances were staged against elaborate backdrops, and the costumes worn theatrical and often lavishly decorated with feathers. The dancers' faces were frequently painted and men dressed up as women, gladiators, animals, and birds.[61] Such large ceremonies also involved bloodletting and trance inducement and were frequently enacted by *ixiptlas*, people who served as deities until they were sacrificed. Other dances were smaller, including circle dances that, as depicted in some of the codices, have strong similarities to the overall form of today's dances.

In general, the Aztecs had two types of dance: *maceualiztli* and *netotiliztli*. The latter were dances of "rejoicing" by which they took "pleasure during their festivals," a form of entertainment (*bailes* in Spanish), whereas the former were more solemn dances "performed in the general festivals and to particular deities and they danced them in the plazas" (*danzas* in Spanish).[62] These were dances of penance not in a sin-purging sense but rather as a service to the gods, in other words, work for the deities from which the dancer later attained recompense.[63]

Although the Concheros' dance can clearly be classified as maceualiztli, the Mexica give their dancing a somewhat different ethos. Although it is claimed to be a dance of the four movements, the nahui ollin—for the Fifth (or Sixth) Sun and thus a dance of respect and retribution that aims to speak to Ometeotl—it is at the same time very much a political performance for Cuauhtémoc and the glory of the Aztec past. The Mexica need to proclaim vindication, to assert themselves, and to make what Motolinía called big dance "gestures."[64] The Mexica are not interested in creating a state of intersubjectivity between dancers, of dancing harmoniously with others in their group and aiming for union and conformity. Rather they dance more rapidly, individualistically, and competitively, each dancer showing off his prowess or even virtuosity with little concern for those in the rest of the circle. Here I use "his" advisedly. Although Mexica groups have adherents who are women, as mentioned previously, they tend to be fewer in number and are often less involved in the dance in part because they find the pace difficult to keep up.

Deren has suggested, *"The sense of the dedicated act is to serve, not oneself, but the object of one's dedication* and it is therefore characterized by a quality of selflessness, discipline and even of depersonalization."[65] She implies that to concentrate on virtuosity (as the Mexica tend to do) is to contradict the sense of dedication and exaltation achieved in ritual dance.[66] The Mexica are perhaps trying to combine both virtuosity and exaltation, but what emerges predominantly is a form of egocentric celebration, not a connection with the divine achieved through ritualization and the development of union among dancers. Rather than an experience of the numinous, most Mexica aim for an individualistic high and use the dance as a means not only to express their desire for self-promotion but also to show off their Aztec self. Their practice concerns their own individual cosmologies and is linked to a proselytizing agenda. For them dance is not so much poetry with its multiple resonances (in xochi, in cuicatl) as a form of prose-like praxis. The Mexica, however, claim that the dance produces a transformation in them, which they describe variously as "a catharsis, a harmony, a stripping off, a force that we maintain," "the offering of sweat to mother earth," and a "game with the energy."[67]

## THE CONTEXT OF THE MEXICA'S DANCE

While the men are dancing flamboyantly, showing off their bodily expertise and frequently stunningly accoutered, the women are usually involved in more mundane matters, such as looking after children and selling *artesanias* (handicrafts) and pamphlets proclaiming the group's philosophy and the aims of Mexicanidad more generally. The dissemination of information about the Aztec past and the Mexica's views on the social present is an integral part of their "show." The Mexica certainly dance less than the Concheros; in some groups, they perform for only about an hour before "resting" so that one or more of them can address anybody who cares to listen for about half an hour. Their line of discourse is often verbose and repetitive and they usually do not tolerate interruptions.

Typically, at the end of a dance, all gather around the leader of the kalpulli (as the Concheros do around their jefes), who often speaks for as long as an hour. The format varies from group to group and according to the occasion but may include an exhortation on the need to speak Nahuatl. One of the arguments for this is that the Spanish speak Spanish and the French speak French, so why are the Mexica(ns) speaking Spanish? Although the Mexica make some effort to learn Nahuatl and certainly use Nahuat terms for most aspects of the dance, few have yet mastered the language for daily use. Indeed, these speeches are always in Spanish. Most of the other themes touched on (such as Catholicism, the United States, and the import of both foreign resources and culture) are developed and propounded in such a way that today's Mexica often come across as just as xenophobic and racist as were the members of the earlier MCRA.

Their stance with respect to the rest of Mexican society is an antagonistic one. They claim to be *guerreros* (warriors) for a better future and "aim to wake up the Mexican people in order to get them out of their ignorance."[68] Whereas the Concheros claim that their clothing is their "armor," their musical instruments their "weapons," and their dance a "battle," the Mexica effectively take these metaphors more literally and are generally belligerent in their approach to the world. Friedlander described the earlier members of the MCRA as cultural extremists, and today's Mexica have been called by equally unflattering names, including "fanatics," "charlatans," "opportunists," and "Aztec imbeciles."[69]

Those kalpultin that dance are as conflict ridden as those more directly involved in cultural politics. Many have undergone one or more splits. The size of these groups is small by comparison to Conchero mesas, most having fewer than thirty members with usually more men than women.[70] Initially, the Mexica danced outside the Museum of Anthropology, but in 1989 the Zocalo was *taken* when it was still against the law to dance there.[71] The Zocalo is considered a far more appropriate place for the reactivation of cosmic forces and moreover a space especially intended for the dance. In Nora's terms, it is a milieu de memoire with a difference, having suffered 500 years of disuse.[72] Three kalpultin dance there regularly at set times and in particular locations but often in competition with other events, many of which are related to the political mainstream.[73] Also held in the Zocalo are a number of special ceremonies that all Mexica kalpultin celebrate together, such as Dia de la Mexicanidad.[74] Some ceremonies involve the Concheros and other organizations, in particular the celebration for the Heroic Defense of Mexico-Tenochtitlan on August 13 and for Dia de la Raza, renamed the Day of Dignity and Resistance of the Indian, on October 12 (Chapter 11).

## IS IT JUST SHOW?

The Concheros talk simply from the heart and, if persuaded, may tell you what the dance means to them. The Mexica, however, use the dance as a prop for their speechifying. Their dance, rather than being an ontological experience to be learned from, is an ostentatious display, a theater of ethnic spectacle staged for others and deployed instrumentally to attract not only attention to themselves but also followers. Most immediately, the Mexica aim to draw bystanders, those people who having stopped to watch the dance look at what is for sale and listen to the disquisitions from which the Mexica hope their audience may learn more about the Aztec past.[75] In TV programs and films (both Mexican and foreign), the media have paid (and still pay) considerable attention to the Mexica for the theatricality and vivacity of their dances are attractive to the camera. They thus catch the attention of tourists too who are as interested in "sights" as "sites" and who increasingly are looking for happenings at tourist locations.[76] The Mexica's attitude to tourism is ambivalent for they sense that they are being used as a resource for tourist propaganda by the hegemonic powers.[77] On the other hand, Mexicanidad (just as the MCRCA before it) has been instrumental in bringing visitors to otherwise rarely visited locations. The small island of Mezcaltitlán (or Mexcatitlán) off the west coast (in the State of Nayarit) was declared to be the place from which the Aztecs had come. The state governor officially recognized it as Aztlán in 1986, and this attracted the attention of many visitors—although according to mythology, the Aztecs originated in the eight caves of Chicomoztoc in northwest Mexico.[78]

Although indigenous rituals in the past were usually forbidden, on many archaeological sites today these are now accepted by the authorities, such as ceremonies for the equinoxes, the zenith crossing of the sun, and the New Fire. The Mexica demand that such sites be recognized as animate centers of cosmic energy. These freedoms seem to indicate that even if the Mexica are against the state, the state is not necessarily against them and is happy to accommodate their movement in the interests of tourism and nationalism.[79]

The ideology created by Nieva and others of the MCRA helped develop a vision of Mexico that by being anti-mestizo could perhaps be claimed to be Indianist.[80] However, the "ethnic" identities that its followers sought and still seek to develop—such as learning Nahuatl and adopting Nahuat names—have little to do with Mexico's present-day indigenous peoples. Similarly, it is not state nationalism that the Mexica are pushing for but a more "radical" or extreme nationalism "of autochthonous inspiration."[81] Although they cause offense to many Mexicans, they do seem to represent a form of Mexican-ness, which is part of the current zeitgeist, and the government has no doubt realized this. By articulating meanings taken from the pre-colonial past, they are creating a new kind of Mexican who has little connection with the mestizo man that the indigenismo of the twentieth century sought to create.[82] In reality, most Mexica are mestizos, but they are not proud of that identity. It is, after all, the Gauchupine aspect of their identity that they so desire to discard (even if, in fact, they have few or no Spanish ancestors).

As a form of proto-nationalism, Mexicanidad is largely performative and informational. It has its own flag, which differs from the national banner in an important respect: the eagle sitting on a nopal cactus no longer has a snake in its mouth because the snake is claimed to be related to the Spanish but rather a glyph, the *atlachinolli*.[83] This flag is said to be similar to that taken from Cuitlahuac by the Spaniards, the original of which is currently hidden somewhere in the Vatican. The State of Mexico strictly controls the use of the official flag, but the Mexica, by reverting to an earlier (possibly imagined) form of it linked to their use of the Zocalo (where the official flag is raised daily), are laying claim to being *the* legitimate inheritors of Tenochtitlan.[84]

As I indicated at the beginning of this chapter, it is difficult to classify Mexicanidad. The founders of the MCRA were more concerned with race than class, whereas today's affiliates are masking a subordinate class position with ethno-cultural elaboration. Although Mexicanidad is in part socio-cultural, it might be better classified as a politico-cultural movement.[85] In that sense, it also signals a subculture that expresses the fundamental tension between those in power and those condemned to second-class lives in subordinate positions.[86] Their collective imaginary, however, is not a challenge to the Mexican state as it is currently constituted. Mexicanidad has no program for social change (although Bernadina Green, a Freemason and one of the few woman leaders in the movement at present, is adamant that change is essential). There is little possibility in the near future that the Mexica will be able to form a political party, even if its proponents desired to do so, because of the movement's extreme heterogeneity. The right-wing elitist club of Nieva has only a few points of contact with the autochthonous Mexicanidad, which today is strongly influenced by Tlakaelel's *Nahui Mitl*, and is different from, although linked to, the more global New Age esotericism of Velasco Piña and the Reginas. Most are caught up in a politics of what Heelas has called "indulgent experience."[87] As Mexicanidad lacks a coherent ideology, and as ideology is all important to them, the differences tend to come out. During a ceremony in 1992, some Mexica disrupted a ritual organized by Velasco Piña, who had invited seven Tibetan monks to Mexico City. The Mexica's view was that those of another religion could not hold such an important ritual on a site that they claimed. As in the earlier MCRA, the nationalism of today's Mexica can easily become racist.

# EPILOGUE

"The historical contacts and impurities that are part of ethnographic work . . .
signal the life, not the death, of societies."

—J. CLIFFORD[1]

In the last chapter, I elaborated on the Mexica and why they have appropriated
the Concheros' dances and their various associated practices into the larger context of their multifaceted and essentialist movement of Mexicanidad. Despite
the frequent assertions made during the 1990s by the older generation of dancers (including Jefe Ernesto) that the obligations never change, most aspects of
the dance have historically always been open to outside influences and hence in
a state of flux. Today the dance is as vital and the *mesas* as numerous as at the
time of the celebrations of 1992 for the "discovery" of the Americas. In part,
this is because the Mexica's way of dancing has revitalized a form that especially
in the eyes of a younger generation had become too staid and unchanging,
too Roman Catholic, and lacking in dynamism. In part, this has also occurred
because as many of the older *jefes*—who came in from the countryside and who
were staunch Catholics with indigenous contacts—have died, and their succes-
sors have been much more interested in and open to the political rhetoric and
practices of Mexicanidad.

Here I assess how the Concheros' practices have been affected by the various ways in which the Mexica have reformulated aspects of the dance and place
those changes that are recent in the context of those that are longer term.

**11.1.** Dancers resting and eating their *comida* in the early afternoon before resuming the dance.

Although the forms of the actual dances appear to have constancy through time, transformations in practice are always historically difficult to assess. Will the Concheros' dancing become with time much less to do with inner spirituality, the quest for self-knowledge, and the emergence of religiosity? Will following the word continue to lead to the attainment of a transcendent state in a public place, thereby extending a spiritual ontology to others, or will it become more like the dancing of the Mexica, which is concerned with external attainment and identity politics.

Recent modifications in many of the Concheros' other representations have been more rapid and wide-ranging than at any other time in the second half of the twentieth century. Although stimulated in the last decade by the Mexica and their ideology, many have also been brought on by more general social transformations that are linked to a changing sense of what it is to be Mexican. Broadly, these have been occasioned in part by the dwindling significance of the Roman Catholic Church as a spiritual mentor, which is closely related to its declining power in a society that has seen a vast rise in Protestant sects and furthermore is becoming increasingly ecumenical and even secular.[2] Changes have been occasioned too by the burgeoning of the media and particularly the

Internet, which has created a greatly increased global interdependence that is as much cultural as economic.[3] Changes have also resulted from migration, not so much to Mexico City but rather from there (and the countryside) to the United States, as well as other parts of Mexico; migrants can now be as much a part of the association elsewhere as when living in Mexico City. At the same time, the linked and increasingly pluralistic nature of culture generally has fostered an intensified awareness of what is local, particular to, and part of the nation's heritage, as seen in the rise of indigenous *reivindicación* movements.[4]

In many parts of the world, most live in increasingly multicultural societies where peoples of many different ethnic backgrounds seek to coexist. Differences still remain but are usually cultural rather than political and are not detrimental to the construction of a greater social cohesion.[5] In Mexico the program of *mestizaje* inaugurated this process early in the twentieth century. Yet, recently in the search for ethnic origins, many have attempted to resurrect ethnic differences or identities that have long since been transformed through time or have simply been elided. This re-creation is thus predominantly performative and enacted for the benefit of those concerned and sometimes too for outsiders, often tourists. The literature on this trend is a growing one: the Mexica are just one of a multitude of examples of an attempt by means of cultural bricolage to introduce small-scale heterogeneity into the increased homogeneity found at a larger scale.[6] Unlike many indigenous groups, however, the Mexica are not so much involved in a *rescate* of the old as in the creation of new identities.

The attitude of the Roman Catholic Church to the dance has also changed significantly. Whereas during the late 1980s the dancers were not exactly ignored but certainly not encouraged, the Church has now begun to want to involve the dancers in some of their ceremonies, but this reaching out does not mean that the Church has as yet understood the Concheros' practices. In 2001, I attended a meeting in the inner recesses of La Villa convened by a monsignor. Many jefes from the Association of La Gran Tenochtitlan had been invited and seven mesas had sent representatives. The discussion centered on the various events to be organized by the Church for the celebration of the twenty-fifth anniversary of the building of the new basilica. La Villa is where the Concheros enact on December 12 in honor of the Virgin of Guadalupe; to be included was thus apposite. Discussions, however, soon broke down for what the monsignor was requesting was a "performance." He wanted to elicit a pre-planned program of the dances that the Concheros intended to enact in the two-hour slot he was allocating them. Those present and especially, interestingly, some of the younger dancers were at pains to explain to him that the dancers can never know what will happen in advance as nothing is pre-planned. They also made clear that with the proposed number of groups dancing together, the need for

211

each group to go through the *permiso* with every other before the dances themselves could begin would take time, and one even implied that it might take up the allotted two hours. Above all, although there would be many *jefes* present, no one would be *the* jefe for the event as a whole and that the positions of first and second *palabras* would be determined by who turned up that day.

The dance itself has also migrated. Formerly found predominantly in the Bajio and since the late nineteenth century in the central Valley of Mexico, it has now spread to a variety of other locations. Santo Niño de Atocha has other newer mesas to the east in Cancun (in the Yucatan) and to the north in New York and Chicago.[7] In addition, many mesas have been established in the southern United States by Andres Segura. In Germany, a mesa was started by a Mexican who had danced with Santo Niño in Mexico City,[8] and in Spain the Insignias Aztecas (from the other *palabra*) instigated a group. The dance is also to be found in other parts of Mexico, such as the association in Guadalajara formed in the middle decades of the twentieth century.[9] With the growth in capitalism generally in Mexico and the increase in the global mobility of labor, it is likely that the dance will continue to spread as people are now leading more peripatetic lives. A number of the dancers I knew in the early 1990s are no longer around, although some still come to Mexico City for the major obligations.[10]

Many of the transformations that the dance has witnessed recently have not been the result of external and more global factors but internal changes. The deaths of most of the older jefes during the last decade of the twentieth century created a hiatus. During their lifetimes in the middle decades of that century, most Concheros were mestizo and at least ostensibly Roman Catholic. The older jefes had generally insisted that practices be carried out as they always had been, despite the growing prominence of a different zeitgeist more aligned with that of the Mexica. The lacunae created by the deaths of these jefes have allowed a new generation of younger jefes and dancers to "carry the word" and many of them have developed what appear to be more Mexica-like ambitions for the dance and, in particular, the desire to (re)turn it to a more autochthonous form.

Importantly, and linked to these deaths, there has also been a rapid demise in the oral transmission of the practices. For generations, the dance of the Concheros was not open to outsiders and the tradition passed from father to son by practice alone, predominantly by those with little formal education, which aided in its preservation and lack of self-consciousness. Now with more outsiders joining and in a more literate ambience closely linked to the growth in the media, a pressure to inscribe what had previously been passed on by practice alone has recently been felt.

Before I develop this strand further, I will summarize the differences between the Concheros and the Mexica to emphasize further that as communities they have little in common. To begin with, their aspirations are distinct. As already discussed, the Concheros work is of an inner spiritual nature linked predominantly to a search for an often loosely defined deity by means of the dance, for to dance is to *orar* (pray). The dance of the Mexica, however, is more external and political and almost a subculture. It consists of building an individualized identity instigated by the overall ideology of Mexicanidad, an identity that can be exhibited to others by means of dance, but more importantly as rhetoric in the hope of politicizing their views and convincing or converting observers to their cause.[11] The Mexica do not value the dancing as a medium that can teach or as a source of experience or self-expression but rather as a means to proselytize. Their way of dancing is less a reinterpretation of the moment that comes from within than a pre-prepared political statement. What for the Concheros is constitutive of experience is for the Mexica much more regulative.[12]

More specifically, the two communities are quite different in form; the Concheros' community is predominantly descent-based, whereas that of the Mexica is founded on assent.[13] Each Conchero mesa is linked to a specific location, usually the place of its inception, and has a temporal continuity, the depth of which is in part dependent on the date its standard was raised but more particularly on where its membership lies in the wider association. There is too an even greater temporal depth that is myth-based. Those born into a mesa become members automatically, and today those who choose to dance join an already formed family. Much is based on taken-for-granted assumptions. Assertions of belief are of secondary importance, and the Concheros do not talk much about them because they do not feel the need to reach consensus. Indeed, many still claim to be *fieles* (of the faith), if not actually practicing Catholics. The various leitmotifs, both visual and verbal, act as pointers toward practice rather than being precise determinants of it. The Concheros' religiosity can be said both to be incorporated into and to emerge from their practices, practices that have been "bequeathed them by their ancestors." Their overall political concerns, as suggested by the meeting of jefes, are about internal continuity—primarily stability and succession. They do not have a strictly regimented hierarchy, and although their nomenclature may seem to imply otherwise, their hierarchy is metaphorical rather than coercive; it has to do with inner achievement rather than external power. Finally, as a community, they are pluralistic. Mesas tend to be different one from the other, even idiosyncratic, and the differences emanate from the jefe. Unlike the Mexica, the Concheros are tolerant of dancers who have different ideas. They are inclusive rather than exclusive.

The Mexica, on the other hand, cannot accept pluralism. They aim rather for essentialist and idealized formulations that create their political agenda and their "work." Each Mexica group has its own ideology to an extent, but that ideology is grounded in Mexicanidad, which is partially based on an invented Aztec past. Their religiosity, if it can be so-called, is rooted in what they know of the beliefs and practices of the Aztecs. Thus, it is external rather than felt and not an integral part of practice and certainly not of the dance. Instead, it is abstract and theorized and based on claims of genealogical descent and the reintroduction of Aztec deities. For most it is just one part of a larger project: Tlakaelel's recent registering of *In Katonal* (La Casa del Sol) is an extreme case in point.

Morris suggests that communities of assent, as they are posterior to communities of descent, are "continually engaged in the process of their own formation." Such communities require "a progressive narrative" of their own temporal "supersession" and replacement of the community of descent. This is certainly true of the Mexica, for by claiming descent from the Aztecs, this paradoxically gives them a greater time depth than does the mythologized past of the Concheros. They can thereby convincingly maintain that their practices are "more authentic" than are those of the Concheros.[14]

The Mexica aim for a community that is unattainable; it can only ever be imaginary and they will be forever involved in its "future completion." Their communion "has an ultimate and fixed identity"—a goal—"and as such cannot accommodate the exposure of the temporal singular being." Yet the Mexica present many examples of an incapacity to surmount their individual desires in the interests of their idealized pronouncements. This is partly shown in the individualistic, overtly expressive, and exaggerated content of much of their dancing. Their quest involves such a leap of the imagination, which is necessarily individual, that this cannot and does not lead to the brotherhood that they so anticipate.[15] Theirs is essentially a "communion" that is unattainable because of their inability to overcome singularity in the interests of "unicity."[16]

Pluralism is also not tolerated by their not-so-formally recognized jefes who each want a band of adepts to follow their particular precepts, nor is it tolerated by the various members themselves, each of whom is busy trying to proselytize their often individual interpretations to others. The success of communities of assent is based on rhetorical persuasion, which can become coercive or even imperialistic, because they want to catch and convert followers. The Mexica can be "fanatically anti-pluralistic and intolerant" (and here I am quoting Morris and not the various critiques made of the Mexica).[17] This behavior also leads to a sense of frustration at the lack of self-fulfillment, which often results in aggression toward others.

Perhaps most significantly, the Mexica's community of assent can only "generate common being but never the being-in-common of singular beings," which is what the Concheros' community of descent nourishes.[18] The desire for unicity demands a form of fundamentalism that militates against a way of being-in-common that can accommodate a range of ontologies. The lack of tolerance of other ways of being among the Mexica accounts for why so many of the older generation of jefes, and Compadre Ernesto in particular, were so concerned during the 1990s about the Mexica's influence on the Concheros.

There can be little doubt that the celebrations for the "discovery" of the Americas in 1992 raised awareness about the nation's pre-Hispanic past. The number of those interested in Mexicanidad multiplied rapidly at that time as did the number of Concheros, whose association was a part of these events. Before these celebrations, the Concheros and the followers of Mexicanidad had formed two distinct organizations with comparatively little shared ground—for few Mexica as yet danced—but the celebrations brought them together.

Many Conchero mesas were invited to cooperate in the "invasion" or "colonization" events, as they were dubbed by some, held in support of today's indigenes, such as the Day of Dignity and Resistance for the Indian People, which was coordinated by COREPI in 1989.[19] This was an event that mainly drew residents of Mexico City, Concheros, and Mexica, although indigenous people from other parts of Mexico were also present. In general, this was a time characterized by a flurry of activity in the dance and of extra obligations, which was for many Concheros an exciting phase of interpenetration. The Mexica who danced brought to the Conchero mesas with which they enacted (which included Santo Niño de Atocha) their Mexicayotl ideas and were willing, if not desperate, to impart these to whomever would listen. Especially fertile ground for the Mexica were the bigger dances at which many mesas danced together. Younger Conchero dancers, usually relative novices, hearing about the Aztec past through the media on an almost daily basis, were ineluctably drawn to Mexicanidad. Many involved themselves in its more political aspects and occasionally succumbed to a desire to enact faster and more flamboyantly, as they surreptitiously danced with one of the mesas with strong Mexica sympathies, which were at that time still few in number.

The celebrations of 1992 created a self-consciousness in and about the Concheros' dance that it had not previously had. For the first time people who were other—that is, the Mexica, who were not part of the association—were performing the very same dances but in a different way. As the number of Mexica who danced grew, some Concheros began to be disconcerted by the Mexica's manipulation of the forms. Many jefes, including Compadre Ernesto, had little patience with the Mexica's more gymnastic approach to the dance,

**215**

although Compadre Ernesto had danced more flamboyantly and faster himself when younger, as testified by the film *El es Dios*. For him, it was their drive toward Nahuatlization that he particularly disliked. He considered the attempt to speak Nahuatl absurd because so few could understand it. He also did not approve of the Mexicaization of the other aspects of their obligations. During his lifetime, no one would have dared to turn up for a vigil with the idea of making the flower form in the shape of a nahui ollin, not only because doing so meant that the form had been predetermined but also because it was a form that had no direct links with the long-term traditions of the dance as he had known it.[20] In his last few years, he found himself under a certain amount of pressure to pass his palabra to an adept who was an outsider and, in terms of the dance, a comparative neophyte. As mentioned, he resisted and finally bequeathed it to his great-nephew, Ricardo (although Ricardo had never danced). By so doing, Compadre Ernesto reinforced the importance of kin, a basic, unwritten tenet of not just Santo Niño de Atocha but all Conchero mesas. A family member is more likely to respect the *animas* of the *antepasados* (ancestors), some of whom are their kin. Among the Concheros, a dancer is not made a jefe because he is a politician involved in identity politics, or brings innovative changes to a mesa but rather because he offers the continuity of kinship and the beliefs and practices linked to that. Ricardo may not have danced previously, but as a member of a family, the older generation of which had been involved in the dance for at least some of their lives he knew about most of the practices. His mother, Carmela, for example, had frequently provided the food for dances when Compadre Ernesto was still alive. He had gained some knowledge of the dance from watching from time to time when younger and of its organization from conversations overheard at home during the compadre's later years. As a man from a younger generation, however, he conceived of the dance differently from his great uncle. He costumes himself in full Aztec style with much plastic silver and gold, and although he does not have full Mexica sympathies, he is open to certain aspects of Mexicanidad and dances considerably faster than the majority of the older members of Santo Niño de Atocha.

Small-scale change over a period of time is often difficult to assess. The process of social change, labeled as "detraditionalization" by some analysts, is in reality much more complex.[21] Change does not necessarily imply loss (a "de-") but may rather imply an awareness of, an opening up to, or an inclusion of what was once seen as other; it may even involve the fusion of incompatibles.[22] Slow, sometimes imperceptible change is inevitable in any organization or association, and particularly one whose practices are or were predominantly transmitted orally. Ritual is not invariant through time but undergoes alterations that emerge "from within and through its own interior dynamics," that is, change on a microscale.[23] On a more macroscale, the new or the different may occur little by little in "the conceiving of resonances and multiple readjustments," for not only does the new modify the old but also the old appears in the new.[24]

Although it may be tempting to suppose that the effects of Mexicanidad on the Concheros have been sudden and invasive, in reality the beginnings of an attempt to Aztecize (and I use this term to distinguish this process from the more recent Mexica-ization) some of the representations of the dance go back much further than 1992 or even 1969, when Nieva's book *Mexicayotl* was published. If, as is generally believed, the Concheros' dance came to Mexico City from the Bajio in the late nineteenth century, where according to myth it took its current form, it cannot be said to be Aztec but rather Chichimec (or Otomi).[25] This geographical disjuncture creates a conceptual difficulty with which the dancers have been grappling and trying to efface for most of the twentieth century. An early interest in the Aztec past and the appearance of an Aztec aesthetic in the dance dates back to at least the 1930s, when the dancers of the mesa of La Gran Tenochtitlan sported an abundance of Aztec designs on their flowing garments. By the late 1950s, many dancers had costumes that although still Chichimeca in style (i.e., long and flowing), were covered in lavish plasticized Aztec-style silver and gold decorations. The shift from a Chichimeca ethos to the assumption of Aztec roots was gradual and ongoing throughout the middle decades of the century. As some dancers became more interested in historical veracity, the already-established trend toward a more minimal style was pushed further as they began to fabricate costumes from more natural materials, such as feathers that had not been dyed. Even though the Mexica have pushed this tendency still further with their insistence on only minimal costumes made exclusively from natural materials based as closely as possible on the depictions in the codices, this practice has not yet been taken up by the Concheros, probably because of the felt differences between them. The Concheros are not aiming for individual virtuosity, unlike the Mexica, but for what participatory collaboration can achieve. Moreover, most want to continue to differentiate themselves from the Mexica "other" by maintaining a certain distance.

Perhaps as important, the growing desire to place the origins of the dance in the Valley of Mexico rather than the Bajio can be seen in the changing words of the *alabanzas*. The words of the frequently sung "Cuando nuestra America fue conquistada" (When Our America Was Conquered), for example, have shifted considerably since the 1930s. As sung at that time, the alabanza still celebrated strong Bajio-centric roots.[26] In a version from Santo Niño de Atocha, taped originally in 1969, all references to the Bajio have gone and the emphasis is on the Aztecs: it is they rather than the Chichimecas who are being baptized.[27] By the 1990s, in a version recorded verbally, six of the eighteen verses[28] concentrate on telling the story of the Conquest and downfall of Tenochtitlan.[29]

The modifications that have occurred to the words since the 1930s have undoubtedly been influenced by the dance's location in Mexico City and its environs. The growing attention given there to the Aztec past has meant that that past has become the one of most significance to the dance, completely eclipsing the history that related it to the Bajío. Initially this interest in the Aztec past was the purview of intellectuals and the avant-garde but it gradually filtered down into more popular forms of culture, where it found expression as a cultural rather than political movement and was expressed as an aesthetic. The Mexica do not sing alabanzas, thus any recent Mexica-ization, or rather Aztecization, of existing alabanzas (or the newly written) is the result of the Concheros' increased interest in the Aztec past and their desire to celebrate it.

The changes in the words are also related to the slow transition from a predominantly oral tradition to a more inscribed one. That there were still various versions of the alabanza "Cuando nuestra America" being sung in the late 1990s indicates that the tradition, even if now more literate, had preserved much of its heterogeneity. Among mesas, there is still a good deal of variation and also between urban and rural parts of the association. In 1989, no compendium of the words of the alabanzas had yet been made by Santo Niño de Atocha. Just about the only place to find hard-copy versions, and then predominantly only of the more Catholic ones, was in the printed *Alabanzera* from Atontonilco in Guanajuato.[30] The majority simply had to be learned by heart, as did the names of the dances, the future locations and dates of the obligations, and of course the steps of the dances. But in 1992, in a move away from orality, a typed list of the annual obligations was produced for the mesa's dancers. This became more detailed with every passing year and presaged the appearance of a loose-leaf book (of which Compadre Ernesto never would have approved) put together for the use of those in named positions at vigils. This contained the words of the alabanzas (including the version of "Cuando nuestra America" with the eighteen verses mentioned above) and indicated the appropriate use for each one. It included too the most frequently used prayers, such as the *agradecimiento* (thanks) and the *misterios* said after a death.

The book was an attempt to bring the various components of an oral tradition into an ordered whole and to provide a source for reference. It is significant that recently, rather than trusting to precedent or to inner-voiced knowledge based on experience—that is, intuition or inspiration—to determine which alabanza to sing next, dancers have begun to look toward external sources to instruct them on how to proceed. Divided into sections (e.g., Dances, Marches,

Meals, and Vigils), this book is now often consulted to find the appropriate ala-banza for a particular situation. Those who have joined Santo Niño de Atocha during the 1990s, instead of relying on memory, have begun to depend on a primer, a small pamphlet outlining the basic representations of the dance that each dancer is now given when he or she has been dancing for a while.

The ongoing project of the loose-leaf book was not, I was assured, initi-ated with any intent to fix or curtail practice. Rather it was started out of a concern that the changes that were occurring were so rapid and wide-ranging that they seemed to threaten the authenticity of the tradition, although perhaps paradoxically many of those transformations are included in the book. It has a section named "Mexica" for recently composed alabanzas and lists the names of the dances in Nahuatl (see Appendix 3). In 1992, however, it would still have been unthinkable for the dancers of Santo Niño de Atocha to have referred to the dances by Nahuatl names.

This attempt to inscribe as many of the words and their associated prac-tices as possible has given these an external, material, and long-term form that previously they did not have. When part of a ritualized whole and committed to memory, they existed only in the moment of their production and were in a sense beyond conscious manipulation.[31] Most dancers cannot reel off the words of the *agradecimiento* or of an alabanza if requested to do so. They know them only in the context of the wider practices. When involved in a vigil, for example, the words come, one line leading to the next, just as during a dance one step leads to the next.

The recording of the alabanzas means that one version may now be given a hegemony that was not possible when each mesa, each palabra, and many of the dancers knew them all by heart, each dancer's version being "correct" but perhaps slightly different. Disagreements about substance (or in the case of the dances, form) could be hammered out during or immediately after an obligation. This is how, after all, almost imperceptible change that is not con-sciously intended occurs through time. On the other hand, the recording of the practices has also meant that they are now much more open to scrutiny, to comparison and analysis and the possibilities of tidying up or even alteration. The eighteen-verse written version of "Cuando nuestra America," discussed above, may well consist of the conjoining of several versions. I do not want to imply that these changes are more typical of Santo Niño de Atocha than of other mesas about whom I know much less. My impression was that this is a wide-spread process that is occurring throughout the dance. The ability to read and write is more common than it was a few decades ago, and once people have acquired these abilities, they want to use them. Even country groups quite often now have handwritten copies of the words of the alabanzas. However, certain aspects of the Concheros' practices are still well concealed and some are considered to be esoteric—I never attended a the ritual for the raising of a new mesa (*levantamiento*), for example, and no one ever really wanted to talk to me about it—but generally they are not so much secret as particular.

It is probable that some Concheros will go back to the earliest recordings in search of more "authentic" forms of the alabanzas, just as some—as, for example, the dancers of the Corporación de Concheros—have re-created the Chichimeca style in their dress and a concha made from a gourd rather than an armadillo's shell, used, they claim, in the late nineteenth century. In general, the drive for authenticity, by being marked as such, ceases to be authentic and can only ever be "staged."[32] As Culler has remarked in relation to the places that tourists go, the dilemma of authenticity is that a place once marked as such becomes mediated, a sign of itself and hence not authentic in the sense of being unspoiled.[33] Once so marked and now more self-consciously manifested, the Concheros' representations may cease to have the fluidity they once had, which is given by a process of an ad hoc contingency or bricolage that so typifies an oral tradition.

The Concheros dance has now entered a new phase. Contradictorily but perhaps not unexpectedly, the rise in awareness of the need to preserve, and hence value, this long-term tradition has led to a greater elaboration of many of the ritual procedures (although it is difficult to pinpoint the precise beginnings of these embellishments). During a vigil and at the beginning but perhaps more particularly at the end of a dance, many additions have clearly been added during the last few decades of the twentieth century. As an example, in the 1960s, during a vigil in the mesa of Santo Niño de Atocha, the lighting of the candles was done without ceremony (as it still is in the Bajio), but this has now become the focus of a ritualized technique that for some dancers is quite elaborate.[34] Further, in the Bajio during a vigil, work on the flower form does not stop when the music ceases as it does in Mexico City. At dances, the complex ritualized forms of disengagement enacted by many mesas (including Santo Niño de Atocha) at the end of an obligation, particularly in comparison to those mesas still headed by older jefes, are often so complex that they seem almost ritualistic.

This is undoubtedly because the dances are no longer the taken-for-granted practices passed on unthinkingly from one generation to the next, conceptualized as the work that needs to be done (as they still predominantly are in the Bajio) but have become much more self-conscious. This is in part because many outsiders (*gente de la banqueta* or the middle classes) who have taken up the practices tend to see them in a rather different way. They are either very aware and respectful of the tradition's longevity and want to (re)create a degree of elaboration that they believe the original indigenous practices have lost through time—in this sense, it might be said that they are even more respectful of the tradition than dancers of an older generation. Or they see the practices as being if not exactly negotiable, at least open to creative embellishment—in other words, a base on which to hang new ideas.

At this point I turn to the dance itself and assess the extent to which the forms of the various dances, the most deeply embodied of all the practices, have been transformed by the passing of time and more recently by the way that the Mexica and Conchero neophytes enact. If changes are occurring to the dance itself, what might this imply for the future of the Concheros' dance? In a sense, Compadre Ernesto was correct when he claimed that the dance exists in an eternal present. Dance is a ritual in its own right that is largely unaffected by, and does not affect, the context in which it is found.[35] As Connerton suggests, "incorporating practices," such as dance, are "largely traceless." The dances do "not exist 'objectively,' independently" of their enactment. Because they have to be learned by doing and, because of their formalization, "they do not require explicit reflection on their performance." They are deeply embedded (more so than the other representations) and as such are not open to critical scrutiny. They thus provide "a measure of insurance against the process of cumulative questioning entailed in all discursive practices."[36]

Just as we can know little about the forms of the Aztec dances—extant descriptions give some detail but the few depictions can say very little about the forms themselves—so also it is difficult to assess more recent changes for lack of documentation. As forms, the dances have not been inscribed and, until the advent of film and more recently video, existed only in the embodied memories of their enactors and the moment of their enactment or in still photos, which give little sense of the overall form. Even today in the actuality of the dance, their existence is fleeting and dancers still learn by doing, by watching and copying others, not from videos.

The so-called Mexica acquired the dance forms by means of enacting as part of Conchero mesas only a few decades ago. However, as the Mexica believe that the forms have come down directly from the Aztecs, they have made no conscious attempt to alter them. The Mexica's more mannered way of dancing has undoubtedly influenced the Concheros but has not changed the overall forms of the dances, although it has to an extent revitalized the dance by greatly enlivening it.[37] The young, such as the new jefe Ricardo, have an energy that they want to manifest when they dance. They do not see any necessity to deny themselves the desire to stimulate, stretch, and feel their bodies, but this need not negate the process of ritualization, provided they move in tempo to the music and to the other dancers and take up the ritual stance.[38]

**221**

More dancers than ever before, however, do not understand this prerequisite. "Carrying the word" by dancing in a disciplined way and as much like everyone else as possible (at least while still neophytes) to achieve a state of communion with the other dancers is not for them. For these younger dancers, the conventional forms of the dances are just not enough. They cannot resist the desire to dance faster than others, to add embellishments to their steps, and to move individualistically and separately, as they see the Mexica doing. They have not understood that to dance is to *orar* (pray), that the dance is a form of religiosity, not a performance of the self.

On the other hand, it is possible in the longer run that increased awareness and an inscribed knowledge of the detailed steps of the dances may mean that the dance as a phenomenon becomes less open to individual interpretation. The various Conchero mesas may no longer encourage through dance the "being-in-common of singular beings" and rather begin to insist on a "common being," a common way of dressing and a style of dancing, for example, in which enactors literally dance in an identical way, as in a staged performance.

The word "insist" is worth exploring further here. Compadre Ernesto may have been of the opinion that the forms should be kept unchanging, that innovations should not be made, but he did not insist; there was never any obduracy to his avowals. Dancers were encouraged to feel out bit by bit what was right for them. If a dancer over time ended up enacting somewhat differently from others, that was accepted. Dancers of the mesa of Santo Niño de Atocha did not have, and still do not have, any sense that an obligation is in any way predetermined.

Importantly for the Concheros, the Mexica have shifted their ground during the last decade. The Concheros now see the Mexica as being supportive of their dance rather than a threat to its continuity, because today the Mexica take a less political stance than they did in the early 1990s. They are more open to the possibility and value of ritualization; some groups now ask permission before dances in a way that is very similar to that of the Concheros. The Mexica have also not been able to ignore the powerful effects of the dance on the self.

Furthermore, as the practices become increasingly regulated because they are now inscribed, as they change less and the dance is seen to have a constancy and hence an external homogeneity, the *associating* of the Concheros may become less spiritual and more political. The dance would then become folkloric and no longer necessarily perceived as a path to individual transformation of the self, "the forming of the self."

Dancing can be an intense intersubjective experience that transcends barriers of nationality, ethnicity, class, race, gender, and, in particular, power because it creates bonds among people that are markedly different from those developed by other means, particularly the spoken word. Dance has its own very specific body language that relates directly to emotions, inner feelings, and the self. It is a means of bringing people together that creates a strong form of sociability. The dance community is an important source of identity, although those who dance are all very much individuals with distinct personalities. The practices they enact are the raison d'être for their being Concheros, but the mixing and mingling with other dancers in their own mesa and with those from other mesas, and contact with others more generally, are also of the greatest significance to them. No Conchero can hold a vigil alone nor dance without the cooperation of others. If this were not so, the dance would not spread and the "word" would not continue to be "carried."

Although most Mexicans are raised as Catholics, the religiosity of the Concheros is not determined by a prescribed ideology but rather is one that emerges during their vigils and dances, changing to meet the contingencies of space and time. The dance is, to use a metaphor employed by one of the dancers, a "war against the circumstances" carried out under the protection of the power of the animas. Dancers may all *try* to dance the same steps but beliefs vary and are ultimately individual. They will differ from mesa to mesa based in part on the religiosity of the jefe, but they also vary from dancer to dancer. Individual Concheros come together to hold a vigil not necessarily because they all hold the same beliefs but because that something they seek can only be gained by means of a shared ritualized experience.

This book has presented the reader with a vast array of people and places because both are of the greatest importance to the Concheros. Their vigils and dances are strongly linked to particular locations, imbuing them with a strong mnemonic and chthonic quality—in Nora's words, *milieux de memoire*. They are also associated with particular individuals: the jefe is extremely important for the development and longevity of a mesa's practices. A jefe forges strong relationships not only with his dancers but also with jefes from other mesas. However, should the Concheros take on an external ideology, whether religious or otherwise (as did the Mexica), that becomes more important to them than the dancing itself and what that can teach them, then the dance as it is enacted today will be under threat. Also imperiling the dance is the move to do the practices by the book, which is the long-term danger that inscription poses. Most Concheros dance because for them it is one of the most important things in their lives; it puts them in touch with others but, more importantly, with themselves, with an internally and individually engendered and inherently spiritual form of empowerment. Once a dancer has become accustomed to this type of religiosity, he or she is loath to be without it.

# APPENDICES

## APPENDIX 1: TIMELINES FOR SANTO NIÑO DE ATOCHA

**1880**
| | |
|---|---|
| 1883 | Santiago Tlatelolco establishes its palabra in Mexico City. |
| 1876 or 1887 | Jesus Gutierrez raises the Reliquia's standard in Mexico City and assumes position of Capitan General de las Danzas de Tenochtitlan. |

**1890**
| | |
|---|---|
| 1891 | Jesus Gutierrez returns to the Bajio. |
| 1897 | Manuel Luna born. |

**1900**
| | |
|---|---|
| 1902 | Ernesto Ortiz Ramirez born. |
| 1908 | Manual Luna raises mesa. |

**1910**
| | |
|---|---|
| 1910 | Ernesto Ortiz comes to Mexico City. |

**1920**
| | |
|---|---|
| 1922 | Ernesto becomes a captain of the mesa of San Juan de los Lagos. |
| 1924 | Ernesto Ortiz marries Maria Robles. |

**1930** Jesus Gutierrez dies.
| | |
|---|---|
| 1930s | Manuel Luna becomes general of Santiago Tlatelolco. |
| 1933 | Ignacio Gutierrez Rodriguez (Tata Nacho) becomes general of the Reliquia. |

**1940**
| | |
|---|---|
| 1942 | Oratorio of Ernesto Ortiz's mesa of San Juan de los Lagos burns down. |

## APPENDIX I—CONTINUED

| | |
|---|---|
| 1948 | Ernesto Ortiz joins Gabriel Osorio. |
| **1950** | |
| 1951 | Andres Segura dances for the first time at La Villa (Poveda 1981:283). |
| 1958 | Gabriel Osorio dies. |
| **1960** | |
| 1960 or 1968 | General Ignacio Gutierrez dies. |
| **1970** | |
| 1973 | Ernesto Ortiz's sister Dolores dies. |
| 1974 | Maria Robles (wife of Ernesto Ortiz) dies. |
| 1976 | Ernesto Ortiz's mesa visits the Mohawk reservation in the United States and other locations, invited by Blancas raíces de la Paz of the Mohawk reservation, Akeswasne, New York. |
| 1977 | Ernesto Ortiz visits Guatemala. |
| 1978 | Pilgrimage of Ernesto Ortiz and others, including Andres Segura, to Santiago de Compostela. Angelica made sahumadora. |
| 1979 | Andres Segura forms his own mesa, Danza Azteca Xinachtli. |
| **1980** | Ernesto Ortiz officially adopts Santo Niño de Atocha. Beginning of involvement with ceremonies at the Templo Mayor and in the Zocalo. |
| 1988 | Ernesto Ortiz's mesa visits the Sufi group Neredin in New York. |
| **1990** | |
| 1991 | Ernesto Ortiz raises his pillars to status of captains. |
| 1992 | The pillars establish their own mesa. Ernesto Ortiz, with the mesa Insignias Aztecas, visits Santiago de Compostela, where the latter raises a mesa (Santa Cruz Espiral del Senor Santiago de Compostela). |
| 1993 | Manuel Luna dies. |
| 1995 | Ernesto Ortiz recognized as a general. Ricardo López Ortiz (his nephew) named as inheritor. |
| 1997 | Ricardo López Ortiz made captain in Fresnillo, Zacatecas. Ernesto Ortiz Ramirez dies (November 5). |

## APPENDIX 2: SPANISH AND ENGLISH
## NAMES OF DANCES, 1989

| | |
|---|---|
| Aguila Blanca | White Eagle |
| Conchero Viejo | Old Conchero |
| Cruz | Cross |
| Escojido | Hidden |
| Fuego | Fire |
| Fuego Viejo | Old Fire |
| Guadalupe | Guadalupe |
| Guajalote | Turkey |
| Guajito | Inducement |
| Lluvia | Rain |
| Maíz | Corn |
| Paloma | Dove |
| Pólvora | Lively |
| Pulquita | Little Pulque |
| Sapito | Toad |
| Sembrador | Sower |
| Sol | Sun |
| Venado | Deer |
| Venado II | Deer II |
| Viento | Wind |

*Source*: Compiled from my fieldwork notes 1989/90.

## APPENDIX 3: SPANISH AND NAHUATL NAMES OF SANTO NIÑO DE ATOCHA'S DANCES, 2001

| *Spanish* | *Nahuatl* |
|---|---|
| Águila blanca (White Eagle) | Iztacuauhtli |
| Apache | — |
| Borrachito (Drunk) | Pantécatl |
| Caballo (Horse) | — |
| Cascabeles | Ayoyotes or Coyoxauhqui |
| Changuito | Ozomatzin |
| Cojito | Tezcatlipoca |
| Conchero Viejo (Old Conchero) | Tlamatinime |
| Conejo (Rabbit) | Tochtli |
| Corazón Santo (Saintly Heart) | Ehécatl |
| Cruz (Cross) or Maíz (Corn) or Sembrador (Sower) | Centéotl |
| Cruz Alabada (Praised Cross) | — |
| Fuego (Fire) | Tlétl, Xiutecutli |
| Fuego Nuevo (New Fire), Cuatro Vientos (Four Winds) | Malinalli |
| Guadalupana (Guadalupe) | Tonantzin |
| Guajito | — |
| Guajolote (Turkey) | Totolito or Hueytotollin |
| Guerrero (Warrior) | Chichimeca |
| — | Hueychichimecáyotl |
| — | Hueyquetzalcóatl Citlanicue |
| — | Huitzilopochtli |
| Lluvia (Rain) | Tláloc |
| — | Mayahuel |
| Paloma (Dove) | Miquiztli |
| Pólvora | — |
| Providencia (Providence) | Xipe Tótec, Quetzalcóatl |
| San Miguel. (Saint Michael) | — |
| Sapito (Little Toad) | Tlamazoltzin |
| Serpiente (Serpent) or Víbora (Viper) | Cóatl |
| Señor de la Misericordia, Ya Resuenan los Clarines | Toteuh |
| Sol (Sun) | Tonatiuh |
| Sol Viejo (Old Sun) | Hueytonatiuh |
| Venado (Deer) | Mázatl. |
| Venado II (Deer 2) | Ome Mázatl |

*Source*: Compiled by Angelica for the mesa of Santo Niño de Atocha.

# APPENDIX 4: PRINCIPAL MESAS IN MEXICO CITY OF SIGNIFICANCE TO SANTO NIÑO DE ATOCHA[1]

| Jefe | Name of mesa | Standards | Date of raising/adoption or inheritance |
|---|---|---|---|
| RELIQUIA GENERAL | | | 1876 |
| Grl. Ignacio Gutierrez Rodriguez († 1960's)[2] <br> (i) Jesus Gutierrez[3] <br> (i) Florencio Gutierrez | | | 1933 |
| Gabriel Osorio († 1958) | San Juan de los Lagos | San Juan de los Lagos <br> Virgen of Dolores <br> Señor of Chalma | 1903 |
| Teresa Mejia Osorio <br> (with Cruz Hernandez) | Santo Niño de Atocha | | 1975 |
| Grl. Ernesto Ortiz Ramirez († 1997) | Virgen de San Juan de Los Lagos <br> Santo Niño de Atocha | | 1922 <br> 1980 |
| (i) Ricardo López Ortiz († 2008) | | | 1997 |
| (i) Maria Mercedes Lopez Ortiz | | | 2008 |
| Grl. Felix Hernandez († 1990s) <br> (i) Grl. Guadalupe Hernandez Zarco | Virgen de San Juan de los Lagos | | late 1960s |

*continued on next page*

1. This table primarily includes the mesas with which Santo Niño de Atocha had contact in Mexico City and excludes most of the country mesas with which it is allied.
2. The symbol † indicates deceased.
3. The notation (i) indicates inheritor.

APPENDIX 4—CONTINUED

| Jefe | Name of mesa | Standards | Date of raising/adoption or inheritance |
|---|---|---|---|
| Grl. Andres Segura Granados (†) | Danza Azteca Xinachtli | Virgen de Dolores | 1979 |
| Grl. Faustino Rodriguez († 1989) | Dulce Nombres de Jesus | | |
| (i) Justino Rodriguez and | | | 1990 |
| (i) Herman Tecoapa | | | 1990 |
| Grl. Alberto Guiterrez († 1980's) | Santo Niño de Atocha. | | 1987 |
| (i) Miguel Gutiérrez (Chicago, Illinois) | | | |
| Doroteo (†) | Santo Niño de Atocha | | |
| Gaudalupe Torres (†) | Santo Niño de Atocha | | |
| Teresa Osorio | Santo Niño de Atocha | | 1975 |
| Remedios Osorio | Santo Niño de Atocha | | |
| Florencio Osorio (†) | Santo Niño de Atocha | | |
| Mesa formed by Ernesto Ortiz's pillars | Santo Niño de Atocha | | 1992 |
| SANTIAGO TLATELOLCO | | | 1883 |
| Grl. Manuel Luna († 1993) | Danzas Religiosas del Apostol de Santiago Tlateloloco | | 1908/1930 |

| | | |
|---|---|---|
| (i) Tiburcio Luna (†) and Miguel Luna | | 1993 |
| Grl. Gaudalupe Jimenez Sanabria (†) | Insignias Aztecas | 1922 |
| (i) Jesus Leon Jiménez and four others | | 1994 |
| Ignacio Cortez | Tenoch | |

## INDEPENDENT

| | | |
|---|---|---|
| Grl. Camillo Bastenos Bársenas (†) | Plan de Toluca | |
| Felipe Hernandez (†) | Corporacion de Concheros Sociedades Unidos | 1938 |
| (i) Carlos y Manuel Barrera | Corporacion de Concheros de Mexico | |
| (i) Felipe Aguilar | | |
| Grl. Felipe Aranda (†) | | |
| (i) Felipe Aranda (†) | Virgen de la Soledad | |
| (i) Conchita Aranda | | |
| Miguel Alvarado | San Juanita de los Lagos | |
| Luis Solis (†) | Madre Santissima de Guadalupe | |

And the mesas of General Fidel Morales (†), Hermilio Jimenez, Manual Cruz, Virginio Hernandez, Francisco Diez, Miguel Avalos, Lupita Jimenez, Miguel Abasolo, and Guadalupe Alvarez.

# APPENDIX 5: GENEALOGY OF THE MESAS OF SANTO NIÑO DE ATOCHA AND SAN JUAN DE LOS LAGOS

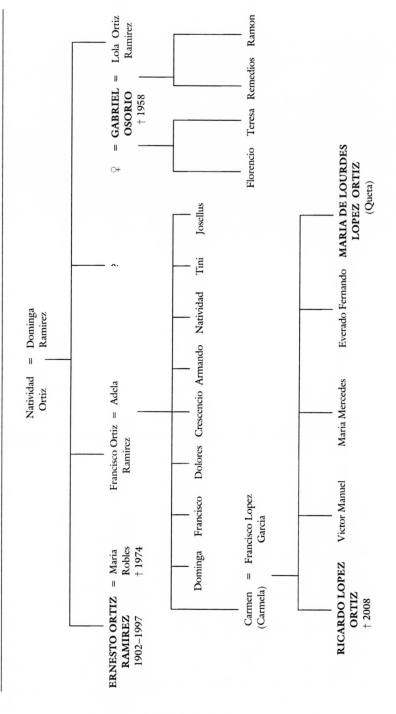

# NOTES

## PREFACE AND ACKNOWLEDGMENTS

1. Weiner 1994:55; Taylor 1994:xiii.
2. Geertz 1988:4–5; Favret Saada 1980:22.
3. There is now, however, a growing literature on the dance. Articles: Solorzano and Guerrero 1941; Kuruth 1946; Hanna 1974; Moedano 1972, 1984, 1985, 1988; Gonzalez M.A. 1988, 1996; Sanchez Venture 1990; Rostas 1991, 1994, 1996, 1998a, 2008; de la Torre 2005, 2008. Dissertations: Mansfield 1953; Kamfer 1985; Bruhn 2001. Books: Fernandez 1941 (a short monograph); Stone 1975 (largely anecdotal, as is the section on the Concheros in Galovic 2002). The most recent is a history by Y. Gonzalez Torres (2005).

## CHAPTER 1: INCONGRUOUS BEGINNINGS

1. Rostas 1987.
2. Dubet 1994.
3. Quoted in Bloch 1986:23–31.
4. In the last few decades much more attention has been given to experience in the literature: see Turner and Bruner 1986; Csordas 1994a; Geertz 1986; Hastrup and Hervik 1994; Howes 1991; Kratz 1994; Turnbull 1990; Young and Goulet 1994.
5. Leder 1990:5.
6. Ibid., 3. Many turn to sports such as football or swimming or to a form of human contact that has to be paid for, such as therapies of various kinds, or join consciousness-raising groups (Bourdieu 2000 [1993]).

7. Leder (1990:5–7) discusses the use of the German terms *Korper* and *Leib*, which differentiate clearly between the physical body, of bone, muscle, skin, nerves, all of which are material, and the energized, alive body that "breathes, perceives, speaks and reasons" (ibid., 6). The latter not only embraces *Korper* but is more than the sum of its parts (see also Ots 1994).

8. Anthropologists have looked at the social and symbolic significance of the body or aspects of it (e.g., Blacking 1977; Benthall and Polhemus 1975; Howes 1991; Leach 1958; and Obeyesekere 1981); as have historians (Feher 1989; Classen 1993, 1994), sociologists (Turner 1995 [1985]; Featherstone et al. 1991), and literary critics (Scarry 1985). First Foucault (1979) and then, for example, the Comaroffs (1991), Taussig (1993), and Stoller (1995) have looked at the significance of historical processes in its shaping. Following earlier analyses (such as Mauss 1979 [1936]; Hertz 1973 [1909]; Douglas 1970 [1960]), there has recently been a rise in interest in a more phenomenological approach to the body (Jackson 1983; Desjarlais 1992; Daniel 1984; Leder 1990; Lowell Lewis 1995; Csordas 1990, 1994a). See Lock 1993 for a recent review of this literature.

9. Csordas 1993:136; Csordas 1990:51.

10. Lowell Lewis 1995:221.

11. Schieffelin 1996:60.

12. Piot 1999:19.

13. Csordas 1994b:xi.

14. Bourdieu 1977:124; Csordas 1990:7; and see Rostas 1998a.

15. Bourdieu 1977, 1979, 1990; de Certeau 1980, 1984; Giddens 1979, 1984.

16. Bourdieu 1977:72, 79.

17. "Because the dispositions . . . inculcated by objective conditions . . . engender aspirations and practices objectively compatible" with requirements, it follows that "the most improbable practices are excluded . . . as *unthinkable*" and incline agents "to love the inevitable" (Bourdieu 1977:77, italics in the original).

18. Comaroff 1985:5. Critiques of Bourdieu are numerous (see, e.g., Dubet 1994:76; Csordas 1990; Lowell Lewis 1995; Jackson 1996:21). See Knauft for a beginner's critique (1996:122–128).

19. Jackson 1996:22.

20. The word *practice* "draws with it a cloud of associations" that they "feel are unproven for ritual action in general, namely, the idea that ritualization produces 'practical knowledge' and 'the ability to deploy, play, and manipulate basic schemes in ways that appropriate and condition experience effectively'" (Humphrey and Laidlaw 1994:4, quoting Bell 1992:221).

21. Humphrey and Laidlaw 1994:4, quoting Charles Taylor (1985).

22. Ibid., 4.

23. Ibid., 5, 64.

24. Ibid., 5.

25. Ritualization consists of a "departure from how things are normally done": it is not a necessary feature of all action "but a particular, occasional *modification* of an intrinsic feature of [any] action, namely its intentionality" (Humphrey and Laidlaw 1994:73).

26. Deren 1953:229.

27. Hastrup 1998:37.

28. Csordas 1990:35.

29. Deren 1953:229–230.

30. "Palimpsest" can be defined as "a site where texts have been superimposed onto others in an attempt to displace earlier and competing histories" (Cooper Alarcón 1997: xiv) and thus is particularly relevant to the metaphor of culture as text (Geertz 1973).

31. During the 1970s and 1980s, the principal temple to Huitzilopochtli and Tlaloc—the Templo Mayor, which is situated between these two buildings—was excavated and is now open to the public as an archaeological site and museum.

32. Cooper Alarcón 1997.

33. For example, the Aztec past has not been emphasized in school history books (Gutiérrez 1999). However, in the run up to the celebrations to commemorate the discovery of the Americas in the early 1990s, a flood of new mainstream assessments of the Aztecs appeared (Clendinnen 1991; Gruzinski 1992; Cypess 1991) and about Latin America in general (Todorov 1982; Greenblatt 1993). See also Bartra 1992; Lomnitz Adler 1992, 2001; and Bonfil Batalla 1990 (1987) for reassessments of Mexican society today.

34. Nora 1996:1.

35. Feld and Basso 1996.

36. Casey 1996:24.

37. Nora 1996:1.

38. Appadurai 1995:207.

39. Lovell 1998.

40. Fabian 1983.

41. Connerton 1989:102.

42. "Mexicanidad" literally means "Mexican-ness" but the Mexica use the term to imply the reinvention of the Aztec past (see Chapter 10).

43. Tilley 1997:74.

44. Garcia Canclini 2001:253, 256.

45. Ibid.; Harvey 1989; Featherstone 1990, 1993; Appadurai 1990.

46. Comaroff and Comaroff 1992:10, 16.

47. Leder 1990:153.

48. In part, too, because the word "performance" does not exist in Spanish. The verb closest to perform is *desempeñar* (to act or to discharge), but Mexicans do not talk about a dance performance as a *desempeño*, although the word exists; for a theater, they use *estreño* (for the first night) and thereafter describe it as a *funcion* or *representacion*. Many Spanish-language writers overcome this difficulty by using the English term "performance" (e.g., Citrio 2000).

49. The *Shorter Oxford English Dictionary* (1989) defines "enact" as "to represent on . . . or as on the stage": that is, in a specially framed space such as the theater, during a performance or as part of a ritual, all of which are usually separated from ordinary everyday life by both spatial and temporal constraints. Turner has defined "frame" as "that often invisible boundary . . . around activity which defines participants, their roles, the 'sense' . . . ascribed to those things included within the boundary, and the elements

within the environment of the activity" (Turner 1982:54). "Framing" is often reflexive in that a part of activity is given "a bordered space and a privileged time within which images and symbols of what has been sectioned off can be 'relived,' scrutinized, assessed, revalued and, if need be, remodelled and rearranged" (Turner 1982:140).

## CHAPTER 2: THE CONCHEROS

1. Evans Pritchard 1940:5.

2. Ots exemplifies well the stance taken by the Concheros. Talking about the practice of *qigong*, a form of cathartic movement in China in the early 1980s, he quotes one of his informants as saying "[o]rganization means rules and control. Under organizational control we could not move as freely as we do now. After a time our group would cease to exist" (Ots 1994:130).

3. "Mesa" glosses as table but is used also to describe a group that heads an organization, rather like "board" in English. Its use by the Concheros refers to a grouping of celebrants in an oratory around an altar (a form of table) and may also have shamanic connotations (Sharon 1978).

4. The Concheros dance at Amecameca on Ash Wednesday in February/March, at Chalma in May or early June, depending on the date of Easter (on the first Thursday after Thursday of Ascension); followed in September by the dance at Los Remedios.

5. The principal obligations have become much shorter over the years. At present, many dancers go to Chalma on Wednesday to hold the vigil that night and dance the following day. In the mid 1900s, they arrived on Monday, danced for four days from Tuesday to Friday, with the vigil, as at present, on Wednesday evening. Onlookers may get the impression that the celebrations still last four days, but this is because some groups of Concheros dance earlier, some later. There are also other dance groups present, such as the Contradanzantes, who enact rather differently. In 1987, I witnessed a group dancing dressed in football shirts and shoes that had come from the United States.

6. Shadow Rodríguez and Shadow 2000:139; Turner and Turner 1978:55, 63, passim.

7. Her representation varies according to her location unlike the iconicity of the Virgin of Guadalupe. But whereas the Virgin of Guadalupe is completely indigenous, the Virgin of los Remedios is definitely Gauchupine (i.e., Spanish) in origin (Turner and Turner 1978:98).

8. Lafaye 1976; Brading 1983, 2001.

9. In relation to Santiago Tlatleloco, Amecameca is to the east (southeast), Chalma to the south (southwest), Los Remedios to the west, and Tepeyac (La Villa) to the north. The winds to the east and the south are associated with male saints, those to the west and north, with female.

10. This dance took place on November 4/5, 1989.

11. Ortiz de Zarate 1990:2.

12. For the Day of the Dead, the house of one of the mesa's dancers was usually used, and for the annual meeting and vigil, held on Corpus Christi in July, a nearby church, the Iglesia del Perpetuo Socoro.

13. Warman estimated that in 1940 there were some 40,000 practitioners throughout the republic and some 5,000 in Mexico City, and the dance has certainly expanded since then (1985 [1972]:125). Solorzano and Guerrero thought there were some 40 mesas in 1939 with about 100 dancers each (1941:454). Toor, writing in 1947, estimated 50,000 in and around Mexico City (Toor 1947). Moedano's more conservative estimate came to only 40,000 in Mexico City and the States of Mexico and Guanajuato in 1990 (verbal communication, 1990).

14. If he has no wife (or his wife has died, as was the case with Jefe Ernesto) or the leader is a woman, the sahumadora will be chosen from among dancers of the group.

15. The "Estatutos de Disciplina" (1930). Known also as the Reglamento de Conquista, this document indicates broadly the responsibilities of the jefe and all other members and notes specifically the prerequisites of each. It mentions too what the punishments for infringement of these rules of discipline should be. The document had been signed by the Jefe Ernesto Ortiz, his wife, Maria, and others.

16. Solorzano and Guerrero (1941:454) indicate that in the group they studied in the 1930s all women dancers were known as "malinches." Malinche was the name of the indigenous woman given to Cortés at the time of the Spanish Conquest who became his translator, mistress, and mother of his children. For Santo Niño de Atocha, Malinche has positive connotations because she "translates"—that is, resolves differences between dancers. In general, to be a malinchista implies a love of the foreign: it is claimed that she made the conquest easier for the Spaniards by betraying the Aztecs (Rostas 1996:220; Franco 1989; Harris 1996).

17. I did not attend a ceremony of *recibimiento*; nor was I able to get much information about the rate of those being received, although in 1993 five dancers were received into Santo Niño de Atocha. Most dancers who hold positions are usually required to have been received before being given such prominence.

18. Although some of those who are no longer as involved usually only come to La Villa on December 12 and to the vigil for All Souls (the Day of the Dead).

19. Tepito, the area in the center of Mexico City that Oscar Lewis wrote about, is quite similar. Both are comparatively unchanged, with many families still residing in vecindades that have a tap in the courtyard and communal lavatories and showers (although Angelica's accommodation had its own WC).

20. For offences in the 1930s, ten *arrobas* were given. An arroba, according to Solorzano and Guerrero (1941:454), consisted for men of twenty-four whippings whereas women received ten half arrobas (i.e., ten sets of twelve). Apart from this bodily castigation was the "penance" that consisted of moving around the atrium of the church while kneeling and blindfolded (ibid., 454).

21. A vigil in Tetelcingo in the State of Morelos on Saturday night and then a dance on Sunday, the latter attended by others from Compadre Ernesto's mesa. Susana then attended a vigil on Monday night followed by a dance on Tuesday in San Rafael (in the State of Mexico), and on Wednesday night a vigil in Mexico City convened by Santo Niño de Atocha for a writer friend of Antonia's who had died.

22. Stone 1975:50; Solorzano and Guerrero 1941:451. There are currently general rehearsals in the Zocalo on Monday, Wednesday, and Friday nights.

## CHAPTER 3: THE OBLIGATIONS: FRAMING THE CONTEXT

1. Colonia Juan Gonzalez Romero, September 22–23, 1989.

2. The Nuestra Madre had a Christ child in her arms and was housed in a large glass box lit by several of its own light bulbs.

3. In the past, a distinction could be drawn between the sergeant of the field for a dance (sargento de campo) and the sergeant of the table (sargento de mesa). In many groups today the same person carries out both roles.

4. On this occasion, the alabanzas sung were "Santo dios y Santo fuerte y santo immortal libranos senor de todo mal" (Saintly God and the immortal Saint free us from all evil) and "Estos son las flores" (These are the flowers).

5. According to one dancer the slower mode is called "alabado" and the other, more usual one, "conquista." However, an alabado is also a type of song (distinct from the alabanza) that dates from the seventeenth century, is typical of the Bajio, and is still sung there (Los Concheros al Fin de Milenio 1997:19).

6. Warman 1965. Stone (1975:22) indicates that vigils should start at midnight, but those I attended started between 11:15 PM and 11:45 PM. The jefe Teresa Mejia indicated that vigils in the past began at sunset (6:00 PM) with the jefe standing on the doorstep, checking all his dancers as they arrived, and that they were well under way by 8:00 PM.

7. The Spanish word for "candle" is *vela*, and the verb *velar*, "to watch over," is suggestive of the process of all night vigilance, a velación.

8. *Cuenta* and *planta* are difficult to gloss but can be loosely translated as the "account of" or "state of."

9. It was indicated by dancers from other mesas that these helpers should be the palabras, but at the vigils of Compadre Ernesto's mesa usually different people were appointed to carry out each part of the work.

10. The flower form can also be constructed on a base of powdered lime (cal), which is spread carefully on the floor in the form of a cross. The flowers are then laid out on top. Stone (1975:128–135) reports that during the early 1940s in Mexico City, the body itself was laid out on a larger lime cross. After its burial, a flower form was then constructed on a long table above, exactly to the dimensions of the cross beneath.

11. Castro Manrriquez (n.d.): "Virgen del Cielo" (the Virgin in Heaven), "A voz a Cielo" (A voice from Heaven), "La Virgen Maria" (the Virgin Mary), and also "¿Quien es este estrella?" (Who is this star?). This volume contains only those alabanzas with Catholic themes.

12. See Stone 1975:163.

13. At one vigil I attended, the flowers and then the lime and its scoop were placed in a box and a black ribbon tied around it. This was then passed around to everyone, accompanied by salt and water and, later, plates of food. If the deceased's ashes are present, the flowers and the lime will eventually be added to them, but for those already interred, the box is usually buried at the foot of the grave at a later date.

14. Gloriosas are said on Wednesdays, Saturdays, and Sundays; Gozosas for Mondays and Thursdays; and Dolorosas for Tuesdays and Fridays.

15. Little skeletons performing a wide variety of pastimes, duties, or work tasks are sold on the streets of Mexico. See Carmichael and Sayer 1991; Medina and Cadena 2002.

16. Stone 1975:24.

17. In the Bajio, they are kept for a full year and the dry flowers burned just before the next velación de ánimas.

18. I never saw this done. It is reported by Solorzano and Guerrero for the 1930s (1941:471), but in the film *El es Dios* (Bonfil and Muñoz 1965) the candles were simply lit with a match.

19. The date of this vigil was November 2, 1989.

20. This figure was probably Nuestra Señora de los Remedios.

21. This dance took place on September 9, 2001.

22. This also occurred at a vigil I attended in a house in the Bajio in August 2002.

23. This was a relatively small gathering because five mesas had simply not appeared, and of those present, many more of their dancers were coming the following day.

24. Most of their mandolins were made from guache (dried gourd).

25. At this particular vigil there were few candles or flowers. It was often difficult to get any sense of what an obligation would be like beforehand.

26. See Jáuregui and Bonfiglioni 1996 for an alternate version of this ritual.

27. Those named for Aztec deities are Huitzilopochtli, Tezcatlipoca, Tlaloc, and Xipe; for animals, *la aguila* (the eagle), *el venado* (the deer), *el sapo* (the toad), and *la paloma* (the dove); for natural entities or elements, *el sol* (the sun), *la lluvia* (the rain), *el viento* (the wind), and *el fuego* (the fire); for agricultural practices, *el sembrador* (the sower) and *el pulquita* (the little pulque).

28. A recent list made by Angelica named some thirty-five dances, fourteen of which are frequently enacted. Many now also have Nahuatl names and two have only Nahuatl names (see Appendix 3).

29. Today few urban dancers are sufficiently fit and practiced to be able to enact it but it can be seen in photographs from the 1960s.

30. Tambiah 1985b:138.

31. From the alabanza "La Gran Tenochtitlan," the first verse of which is *Estas son las flores / Que el Señor mando / Para la conquista / Del Santa Reliquia* ("These are the flowers / that the Lord sent / for the Conquest / of the Saintly Reliquia").

## CHAPTER 4: AGENCY AND THE DANCE: RITUALIZATION AND THE PERFORMATIVE

1. Turner 1967, 1969; Schechner 1985.

2. Bell 1992:39.

3. Goody 1977.

4. Moore and Meyerhoff 1977.

5. Goody 1977:27; Bocock 1974:15.

6. "The performative . . . is a cultural act, a critical perspective, a political intervention" (quoted by Roach [1995:46] from "The Editors Note," *PMLA* 107 [1992]:425).

7. Bell is critical of "performance theory" for, as she points out, "although performance may become a criteria for what is or is not ritual, insofar as performance is broadly used for a vast spectrum of activities, there is no basis [on which] to differentiate among ways of performing" (1992:42). See Bell 1992, for two further critiques.

8. Tambiah 1985b (1981):125.

9. Gerholm 1988.

10. Tambiah 1985b (1981):124–5; Bauman 1992:42.

11. Humphrey and Laidlaw 1994:69, 263.

12. Ibid., 64.

13. Tambiah 1985b (1981):132.

14. Tambiah 1985b (1981):161; Staal 1979; Rostas 1998a.

15. The term "habitus" was first used by Mauss (1979 [1936]) and then Bourdieu (1977). If I take washing the body as an example, this is precisely the kind of action that is done according to habitude. It is done frequently, usually in more or less the same way, with attention but not conscious intention other than that of getting one's body clean (an intention formed usually subconsciously before the action is begun), and carried out principally by means of embodied habitual activity. See Miner 1956.

16. Humphrey and Laidlaw 1994:5.

17. Ibid., 73.

18. Ibid., xx.

19. Lewis 1980; Humphrey and Laidlaw 1994:88, 94.

20. Tambiah 1985b (1981):133; Humphrey and Laidlaw 1994:96, 99, 12.

21. Tambiah 1985b (1981):133; Langer quoted in Tambiah 1985b (1981):134.

22. Irvine 1979:778; Geertz 1973 (1966). Strongly ritualized acts, however, "evoke responses [in the actors] and these responses may be as various as the interpretive vantage points in the everyday world from which people approach ritual" (Humphrey and Laidlaw 1994:12).

23. Humphrey and Laidlaw 1994:88.

24. Schieffelin 1998:196.

25. I want here to distinguish between the unintentional (the doing of something unintentionally) and action that is purposively not intentional (the non-intentional). In this instance, by non-intentional action I mean that the dancer attempts not to add anything that is of herself consciously and to act only non-intentionally—to go with the flow with her whole being.

26. Douglas 1973:41; Tambiah 1985b (1981):128, 138, 132. Staal discusses extensively the idea of ritual activity being without meaning (1979, 1986). "Like rocks and trees, ritual acts and sounds may be provided with meanings, but they do not require meanings and do not exist for meaning's sake." He suggests that, like languages, religions are "governed by rules, but unlike language in that they do not express meanings" (Staal 1986:217, 218).

27. See Battaglia 1995.

28. Ibid., 2.

29. Connerton 1989:103.

30. Csordas 1993:138.

31. Hymes 1975:13.

32. Ritual is discussed by other disciplines en passant, whereas performance has been a significant focus for a variety of disciplines, including linguistics, sociology, psychology, cultural studies, feminist studies, and dance and theater studies.

33. Carlson (1996:5), writing from a theater/literature perspective, discusses anthropological (i.e., folkloric), sociological, and linguistic perspectives on performance, as indeed does Csordas (1996). See also Sullivan 1986 for a summation and nuanced overview of other scholar's views on the rise in interest in performance. A writer on the theater recently observed that the word "performance is still ramifying" [*sic*] and thinks that a semiotic definition is an impossibility (States, quoted by Crease 1997:214).

34. Schieffelin 1998:194–195, but see also Schieffelin 1985, 1996.

35. Schieffelin 1998:194; Csordas 1996:92.

36. Schieffelin 1998:195.

37. Turner 1982:13.

38. *The Shorter Oxford English Dictionary* 1973.

39. Geertz 1986:380.

40. Goffman 1959; Bauman, quoted in Carlson 1996:5.

41. Searle 1969, 1979; Austin 1975 (1962).

42. That metalanguage would need perhaps to include a semantics of body language (Kaeppler 1989:454) or a dissection of components of behavior known as kinesics (Hymes 1975:13n6). Birdwhistell (1970) developed a complete linguistic system for measuring body movements, but to my knowledge, little work has been done in this area recently.

43. Bell on Wuthnow 1992:38.

44. Tambiah 1985b:138. Barba has suggested that in performance, extra-daily techniques replace the usual daily techniques of the body and are a source of information because "they . . . *put the body in-form*," that is, they can "in-form." This he sees as lying somewhere between what the everyday body communicates and virtuosity, which amazes and transforms the body but (rather surprisingly) apparently does not inform, perhaps because he sees virtuosity as pure ritualization (Barba 1991:10).

45. Tambiah 1985b (1981):138.

46. Turner 1982, 1986; Schechner 1985, 1988; Schechner and Appel 1991.

47. Schechner 1986.

48. Brooke 1968.

49. Tambiah 1985b (1981):139.

50. Roach 1995:46.

51. Ibid., 47.

52. Hymes 1975:13.

53. Schieffelin (1996) has written about the dangers of using the theater as an analogy for the kinds of performances that anthropologists study largely because of the separation between the actors and their audience and the effects that the former have on the latter. He claims too, perhaps mistakenly, that what the actors are enacting is only a simulacrum: it is not real.

54. Schieffelin 1996:61.

55. I have elsewhere used the example of washing up to illustrate this point, but see also a critique of this position by Scheiffelin (1998:197).

56. Hymes 1975.

57. Humphrey and Laidlaw 1994.

58. Phelan 1993:146.

59. Crease 1997:218–219.

60. Schieffelin 1998:194; Zarrilli 1990:133; see also Freedburg 1989:27.

61. Rostas 1998a:96; Parkin 1992:24.

62. Bateson 1973.

63. Connerton 1989:94.

64. Ibid., 101.

65. Further clarification on this can be found in writings on shamanism. Most shamans, initially at least, fake the curing process by sleight of hand. At some level this is deliberate but "perhaps not deeper than the foreconscious" (Kroeber, quoted by Goffman 1959:32). If the would-be shaman is not a good enactor and cannot begin by faking it while at the same time letting go, then the desired powers will not come. Kendell discusses the case of a young woman in Korea, Chini, who does not succeed as a shaman "because she fails to act like a shaman." She cannot quieten her mind and "give herself over to the flow of inspiration conjured by drum beats, dancing, [and] costumes" (Kendell 1996:50), thereby losing herself. "She fails because she is self-conscious and inhibited" (Laderman and Roseman 1996:6).

66. Humphrey and Laidlaw 1994:102.

67. But the reverse can also happen. Connerton has pointed out that incorporating practices cannot be "well accomplished without a diminution of the conscious attention paid to them" (1989:101). To think about the movement, to become conscious of it, tends to interrupt its flow. Hence, the dancer from another group who dances more flamboyantly cannot easily and immediately modify his dance.

68. Tambiah 1985b (1981):145.

69. Battaglia 1995:7.

70. Hastrup 1998.

71. Leder 1990:150.

72. Barba 1991:13, 12, italics in the original.

73. Schieffelin 1998:199, italics in original. This is his definition of performativity.

74. Ibid., 199.

75. Turner 1986:133.

76. Tambiah 1985b (1981):145.

77. Turner 1986; Csikszentmihalyi 1992.

78. Turner 1986:44; Tambiah 1985b (1981):145.

79. Turner 1986:44.

80. Tambiah 1985b (1981):145.

# CHAPTER 5: CONCHERO SPEAK: CARRYING THE WORD

1. Angelica indicated how dependent a mesa can be on its leader when she recounted the confusion at a vigil of another mesa after the death of its jefe (Don Faustino). The

two captains of the group did not really know what was expected of them while acting as palabras because their now defunct jefe had always instructed them as to what to do.

2. In Spanish as in English, "general" can mean the chief of a religious order: "prelado superior de una ordern religiosa" (Real Academia Espanol, *Diccionario de la Lengua Espanol*, 1992).

3. In the past there were few generals but, as one dancer said, "today every other jefe considers himself a general."

4. Sanchez Ventura 1990:2.

5. Csordas 1990:25.

6. McDowell in Bauman and Briggs 1990.

7. Boyer 1990; Derrida in Keane 1997:56.

8. Tambiah 1985b (1981):138.

9. Csordas 1990:11.

10. Kleinman and Kleinman 1994:712.

11. Cf. Coleman (1996:112), who discusses how Word of Life supporters talk about "walking on the Word . . . as if it were a solid foundation for physical as well as spiritual support."

12. Boyer 1990:112.

13. He explained his use of "sombra" here, saying that there are things that we do not see: the power of the standard cannot be captured visually. This is closely linked to *cuenta* and *planta* (see Chapter 3).

14. Much of the more detailed exegesis was gained by means of semi-structured interviews carried out during my third period of fieldwork in 1995 when I already had a general sense of what was implied by the terms.

15. See Chapter 9. According to Soledad, this name is being used because the dance is currently going through a period of decadence as it changes rapidly and is loosing some of its former spirituality.

16. Many dancers in Santo Niño de Atocha would not agree with her.

17. *Este documento será reconcido en altos y bajios y respectado por todos los comunidades que estan adentro de la orden general de conquista* ("This document shall be acknowledged and respected by all the communities that are within the order of the conquest").

18. Sanchez Ventura 1990:3.

19. Rostas 1987.

20. Fernandéz 1941:15; Moedano 1972:601. See Chapter 9 for more detail.

21. Clendinnen 1991; this suggestion was also made by the jefe Andres Segura (Vento 1994:63n4).

22. The three injunctions (union, conformity, and conquest) may also refer to the three aspects of the Holy Trinity: the Father, Son, and Holy Spirit that in God become one.

23. Tambiah 1985a (1973).

24. Although here "El" is the subject of the sentence and "Dios" the object, the Larousse Spanish dictionary indicates that "el," when part of a phrase like *el que vino ayer*, is translated as "the one who came yesterday." What I am suggesting is that I sensed that it was used in this more encompassing or abstract way as the one (who) is God (like).

The connection is metonymic rather than metaphorical, because the connection in the phrase has been established prior to its use before each dance by the permiso (Leach 1976:14).

25. The reflective use of the verb *endiosar se* usually has the meaning "to be elated with pride," which seems to reflect the Catholic belief that to attempt to become godlike is sinful.

26. To the Aztecs, the deities were immanent and could become incorporated into one another; there is a large body of literature on these beliefs (but see Brundage 1979). Put in another way, there is a bit of "God in every man" that each tries to approach by means of the dance, although no one actually suggested this to me in so many words—an indication, presumably, of the predominance of Catholic thought (Irvine 1982:249). Quakers discuss how God is considered to be inside all human beings and that the spirit moves each to speak as "the spirit dictates" (ibid., 249). During a Quaker meeting there is silence for most of the time and members speak only when moved to do so.

27. Many dancers could not or were reluctant to give an exegesis of "El es Dios." The general Guadalupe Hernandez's gloss of the invocation was pragmatic. He tended to talk about the dance in strictly Catholic terms and as still a dance of conquest, claiming that the expression signified "attention, respect, and obedience." Another linked it to the myth of the appearance of the cross at Sangremal, which ties in with an explanation given to Stone by a dancer of a friar converting Indians in the first days of the Conquest. He was carrying "a Cristo in his hands and when he came upon Indians worshipping idols he pointed to Our Lord on the Cross and called out 'El es Dios.'" (Stone 1975:163).

28. Stoller 1996:168.

29. For the indigenous people in Chamula (Chiapas, Mexico) and other communities, Gossen has described ritual language as "heated" rather than "cool." "Heated" words have a metaphorical sense and a religious significance, because "heat" has a particular meaning in Tzotzil: the principal deity is Htotik K'ak'al (Father Heat) or, in Tzeltal, K'ahkanantik (Hot/Fiery Protector), both of which refer also to the sun. Heated words are important in religious discourse where redundancy is frequent and the constraints on verbal form strong (Gossen 1974:48; Rostas 1987).

30. Sanchez Ventura n.d.:3.

31. Bauman and Briggs 1990:62.

32. Lewis 1980.

33. Tambiah 1985b (1981):163; Tambiah 1985a (1973).

34. Ibid., 145.

## CHAPTER 6: CLOTHING MATTERS

1. Csordas 1993:135.

2. El Guindi 1999; Barnes and Eicher 1992; Cordwell and Schwarz 1979; Eicher 1995; Weiner and Schneider 1989.

3. Tarlo 1996.

4. Sahlins (1976:185–186) uses the Barthian distinction of active as opposed to passive to elaborate a structuralist typology. What is worn on a daily, informal basis is

passive: we are being. But what is worn for an activity, whether sport or dance, is distinct and hence active. Veblen made a similar distinction between clothing for work versus that for leisure: leisure clothing being on the whole more marked than that worn for work (Veblen, in ibid., 186). Sahlins's typology indicates that clothing on both sides of the equation can be both more and less marked as some special occasions are more sacred or ceremonial than others (ibid., 186).

5. See Eicher and Sumberg 1995.

6. Crain 1996; Veber 1992; Canessa 2000.

7. Gell 1986:112.

8. Eicher 1995.

9. Csordas 1994b:14.

10. These skirts are fairly similar to the *nahua* or *nahui* worn in many indigenous communities in central Mexico.

11. Anwalt 1980, 1981; Arthur 1999.

12. But see Behar 1987; Furst and McKeever 1998:218.

13. According to jefe Manuel Luna, the feathers, known as *chililos*, gave their name to a type of headdress made with a plenitude of small white turkey feathers, which was worn in the first half of the twentieth century (Stone 1975:192).

14. Fernández 1941; Solorzano and Guerrero 1941.

15. Fernández 1941:12.

16. Ibid., 12.

17. Ibid., 12.

18. Fernández (1941:12) indicates that in some groups in the Bajio both sexes wore hats.

19. Their "best" clothing consisted of "skirts and blouses or dresses made from loud colors" and "often in their usual style" (Fernández 1941:12; and see Toor 1947:327).

20. Solorzano and Guerrero 1941:461.

21. Ibid., 454.

22. Toor makes a similar observation. In "recent years many of the groups wear brown chamois-skin suits, adorned with beads and leather fringe, feathered crowns as usual and bright silk kerchiefs" (1947:327).

23. Poveda (1981:291) suggests that the costumes looked like the clothing of the Apache. The image of the archetypical fearless Indian warrior in films dates back to the first decades of the twentieth century (Bird 1996). Several dancers suggested that the "Sun Dance" did not originate with the Concheros but came to Mexico possibly during the 1920s, when Mexico was strongly influenced by the United States.

24. Footage from Eisenstein's film *Que Viva Mexico!* (1931) confirms that the costumes of country dancers were often less embellished. They are shown wearing feathered headdresses and long skirts that are predominantly plain although a few have floral patterns or abstract shapes with fringed edges.

25. For example, buildings were designed in Aztec style, such as the edifice for the World Fair in Paris in 1889 (Tenorio 1993).

26. Alonso 2004:463–468; De la Peña 2002:47–50, but see also Chapter 9 of this book.

27. Brading 1988; Dawson 2004:21; Nájera Ramírez 1989:19.

28. This was the precursor to the now well-known Ballet Folklorico, which was started by Amelia Hernandez in 1952 and includes Conchero dances to this day (see Nájera Ramírez 1989:20; Hellier Tinoco 2004:51).

29. Nájera Ramírez 1994. The latter includes a mural by Fernando Leal of "The Dancers of Chalma" (1922) which shows dancers who wear feather (and beribboned headdresses), one of whom beats a drum while another plays a pipe. In the study for the mural it is just possible to read the wording on the banner in the background: "Asociación de Senor del Claustro de Tacuba." The men predominantly wear long sleeved garments with layered trousers, each different in color and trimmed with ribbon (which ties in to an extent with Toor's description of "gay ballet-dancer skirts" (1947:327). They wear strings of beads, sport cloaks and some have masks. The mural very effectively gives the feel of the Concheros' circle dance, but as they lack conchas, it cannot be assumed that these dancers were Concheros. They were probably dancers linked to a *cofradia* as were the Concheros before coming to the city (Ades 1989:156; Rochfort 1993; and see Chapter 9).

30. This was a purely cultural, even aesthetic, form of *Mexicanidad* and should not be confused with the more strident political version that developed later (see Chapter 10).

31. Weston 1990:80; Knight 1994:431.

32. Solorzano and Guerrero 1941:460, 451, 459.

33. Ibid., 450, 459.

34. Stone 1975:192.

35. Ibid., 173. One way of resolving this problem was for the dancer to wear a manta shift under his Aztec-style finery (ibid., frontispiece; Toor 1947:photo 75).

36. Stone 1975:175.

37. Toor 1947:327.

38. Fernández 1941:12.

39. Toor 1947:325; Stone 1975:194.

40. In highland Guatemala, the clothing worn by indigenous women acted as a marker of marital status, age, and social standing. How she tied her hair ribbons, the length she wore her skirt, and the manner of its pleating were all social indicators, part of an intricate semiotic code (Osborne 1965). It has been claimed that the Aztecs had complex sumptuary laws, but according to Anawalt (1980), their strictness has probably been exaggerated.

41. That is, earth, water, wind, and fire or sun.

42. Sahlins 1976:184. Although changes in high fashion can be associated with the trickle-down effect, much of the style of what we wear daily is based much more on what has become appropriate for the zeitgeist. We see fashion as change where an innovation is introduced, accepted, and later discarded, however small in scale, as do the Concheros. See Eicher and Sumberg (1995:299), quoting Roach-Higgins (1991:128), who suggests that if "people in a society are generally not aware of change in form of dress during their lifetime, fashion does not exist in that society."

43. Weiner and Schneider 1989:2.

44. Keali'inihomoku 1979.

45. Toor 1947:327.

46. Turner 1995 (1985):148.

47. Hollander 1993:250, 262. Hollander seems to be implying that dance (and other physical forms) does not speak visually to its audience, which it surely must because it too is a visual form.

## CHAPTER 7: WHY DANCE?

1. Quoted in Fernández 1941:9.

2. Levin 1985:297.

3. Kaeppler 1978:47, passim. Hanna has defined "dance" as human behavior composed, from the dancer's perspective, of purposeful, intentionally rhythmical, and culturally patterned sequences of nonverbal body movement and gesture that are not ordinary motor activities, the motion having inherent and "aesthetic value" (Hanna 1977:212; but see also Copeland and Cohen's 1983 anthology of articles). Suzanne Langer's (1953) theory of dance is of interest, as is Sparshott's book (1988) on the philosophy of dance. Indeed, dance is often used as a trope for life, as in the dance of life. T. S. Eliot in his poem "Burnt Norton" points out that the aim of life is the dance or to dance, whereas for Murakami (1994) "dance" is a way of changing the self.

4. In Japan, for example, three forms—mikagura (performed in Shinto shrines), buyo (performed in relation to or within a Kabuki drama), and bon (performed to honor the dead)—all appear to Western eyes to be forms of dance but are not classified as such by the Japanese. Indeed, any term that could classify these three cultural forms together would also include much of what would not be considered dance from a Western point of view (Kaeppler 1978:46).

5. In Chiapas, Mexico, when the Tenejapans *ahk'ot*, they move their weight slowly from one foot to the other, slightly raising the heel of the weightless foot. Performed only during some festivals, it is a rhythmic and stylized shifting distinct from everyday movement and carried out in response to music. Ahk'ot has generally been glossed as "dance" but were it not for the music, it might be difficult to see it as such (Rostas 1987; see also Slocum and Gerdel 1980; Laughlin 1975).

6. Ness 1992; Lowell Lewis 1995.

7. Lowell Lewis 1992; Ness 1992.

8. Kaeppler 1978:46. In this review article only forty-three references are listed, which include Kaeppler's work and that of Kuruth, Royce, and Hanna, all specialists in dance. Kaeppler points out that Schieffelin's *The Sorrow of the Lonely and the Burning of the Dancers* (1976) was then probably the best anthropological study because it presents the dance in its full ethnographic context.

9. Reed looks at hundreds of references in his 1998 article, but see especially Wulff 1998; Taylor 1998; Ness 1992; Cowan 1990; Parviainen 1998; and Mendoza Walker 2000.

10. Ness 1992:236.

11. Various choreographic notations exist by which dance steps can be recorded, such as the Laban, Benesch, and Noa-Eshkol systems (see Kleinman 1975 for more detail). Easily deciphered only by those who have studied them, the notations are too

specialized for non-dancers but helpful to professionals in recording the finer nuances. They can, of course, say nothing about the experiential aspects.

12. See Ness 1992.

13. Quoted in Bateson 1973:110.

14. In this sense the Concheros' dance is quite different from Morris dancing, a comparison often made by people with whom I have discussed the Concheros. Morris dancing lacks an emerging spirituality probably because the dances were recorded and thus institutionalized by the Sharps in the early decades of the 1900s (Forrest 1985). The Concheros' dances are more like the dances linked to ritual forms found widely in the anthropological record of the less-developed world.

15. Parkin 1992:24; Leder 1990:153.

16. Leder 1990.

17. Geertz 1983:27, referring to Turner.

18. Radcliffe-Brown 1922:249.

19. Blacking 1979:10, 8.

20. Knauft 1979:190; Howes 1991:132.

21. Feld 1991:79; but see also Feld 1990 (1982).

22. Feld 1991:92.

23. Howes 1991:143, 132.

24. Deren 1953:228.

25. Turner has called this state of intersubjectivity "communitas" (Turner 1982, 1986).

26. Interestingly, Eduardo was not interested in informal social dancing.

27. There is an ongoing debate as to whether dance should be seen as instrumental or non-instrumental movement (i.e., goal-oriented or not). This depends not only on the context of its enactment but also on how instrumentality is defined. If we draw the Western distinction between work and leisure, then in many cases dance in general is seen as non-instrumental activity where work is to instrumental activity as leisure is to non-instrumental activity. But this interpretation clearly rests on a materialist definition of instrumentality as work that produces measurable benefit, whereas in many of the societies that anthropologists look at this kind of distinction is not made. As Lowell Lewis points out, some so-called leisure activities in the West are considered central to many people's lives and have goals that are often more spiritual than material (1995:228). Dance can be a form of play, "a movement which carries away the dancer" (Gadamer, quoted by Clendinnen 1991:258), and a way of eclipsing subjectivity "for in play subjectivity forgets itself" (Ricoeur 1981:186).

28. According to Soledad, who works in the theater, the multisensory nature of the dance "keeps the cosmos going . . . the turns and steps serve to carry the energy and at the same time return or transmit it to the circle, to the community."

29. Deren 1953:229.

30. See McNeill 1995 on the potency of marching.

31. The Aztecs danced, sang, and played music. That dance was of central importance to their culture is indicated by the fact that every festival had its dance, but dance was also inseparable from music and song. Many now claim that the Concheros' dances

have descended from those of the Aztecs (see Chapter 6). Certainly the overall form is similar to that of Aztec dancing, according to the depictions that have come down to us, but its practice may have been a reinvention of the early nineteenth century (see Chapter 9). The type of music, the context in which it is performed, and the backgrounds from which dancers now come are so different that comparison is not particularly helpful in thinking about why the Concheros dance.

32. Clendinnen 1991:259.

33. As Eduardo stated, "it's important to feel you are collaborating with the animas. We don't know how to manage the energy that is coming out of the circle. It's powerful. There's a lot of force. Shamanic tunnels or doors are opened and the divine substance flows. However, if the dancer doesn't know what he's doing, and almost nobody knows, it's good when this substance escapes because it's not for you. You are the medium, the opener. . . . Remember, in magic you never ask for yourself only for others."

34. Known elsewhere as *orenda* or *manitou*; see Csordas 1990:42.

35. Clendinnen 1991:259.

36. Tambiah 1985:145.

37. Needham 1967:610.

38. Ibid., 606; Rouget 1985:171, 170; Blacking 1968:313; Rouget 1985:169, 87. I am not qualified to discuss the physiological effects of sounds on the body, but the effect of rhythm and noise (or music) on any one individual must obviously be subjective, because some people can tolerate much louder noise levels than others. Some work has been done to attempt to establish the levels at which non-ordinary states of consciousness are induced by drumming and other percussion instruments (see Neher 1962; Jilek 1982). However, Rouget effectively rubbishes this work by pointing out that "half of Africa would be in trance from the beginning of the year to the end" if they were correct about the levels they propose (1985:172–176). Effective experimental conditions are probably impossible to set up as pure tone produced in a laboratory is much less likely to simulate the intensity achieved during an event.

39. No one commented to me that the lack of music caused any change. In fact, they were quite emphatic that a dancer should be able to transcend whatever is going on around him/her.

40. The jefe Andres Segura claimed that although the dances have a Christian form, they conserve the essence of the ancestors, who cleverly reduced the steps to numbers. Each dance has a determinate number of steps that does not change and that are said to move certain energies (Poveda 1981:291). A recent book written and published by a dancer addressed this aspect: "It has been observed that in the rhythms of all the dances can be found immersed the basic numbers of prehispanic mathematics" (Lara González 1993:69). Many Concheros share this fascination with numerology.

41. See Csikszentmihalyi (1964, 1975) for a discussion of the effects of rock climbing.

42. Another expression Eduardo used was "el mero mero matatero," which can loosely be translated as "the real thing" but which he glossed for me as the animas or the ancestors. Soledad referred to the "creative center" or the "center of benevolence or consent [*voluntad*]" from which all the energy of the cosmos comes.

43. Ots (1994:133), quoting Merleau-Ponty (1964).

44. Angelica said this in relation to Sufi practice. As indicated in Chapter 2, in the 1980s a Sufi master came to Mexico City and joined the dance for a while with the apparent intention of converting the dancers. Many of Compadre Ernesto's group left, some for only a short period; others still danced as Concheros while following Sufi practices (which include dance). Angelica had not become a Sufi, because she felt that "once a member of the Sufis you are part of the conquered."

45. Fabian 1990:261.

46. Ideally in dance, the dancer's body moves in such a way that the movement is seamless. Laban is quoted as saying, "the lasting, uninterrupted flow of organized movement phrases is true dance" (in Sparshott 1988:206).

47. See Rostas 1992:367.

48. Stallybrass has pointed out that the word "individual" has only gained the meaning that it has today comparatively recently and that prior to the seventeenth century, it meant indivisible. (This becomes clearer if you replace "in" by "un"—hence, "undivisible." The undivisible was inextricably linked to another, like the three of the Holy Trinity or the undivisible pair, the divinely linked man and woman.) Thus, at the time of Shakespeare, "individual" appears to have referred to the indivisibility of the two sexes and it was at about that time that it began to gain the opposing sense that it still has today (Stallybrass 1993). Cf. Strathern 1990 (1988):15, 348.

49. Ness 1992:5.

50. Strathern 1990 (1988):13.

51. Deren 1953:229.

52. Leder 1990:5–7.

53. Clendinnen 1991:259.

54. Stoller 1996:181.

55. Merleau-Ponty 1962; Csordas 1994a:270.

56. Deren 1953:229, italics in original.


## CHAPTER 8: ALLIANCES AND IDENTITY POLITICS

1. Jackson 1996:5, 6.

2. Evans-Pritchard 1940:5.

3. Dancers in the Bajio have yet another locational topography. According to de la Peña Martínez, the four winds are located at Zamorano in the north, Cimatario in the south, the sanctuary of La Virgen del Pueblito in the west, and the Santa Cruz de Milagros (on the mountain of Sangremal) in the east (1999:65).

4. Fabian 1990:16.

5. The other two jefes in this group were Manuel Luna, who died in 1993, and Carmillo Bárcenas, who died in the early 2000s.

6. Graniceras are said to be able to dispel hailstorms (*granizadas*) (see Glockner 2000). Black as opposed to white jefes are believed to dabble in black magic. The qualities of the various jefes are frequently discussed in these terms.

7. The other animas mentioned were those of Maria Graciana, the Anima Sola, and Santo Niño de Atocha.

8. Amecameca, San Rafael, Tepetlixpa, and Mexicalcingo (all except San Rafael located in the State of Mexico). At the dance at La Villa in December 1989, two banners of Santo Niño de Atocha were present representing the mesa of Compadre Ernesto and that of Doroteo. Although Doroteo always danced with Compadre Ernesto, he had recently had his own banner made; his mesa is also linked to the Virgen de los Remedios. They were all joined also by the mesa of Miguel Gutierrez (also Santo Niño de Atocha but with different imagery).

9. Compadre Ernesto's mesa also dances in Amecameca at the end of January, at Tetelcingo in the State of Guerrero in October, and in San Rafael also in October, all dances convened by allies of Compadre Ernesto and Don Faustino. These allies are Graviel or Gabriel Hernandez of Amecameca (Mexico), Mariano Zavalo and his inheritor Marciano Zavalo of Tetelcingo (Morelos), and Salvador Contreras of San Rafael (in the State of Mexico). Other allies of them both are Vicente of Cuijingo (Mexico), Fernando of Yecapixtla (Morelos), Lucino of Axocopan (Puebla), Pablino of San Miguel Atlautla (Mexico), and the inheritor of Ermilio Jimenez from Zapotitlan.

10. Some sources indicate that the Corporación had originally been inside the Reliquia but that it later became a palabra in its own right. Guadalupe Hernandez gives Vicente Marquez as founder and the date as February 25, 1922 (see Chapter 9).

11. Predominantly, these locations are in the Bajio some 125 miles northeast of Mexico City, but Aguascalientes is some 125 miles further to the northeast.

12. Present were General Guadalupe Hernandez, General Manuel Luna, Ernesto Ortiz, General Camillo Bársenas, Andres Segura, Jesus Leon, Salvador Contreras, Emilio Segura, and Soledad Ruiz, a captain in Manual Luna's palabra. Guadalupe Hernandez had mentioned in a discussion with me beforehand others whom he had hoped would attend: Miguel Abasolo, Ignacio Cortez, Ermilio Jimenez, Miguel Alvarado, Manual Cruz, Virginio Hernandez, Florencio Osorio, and Teresa Mejia.

13. He has a mesa of his own in San Rafael.

14. He was, however, central to the dance in the 1960s (see Chapter 9).

15. Miguel has now started a mesa in Chicago, where there are an ever-increasing number of Concheros.

16. The group has so far been successful but as yet numbers few dancers (between fifteen and twenty).

17. Ricardo is the eldest son of Carmen, the daughter of the jefe's brother and his wife, Dominga (see Appendix 5).

18. This alliance continued after Ricardo was declared inheritor and Felipe Aguilar, the jefe of the Corporación, was made a godfather to Ricardo.

19. One poet-writer who was studying dance at that time joined up with Andres Segura. She travelled with his mesa almost continuously but finally left after six months as she found it just too demanding and financially insecure. Although as dancers they were fed and housed wherever they went, she felt she needed more time to herself and a steady income.

20. Interestingly, the banner of the mesa from Amecameca, raised in 1988 by Compadre Faustino (see Chapter 5), indicated that they had had the backing (*apadrinado*) of, among others, General Andres Segura.

21. Toward the end of his life, Segura spent an increasing amount of time in the southern United States (which he called Aztlan), where he raised a number of successful groups in California, New Mexico, and Texas (Xinachtli Califaztlan, Novo Mexicaztlan, and Texaztlan, respectively). According to Avila (2000), he had modified some of the practices, establishing weekend festivals rather than holding urban dances, and he was also involved in healing and the training of curandero/as.

22. This peripatetic tendency is most often found among younger dancers, such as Susana (mentioned in Chapter 2). Many dancers say that they really appreciate the experience of dancing with other groups because the feel of the dance is so very different and they find this both stimulating and part of the learning process.

23. The literature on African acephalous societies and segmentary lineages is relevant here. In a sense, the Association of Concheros is rather like an acephalous society, made up of a number of lineages, each with its head but with no overall government. The generals have no executive or judicial authority and are a bit like the leopard-skin chiefs of the Nuer, who as mediators were "sacred person[s] without political authority" (Evans-Pritchard 1940:5). Although the generals tend to be given more respect than other dancers, especially by members of their own mesa, in the end they have no more political authority to control social relations than anyone else.

# CHAPTER 9: ORAL TRADITION, MYTH, AND HISTORY

In the early part of this chapter, the source footnotes are predominantly placed at the end of each paragraph.

1. The "Compendium of the Activities of Santo Niño de Atocha from 1922 Onwards" was produced in 2001 and compiled in part with the aid of my tape recordings of the meeting of jefes in 1990.

2. Documentation is a strong part of current Mexican culture and its significance is indicative of a desire for literacy. For the Concheros, documents are usually set up according to the rules laid down for all associations.

3. Lockhart 1992:374.

4. Circle dances are also found in many other cultures throughout the world (Sten 1990; Oesterley 1923).

5. The year 1531 is also the year when the Virgin of Guadalupe appeared at Tepeyac (La Villa).

6. "Ensinal" glosses as stream, although according to one dancer, "encina" is a type of tree that in large numbers forms a forest, an "encinal."

7. This battle was perhaps a bit like the *guerras floridas* of the Aztecs, which were "fought" with their neighbors not to kill but to take captives for human sacrifice (Burkhart 1989:50).

8. The following is part translation and part paraphrase of "Fragments of the account Don Nicolas de San Luis Montañez" (Beaumont 1932), written most probably in 1744, according to Warman (1985 [1972]:72) and quoted by Fernandez and colleagues (1941:15–16, 39–42), on whom other writers on the Concheros have also relied (e.g., Gonzalez 1996:218; Stone 1975:197).

9. Stone 1975:254.

10. This resistance continued specifically in the Sierra Gorda (Behar 1987; Gruzinski 1986; Marta García Ugarte, personal communication).

11. The Otomis had lived in the region immediately north of Tenochtitlan but were predominantly pushed off their more fertile lands and moved northward into the Bajio during the second half of the fifteenth century.

12. Fernandez 1941:41.

13. Fr. Alonso de la Rea in Fernandéz 1941:16. I witnessed a similar procession in the Bajio in 2002.

14. Warman 1985 (1972):58.

15. Burkhart 1989:50.The *nahui ollin*, a pre-Hispanic symbol in the form of a cross, has four equal-sized arms. Nahui Ollin was also the name of a day in the 260-day calendar. See Burkhart 1989:58; Brotherston 1992:16; Brundage 1979:39.

16. Beaumont quoted in Moedano 1984:5; Fernandez 1941:15; Stone 1975:198.

17. Gruzinski 1986:338, 343.

18. Ibid., 343; passim. In this, Montáñez (not Conín) addresses the Chichimeca chief(s) using terms of the greatest respect. Gruzinski suggests that this is probably an exceptional Indian version that seeks to deny the true nature of the Conquest and "the degradation of the vanquished" (Ibid., 344). This version was penned at a time when the power of the Otomis was dwindling in the area as they became just one indigenous group among many.

19. Ibid., 341–342.

20. Alabanzas are difficult to date. The last two are probably fairly recent as Cuauhtémoc only regained significance toward the end of the nineteenth century. Vasquez de Santa Ana suggests that "Cuando nuestra América" comes from the seventeenth century but gives no source (1953:261).

21. Pueblito de Tlaxcala / No te puedo olvidar / Porque alli fue fundada / La palabra general / Pueblito de Dolores / . . . / Porque alli fue levantada / La reliquia general ("Little town of Tlaxcala / I cannot forget you / For established there / Was the Palabra General / Little town of Dolores / . . . / For raised there / Was the Reliquia General"). The best-known town called Tlaxcala today is the one in the state of that name, located close to Mexico City, although another Tlaxcala existed in the sixteenth century in the "heartland of the Chichimeca group of Guachichiles," today part of the city of San Luis Potosi (Behar 1987:121).

22. The document is a notice announcing the honoring of an important ánima, a general of their confraternity who had died some five years previously. This confraternity has had links with the mesa of Santo Niño de Atocha for some years. I am grateful to Ernesto Cabral for bringing this document to my attention.

23. This occurred in the Puerto de Chamacuero, known today as the Arroyo de Fraile and in the present-day city of San Miguel de Allende.

24. This implies that he was recognized both in the Bajio (the lowlands) and also in *los altos*, (the heights) the region of the other two *conformidades* (see Chapter 2).

25. The indigenous population of the Bajio is today quite small, but the Otomi language is still spoken by about 300,000 people (of whom 9,000 are monolingual). As

Moedano has suggested, it is likely that Otomi became the lingua franca for ritual and was used to preserve religious practices and understandings between groups that had previously been heterogeneous or even hostile to one another (Moedano 1972:603).

26. Behar 1987:119.

27. Moedano 1984:6, quoting Zelaa e Hidalgo; Moedano 1972:602.

28. *Nepantla*, "in the middle," is the Nahuatl term used to describe the state in which people find themselves when they are trying to make sense of two religions: the one that is threatened and the other that has yet to be assimilated or understood. This situation is vividly described in sources from the 1530s to the 1650s (Klor de Alva 1982:353–355; León-Portilla 1974:24).

29. Gruzinski 1990:206; Wolf 1957:186; Gruzinski 1990:210. The complexity of confraternities is not easy to unravel. Not only were they so numerous and varied as to be difficult to classify but the boundaries between *mayordomias*, *hermandades*, and *cofradias* and *devociones* are far from clear. Bearing that in mind, I have kept to the term "confraternity" (*cofradia*) and sometimes use "solidarity" (Gruzinski 1990:211, 210, 205). Reconstructing social history from secondary sources is always difficult, and on dance in relation to confraternities and associations, it is particularly so.

30. Lockhart 1992:219, 223; Gibson 1964:132; Gruzinski 1990:209; Llaguno 1963: 286.

31. Warman 1985 (1972); Gruzinski 1990:206; Bierhorst 1985b:527n19, quoting Sahagún.

32. Códice Franciscano 1941:206, in Alberro 1998:123; Ricard 1966:184; Alberro 1998:126. Today, in indigenous communities, in Chiapas, the indigenes still perform many of their rituals inside the church; however, their rituals are not Catholic and have only a slight Christian gloss (Rostas 1987). During the sixteenth century, outdoor impromptu "churches" were gradually replaced by buildings (see McAndrew 1964).

33. Alberro 1998:123; Gruzinski 1990:207; Gibson 1964:127.

34. Gruzinski 1990:206. This applied particularly to the Otomis, who had fared better initially. In Queretero, by the end of the sixteenth century they were no longer the only indigenous group but just one among many subaltern peoples—including Nahuas, Tarascos, negroes, mulattos, and mestizos—and were beginning to live in "an atmosphere of crisis and social and political decline" (Gruzinski 1986:341).

35. "Santocalli" means saint house or oratory and is a term part Spanish (*santo*, "saint") and part Nahuatl (*calli*, "house") (Lockhart 1992:536n48). Pizzigoni, who has worked on documents from Toluca, indicates that in the seventeenth century "santocalli" was replaced by "ichatzinco dios" (glossed loosely as house of god) and later in the eighteenth century by the Spanish "oratorio" (Pizzigoni 2005).

36. An image of the Virgin of Guadalupe was, it is claimed, to be found in "every house in New Spain" of both the rich and the poor by 1659 (Brading 1991:346, 351). This seems unlikely in the more rural and indigenous communities, as even today the Virgin of Guadalupe is relatively unknown among the indigenes in outlying areas of Mexico, such as Chiapas.

37. Gruzinski 1990:215–218; Lockhart 1992; Beezley 1997:92.

38. Gruzinski 1990:213.

39. Taylor 1996:310, 322, 307, 315; Gruzinski 1990:212; Hall and Jefferson 1989; Beezley, Martin, and French 1994; Chance and Taylor 1985:17.

40. Harris (1993) discusses theatrical performances of the Moors and Christians in the years after the Conquest.

41. Moedano 1984:6, quoting Zelee e Hidalgo 1926:99; Warman 1985 (1972); Clendinnen 1985:50; Warman 1985 (1972):98; Rea quoted in Fernandez 1941:16.

42. Rea points out that previously "they had mixed dances [mitotes y bailes] with the military . . . often there had been from two hundred to three hundred or even more dancers wearing on their heads feather headdresses and each with a large green feather in their left hand" (Fernandez 1941:16).

43. "Mitote" comes from the Nahuatl "mitotia," a term employed in Tenochtitlan, with netotiliztli to indicate dancing of an informal kind as opposed to a more formal form (see Chapter 10). After the Conquest, first "mitotia" and then gradually "mitote" became the term used for most forms of indigenous dance (Motolinía 1971:386; Clendinnen 1991:356; Sahagún 1950–1982, 8:17, 5; Cervantes de Salazar 1914 (1650):462.

44. Warman 1985 (1972):99–101; Bierhorst 1985b:90, quoting Clavijero.

45. In many communities, the "battle" between either the Moors and Christians or the Chichimecas and the Spaniards, which includes dance, survives to this day as sustained by conservatives during the nineteenth century (Warman 1985 [1972]:96). See, for example, the photographic essay of Vértiz and Alfaro (2001) and Harris (1996).

46. Earlier reappraisals had contrasted the Aztecs favorably with the Greeks and Romans and even the Egyptians. Tenenbaum (1994:13) refers to the writings of the Jesuit Manuel Duarte, and Phelan (1960) discusses the widespread influence of Clavijero's work (see also Lafaye 1976; Brading 1985).

47. Carillo y Perez 1979 (1808):105–106, and quoted in part in Albero 1998:128.

48. Moedano 1984:4; Warman 1985 (1972):105, quoting Guillermo Prieto. See Bernal 1980 for a discussion on archaeology during this period.

49. Gibson 1964:131. I thank Edwin Rojas for the suggestion regarding kinship.

50. Taylor 1996; Gruzinski 1990:212; Brading 1991:656; Chance and Taylor 1985:17.

51. Bernal 1980:102; Guzman 1966. According to Guedea (1989:48), 1808 is the date of the first secret society, whereas Greenleaf (1969) suggests 1782.

52. Bastian 1995:449; Gonzalez Torres 1996:5; Bastian 1995:448; Guedea 1989; Guzman 1966. Work on secret societies has focused predominantly on Masonic lodges (such as Los Guadalupes), some but not all of which were involved in insurgency (Guedea 1989). Freemasonry came to New Spain from post-revolutionary France, where it had taken a more liberal form than in other European countries. It was often socialist in its aims to abolish differences of race, color, fatherland, all national hatreds, and fanaticism (Rangel 1932:v). Little has been written about Freemasonry (Francmasonaria) in Mexico, although the Freemasons have played a large, even privileged, role in the political life of the country, especially since the establishment of the federal system of government (Bastian 1995; Guedea 1989:61).

53. Archive of the Bibilioteca de Antropologia, Mexico, D.F.; Guzman 1966; Beezley 1994:174.

54. Bernal 1980:114.

55. Vasquez de Santa Ana 1953:252–259; but he makes no reference to the where-abouts of the documents. Both are quoted by Warman (1985 [1972]:111) and more extensively still by Moedano (1984).

56. Vasquez de Santa Ana 1953:255.

57. Vasquez de Santa Ana tells us that "[t]he commander-in-chief of the distin-guished troops of the dance of the bow and arrow and other annual devotions," who had held the position since 1820, had inherited his command over these "from his ances-tors and others established by arrangement with . . . Sanchez and his secretary . . . who have developed them with great efficiency and punctuality" (Vasquez de Santa Ana 1953:255).

58. Ibid., 256.

59. Moedano claims to have seen documents dating its antecedents to 1531, and the mesa Santa Cruz de los Milagros is said to have various documents including a parchment purportedly dated August 17, 1558, in memory of the priest Julian Campos, the great nephew of Cónin, who the current general claimed was a "fifth grandparent"(Moedano 1984:7, 8).

60. Vasquez de Santa Ana 1953:252.

61. Warman 1985 (1972):111.

62. Guedea (1989:49) points out that in the nineteenth century, hierarchical secret societies chose their members carefully and had certain rituals of membership, such as initiation, to bind those who joined. They usually promised to care for their broth-ers—the raison d'être of the societies—and asked their members never to reveal their existence. They tended also to have certain gestures or symbols by which the adepts were able to recognize each other. A masonic lodge in Jalapa had certain words that had to be spoken to identify a member: union, fortaleza, and valor (ibid., 54). Although "union" is part of the Concheros leitmotif, their terms are never used as passwords, at least today. The Concheros once initiated, however, promise to dance for the rest of their lives till death "cuts off" their steps, to care for other members, and to maintain the organization intact and unchanging.

63. Brading 1991:656; Warman 1985 (1972):106; Knowlton 1976.

64. If the later, it is possible that it was under Masonic influence that the groups became known as "mesas"; a number of dancers claim the date of 1872 in Queretero for this change. However, "mesa" is also the name used for the altar-like arrangements of power objects in various other Latin American curing traditions (see Sharon 1978: 174–183).

65. It is possible that Miguel had mixed up the early twentieth century with the nineteenth century.

66. Witnessing an "Indian dance in the church" in Chalma, Tylor commented that the dancers—Indian boys in short tunics and headdresses of feathers and as many girls—danced a polka "to our unspeakable astonishment'" and than "a Schottish, another waltz and a quadrille." He was assured that this was not the great festival, which took place once a year when "the Indians come from fifty miles around and stay here several days, living in the caves in the rock just by the town, buying and selling in the fair, attending

mass and having solemn dances in the church" (Tylor 1861:210–211). Unfortunately, he did not see these.

67. Bastian 1995.

68. The Kikapoo were Canadian indigenes resettled in Texas who it was feared would join up with Mexican indigenes. Represented in a painting by Beaucé, they are depicted with feathered headdresses that are far more stereotypically "Indian" than those seen in contemporary photographs (Acevedo 2005).

69. Warman 1985 (1972):103.

70. Beezley 1997:96; Brading 2001:289, 312; Beezley 1997:97–98; Brading 2001: 288.

71. Stone 1975:198. This undoubtedly represents a Mexico City–centric view of the dance, as it was more firmly established in the Bajio. Today, as already indicated, it is still common to consult with important jefes in other parts of the association about matters concerning potential new jefes (see Chapter 8).

72. Benjamin 2000:171; Morgan 1994:153–153; Knight 1994; Morgan 1994: 157.

73. Sources for this section are as indicated on page 166 but include too the "Reseña Historica" produced by Santo Niño de Atocha in 2001.

74. The exact date was March 11, 1876, and the location was possibly in San Simon (Guadalupe Hernandez; Fin del Milenio: 8). However, sources differ as to the date. Stone (1975:208) implies that the Reliquia was raised in the city in 1887, whereas Guadalupe Hernandez (probably a more reliable source) claims it was raised in 1876, especially as Gabriel Moedano indicated that there had been a celebration to mark the centenary in 1976 (personal communication).

75. Stone 1975:209.

76. Soledad Ruiz and Guadalupe Hernandez (interviews).

77. According to Stone (1975:208), Ignacio Gutierrez was the nephew and not the son of Jesus Gutierrez.

78. Stone 1975:209.

79. Odena Güemes 1984:82.

80. De la Peña 2002; Brading 2001; Dawson 1998; Knight 1994:408.

81. Stone 1975:209. One analyst suggests that the Corporación was established en contra to the rigid and pyramidal organization of the other mesas (Gonzalez Torres 2000:27).

82. Stone 1975:209; Guadalupe Hernandez (interview). The other mesas are those of Felipe Aranda, Camilo Varsenas, and the Alvarados.

83. Knight 1994:397, 431. See also Chapter 6.

84. Knight 1994:431; Dawson 1998:281.

85. Alonso 2004:484n11; Dawson 1998:284–286.

86. Alonso 2004:403; Knight 1994:404.

87. Quoted in de la Peña 2002:51.

88. Brading 2001:317.

89. According to one dancer, Miguel Gutierrez, the dance had continued in the Bajio throughout this period and the dancers used the churches without problems.

90. Among Ignacio Gutierrez's allies were Felipe Hernandez, Los Hermanos Barrera, Rafael Sanchez, Guadalupe Hernandez, and Ernesto Ortiz, all names mentioned at the meeting of jefes held in 1989. There were undoubtedly many more, such as Felipe Aranda and Manuel Pineda.

91. Teresa Mejia (interview). Guadalupe Hernandez, however, did not inherit the original standard (reliquia), which went to one of the Gutierrez brothers, Florencio, who later assumed the position of a general but does not dance in Mexico City. The reliquia is now kept in Progresso Nacional (in Hidalgo).

92. The following standards (that I photographed) mention his name as their founder: Santiago Apostel (of which Herman Santiago is the current jefe); La Virgen de los Dolores (with jefe Arturo Balverde); La Virgen de Guadalupe (with jefe Adelita Vargas, at Tulpetlan in the State of Mexico); El Senor de Chalma at San Juan Citlaltepec.

93. According to Stone 1975:208.

94. See Chapter 8. According to Manuel Luna (as reported in Stone 1975:208), his predecessors raised their banner before that of the Reliquia, although, as indicated above, this is not supported by the Reliquia. The location of their oratorios in relation to the center of the city is one way of assessing which established its palabra first.

95. Stone 1975:152; Ernesto Cabral. By recognizing the palabras in this way, the Church might have hoped to gain some control over the dance.

96. The date of Ignacio Gutierrez's death has been reported as 1960 (by Teresa Mejia) and 1968 (by Guadalupe Hernandez).

97. This sergeant was probably Ciriaco Gutierrez, mentioned at the vigil on November 2, 1989, in a full list of the animas.

98. Stone 1975:210; but she does not provide a date for this controversy (her book covers a period of twenty-five years beginning in the 1950s).

99. De la Peña 2002:50.

100. Information from Teresa Mejia; Bonfil Batalla and Muñoz 1965. Both the film and the record were produced by the Instituto Nacional de Antropología y Historia (INAH) in 1965.

101. They also danced more sedately in the Plazuela Santo Domingo.

102. One dancer remembers that Pedro Rodriguez became more and more involved in "show" and went frequently to the United States, where he stayed more or less permanently from the early 1980s onward.

103. Those mesas are the ones of Cruz Hernandez, Guadalupe Torres, Remedios Osorio, Teresa Mejia, Ernesto Ortiz, and Florencio Osorio.

104. Gonzalez Torres 1996, 2000.

105. The PRI is the political party that controlled the government for seventy-one years, until 2000.

106. Rostas 2008.

## CHAPTER 10: THE MEXICA AND MEXICANIDAD

1. Rostas 1998b:57; Escobar 1992; Melucci 1985; Evers 1985.

2. De la Peña Martínez 1999:5.

3. Ayala Serrano 2000.

4. Heelas 1996; Woodhead and Heelas 2000:342–347.

5. Linares Aguirre 1995:5.

6. For the Aztecs, teotl was less theistic than the Christian God but not as animate as the Inca concept of a huaca (Bierhorst 1985). Ometeotl, lord of duality, was the origin of all natural forces and, being both masculine and feminine, appeared in various paired aspects that were not necessarily fully anthropomorphic.

7. On display in the museum at the Templo Mayor in Mexico City (adjacent to the Zocalo) are various burial tombs filled with exquisitely fabricated artifacts that were doused in human blood before interment.

8. "Aztec" in this chapter and the book generally refers to the people who lived in Tenochtitlan at the time of the Spanish Conquest, although the Mexica prefer to refer to them also as "Mexica" (as indeed do many archaeologists at present). My usage of "Aztec" helps differentiate between a historical people (the Aztecs) and today's re-inventors of Aztec practices (the Mexica).

9. The term "Mexicanidad" was used in the nineteenth century to mean "Mexicaness," implying an identity neither indigenous nor European and was replaced in the twentieth by "mestizaje." The current link of Mexicanidad with the Aztec past is a reaction to the ideological shift in mainstream politics in which the state had attempted to draw the indigenous population into the mainstream in order to eradicate their cultural differences. Its use today accords with the move to create a multicultural nation (de la Peña 2002:48).

10. Pratt 1992.

11. This book also includes the claims that Mayan Nahuatl-speaking people reached Egypt, where the concept of teotl is reflected in the building of the pyramids; that Christ was born a Maya-Naga (part Mexican, part Kashmiri) and that Plato took Nahuat knowledge to Greece, where it later formed the basis of Christian theology (Friedlander 1975:175; Odena Güemes 1984:76; 1993:106). The author also claimed that Nahuat culture (in the form of the kalpulli) not only influenced the Americas, Europe, and the Middle East but also Africa and Asia. It was even claimed that Mao in China was inspired by the idea of the kalpulli as was the kibbutz movement in Israel (Nieva 1969:39–40; see also de la Peña Martínez 1999:109). This was just one of a number of like-minded publications that appeared at this time. Others, although less extreme, propounded similar themes, such as Magaloni 1969.

12. Such as the Organización Nacional de los Indios de la Republica, founded in 1936 and supported by Andres Molino Enriquez, which was anti-imperialist, anti-fascist, but also anti-communist (Odena Güemes 1993:97).

13. Such as CONFIA, Consejo Organizador Nacional de Fomento Industrial y Agrícola, (Organizing Council for the Furtherance of Industry and Agriculture), which aimed to halt foreign domination of Mexico's agriculture and industry and to work for economic independence. Many Mexicans strongly disliked the United States and its economic domination. By 1925, 51 percent of the land in Mexico was in U.S. hands (Odena Güemes 1984:91); forty-one right-wing groups were recorded in the 1930s (in a city of some 1.5 million inhabitants) (Pérez Monfort and Odena Güemes 1982:56).

14. Friedlander 1975:171. Juan Luna Cardenas was not related to President Lazaro Cardenas.

15. Odena Güemes 1984:115, 118, 90.

16. Friedlander 1975:171. MCRAs were formed in Detroit and Chicago (in 1965) and links developed with South America (Odena Güemes 1984:126).

17. His goals included giving land back to campesinos and setting up rights for workers (Pérez Montfort and Odena Güemes 1982:137).

18. Odena Güemes 1984:107.

19. It was clear from a session I attended in 1989 that her knowledge of grammar was lacking—but her enthusiasm for introducing neologisms was great. Playing with Nahuatl words and finding new meanings in or for them is a pastime of many Mexica.

20. Friedlander 1975:179–80. Friedlander (1975) had heard about Nieva and Mexicanidad before arriving in Mexico to do fieldwork and intended to study the movement, but on finding it not to be an indigenous one, she soon dropped the idea. I witnessed a Mexica wedding (organized by the Maestra in 1990) that appeared to be very ad hoc (although she must have been behind such ceremonies for more than thirty years).

21. Odena Güemes 1984:22.

22. Ayala Serrano 2000:46, quoting a Mexica named Ocelocoatl; my quotation marks.

23. De la Peña Martínez 1999:97, 47.

24. Nieva received word of it from an engineer from Tlahuac (Odena Güemes 1984:107), and Tlacaélel, also a Mexica leader, received it from his father, who "inherited" it from his father (who also claims to have started the MRCA). The tendency to invent claims about and details of the past (both their own and that of the Aztecs) and to exaggerate not only the size of the movement but also their own importance to it seems to be inherent to the many often charismatic characters who have, or claim to have, founded and led or still lead the various organizations.

25. Gonzalez Torres 1996:15.

26. This prophecy was claimed to be linked to the highly respected sixteenth-century Franciscan chronicler Motolínia (de la Peña Martínez 1999:280).

27. She held a post in archaeology at UNAM and is thought to be the originator of the denial of human sacrifice during the Aztec epoch.

28. For an archaeological view on the Fifth Sun, see Brundage 1979.

29. De la Peña Martínez 1999:142; Tlacaélel et al. 1992:47.

30. These traditions included the *temazcal*, a steambath still used by indigenous communities in the central area and by the Mexica and the Concheros from time to time.

31. De la Peña Martínez 1999:149; Gonzalez Torres and Acevedo Martinez 2000.

32. De la Peña Martínez 1999:162.

33. When I attempted to talk to him, I met with little success. He showed me the many scars on his chest to frighten me off. He is said to have had many extrasensory experiences and to be a granicero. He is certainly as powerful as was the Conchero jefe Andres Segura. The latter's power was primarily, I sensed, ego-based (although not all would agree), whereas Tlacaélel's is probably much more deep-seated; he is undoubtedly a brujo and/or curandero.

34. Heelas (1996:27) has suggested that New Agers attach importance to the "essential unity of the human species, scorning nationally or ethnically differentiated modes of being."

35. As predicted in *La Mujer Dormida debe dar Luz*, published under the pseudonym Ayocuan (1972).

36. For example, Ramos 1934; Paz 1950. This continuing concern with Mexican identity is discussed by Bartra (1992) and Lomnitz-Adler (1992).

37. Regina Teuchar was an athlete who planned to compete in the Olympics but was killed at Tlatelolco in 1968 and inspired Velasco Piña. The fictional Regina is steeped in Tibetan esotericism and was predestined to act as a spiritual redeemer of Mexico. With its salvationist message, the book weaves together the beginnings of the Age of Aquarius and the Fifth Sun and links Tibetan knowledge to Mexican indigenous knowledge. Its political aim is to see the end of authoritarian regimes heralded by the reawakening of Mexicanidad (Gonzalez Torres 1996:24; de la Peña Martínez 1999:240, 276).

38. De la Peña Martínez 1999:245.

39. This dance was developed in collaboration with the theater director Nicolas Nuñez (1996), who is interested in anthropocosmic theater and whose group has worked with Grotowski.

40. De la Peña Martínez 1999:248.

41. Gonzalez Torres 2000:22.

42. In Katonal also includes ceremonies more clearly indigenous to Mexico, but these are considered of lesser importance although spaced according to the 260-day ritual calendar, the Tonalpohualli (Gonzalez Torres and Acevedo Martinez n.d.:7).

43. See Gonzalez Torres 2000:22.

44. De la Peña Martínez 1999:6.

45. Linares Aguirre 1995:6.

46. De la Peña Martínez (1999:265) sees their position as an "ideological device, practical and symbolic, by means of which a particular line of belief or consciousness (collective and individual) is constituted, maintained, developed and controlled" (quoting from Hervieu-Léger 1993).

47. Asuntos Religiosos de Gobernacíon (Religious Affairs Ministry).

48. Heelas 1996:15–18.

49. If Heelas's definition of "New Age" is used, the Concheros appear to be more New Age than the Mexica, although I would never classify the former as such.

50. The popular literature on extraterrestrial beings and other esoteric phenomena is large in Mexico. Nieva had little interest in the extrasensory but it has become increasingly popular in recent decades. Latin America–wide New Age forms include the Gran Fraternidad Universal and MAIS (Mancommunidad de la América Iniciática Solar), and internationally there are groups such as Hare Krishna, Theosophy, Transcendental Meditation, Soka Gakkai, the 3HO (Happy, Healthy, and Holy Organization), Silva Mind Control, the Bahai, and Scientology (Gutiérrez Zúñiga 1996:22).

51. Other journals are *El Mitote* and *Tlamatini*. De la Peña Martínez (1999:8) mentions in addition the journals *Tlazeloteotl*, *El Guerrero Solar*, and *Kin Tonatiuh*.

52. Editorial, *Ce-Acatl* 1 (1990–1996):3.

53. De la Peña Martínez 1999.

54. De la Peña Martínez describes adherents as being "hippies, ex-hippies, naturists and esotericists, as well as ecologists, ex-lefties and the young who sell crafts in the street." But he also lists "dancers, actors, musicians; doctors, lawyers, and engineers; government functionaries, bureaucrats, schoolteachers, writers, journalists, university students (many of whom are studying social anthropology) and foreigners." His classification is broader than mine, but he agrees that most are urbanites, are Mestizo in origin, and have some education (1999:8). Ayala Serrano also encountered students, primary schoolteachers, and taxi drivers during his fieldwork (2000:70).

55. Ayala Serrano 2000:73.

56. Ibid., 124, passim; Anawalt 1981:27.

57. Historically, a *quechquemitl* was an unsewn garment worn over a skirt (*cueitl*).

58. The Mexica employ two sorts of drums: the *huéhuetl*, a large vertical standing drum made from a hollowed-out log, covered with a skin, and played with the hands; and the *teponaztli*, a wooden slit drum producing two tones and usually played with two sticks. They also use flutes (*tlapitzalli*) made from bone, clay, or shell; conch shells (*atecococli*); and whistles (*tlototlapitzali*) (Ayala Serrano 2000:130). In addition, they deploy ocarinas (*huilacapitztli*), bone rasps (*omichicahuaztli*), and gourd rattles (known variously to the Aztecs as *ayacachtli*, *cacalachtli*, and *chicahuaztil*). Stevenson's book on Aztec music (1968) does not mention the *tlototlapitzali*, which may be a neologism, but on the whole the Mexica use the Aztec terminology correctly (see Stevenson 1968; Bierhorst 1985:72; Kurath and Martí 1964; and for illustrations, Marti 1978).

59. Sten 1990; and see Chapter 7.

60. Knab 1986; Lockhart 1992:282n.

61. Sahagún 1950–1982, 2:163.

62. Motolinía 1971:386, 387.

63. Clendinnen 1991:356.

64. Motolinía 1971:102.

65. Deren 1953:228, italics in original.

66. Ibid., 231.

67. Quotations culled from various dancers, but see Chapter 7.

68. Ayala Serrano 2000:58.

69. Friedlander 1975:165; Juan Anzaldo Meneses 1990, 1993, quoting Luis Gonzalez de Alba. The movement itself has been labeled grotesque, derisory, an example of Mexican surrealism, and a cultural farce (de la Peña Martínez 1999:16, 25). The Mexica seem generally to arouse only antipathy.

70. See Ayala Serrano 2000:44–75, for details on the various groups.

71. This was done by Xoconochtle (of the kalpultin Mazakoatl and Toltekayotl), who also campaigned for the return of the copilli (headdress) that is claimed to have belonged to Moctezuma and is currently in Vienna (de la Peña Martínez 1999:274).

72. Nora 1996.

73. Ayala Serrano 2000:65, 52.

74. Held on May 3, this celebration coincides with Nieva's birthday.

75. See Gutiérrez 1999.

76. MacCannell 1992.

77. Rostas 2002.

78. Sahagún 1950–1982, 7:6. At the time of the Conquest, the version of the myth told to Durán was that the Aztecs (Mexica) were the last to leave the caves and were the chosen people (above the Tlaxalatecs; that is, those from Tlaxcala). The name Mezcaltitlán is said to mean in Nahuatl the "house of the Mexicans," —and there is thought to be some resemblance between its physical layout and the island of Tenochtitlan (at the time of the Spanish Conquest) (de la Peña Martínez 1999:272).

79. Rostas 2002:35.

80. Odena Güemes 1984:167.

81. De la Peña Martínez 1999:5.

82. Rostas 2002.

83. The eagle symbol comes from the myth that recounts that the travelers from Aztlan would know that they had reached the place that their god Huitzilopochtli had chosen for them when they saw an eagle sitting on a nopal cactus. The snake was added in 1823 to the original flag, designed in 1815.

84. Ayala Serrano 2000:98–101, 95. Beezley points out that the colors on the national flag were adopted from the banner displayed on San Hipolito Day (August 19), the day that Tenochtitlan fell (Beezley n.d.:3).

85. I have suggested elsewhere that Mexicanidad cannot be seen as a social movement in the sense of a political struggle of the dispossessed against hegemonic power but should rather be seen as a cultural struggle involving socio-symbolic elaboration (Rostas 1998b; but see also Rostas 1993, 2002). De la Peña Martínez also discusses this in his thesis (1999:287, passim).

86. Hebdige 1979:132.

87. Heelas 1996:202; but see also Rostas 1998b:57.


# EPILOGUE

1. Clifford 1988:201.

2. There is a vast literature on the rise of Protestantism in Latin America; see, for example, Stoll 1990; Martin 1990.

3. See, for example, Appadurai 1990.

4. Mexico still has a large indigenous population including some 10 million people who speak fifty-six languages. Their desire for more autonomy and better social conditions was (re)awakened and given new impetus by the Chiapas uprising in 1994 under the eponymous Subcomandante Marcos. The literature on this is now vast, but see Harvey 1998; Collier and Quaratiello 2005; Ponce de Leon 2001.

5. This was the case at least during the last few decades of the twentieth century. The situation has changed radically since September 11, 2001.

6. See, for example, Jean-Francois Veran 2005.

7. The mesa in New York was formed by Antonia, who went to the United States in the late 1990s. The one in Chicago was formed by a number of dancers who moved there in search of work.

8. The name of this dancer is Sadie Sesín.

9. Santo Niño de Atocha has only loose links with the groups in Guadalajara. For more on these, see de la Torre 2005.

10. Miguel Gutierrez, for example, now lives in Chicago, but he lacks the necessary means to return to Mexico City for the principal obligations. Others, however, such as Antonia (based in New York) and Margarita (who has a job in the State of Veracruz) can and do.

11. Rostas 2002.

12. Ahern 1982.

13. Morris 1996:238–245. His typological model is based on the differences between the Jewish and Christian traditions, but I found it to be an excellent tool for highlighting the differences between the Concheros and the Mexica.

14. Ibid., 238, 239.

15. Ibid., 238, 233.

16. Morris 1996:233, discussing Nancy 1991.

17. Morris 1996:239.

18. Ibid., 233.

19. COREPI, El Consejo Restaurador de los Pueblos Indios (the Council for the Restoration of the Indian Peoples), organized the Day of Dignity and Resistance for the Indian People in October in cooperation with the FIPI (the Independent Front for the Indian People). FIPI's leader at the time was Margarito Ruiz of the PRD (the Party of Democratic Revolution). Also involved were the Frente Democrático Oriental de México Emiliano Zapata (FDOMEZ-FNLS: The Democratic Eastern Front), representing indigenes from the region of the Huasteca in the state of Veracruz, and the Asamblea de Barrios, led by the activist Superbarrio, who, dressed as Superman, led the fight to improve the lives of the dispossessed in and around Mexico City. Offerings, which had been set up at the statue of Christopher Columbus, were torn down during the day and counter offerings set up at the monument to Cuitlahuac. Later in the cathedral, the statue of Cuauhtémoc was censed before dancing took place in the Zocalo after lengthy political speeches.

20. In Mexico City in 2006, at some vigils, the initial form of the cross made during a vigil had begun to be "transformed" during the course of the night into various other shapes, such as flowers, animals, and even the nahui ollin. The form chosen often had some close relation to the purpose of the vigil and was retained. So only the unused flowers that had not been ritually deployed were tied to a baston and used for a cleansing "al cabo del año" (the vigil held a year after a death).

21. Heelas et al. 1996.

22. Adam 1996:143.

23. Handelman and Lindquist 2004:7.

24. Adam 1996:143.

25. Throughout this book, I have emphasized the Concheros' own views as to whether the dance existed in Mexico City before the late nineteenth century. There is insufficient evidence to make a strong case that it did and those stories that appear to support its existence at that time may well be "invented" (Anderson 1991).

26. This alabanza was sung in the 1930s by the Mesa of La Gran Tenochtitlan. Of its nine verses, three mention the mythical origins in the Bajio—the battle of Sangremal, the founding of Queretero and the baptizing of the Chichimeca (Solorzano and Guerrero 1941:475).

27. Aguila Blanca 1993 (1969).

28. Six of these eighteen verses are identical to those in the 1930s version. It should be noted that alabanzas as recorded on tape or records are often not given in full.

29. One verse, however, does mention that the Chichimecas were part of the battle when Anahuac was conquered.

30. This publication was on sale outside certain churches near the Merced market in Mexico City (Castro Manriquez n.d.)

31. Connerton 1989.

32. Cooper Alarcón 1997:158.

33. Culler quoted in ibid., 158.

34. This ritualized technique is described for the mesa La Gran Tenochtitlan in 1941 (Solorzano and Guerrero 1941:471–472), but this mesa was very aware of the Aztec past.

35. Handelman and Lindquist 2004.

36. Connerton 1989:102.

37. Wallace 1956.

38. As the practices in many churches today are showing, singing to music with a beat is increasingly seen as not contradictory to religiosity.

# GLOSSARY

**Agradecimiento.** Prayer of thanks.

**Alabanza.** The term used for the Concheros' songs of praise (from the Spanish *alabar*, "to praise, to commend").

**Anahuac.** The name of the place to the northwest of Mexico City from which the founders of Tenochtitlan are said to have come.

**Anciano.** Man of knowledge (literally, "old man").

**Anima.** Spirit, soul.

**Animas conquistadoras de los cuatro vientos.** The conquering spirits of the four winds.

**Antepasados.** Those who came before; ancestors.

**Artesanias.** Handicrafts.

**Aztec.** The term used to refer to the inhabitants of Tenochtitlan and its territories at the time of the Spanish Conquest.

**Aztecquismo.** Aztecism.

**Banqueta.** Sidewalk; pavement.

**Banqueteros.** People of the pavement (i.e., city dwellers).

**Brujo.** A man of power or a sorcerer.

**Cabeceras.** The two large candles placed on either side of the altar during a vigil.

**Calzones.** Simple peasant trousers made from manta.

**Campesino.** One who works in the fields (*campo*).

**Cargo.** A position or responsibility.

**Chichimeca.** The name given, usually with pejorative connotations, to those indigenous groups who lived in the northern expanses of what is today Mexico.

**Chimaleros.** The name given to dancers who perform primarily to raise money, which they collect on their shields.

**Chitontiquiza.** The term used by the Mexica for Aztec dance.

**Codices.** The records produced shortly after the Spanish Conquest by the various religious orders in Mexico.

**Comadre/compadre.** Usually glossed as "godmother/godfather" but can be used to indicate benefaction, respect, and friendship between a jefe and a group or between dancers.

**Comida corrida.** The main meal in Mexico, which is usually eaten at 2:00 PM.

**Compañero/a.** The term usually used for a common-law wife or husband (literally, "companion").

**Conformidad.** One of the Concheros leitmotifs (literally, "conformity"), but also a term used for the Concheros' association.

**Congregación.** An alternative name for the association or a part thereof.

**Conquista.** One of the Concheros' leitmotifs (literally, "conquest").

**Consejo de Ancianos.** Council of Elders.

**Consigna.** Order or instruction.

**Criollo.** One of unmixed Spanish blood (as opposed to a mestizo).

**Cuartel general.** Headquarters.

**Cuauhtémoc.** The name of the last Aztec tlatoani (emperor), who was killed by the Spaniards.

**Cuenta.** A term used to describe the state of events usually during a vigil (literally, "account" but better glossed as "account of" or "state of").

**Cuitlahuac.** Tlatoani of Tenochtitlan during the Spanish conquest of Mexico.

**Curandero.** Curer; often a person of indigenous descent or with indigenous or folk knowledge.

**Delegación.** A large-scale administrative area within Mexico City.

**D.F.** Distrito Federal; the Federal District of Mexico City.

**Ensayo.** Rehearsal.

**Fieles.** Of the faith, usually used of Roman Catholics.

**Flor.** In reference to the Concheros' dance, the various phrases that are enacted after each repetition of the core phrase (*planta*).

**Forms/formas.** The term used by Conchero mesas specifically for their dances and sometimes for the various related practices.

**Gauchupine.** A pejorative term for the Spaniards used in Mexico.

**Gente humilde.** The phrase used for those of humble (i.e., lower class or peasant) origins.

**Granicero.** One who is believed to be able to control the weather and also to heal (literally, "rain/hail maker").

**Guerras floridas.** The so-called wars without conflict "fought" between Tenochtitlan and its neighboring enemies to take victims for sacrifice.

**Huaraches.** Typical Mexican sandals with soles usually made from old car tires.

**Huipil.** The name given throughout Mexico for an indigenous woman's handwoven blouse.

**Huitzilopochtli.** The supreme deity of the Aztecs who, if the sun was to rise, had to be placated by daily human sacrifices.

**Indigene.** A person of indigenous or native descent.

**INI.** Instituto Nacional Indigenista (National Indigenist Institute)

**In xochi, in cuicatl.** A Nahuatl phrase used as a metaphor by the Aztecs for the three closely linked practices of singing, playing music, and dancing (literally, "the flower, the song").

**Izcoahuecatl.** The red headband worn by the Mexica and, in particular, the Reginas (the followers of Antonio Velasco Piña).

**Jefe.** Leader or head of a mesa.

**Kalpulli** (pl. **kalpultin**). The Nahuatl term for a small self-governing group or community of Aztecs.

**Maguey.** A cactus whose fruit is used to produce pulque.

**Mando.** Leadership in the sense of caring for.

**Manta.** Unbleached woven cotton that whitens and softens as it is washed.

**MCR(C)A.** Movimiento confederado restaurador (de la cultura) de Anahuac (Confederated Movement for the [Cultural] Restoration of Anahuac).

**Mesa.** Dance group.

**Mesa Central.** An alternative term for the Mexico City–based part of the association.

**Mestizaje.** The process of mixing or crossing races.

**Mestizo.** A person of mixed Spanish and Mexican (indigenous) blood.

**Mexica.** The followers of Mexicanidad, who are intent on re-creating the Aztec past.

**Mexicanidad.** In the context of the Mexica, the current movement that proclaims Mexicanity with strong New Age tendencies (but literally, "mexicaness").

**Mexicayotl.** The name by which Mexicanidad was known in the middle of the twentieth century; also the title of a book by Rodolfo Nieva.

**Nahuatl or Nahuat.** The language spoken by the Aztecs in Tenochtitlan.

**Nahui Mitl.** The four arrows ritually thrown in the thirteenth century that brought together indigenous peoples from the four directions.

**Nahui ollin.** A cross-shaped symbol that glosses as the four movements; also the insignia of the MCRCA.

**Obligation/obligación.** The term used by the Concheros for the various commitments that they have throughout the year.

**Ocote.** Resinous pine used to light fires.

**Palabra.** A term used to mean a position or a grouping (literally, "word").

**Pan dulce.** Sweet bread.

**Pedir permiso.** To ask permission.

**Planta.** The opening phrase in a Conchero dance; it is repeated after each repetition of the core phrase (*flor*).

**Porfiriato.** The period when Porfirio Diaz was president of Mexico (from 1876 to 1880 and 1884 to 1911).

**Pozole.** A thick soup made from corn with added pork and various vegetables.

**PRD.** Partido de la Revolución Democrática (Party of Democratic Revolution)

**PRI.** Partido Revolutionario Institucional (Institutional Revolutionary Party).

**Pulque.** A fermented drink made from the maguey cactus.

**Rangos.** The different levels of hierarchical responsibility in the dance.

**Recibimiento.** The ceremony when a dancer is received.

**Reivindicación.** Re-creation or recovery (literally, "re-vindication").

**Sacerdote.** A sage or priest.

**Sahumadora.** The woman responsible for the incense burner (*sahumar*).

**Santa Xuchil.** Name given to the special flower form constructed during the vigil for the Day of the Dead.

**Sextennial.** The six-year term of a Mexican president.

**Sombra.** Soul of a dead person (literally, "shadow").

**Sope.** A snack-sized meal consisting of a corn base with beans and other garnishes.

**Temazcal.** The Nahuatl term for steambath.

**Teocalli.** A temple (literally, "god house" or "divinity house").

**Terreno.** A landholding.

**Tlatoani.** The Nahuatl term for the emperor during the Aztec era.

**Tonalamatl.** A pre-Colombian codex of destiny based on the 260-day calendar (the *tonalpohualli*); also the name adopted by the Mexica for their renaming ceremony.

**Tonantzin.** The name used for a range of Aztec female deities who represent the power of the earth; Mother Earth or Our Mother.

**Traje.** Indigenous clothing or costume.

**Tuna.** The fruit of the prickly pear cactus.

**UNAM.** Universidad Nacional Autonoma de Mexico (Autonomous Nacional University of Mexico).

**Uniforme.** The term the Concheros use for their dance clothing (literally, "uniform").

**Union.** One of the Concheros' leitmotifs (literally, "union").

**Union General.** An alternative name for the central segment of the association.

**Velación.** All-night vigil.

**Voceador.** A town crier; the name now given to those who sell newspapers.

# BIBLIOGRAPHY

Acevedo, E. 2005. "The Influence of New Representational Media Strategies on Visual History in Mexico 1863–1867." Conference Paper for The Conundrum of Vision: Reflexivity in Latin American Visual Culture. CRASSH Cambridge, February 18–19.

Adam, B. 1996. "Detraditionalization and the Certainty of Uncertain Futures." In Heelas, Lash, and Morris 1996.

Ades, D. 1989. *Art in Latin America, the Modern Era, 1820–1980.* London, South Bank Centre.

Ahern, E. 1982. "Rules in Oracles and Games." *Man* 17:302–312.

Alberro. 1998. "Bailes y mitotes coloniales como producto y factor sincrético." In *La cultura plural: Homenaje a Italo Signorini*, ed. A. Lusi and A. López Austin, 119–137. Mexico City, UNAM.

Alonso, A-M. 2004. "Conforming Discontinuity: 'Mestizaje,' Hybridity, and the Aesthetics of Mexican Nationalism," *Cultural Anthropology* 19:459–490.

Anawalt, P. 1980. "Costume and Control: Aztec Sumptuary Laws." *Archaeology* (January/February): 33–43.

———. 1981. *Indian Clothing before Cortes: Mesomaerican Costumes from the Codices.* Norman: University of Oklahoma Press.

Anderson, B. 1991 [1983]. *Imagined Communities: Reflections on the Origins and Spread of Nationalism.* London, Verso.

Anzaldo Meneses, J. 1990. Editorial. *Ce-Acatl* 1 (November 7):3.

———. 1993. "Fanatismo, mexicanidad y las culturas autoctonas." *Ce-Acatl* 41 (March 12–31):8–12.

Appadurai, A. 1986. *The Social Life of Things.* Cambridge, Cambridge University Press.

———. 1990. "Disjuncture and Difference in the Global Economy." In Featherstone 1990.

————. 1995. "The Production of Locality." In Fardon 1995.

————, ed. 2001. *Globalization*. Durham, NC, Duke University Press.

Argyaridis, K., R. de la Torre, C. Gutiérrez Zúñiga, and R Aguilar, eds. 2008. *Raíces en movimiento: Prácticas religiosas tradicionales en contextos translocales*. Mexico, El Colegio de Jalisco/CIESAS/IRD/CEMCA/ITESO.

Arthur, L. B., ed. 1999. *Religion, Dress, and the Body*. London, Berg.

Austin, J. L. 1975 [1962]. *How to Do Things with Words*. Oxford, Clarendon Press.

Avila, E. 2000. *Woman Who Glows in the Dark*. London, Thorsons.

Ayala Serrano, L. E. 2000. "Tempo Indigena: La Construccion de Imaginarios Prehispanicos." Master's thesis, Universidad Iberamericana, Mexico, D.F.

Ayocuan. 1972. *La mujer dormida debe dar a luz*. Mexico, D.F., Editorial Jus.

Barba, E. 1991. "Theatre Anthropology." In *A Dictionary of Theatre Anthropology: The Secret Art of the Performer*, ed. E. Barba and N. Savarese. London, Routledge.

Barnes, R., and J. Eichler, eds. 1992. *Dress and Gender: Making and Meaning in Cultural Contexts*. Oxford, Berg.

Bartra, R. 1992. *The Cage of Melancholy: Identity and Metamorphosis in the Mexican Character*. Trans. C. Hall. New Brunswick, New Jersey, Rutgers University Press.

Bastian, J-P. 1995. Una Ausencia notoria: La francomasoneria en la historiografica mexicanista. *Historia Mexicana* 20 (3):439–460.

Bateson, G. 1973. *Steps to an Ecology of Mind*. England: St. Albans, UK, Paladin.

Battaglia, D., ed. 1995. *Rhetorics of Self-Making*. Berkeley, University of California Press.

Bauman, R. 1992. "Performance." In *Folklore, Cultural Performances and Popular Entertainments*, ed. R. Bauman. Oxford, Oxford University Press.

Bauman, R., and C. Briggs. 1990. "Poetics and Performance as a Critical Perspective on Language and Social Life." *Annual Review of Anthropology* 19:59–88.

Beaumont, Fr. P. 1932. "Fragments of the Account of Don Nicolas de San Luis [Montañez]." *Crónica de Michoacán: Mexico*. Mexico, D.F., Edicion del Archivo General de la Nacion.

Beezley, W. 1994. "The Porfirian Smart Set Anticipates Thorstein Veblan in Guadalajara." In Beezley, Martin, and French 1994.

————. 1997. "Home Altars: Private Reflections of Public Life." In *Home Altars of Mexico*, ed. D. Salvo. London, Thames and Hudson.

————. N.d. "Recreating the Creation of Mexico: Pondering Nineteenth-Century Celebrations of Independence." Paper given at the Centre for Latin American Studies, Cambridge, ca. 1994.

Beezley, W., and L. A. Curcio-Nagy, eds. 2000. *Latin American Popular Culture*. Wilmington, Delaware, SR Books.

Beezley, W., C. E. Martin, and W. French, eds. 1994. *Rituals of Rule, Rituals of Resistance: Public Celebrations and Popular Culture in Mexico*. Wilmington, DE, SR Books.

Behar, R. 1987. "Visions of a Guachichil Witch 1599: A Window on the Subjugation of Mexico's Hunter-Gatherers." *Ethnohistory* 34 (2):115–137.

Bell, C. 1992. *Ritual Theory, Ritual Practice*. Oxford, Oxford University Press.

————. 1997. *Ritual*. Oxford, Oxford University Press.

Benjamin, T. 2000. "From the Ruins of the Ancient Regime: Mexico's Monument to the Revolution." In Beezley and Curcio-Nagy 2000.

Benthall, J., and T. Polhemus. 1975. *The Body as a Medium of Expression*. London, Allen Lane, Penguin Books.

Bernal, I. 1980. *A History of Mexican Archaeology: The Vanished Civilizations of Middle America*. London, Thames and Hudson.

Bierhorst, J. 1985. *Cantares Mexicanos: Songs of the Aztecs*. Stanford, California, Stanford University Press.

Bird, E., ed. 1996. *Dressing in Feathers*. Boulder, Colorado, Westview Press.

Bird, J., et al., eds. 1993. *Mapping the Future*. London, Routledge.

Birdwhistell, R. L. 1970. *Kinesics and Context*. Philadelphia, University of Pennsylvania Press.

Blacking, J. 1968. "Percussion and Transition." *Man* n.s. 3 (2):313–314.

———, ed. 1977. *The Anthropology of the Body*. London, Academic Press.

———. 1979. *The Performing Arts*. The Hague: Mouton Publishers.

Bloch, M. 1986. *From Blessing to Violence*. Cambridge, Cambridge University Press.

Bocock, J. 1974. *Ritual in Industrial Society*. London, Chatto and Windus.

Bondi, L. 1993. "Locating Identity Politics." In *Place and the Politics of Identity*, ed. M. Keith and S Pile. London, Routledge.

Bonfil Batalla, G. 1990 [1987]. *México Profundo*. Mexico, D.F., Grijalbo.

Bonfil Batalla, G., and G. Muñoz. 1965. *El es Dios*. Film. Mexico, D.F., Instituto Nacional de Antropología y Historia.

Bourdieu, P. 1977. *Outline of a Theory of Practice*. Cambridge, Cambridge University Press.

———. 2000 [1993]. "How Can One Be a Sports Fan." In *The Cultural Studies Reader*, S. During, 427–440. London, Routledge.

Boyer, P. 1990. *Tradition as Truth and Communication: A Cognitive Description of Traditional Discourse*. Cambridge, Cambridge University Press.

Brading, D. 1983. *Prophecy and Myth in Mexican History*. Cambridge, Centre for Latin American Studies.

———. 1985. *The Origins of Mexican Nationalism*. Cambridge, Centre for Latin American Studies.

———. 1988. "Manuel Gamio and Official Indigenismo in Mexico." *Bulletin for Latin American Research* 7 (1):75–89.

———. 1991. *The First America: The Spanish Monarchy, Creole Patriots and the Liberal State, 1492–1867*. Cambridge, Cambridge University Press.

———. 2001. *Mexican Phoenix: Our Lady of Guadalupe; Image and Tradition across Five Centuries*. Cambridge, Cambridge University Press.

Brooke, P. 1968. *The Empty Space*. London, Penguin.

Brotherston, G. 1992. *Book of the Fourth World: Reading the Native Americas through Their Literature*. Cambridge, Cambridge University Press.

Bruhn, A. 2001. *Chichimekische Tanztradition der Concheros in Mexiko: Bewegungskultur als Überlebensstrategie*. Immenhausen, Institut F. Bewegungslehre u. Bewegungsforschung.

Brundage, B. C. 1979. *The Fifth Sun: Aztec Gods, Aztec World*. Austin, University of Texas Press.

Burkhart, L. 1989. *The Slippery Earth: Nahua Christian Moral Dialogue in Sixteenth-Century Mexico*. Tucson, University of Arizona Press.

Butler, J. 1993. *Bodies That Matter*. London, Routledge.

———. 1995. "Burning Acts—Injurious Speech." In Parker and Sedgwick 1995.

Canessa, A. 2000. "Contesting Hybridity: Evangelistas and Kataristas in Highland Bolivia." *Journal of Latin American Studies* 32 (1):55–84.

Carillo y Perez, I. 1979 [1808]. Facsimile, *Lo maximo en lo minimo*. Mexico, D.F., Don Mariano de Zuñiga y Ontiveros.

Carlson, M. 1996. *Performance: A Critical Introduction*. London, Routledge.

Carmichael, E., and C. Sayer. 1991. *The Skeleton at the Feast*. London, British Museum Press.

Casey, E. 1996. "How to Get from Space to Place in a Fairly Short Stretch of Time: Phenomenological Prolegomena." In Feld and Basso 1996.

Castro Manriquez, M. N.d. *Alabanzas que se cantan en el Santuario de Nuestro Padre Jesus de Atontonilco, Guanajuato*. Mexico, D.F., n.p.

*Ce-Acatl*. 1990–1996. Revista de la Cultura de Anáhuac. Published each 20-day month. Mexico, D.F., Centro de Estudios Ce-Acatl.

Cervantes de Salazar, F. 1914 [1550]. *Cronica de la Nueva Espana*. New York, Hispanic Society of America.

———. 1985. *Crónica de la Nueva España*. Mexico, Porrua.

Chance, J. K., and W. B. Taylor. 1985. "Cofradias and Cargos: An Historical Perspective on the Mesoamerican Civil-Religious Hierarchy." *American Ethnologist* 12 (1):1–26.

Citro, S. 2000. "El cuerpo de las Creencias." *Suplemento Antropológico*, Revista del Centro de Estudios Antropológicos de la Universidad Católica, Asunción, Paraguay 35 (2):189–242.

Classen, C. 1993. *Worlds of Sense: Exploring the Senses in History and across Cultures*. London, Routledge.

———. 1994. *Aroma: The Cultural History of Smell*. London: Routledge.

Clendinnen, I. 1985. "The Cost of Courage in Aztec Society." *Past and Present* 107:44–89.

———. 1990. "Ways to the Sacred: Reconstructing Religion in Sixteenth-Century Mexico." *History and Anthropology* 5:105–141.

———. 1991. *Aztecs*. Cambridge, Cambridge University Press.

Clifford, J. 1986. "Introduction: Partial Truths." In Clifford and Marcus 1986.

———. 1988. *The Predicament of Culture*. Cambridge, Massachusetts, Harvard University Press.

Clifford, J., and G. Marcus. 1986. *Writing Culture*. Berkeley, University of California Press.

Coleman, S. 1996. "Words as Things." *Journal of Material Culture* 1 (1):107–128.

Collier, G., and E. Lowery Quaratiello. 2005. *Basta! Land and the Zapatista Revolution*. San Francisco, Food First.

Comaroff, J. 1985. *Body of Power, Spirit of Resistance: The Culture and History of a South African People*. Chicago, University of Chicago Press.

Comaroff, J., and J. L. Comaroff. 1991. *Of Revelation and Revolution: Christianity, Colonialism and Consciousness in South Africa*. Chicago, Chicago University Press.

Comaroff, J. L., and J. Comaroff. 1992. "Ethnography and the Historical Imagination." In *Ethnography and the Historical Imagination*, ed. J. Comaroff and J. Comaroff. Boulder, Colorado, Westview Press.

Connerton, P. 1989. *How Societies Remember*. Cambridge, Cambridge University Press.

Cooper Alarcón, D. 1997. *The Aztec Palimpsest*. Tuscon, University of Arizona Press.

Copeland, R., and M. Cohen. 1983. *What Is Dance? Readings in Theory and Criticism*. Oxford, Oxford University Press.

Cordwell, J., and R. Schwarz. 1979. *The Fabrics of Culture*. The Hague: Mouton Publishers.

Cowan, J. 1990. *Dance and the Body Politic in Northern Greece*. Princeton, New Jersey, Princeton University Press.

Crain, M. 1996. "The Gendering of Ethnicity in the Eucadorean Highlands: Native Women's Self-Fashioning in the Urban Marketplace." In Melhuus and Stolen 1996.

Crease, R. P. 1997. "Responsive Order: The Phenomenology of Dramatic and Scientific Performance." In Sawyer 1997.

Csikszentmihalyi, M. 1964. "The Americanization of Rock Climbing." *The University of Chicago Magazine* 61 (6):484–488.

———. 1975. "Play and Intrinsic Rewards." *Journal of Humanistic Psychology* 15 (3):41–63.

———. 1992. *Flow: The Psychology of Happiness*. London, Rider.

Csordas, T. 1990. "Embodiment as a Paradigm for Anthropology." *Ethos* 18:5–47.

———. 1993. "Somatic Modes of Attention." *Cultural Anthropology* 8:135–156.

———, ed. 1994a. *Embodiment and Experience: The Existential Ground of Culture and Self*. Cambridge, Cambridge University Press.

———. 1994b. *The Sacred Self: A Cultural Phenomenology of Charismatic Healing*. Berkeley, CA, University of California Press.

———. 1996. "Imaginal Performance and Memory in Ritual Healing." In Laderman and Roseman 1996.

Cypess, S. M. 1991. *La Malinche in Mexican Literature: From History to Myth*. Austin, University of Texas Press.

Daniel, E. V. 1984. *Being a Person the Tamil Way*. Berkeley, University of California Press.

Dawson, A. 1998. "From Model for the Nation to Model Citizens: Indigenismo and the 'Revindication' of the Mexican Indian, 1929–1940." *Journal of Latin American Studies* 30:279–308.

———. 2004. *Indian and Nation in Revolutionary Mexico*. Tucson, University of Arizona Press.

De Certeau, M. 1980. "On the Oppositional Practices of Everyday Life." *Social Text* 3 (Fall):1–43.

———. 1984. *The Practice of Everyday Life*. Berkeley, University of California Press.

De la Peña, G. 2002. "El futuro del indigenismo en Mexico: Del mito del mestizaje al la fragmentación neoliberal." In *Estados Nacionales, etnicidad y democracia en America Latina*, ed. M. Yamada and C. I. Degregori. National Museum of Ethnology, Osaka, Japan.

De la Peña Martínez, F. 1993. "La construcción imaginaria de la mexicanidad." *La Jornada*, Sunday Supplement (July 4):31–34.

———. 1999. "Le Mouvement de la Mexicanité ou l'invention de l'autre: neo-tradicion, millénarisme et imaginaire indigene." Ph.D. dissertation, Ecole de Hautes Etudes en Sciences Sociales (EHSS), Paris. (Published in 2002 as *Los hijos del sexto sol* [Mexico, D.F., INAH].)

De la Torre, R. 2005. "Danzar: Una manera de practicar la religión." *Estudios Jaliscienses*, Colegio de Jalisco, Mexico 60:6–18.

———. 2008. "La estetización y los usos culturales de la danza conchera-azteca." In Argyaridis et al. 2008.

De Leon, P., ed. 2001. *Our Word Is Our Weapon: Selected Writings of Marcos, Subcomandante Insurgente*. London, Serpent's Tail.

Deren, M. 1953. *Divine Horsemen: The Living Gods of Haiti*. London, Thames and Hudson.

Desjarlais, R. 1992. *Body and Emotion: The Aesthetics of Illness and Healing in the Nepal Himalayas*. Philadelphia, University of Pennsylvania Press.

Douglas, M. 1970 [1966]. *Purity and Danger*. London, Penguin Books.

———. 1973 [1970]. *Natural Symbols: Explorations in Cosmology*. London, Barry and Jenkins.

Dubet, F. 1994. *Sociologie de l'Expérience*. Paris, Seuil.

Eicher, J., ed. 1995. *Dress and Ethnicity: Change across Space and Time*. Oxford, Berg.

Eicher J., and B. Sumberg. 1995. "World Fashion, Ethnic and National Dress." In Eicher 1995.

Eisenstein, S., director. 1930. *Que Viva Mexico!* Film. Moscow, Mosfilm.

El Guindi, F. 1999. *Veil: Modesty, Privacy and Resistance*. Oxford, Berg.

Escobar, A. 1992. "Culture, Economics and Politics in Latin American Social Movement Theory and Research." In Escobar and Alvarez 1992.

Escobar, A., and S. Alvarez. 1992. *The Making of Social Movements in Latin America*. Boulder, Westview Press.

Evans-Pritchard, E. 1928. "The Dance." *Africa* 1:446–462.

———. 1930. "Estatutos de Disciplina." Unpublished document.

———. 1940. *The Nuer*. Oxford, Oxford University Press.

Evers, T. 1985. "Identity: The Hidden Side of New Social Movements in Latin America." In Slater 1985.

Fabian, J. 1983. *Time and the Other: How Anthropology Makes Its Object*. New York, Columbia University Press.

———. 1990. *Power and Performance*. Madison, University of Wisconsin Press.

Fardon, R., ed. 1995. *Counterworks: Managing the Diversity of Knowledge*. London, Routledge.

Favret-Saada, J. 1980. *Deadly Words: Witchcraft in the Bocage*. Cambridge, Cambridge University Press.

Featherstone, M., ed. 1990. *Global Culture: Nationalism, Globalization and Modernity*. London, Sage Publications.

———. 1993. "Global and Local Cultures." In Bird et al. 1993.

Featherstone, M., M. Hepworth, and B. Turner. 1991. *The Body, Social Process and Cultural Theory*. London, Sage.

Feher, M. 1989. *Fragments for a History of the Human Body*. New York, Zone.

Feld, S. 1990 [1982]. *Sound and Sentiment*. Philadelphia, University of Pennsylvania Press.

———. 1991. "Sound as a Symbolic System: The Kaluli Drum." In Howes 1991.

Feld, S., and K. Basso. 1996. *Senses of Place*. Santa Fe, New Mexico, School of American Research Advanced Seminar Series.

Fernandez, J. [with V. T. Mendoza and A. Rodriguez Luna]. 1941. *Danzas de los Concheros en San Miguel de Allende*. Mexico, D.F., Colegio de Mexico.

Forrest, J. 1985. "Here We Come A-Fossiling." *Dance Reasearch Journal* 17 (1):27–42.

Foucault, M. 1979. *Discipline and Punish: The Birth of a Prison*. Harmondsworth, Penguin.

Franco, J. 1989. *Plotting Women: Gender and Representation in Mexico*. London, Verso.

Freedburg, D. 1989. *The Power of Images*. Chicago, University of Chicago Press.

Friedlander, J. 1975. *Being Indian in Hueyapan*. New York, St. Martin's Press.

Furst, J., and L. McKeever. 1998. "The Nahualli of Christ: The Trinity and the Nature of the Soul in Ancient Mexico." *Res* 33 (Spring):209–224.

Galovic, J. 2002. *Los grupos místico-espirituales de la actualidad*. Mexico, D.F., Plaza y Valdes.

Gamio, M. 1916. *Forjando patria*. Mexico, D.F., Porrua.

Garcia, I. 2004. "Mimi Derba y la Azteca Films: Nacionalismo y la primera realizadores de cine de Mexico." In *Mujeres y nacionalismos en America Latina*, coord. N. Guiterrez Chong. Mexico, D.F., UNAM.

Garcia Canclini, N. 1982. *Las culturas populares en el capitalismo*. Mexico, D.F., Editorial Nueva Imagen.

———. 1989. *Cultural Híbridas: Estrategias para entrar y salir de la modernidad*. Mexico, D.F., Grijalbo.

———. 1995. "Mexico: Cultural globalization in a disintegrating city." *American Ethnologist* 22 (4):743–755.

———. 2000. "From National Capital to Global Capital: Urban Change in Mexico City." In Appadurai 2000.

Gardiner, D. S. 1983. "Performativity in Ritual." *Man* n.s. 18:346–360.

Geertz, C. 1973 [1966]. "Person, Time and Conduct in Bali: An Esssay in Cultural Analysis." *Cultural Report Series*, No. 14. New Haven, CT, Yale Southeast Asia Program.

———. 1973. *The Interpretation of Cultures*. New York, Basic Books.

———. 1983. *Local Knowledge*. New York, Basic Books.

———. 1986. "Making Experience, Authoring Selves." In *The Anthropology of Experience*, ed. V. Turner and E. Bruner. Stanford, California, Stanford University Press.

Gell, A. 1986. "Newcomers to the World of Goods: Consumption among the Muria Gonds." In Appadurai 1986.

Gerholm, T. 1988. "On Ritual: A Postmodernist View." *Ethnos* 53:190–203.

Gibson, C. 1964. *The Aztecs under Spanish Rule: A Hisory of the Indians of the Valley of Mexico, 1519–1810*. Stanford, California, Stanford University Press.

Giddens, A. 1979. *Central Problems in Social Theory: Structure and Contradiction in Social Analysis*. Berkeley: University of California Press.

———. 1984. *The Constitution of Society: Outline of the Theory of Structuration*. Berkeley: University of California Press.

Glockner, J. 2000. *Asi en el cielo como en la tierra: Pedidores de lluvia del volcán*. Mexico, D.F., Grijalbo.

Goffman, E. 1959. *The Presentation of Self in Everyday Life*. Garden City, New York, Doubleday.

Gonzalez, M. A. 1988. "La danza de concheros: Una tradición sagrada." *Mexico Indigena* 4 (20):59–62.

———. 1996. "Los Concheros: La (re)conquista de Mexico." In Jáuregui and Bonfiglioni 1996.

Gonzalez Torres, E., and V. Acevedo Martinez. 2000. "In Kaltonal: 'La Casa del Sol' Iglesia del Movimiento de la Mexicayotl." Undergraduate thesis, Escuela Nacional de Antroplogia e Historia (INAH), Mexico, D.F.

———. N.d. "La Casa de Sol: Una alternativa religiosa en el Movimiento de la mexicanidad." Manuscript in authors' possession.

Gonzalez Torres, Y. 1996. "The Revival of Mexican Religions: The Impact of Nativism." *Numen* 43:1–31.

———. 2000. "El Movimiento de la Mexicanidad." *Religiones y Sociedad*. Mexico, D.F., Gobernación, 9–35.

———. 2005. *Danza tu palabra: La danza de los concheros*. Mexico, D.F., Plaza y Valdés.

Goody, J. 1977. "Against Ritual: Loosely Structured Thoughts on a Loosely Defined Topic." In Moore and Meyerhoff 1977.

Gossen, G. 1974. *Chamulas in the World of the Sun*. Cambridge, Massachusetts, Harvard University Press.

———. 1986. *Symbol and Meaning beyond the Closed Community: Essays in Mesoamerican Ideas*. Studies in Culture and Society, Institute of Mesoamerican Studies. Albany, State University of New York.

Greenblatt, S., ed. 1993. *New World Encounter.* Berkeley: University of California Press.

Greenleaf, R. E. 1969. "The Mexican Inquisition and the Masonic Movement." *New Mexico Historical Review* 44 (2):99–117.

Gruzinski, S. 1986. "Mutilated Memory: Reconstruction of the Past and the Mechanisms of Memory among Seventeenth-Century Otomis." *History and Anthropology* 2: 337–353.

———. 1990. "Indian Confraternities, Brotherhoods and Mayordomias in Central New Spain: A List of Questions for the Historian and Anthropologist." In *The Indian Community of Colonial Mexico: Fifteen Essays on Land Tenure, Corporate Organizations, Ideology and Village Politics*, ed. A. Ouweneel and S. Miller. Amsterdam, CEDLA.

———. 1992. *The Aztecs: Rise and Fall of an Empire.* London, Thames and Hudson.

Guedea, V. 1989. "Las sociedades secretas durante el movimiento de independicia." In *The Independence of Mexico and the New Nation*, ed. O. J. Rodriguez. Los Angeles, UCLA Latin American Center.

Gutiérrez, N. 1999. *Nationalist Myths and Ethnic Identities: Indigenous Intellectuals and the Mexican State.* Lincoln, University of Nebraska Press.

Gutiérrez Zúñiga, C. 1996. *Nuevos Movimientos Religiosas: La Nueva Era en Guadalajara.* Jalisco, El Colegio de Jalisco.

Guzman, J. 1966. "Proscripcion de sociedades secretas en 1828." *Boletin del Archivo General de la Nacion* 7:693–790.

Hall, S., and T. Jefferson, eds. 1989. *Resistance through Rituals.* London, Hutchinson.

Handelman, D., and G. Lindquist, eds. 2004. *Ritual in Its Own Right.* Oxford, Berghahn Books.

Hanna, J. L. 1974. "Dances of Anahuac—for God or Man; an Alternative Way of Thinking about Prehistory." *Dance Research Journal* 7 (1):13–27.

———. 1977: "To Dance Is Human." In Blacking 1977.

Harris, M. 1993. *The Dialogocal Theatre: Dramatizations of the Conquest of Mexico and the Question of the Other.* London, St. Martin's Press.

———. 1996. "Moctezuma's Daughter: The Role of La Malinche in Mesoamerican Dance." *The Journal of American Folklore*, 109 (432):149–177.

———. 2000. *Aztecs, Moors and Christians: Festivals of Reconquest in Mexico and Spain.* Austin, University of Texas Press.

Harvey, D. 1989. *The Condition of Postmodernity: An Enquiry into the Origins of Cultural Change.* Oxford, Basil Blackwell.

———. 1993. "From Space to Place and Back Again." In Bird et al. 1993.

Harvey, N. 1998. *The Chiapas Rebellion: The Struggle for Land and Democracy.* Durham, North Carolina, Duke University Press.

Hastrup, K. 1998. "Theatre as a Site of Passage: Some Reflections on the Magic of Acting." In Hughes-Freeland 1998.

Hastrup, K., and P. Hervik. 1994. "Introduction." In *Social Experience and Anthropological Knowledge*. London, Routledge.

Hebdige, D. 1979. *Subculture: The Meaning of Style.* London, Methuen and Co.

Heelas, P. 1996. *The New Age Movement: The Celebration of the Self and the Sacralization of Modernity.* Oxford, Blackwell.

Heelas, P., S. Lash, and P. Morris. 1996. *Detraditionalization.* Oxford, Blackwell.

Hellier Tinoco, R. 2004. "Power Needs Names: Hegemony, Folklorization, and the Viejitos Dance of Michoacán, Mexico." In *Music, Power and Politics*, ed. A. Randall. London, Routledge.

Herrera, F., dir. 1993. *Concheros Somos.* Video. Mexico, D.F., Ixtac.

Hertz, R. 1973 (1909). "The Pre-eminance of the Right Hand: A Study in Religious Polarity." In *Right and Left, Essays on Dual Symbolic Classifications*, ed. R. Needham. Chiacago, University Press of Chicago.

Hervieu-Léger, D. 1993. *La Religion pour Memoire*. Paris, CERF.

Hobsbawm, E., and T. Ranger. 1992 (1983). *The Invention of Tradition*. Cambridge, Cambridge University Press.

Hollander, A. 1993. *Seeing through Clothes*. London, Penguin.

Howes, D., ed. 1991. *The Varieties of Sensory Experience: A Sourcebook in the Anthropology of the Senses*. Toronto, University of Toronto Press.

Hughes-Freeland, F. 1998. *Ritual, Performance, Media*. London, Routledge.

Hughes-Freeland, F., and M. Crain. 1998. *Recasting Ritual: Performance, Media, Identity*. London, Routledge.

Humphrey, C., and J. Laidlaw. 1994. *The Archetypal Actions of Ritual*. Oxford, Clarendon Press.

Hymes, D. 1975. "Breakthrough into Performance." In *Folklore: Performance and Communication*, ed. D. Ben-Amos and K. S. Goldstein. The Hague, Mouton.

Irvine, J. 1979. "Formality and Informality in Communicative Events." *American Anthropologist* 81:773–779.

———. 1982. "The Creation of Identity in Spirit Mediumship and Possession." In Parkin.

*Izkalotl*. 1960–. Newspaper of El Movimiento Confederato Restaurador de Anauak. Mexico, D.F.

Jackson, M. 1983. "Thinking through the Body: An Essay on Understanding Metaphor." *Social Analysis* 14 (December):127–148.

———. 1996. *Things as They Are*. Bloomington, Indiana University Press.

Jáuregui, J., and C. Bonfiglioni, eds. 1996. *Las Danzas de Conquista: I. Mexico Contemporaneo*. Mexico, D.F., Consejo Nacional para la Cultura y las Artes and Fondo de Cultura Económica.

Jilek, W. 1982. "Altered States of Consciousness in North American Indian Ceremonials." *Ethos* 10 (4):326–343.

Kaeppler, A. 1978. "Dance in Anthropological Perspective." *Annual Review of Anthropology* 7:31–49.

———. 1989. "Dance." In *International Encyclopaedia of Communications*, ed. E. Barnouw. Oxford, Oxford University Press.

Kamfer, C. 1985. "El Arte de La Danza." Undergraduate dissertation. ENAP/DED, Mexico, D.F.

Keali'inohomoku, J. 1979. "You Dance What You Wear, and You Wear Your Cultural Values." In Cordwell and Schwarz 1979.

Keane, W. 1997. "Religious Language." *Annual Review of Anthropology* 26:47–71.

Kendall, L. 1996. "Initiating Performance: The Story of Chini, a Korean Shaman." In Laderman and Roseman 1996.

Kleinman, A., and J. Kleinman. 1994. "How Bodies Remember: Social Memory and Bodily Experience of Criticism, Resistance, and Deligitimation Following China's Cultural Revolution." *New Literary History* 25:707–723.

Kleinman, S. 1975. "Movement Notation Systems: An Introduction." *Quest: The Language of Movement* 23:33–56.

Klor de Alva, J. J. 1982. "Spiritual Conflict and Accomodation in New Spain." In *The Inca and Aztec States, 1400–1800: Anthropology and History*, ed. G. Collier, R. Rosaldo, and J. Wirth. New York, Academic Press.

Knab, T. 1986. "Metaphors, Concepts and Coherence in Aztec." In Gossen 1986.

Knauft, B. 1979. "On Percussion and Metaphor." *Current Anthropology* 20 (1):189–191.
———. 1996. *Genealogies for the Present in Cultural Anthropology*. London, Routledge.
Knight, A. 1990. "Racism, Revolution and Indigenismo: Mexico 1910–1940." In *The Idea of Race in Latin America, 1870–1940*, ed. R. Graham. Austin, University of Texas Press.
———. 1994. "Popular Culture and the Revolutionary State in Mexco, 1910–1940." *Hispanic American Historical Review* 74 (3):393–444.
Knowlton, R. 1976. *Church Property and the Mexican Reform, 1856–1910*. Dekalb, Northern Illinois University Press.
Kratz, C. 1994. *Affecting Performance: Meaning, Movement and Experience in Okiek Women's Initiation*. Washington, DC, Smithsonian Institution Press.
Kuruth, G. P. 1946. "Los Concheros." *Journal of American Folklore* 59: 387–399.
Kuruth, G. P., and S. Martí. 1964. *Dances of Anahuac: The Choreography and Music of PreCortesian Dances*. Chicago, Aldine.
Laderman, C., and M. Roseman. 1996. *The Performance of Healing*. London, Routledge.
Lafaye, J. 1976. *Quetzalcoatl and Guadalupe: The Formation of Mexican National Consciousness, 1531–1813*. Chicago, University of Chicago Press.
Langer, S. 1953. *Feeling and Form: A Theory of Art*. London, Routledge and Keegan Paul.
Lara González, E. 1993. *Matematica y simbolismo en la danza autoctona de Mexico*. Mexico, D.F., self-published.
Laughlin, R. 1975. *The Great Tzotzil Dictionary of San Lorenzo Zinacantán*. Smithsonian Contributions to Anthropology series, no. 19. Washington, DC, Smithsonian Institution Press.
Leach, E. 1958. "Magical Hair." *Journal of the Royal Anthropological Institute* 88:147–164.
———. 1976. *Culture and Communication*. Cambridge, Cambridge University Press.
Leder, D. 1990. *The Absent Body*. Chicago, University of Chicago Press.
León-Portilla, M. 1974. "Testimonios nahuas sobre la conquista espiritual." *Estudios de Cultura Nahuatl* 11:11–36.
Levin, D. M. 1985. *The Body's Recollection of Being: Phenomenological Psychology and the Deconstruction of Nihilism*. London, Routledge and Kegan Paul.
Lewis, G. 1980. *Day of Shining Red: An Essay on Understanding Ritual*. Cambridge, Cambridge University Press.
———. 1986. "The Look of Magic." *Man* n.s. 21:414–437.
Lewis, O. 1961. *The Children of Sanchez*. London, Penguin Books.
Linares Aguirre, V. 1995. "Acerca de la raiz: Teotl o Deo Ignoto." *Ce-Acatl* 67:5–7.
Little, W., et al. 1973. *The Shorter Oxford English Dictionary*. Oxford, Clarendon Press.
Llaguno, J. A. 1963. "Decretos del III Concilio Provincial Mexicano." In *La Personalidad juridica del indio y el III Concilio Provincial Mexicano*. Mexico, D.F., Editorial Porrua.
Lock, M. 1993. "Cultivating the Body: Anthropology and Epistemologies of Bodily Practice and Knowledge." *Annual Review of Anthropology* 22:133–135.
Lockhart, J. 1992. *The Nahuas after the Conquest: A Social and Cultural History of the Indians of Central Mexico, Sixteenth through Eighteenth Centuries*. Stanford, Stanford University Press.
Lomnitz-Adler, C. 1992. *Exits from the Labyrinth: Culture and Ideology in the Mexican National Space*. Berkeley, University of California Press.
———. 2001. *Deep Mexico, Silent Mexico: An Anthropology of Nationalism*. Minneapolis, University of Minnesota Press.

*Los Concheros al Fin de Milenio*. See Musicology.

Lovell, N., ed. 1998. *Locality and Belonging*. London, Routledge.

Lowell Lewis, J. 1992. *Ring of Liberation: Deceptive Discourse on Brazilian Capoeira*. Chicago, University of Chicago Press.

———. 1995. "Genre and Embodiment: From Brazilian Capoiera to the Ethnology of Human Movement." *Cultural Anthropology* 10 (2):221–243.

Lynne Hanna, J. 1974. "Dances of Anahuac—for God or Man." *Dance Research Journal* 7 (1):13–27.

MacCannell, D. 1992. *Empty Meeting Ground*. London, Routledge.

Magaloni Duarte, I. 1969. *Educatores del Mundo*. Mexico, D.F., B. Costa-Amic.

Mansfield, P. 1953. "The Concheros Dancers of Mexico." Ph.Ed.D. thesis, New York University, New York.

Marti, S. 1978. *Music before Columbus*. Mexico, D.F., Ediciones Euroamericanas.

Martin, D. 1990. *Tongues of Fire: The Explosion of Protestantism in Latin America*. Oxford, Basil Blackwell.

Mauss, M. 1979 (1936). "Body Techniques." In *Sociology and Psychology Essays*. London, Routledge and Kegan Paul.

McAndrew, J. 1964. *The Open-Air Churches of Sixteenth-Century Mexico*. Cambridge, Massachusetts, Harvard University Press.

McNeill, W. 1995. *Keeping Together in Time: Dance and Drill in Human History*. Cambridge, MA, Harvard University Press.

Medina, L., and G. Cadena. 2002. "Dias de los Muertos: Public Ritual, Community Renewal, and Popular Religion in Los Angeles." In *Horizons of the Sacred: Mexican Traditions in U.S. Catholicism*, ed. T. Matovina and G. Riebe-Estrella. Ithaca, NY, Cornell University Press.

Melhuus, M., and K-A. Stolen. 1996. *Machos, Mistresses, Madonnas: Contesting the Power of Latin American Gender Imagery*. London, Verso.

Melucci, A. 1985. "The Symbolic Challenge of Contemporary Movements." *Social Research* 52 (4):789–816.

Mendoza (Walker), Z. S. 2000. *Shaping Society through Dance*. Chicago, University of Chicago Press.

Merleau-Ponty, M. 1962. *Phenomenology of Perception*. London, Routledge.

———. 1964. *The Primacy of Perception*. London, Routledge.

Miner, H. 1956. "Body Ritual among the Nacirema." *American Anthropologist* n.s. 58 (3):503–550.

Moedano, G. Navarro. 1972. "Los hermanos de la Santa Cuenta: Un culto de crisis de origen Chichimeca." *Religion en MesoAmerica*, XII Mesa Redonda de Antropologia, Sociedad Mexicana de Antropologia, 599–609.

———. 1984. "La Danza de Los Concheros de Queretero." *Universidad* 23/24:3–10.

———. 1985. "El tema de la conquista en la tradicion literaria-musical de los Concheros." *I Congreso Sociedad Mexicana de Musicologia*, Cuidad Victoria, Tamaulipas, 62–74.

———. 1988. "Expresiones de la religiosidad popular guanajuatense: Las velaciones." *Arquelogia e Historia Guanajuatense* (Homenaje a Wigberto Jimenez), El Colegio del Bajio, 105–115.

Monsivais, C. 1995. *Los rituales del Caos*. Mexico, D.F., Ediciones Era.

Moore, S. F., and B. Meyerhoff. 1977. *Secular Ritual*. Assen, Van Gorcum.

Mora, C. J. 1989 (1982). *Mexican Cinema: Reflections of a Society 1986–1988*. Berkeley, University of California Press.

Morgan, T. 1994. "Proleterians, Politicos, and Patriarchs: The Use and Abuse of Cultural Customs in the Early Industrialization of Mexico City, 1880–1910." In Beezley, Martin, and French 1994.

Morris, P. 1996. "Community beyond Tradition." In Heelas, Lash, and Morris 1996.

Motolinia, Fray T. de Benavente. 1971. *Memoriales: Libro de las cosas de la Nueva España y de los naturales de ella*, ed. E. O'Gorman. Mexico, D.F., Universitaria Autonoma Nacional de Mexico.

Murakami, H. 1994. *Dance Dance Dance*. London, Hamish Hamilton.

Nájera Ramírez, O. 1989. "Social and Political Dimensions of Folklorico Dance: The Binational Dialectic of Residual and Emergent Culture." *Western Folklore* 48 (1): 15–32.

———. 1994. "Engendering Nationalism: Identity, Discourse and the Mexican Charro." *Anthropological Quarterly* 67 (1):1–14.

Nancy, J-L. 1991. *The Inoperative Community*. Minneapolis, University of Minnesota Press.

Needham, R. 1967. "Percussion and Transition." *Man* n.s. 2:606–614.

———, ed. 1973. *Right and Left: Essays on Dual Symbolic Classification*. Chicago, University of Chicago Press.

Neher, A. 1962. "A Physiological Explanation of Unusual Behaviour in Ceremonies Involving Drums." *Human Biology* 34:151–160.

Ness, S. A. 1992. *Body, Movement and Culture*. Philadelphia, University of Pennsylvania Press.

Nieva, M. 1969. *Mexicayotl*. Mexico, D.F., Editorial Orion.

Nora, P. 1996. "Between Memory and History: General Introduction." In *Realms of Memory*, ed. P. Nora. New York, Columbia University.

Nugent, S., and C. Shore, eds. 1997. *Anthropology and Cultural Studies*. Cambridge, Pluto Press.

Núñez, N. 1996. *Anthropocosmic Theatre: Rite in the Dynamics of Theatre*. Amsterdam, The Netherlands, Harwood Academic Publishers.

Obeyesekere G. 1981. *Medusa's Hair: An Essay on Personal Symbols and Religious Experience*. Chicago, University of Chicago Press.

Odena Güemes, L. 1984. *Movimiento Confederado Restaurador de la Cultura Anahuac*. Mexico, D.F., Centro de Investigaciones y Estudios Superiores en Antropologia Social (CIESAS).

———. 1993. "En Busca de la Mexicanidad." In *Nuevas Identidades Culturales en Mexico*, ed. G. Bonfil Battala. Mexico, D.F., Consejo Nacional para la Cultura y Les Artes.

Oesterley, W. 1923. *The Sacred Dance*. Cambridge, Cambridge University Press.

Ong, W. 1969. "World as View and World as Event." *American Anthropologist* 71:634–647.

———. 1982. *Orality and Literacy*. London, Routledge.

Ortiz de Zarate, A. 1990. Untitled notes on the Concheros. Xerox.

Osborne, L., de Jongh. 1965. *Indian Crafts of Guatemala and El Salvador*. Norman, University of Oklahoma Press.

Ots, T. 1994. "The Silenced Body—The Expressive Leib: On the Dialectic of Mind and Life in Chinese Cathartic Healing." In Csordas 1994a.

Parker, A., and E. K. Sedgwick, eds. 1995. *Performativity and Performance*. London, Routledge.

Parkin, D., ed. 1982. *Semantic Anthropology*. London, Academic Press.

———. 1992. "Ritual as Spatial Direction and Bodily Division." In *Understanding Rituals*, ed. D. de Coppet. London, Routledge.

Parviainen, J. 1998. *Bodies Moving and Moved: A Phenomenological Analysis of the Dancing Subject and the Cognitive and Ethical Values of Dance Art*. Tampere, Finland, Tampere University Press.

Paz, O. 1950. *El laberinto de la soledad*. Mexico, D.F., Fondo de Culture Economica.

———. 1972. *The Other Mexico: Critique of the Pyramid*. Trans. Lysander Kemp. New York, Grove Press.

Pérez Monfort, R., and L. Odena Güemes. 1982. *Por la Patria y por la Raza: Tres movimientos nacionalistas 1930–1940*. Documentos. Mexico, D.F., Cuardenos de la Casa Chata, CIESAS.

Phelan, J. L. 1960. "Neo-Aztecism in the Eighteenth Century and the Genesis of Mexican Nationalism." In *Culture in History: Essays in Honor of Paul Radin*, ed. S. Diamond. New York, Columbia University Press.

Phelan, P. 1993. *Unmarked: The Politics of Performance*. London, Routledge.

Piot, C. 1999. *Remotely Global: Village Modernity in West Africa*. Chicago, University of Chicago Press.

Pizzigoni, C. 2004. "The Life Within: Local Indigenous Society in Colonial Mexico (Eighteenth Century)." Unpublished seminar paper, Centre for Latin American Studies, Cambridge.

Poveda, P. 1981. "Danza de Concheros en Austin, Texas: Entrevista con Andres Segura Granados." *Latin American Music Review* 2 (2):280–299.

Pratt, M-L. 1992. *Imperial Eyes: Travel Writing and Transculturation*. London, Routledge.

Radcliffe-Brown, A. R. 1922. *The Andaman Islanders*. Cambridge, Cambridge University Press.

Ramos, S. 1934. *El perfil del hombre y la cultura en México*. Mexico, D.F., Imprenta Mundial.

Rangel, N. 1932. "Introduction." *Los precursores Ideológicas de la Guerra de Independencia: La Masóneria en Mexico* (Siglo XVIII, tomo II. XXI La vida colonial). Mexico, D.F., Archive General de la Nación, Talleres Graficos de la Nación.

Real Academia Español. 1992. *Diccionario de la Lengua Español*. Madrid: Espasa-Calpe.

Reed, S. 1998. "The Politics and Poetics of Dance." *Annual Review of Anthropology* 27:503–532.

Ricard, R. 1966. *The Spiritual Conquest of Mexico*. Berkeley, University of California Press.

Ricoeur, P. 1981. *Hermeneutics and the Human Sciences: Essays on Language, Action and Interpretation*, ed. and trans. J. B. Thompson. Cambridge, Cambridge University Press.

Roach, Joseph. 1995. "Culture and Performance." In Parker and Sedgwick 1995.

Roach-Higgins, M. E. 1991. "Fashion." In *Perspectives on Fashion*, ed. G. Sproles. Minneapolis, Burgess Publishing.

Rochfort, D. 1993. *Mexican Muralists: Orozco, Rivera Siqueiros*. London, Laurence King.

Rodriguez, F. 1981. "Quelques apports à l'archéologie des Chichimèquea: Les Guachichiles de San Luis Potosi." *Bulletin Mission Archéologoque Ethnologique Française au Mexique* 35–38.

Rodriguez, O. J., ed. 1989. *The Independence of Mexico and the Creation of the New Nation*. Los Angeles, UCLA, Latin America Center Publications, University of California, Irvine.

Roseman, M. 1991. *Healing Sounds from the Malaysian Rainforest*. Berkeley, University of California Press.

Rostas, S. 1987. "From Ethos to Identity: Religious Practice as Resistance to Change." Ph.D. dissertation, Sussex University, Falmer, Sussex.

———. 1991. "The Concheros of Mexico: A Search for Ethnic Identity." *Dance Research* 9 (2):3–17.

———. 1992. "Mexican Mythology." In *The Feminist Companion to Mythology*, ed. D. Larrington. London, Pandora Press.

———. 1993. "The Mexica's Reformulation of the Concheros Dance: The Popular Use of Autochthonous Religion in Mexico City." In *The Popular Use of Popular Religion in Latin America*, ed. S. Rostas and A. Droogers. Amsterdam, CEDLA Latin America Studies 70.

———. 1994. "The Concheros of Mexico: Changing Ideas of Indianity." In *Living Traditions: Continuity and Change, Past and Present*, ed. A. Herle and D. Phillipson. *Cambridge Anthropology* 17 (2):38–56.

———. 1996. "The Production of Gendered Imagery: The Concheros of Mexico." In Melhuus and Stølen 1996.

———. 1998a. "From Ritualization to Performativity: The Concheros of Mexico." In *Ritual, Performance, Media*, eds. F. Hughes-Freeland. London, Routledge.

———. 1998b. "Performing 'Mexicanidad': Popular 'Indigenismo' in Mexico City." In *Encuentros Antropológicos: Power, Identity and Mobility in Mexican Society*, ed. V. Napolitano and X. Leyva-Solano. London, Institute of Latin American Studies, London University.

———. 2002. "Mexicanidad: The Resurgence of the Indian in Popular Mexican Nationalism." *Cambridge Anthropology* 23 (1):20–38.

———. 2008. "Los concheros en un contexto mundial: Mexicanidad, espiritualidad New Age y Sufismo como influencias en la danza." In Argyaridis et al. 2008.

Rouget, G. 1985. *Music and Trance: A Theory of the Relations between Music and Possession*. Chicago, University of Chicago Press.

Sahagún, Fray B. de. 1950–1982. *Florentine Codex: General History of the Things of New Spain*, trans. from Nahuatl by J. O. Anderson and C. Dibble. 13 parts. Santa Fe, NM, School of American Research.

Sahlins, M. 1976. *Culture and Practical Reason*. Chicago, University of Chicago Press.

Sanchez Ventura, F. 1990. "Los Concheros: Devocionario del rito solar." *Lo mejor de Mexico desconocido*. Mexico, D.F., Jilguero SEP.

Sawyer, R. K. 1997. *Creativity in Performance*. London, Ablex Publishing.

Scarry, E. 1985. *The Body in Pain: The Making and Unmaking of the World*. Oxford, Oxford University Press.

Schechner, R. 1985. *Between Theatre and Anthropology*. Philadelphia, University of Pennsylvania Press.

———. 1986. "Magnitudes of Performance." In Turner and Bruner 1986.

———. 1988. *Performance Theory*. New York, Routledge.

Schechner, R., and W. Appel. 1990. *By Means of Performance*. Cambridge, Cambridge University Press.

Schieffelin, E. 1976. *The Sorrow of the Lonely and the Burning of the Dancers*. New York, St. Martin's Press.

———. 1985. "Performance and the Cultural Construction of Reality." *American Ethnologist* 12 (4):707–724.

———. 1996. "On Failure and Performance: Throwing the Medium out of the Séance." In Laderman and Roseman 1996.

———. 1998. "Problematizing Performance." In Hughes-Freeland 1998.

Searle, J. 1969. *Speech Acts*. Cambridge, Cambridge University Press.

―――. 1979. *Expression and Meaning: Studies in the Theory of Speech Acts*. Cambridge, Cambridge University Press.

Segura, A. N.d. Leaflet reproduced by Mario E. Aguilar. www.aguila-blance.com/segura2.htm.

Shadow Rodríguez, M., and R. Shadow. 2000. *El pueblo del Señor:Llas fiestas y peregrinaciones de Chamla*. Toluca, Mexico, Universidad Autonoma del Estado de Mexico.

Sharon, D. 1978. *The Wizard of the Four Winds: A Shaman's Story*. New York, Macmillan.

Slater, D. 1985. *New Social Movements and the State in Latin America*. Amsterdam, CEDLA.

Slocum, M., and F. Gerdel. 1980. *Vocabulario Tzeltal de Bachajon*. Mexico, D.F., Summer Institute of Linguistics.

Solorzano, A., and R. Guerrero. 1941. "Ensayo para un Estudio sobre la 'Danza de los Concheros de la Gran Tenochtitlan.'" *Boletín Latino-Americano de Música* 5:449–476.

Sparshott, F. 1988. *Off the Ground: First Steps in a Philosophical Consideration of Dance*. Princeton, New Jersey, Princeton University Press.

Staal, F. 1979. "The Meaninglessness of Ritual." *Numen* 26 (1):1–22.

―――. 1986. "The Sounds of Religion: Parts IV–V." *Numen* 33 (2):185–224.

Stallybrass, P. 1993. "Shakespeare, the Individual and the Text." In *Cultural Studies Reader*, ed. S. During. London, Routledge.

Sten, M. 1990. *Ponte a bailar tu que reinas: Antropologia de la danza prehispanica*. Mexico, D.F., Editorial Joaquín Mortiz.

Stevenson, R. 1968. *Music in Aztec and Inca Territory*. Berkeley, University of California Press.

Stoll, D. 1990. *Is Latin America Turning Protestant?The Politics of Evangelical Growth*. Berkeley, University of California Press.

Stoller, P. 1989. *The Taste of Ethnographic Things: The Senses in Anthropology*. Philadelphia, University of Pennsylvania Press.

―――. 1995. *Embodying Colonial Memories: Spirit Possession, Power and the Hauka in West Africa*. London, Routledge.

―――. 1996. "Sounds and Things: Pulsations of Power in Songhay." In Laderman and Roseman 1996.

Stone, M. 1975. *At the Sign of Midnight: The Concheros Dance Cult of Mexico*. Tuscon, University of Arizona Press.

Strathern, M. 1990 (1988). *The Gender of the Gift*. Berkeley, University of California Press.

Sullivan, L. E. 1986. "Sound and Senses: Towards a Hermeneutics of Performance." *History of Religions* 26 (1):1–33.

Tambiah, S. J. 1985a (1973). "The Magical Power of Words" in *Culture, Thought and Social Action: An Anthropological Perspective*. Cambridge, Massachusetts, Harvard University Press.

―――. 1985b (1981). "A Performative Approach to Ritual." In *Culture, Thought and Social Action: An Anthropological Perspective*. Cambridge, Massachusetts, Harvard University Press.

Tarlo, E. 1996. *Clothing Matters: Dress and Identity in India*. London, Hurst and Company.

Taussig, M. 1993. *Mimesis and Alterity: A Particular History of the Senses*. London, Routledge.

Taylor, C. 1985. *Human Agency and Language*. Philosophical Papers 1. Cambridge, Cambridge University Press.

Taylor, J. 1998. *Paper Tangos*. Durham, North Carolina. Duke University Press.

Taylor, L., ed. 1994. *Visualizing Theory: Selected Essays from V.A.R. 1990–1994*. London, Routledge.

Taylor, W. B. 1996. *Magistrates of the Sacred: Priests and Parishioners in Eighteenth-Century Mexico*. Stanford, CA, Stanford University Press.

Tenenbaum, B. 1994. "Streetwise History: The Paseo de la Reforma and the Porfirian State, 1876–1910." In Beezley, Martin, and French 1994.

Tenorio, M. 1993. "Crafting a Modern Nation: Modernity and Nationalism at World's Fairs 1880s–1920s." Ph.D. thesis, Stanford University, Stanford, California.

Thompson, C. D., Jr. 2000. "The Unwieldly Promise of Ceremonies: The Case of the Jakalteko Maya's Dance of the Conquest." In *Indigenous Religions*, ed. G. Harvey. London, Cassell.

Tilley, C. 1997. "Performing Culture in the Global Village." *Critique of Anthropology* 17 (1):67–89.

Tlakaelel, et al. 1992. *Nahui Mitl* (Los cuatro flechas). Mexico, D.F., Universidad Autonoma Metropolitana.

Todorov, T. 1982. *La Conquete de L'Amerique: La Question de L'Autre*. Paris, Seuil.

Toor, F. 1947. *A Treasury of Mexican Folkways*. New York, Crown Publishers.

Turnbull, C. 1990. "Liminality: A Synthesis of Subjective and Objective Experience." In Schechner and Appel 1990.

Turner, B. 1995 (1985). *Body and Society: Explorations in Social Theory*. New York: Basil Blackwell.

Turner, V. 1967. *The Forest of Symbols: Aspects of Ndembu Ritual*. Ithaca, New York, Cornell University Press.

———. 1969. *The Ritual Process: Structure and Anti-Structure*. Ithaca, New York, Cornell University Press.

———. 1982. *From Ritual to Theatre: The Human Seriousness of Play*. New York, Performing Arts Journal.

———. 1986. *The Anthropology of Performance*. New York, Performing Arts Journal.

Turner, V., and E. Turner. 1978. *Image and Pilgrimage in Christian Culture*. New York, Columbia University Press.

———. 1986. *The Anthropology of Experience*. Urbana, University of Illinois Press.

Tylor, B. T. 1861. *Anahuac or Mexico and the Mexicans, Ancient and Modern*. London, Longman, Green and Roberts.

Vansina, J. 1985. *Oral Tradition as History*. London, James Currey.

Vasconcelos, J. 1979 (1925). *The Cosmic Race: La raza cósmica*. Baltimore, John Hopkins University Press.

Vasquez de Santa Ana, H. 1953. *Fiestas y costumbres mexicanas*. Mexico, D.F., Ediciones Botas.

Vásquez Hernández, J. de J. 1999. "Nacionalismo y racismo en Mexico, el caso de la Mexicanidad (Mexicayotl)." Master's thesis, Universidad Autonoma Metropolitano (UAM), Mexico, D.F.

Veber, H. 1992. "Why Indians Wear Clothes . . . Managing Identity across an Ethnic Boundary." *Ethnos* 57 (1–2):51–60.

Velasco Pina, A. 1979. *Tlacaelel*. Mexico, D.F., Editorial Jus.

———. 1987. *Regina*. Mexico, D.F., Editorial Jus.

———. 1990. *El Despertar de Teotihuacan*. Mexico, D.F., Editorial Jus.

———. 1994. *El retorno de lo Sagrado*. Mexico, D.F., Circulo Cuadrado.

Vento, A. C. 1994. "Aztec Conchero Dance Tradition: Historic, Religious and Cultural Significance." *Wicazo Sa Review* 10 (1):59–64.

Veran, J. F. 2005. "The Dialectics of Ethnicity: A Source of Strength for Some and of Constraint for Others." Mestizajes Conference, Centre for Latin American Studies, Cambridge.

Vértiz, J., and A. Alfaro. 2001. *Moros y Cristianos: Una batalla cósmica.* Mexico, D.F., Artes de Mexico.

Wallace, A. 1956. "Revitalization Movements." *American Anthropologist* 58:264–281.

Warman, A. 1965. Notes on the record sleeve, "Danzas de la Conquista."

———. 1985 (1972). *La danza de moros y cristianos.* Mexico, D.F., Instituto Nacional de Antropologiá e Historia.

Weiner, A. 1994. "Trobrianders on Camera and Off." In *Visualizing Theory: Selected Essays from V.A.R. 1990–1994,* ed. L. Taylor. London, Routledge.

Weiner, A., and J. Schneider, eds. 1989. *Cloth and Human Experience.* Washington, DC, Smithsonian Institution Press.

Werbner, R. 1989. *Ritual Passage, Sacred Journey: The Process and Organization of Religious Movements.* Washington, DC, Smithsonian Institution Press.

Weston, E. 1990 (1973). *The Daybooks of Edward Weston,* vols. 1 and 2: *Mexico and California,* foreword by B. Newhall, ed. N. Newhall Millerton. New York, Aperture Books.

Whitehead, C. 2001. "Social Mirrors and Shared Experiential Worlds." *Journal of Consciousness Studies* 8 (4):3–36.

Widdifield, S. 1996. *The Embodiment of the National.* Tucson, University of Arizona Press.

Wolf, E. 1957. "The Mexican Bajio in the Eigtheeth Century." *Synoptic Studies of Mexican Culture* 17:180–198. Tulane University, Middle American Research Institute.

———. 1982. *Europe and the People without History.* Berkeley, University of California Press.

Woodhead, L., and P. Heelas. 2000. *Religion in Modern Times: An Interpretive Approach.* Oxford, Blackwell.

Woodside, L., V. K. Kumar, and R. Pekala. 1997. "Monotonous Percussion Drumming and Trance Postures: A Controlled Evaluation of Phenomenological Effects." *Anthropology of Consciousness* 8 (2–3):69–87.

Wosien, M-G. 1974. *Sacred Dance.* London, Thames and Hudson.

Wulff, H. 1998. *Ballet across Borders.* Oxford, Berg.

Wuthnow, R. 1987. *Meaning and Moral Order: Explorations in Cultural Analysis.* Berkeley, University of California Press.

Young, D., and J-G. Goulet. 1994. *Being Changed by Cross-cultural Encounters: The Anthropology of Extraordinary Experience.* Peterborough, Ontario, Canada, Broadview Press.

Zaner, R. 1981. *The Context Self: A Phenomenological Enquiry into Medicine as a Clue.* Athens, Ohio University Press.

Zarrilli, P. 1990. "What Does It Mean to 'Become the Character': Power, Presence, and Transcendence in Asian In-body Disciplines of Practice." In Schechner and Appel 1990.

## FILMOLOGY

Bonfil Batalla, G., and G. Muñoz, dirs. 1965. *El es Dios.* Film now on video. Mexico, D.F., Instituto Nacional de Antropologia y Historia.

Eisenstein, S., dir. 1930. *Que Viva Mexico!* Video. Moscow, Mosfilm.

Herrera, F., dir. 1993. *Concheros Somos*. Video. Mexico, D.F., Mexico, Ixtac.
Mansfield, P., dir. 1953. *The Concheros Dancers of Mexico*. Film. New York, Performing Arts Research Collections, New York Public Library.


## MUSICOLOGY

*Danzas de la Conquista*. N.d. (ca. 1965). Vinyl. Recording and notes by A. Warman. Vol. 2, INAH/SEP.

*El Aguila Blanca*. 1993. Tape. Conjunto Los Concheros de Capitan Ernesto Ortiz. Mexico, D.F., Bertelsmann de Mexico.

*El Grupo Nahucalli*. N.d. Tape. Danzas de Concheros y Musica Nayarita, Discos Ehecatl.

*Los Concheros al Fin de Milenio*. 1997. Tape and booklet. Homenaje al antropologo Guillermo Bonfil Batalla, INAH.

*Maria Anzures, Canto Mexica*. N.d. Tape. Tech. prod., H. Magaña Alondo. Booklet by A. Zuñiga Peña and N. Rodriguez Carrasco. Mexico, D.F., Grupo Tlapitzalco, Producciones Diamante.

# INDEX

Action. *See* Intentional Action; Ritual; Ritualization

Aesthetic: Aztec, 120, 217, 218; of clothing, 106–107, 126, 144; Mexica aesthetic, 117–118, 126; of music, 139; personal, 106, 122; and style, 119

Age of Aquarius, 197, 261(n37)

Agency, 4–7, 67, 184; clothing as form of agency, 106; double agency, 7–8, 81

Agradecimiento. *See* Prayers

Aguascalientes, 154, 251(n11)

Aguilar, Eduardo, 35, 136–138, 140–142, 159, 160, 243(n13), 248(n26); on animas, 249(nn33, 42); on power, 138; on standards, 91

Ahuehuete, 2. *See also* Chalma

Alabanzas (songs): change through time, 217–21; content, 53, 63; for a dance, 58–64 passim; dating of, 253(n20); for Day of the Dead, 52–3; during a vigil, 45–51, 55–57, 98, 238(n11); form of, 45; as history of dance, 165–170 passim; for a limpia, 50; Mexica's rejection of, 193, 203, 218; mode of accompaniment, 238(n5); as oral tradition, 10, 218; printed book of, 218; recordings of, 220; writing of, 159. *See also* Concheros; Dances of the Concheros; Music; Singing

Alberto, 38, 122

Alferez. *See* Lieutenant

Altar(s): of Ernesto Ortiz, 28; for Day of the Dead, 52–54; link to "mesa," 236(n3), 256(n64); in oratories, 27; post-Colonial rural, 174; at a vigil, 44–51 passim; for vigil after a death, 52. *See also* Oratorio; Permiso; Santocalli

Alliances: with the animas, 138; between mesas, 24, 94, 151, 153–154; with the Corporación de Concheros, 153; counter to kinship, 157; Cresencio, 152; Faustino Rodriguez, 152; Jesus Leon, 153; personal, 154; Santo Niño with Alberto Gutierrez, 152. *See also* Animas; Mesas; Santo Niño de Atocha

All Souls. *See* Day of the Dead

Alvarado, Miguel, 131, 162, 251(n12), 257(n82)

Amátlan, 198

Amecameca: banner from, 251(n20); cerro de Sacromonte, 26; date of dance in, 150, 251(n9); as group, 251(nn8, 9); as location of dance, 25, 26, 150, 152, 236(nn4, 9); as a wind, 26

Anahuac, 179, 197; Confederated Movement for the Restoration of, 195–196; Congress of, 202; conquest of, 265(n29)

Anciano: Consejo de Ancianos, 163, 196; role of, 136

Angelica. *See* Ortiz de Zarate

Animas, 49, 143–144, 175, 197; Anima Sola, 27, 250(n7); beliefs about, 56; dance to

Partido, Roberto, 36–37, 44, 126, 145, promesa of, 36
Party of Democratic Revolution (PRD), 264(n19)
Payata (dancer), 38
Performance, 67–69, 74–79; defined, 74; etymology of, 75; as extra-daily techniques, 241(n44); relation of performance to ritual, 68; Spanish terms for, 235(n48); theatre as analogy for, 241(n53)
Performative/performativity, 5, 7–8, 73–79; defined, 17, 74–75, 78, 83; everyday action as performance, 78; link to ritualization, 73; as mode of communication, 74, 78; relationship of performativity to ritualization, 79, 81–85; as self-expression, 73; sense of presence, 79, 138. See also Ritualization; Transcendence
Permiso, 82, 53; with feet, 59, 70, 80, 82, 140, 212; form of, 140; link to ritualization, 79, 82; verbal permission, 45–46, 53–58 passim, 90, 99; words of, 46. See also El es Dios
Peyote, 174
Phelan, P., 78
Pilgrimage, 18, 161; to San Juan Nuevo de los Milagros, 161; to Santiago de Compostela, 188. See also Chalma; Los Remedios
Piña, Carlos, 38, 136
Pineda, Manual, 165, 250(n90)
Ponce, Alfredo, 35; and Sufis, 159
Ponce, Linda, 35, 71, 94
Porfiriato (President Porfirio Diaz), 111, 180, 181–182
Power. See Empowerment
Practice, 5–6; incorporating practices, 221, 242(n67)
Prayers, 3, 24, 51, 90, 142; Agradecimiento, 49, 218, 219; Ave Maria (sung), 48; dance as prayer, 213; during a vigil, 46–48, 49, 238(n14); lack of records of, 10; for limpia, 50; Lord's Prayer, 48, 59; misterios, 51, 218; for specific animas (Day of the Dead), 52
PRD. See Party of Democratic Revolution
Precepts: as ideology of dance, 95; as injunctions, 99; lack of consensus as to meanings of, 95, 101; as mnemonics, 15, 102; parallelism, 101; in relation to the Trinity, 243(n22); slippage between, 95, 96; use of in daily life, 95. See also Conformity; Conquest; Union
Protestantism, rise of, 200, 210, 263(n2)
Proto-nationalism, Mexicanidad as form of, 191, 207
Puebla (State of), 22, 31
Pulque, 60; at los Remedios, 25; name of dance, 227, 239(n27)

Quakers, 244(n26)
Queretero: city, 265(n26); state, 22, 154, 254(n34)
Quetzalcoatl, 9, 117, 199; name of dance, 228

Race, 112, 184; Dia de la Raza, 26; and Masons, 255(n52); and MRCA, 207; transcendence of, 222
Radcliffe-Brown, A.R., 131, 134
Redfield, R., xvi
Regidor, de danzas, 58, 60
Reginas. See Velasco Piña, Antonio
Rehearsals. See Mesas: rehearsals
Religiosity: of dancers, 22, 143, 223, 244(n26); as rejoining, 4. See also Catholicism; Indigenous religiosity
Reliquia General (The Reliquia), Palabra of, 24, 149–150, 154, 183–185; Actas de la Reliquia General, secretary of, 152 locations of dances, 150; origin of, 120, 257(n74); physical standard of, 183, 258(n91). See also Association of Concheros
Reivindicación (re-conquest movement), 190, 191, 204. See also Mexicayotl
Ribera y Argomanis, Josefus de, 176, 177
Ricardo. See Lopez Ortiz, Ricardo
Ritual: as being without meaning, 240(n26); change through time, 216, 221; defined, 67; getting it right, 7, 71–72, 78, 84; as non-communicative action, 72; ritual commitment, 70–72, 80–81; ritual as communicative action, 72; ritual language, 90, 102, 244(n29); ritual ruling, 70; ritual stance, 70–72, 78–81 passim, 100, 221
Ritualization/ritualized, 5, 67–73, 80; how achieved, 6–7, 69–72; how differs from everyday action, 6, 68; the emergence of transcendence, 84, 135, 142; as prescribed action, 69, 71; relationship of to the performative, 69, 73, 79, 81–85. See also Double agency; Performative; Transcendence
Rivera, Diego, 114, 197
Roach, J., 68, 77
Robles, Maria. See Ortiz, Ernesto
Rodriguez, Faustino, 53, 96, 152–153, 156–157, 188, 242(n1); inheritors of, 155; and Regina, 198, 201
Rodriguez, Justino (nephew of Faustino), 96, 155–158, 230
Rodriguez, Pedro, 188, 258(n102)
Rojas, E., xviii, 255(n49)
Rosa-Elia, Correa, 37, 46; and clothing, 124–126; and sisters, 39; and spirituality, 83, 142
Rouget, G., 139, 249(n38)
Ruiz, Soledad, 144–146, 163, 231, 251(n12); beliefs of, 248(n28), 249(n42); on the precepts, 93, 95; on transcendence, 142–143

CPSIA information can be obtained at www.ICGtesting.com
Printed in the USA
LVOW060921291011

252641LV00003B/3/P

9 781607 321385